Performing Blackness

Performing Blackness offers a challenging interpretation of black cultural expression since the Black Arts Movement of the 1960s. Exploring drama, music, poetry, sermons, and criticism, Benston offers an exciting meditation on modern black performance's role in realizing African-American aspirations for autonomy and authority.

Artists covered include:

- Ntozake Shange
- Ed Bullins
- John Coltrane
- Amiri Baraka
- Adrienne Kennedy
- Michael Harper

Performing Blackness is an exciting contribution to the ongoing debate about the vitality and importance of black culture.

Kimberly W. Benston is Kenan Professor of English at Haverford College. He is the author of *Baraka: The Renegade and the Mask* and editor of *Speaking of You: The Vision of Ralph Ellison.*

Performing Blackness
Enactments of African-American modernism

Kimberly W. Benston

London and New York

First published 2000 by Routledge
11 New Fetter Lane, London EC4P 4EE

Simultaneously published in the USA and Canada
by Routledge
29 West 35th Street, New York, NY 10001

Typeset in Garamond by
Florence Production Ltd, Stoodleigh, Devon.
Printed and bound in Great Britain by Biddles Ltd, Guildford and King's Lynn

British Library Cataloguing in Publication Data
A catalogue record for this book is available from the British Library

Library of Congress Cataloging in Publication Data
Benston, Kimberly W.
    Performing blackness : enactments of African-American modernism /
    Kimberly W. Benston.
        p. cm.
    Includes bibliographical references and index.
    1. American literature—Afro-American authors—History and criticism.
    2. American literature—20th century—History and criticism.
    3. Performing arts—United States—History—20th century.
    4. Modernism (Literature)—United States. 5. Afro-Americans
    in literature. 6. Afro-American arts. I. Title.
    PS153.N5 B45 2000
    810.9'896073—dc21
                                                    99–054173

ISBN 0–415–00948–0 (hbk)
ISBN 0–415–00949–9 (pbk)

**For Sue, Shawna, Cliff
&
The Family**

*a love supreme, a love supreme
a love supreme, a love supreme*

Contents

    theatrical prefaces of Adrienne Kennedy   228

    PART IV
    **I was myself within the circle: vernacular
    and critical paradigms of expressive agency**   245

7   Improvising blackness: telling and testifying in the
    modern chant-sermon   247

8   Re-calling blackness: recollection and response in
    contemporary black autocritography   283

    Epilogue: re:presenting blackness   307

    Appendix A: Coltrane Poems   313
    Appendix B: sermon transcripts   331

    Notes   352
    Index   375

Plates

Acknowledgements

One of the principal figures of this book, John Coltrane, proclaimed often and passionately his indebtedness to the seekers and masters who preceded him. With enviable eloquence, he indicated that each musical phrase, indeed each note, that emerged from his wondrous horn was in itself an acknowledgement of all who had taught and inspired him through a life-time of apprenticeship, a crucial dimension of which was attentive listening. Though the analogy otherwise has its limits, as with Coltrane's notes, so with my words: each one bears the imprint of some teacher, colleague, friend, student, or kin who has taught me something over the years, and the specific acknowledgements that follow are themselves only the trace of this intricate, endless web of nurture.

First, to two teachers, long passed but still warmly remembered and appreciated, I owe the foundation of my study in the Black Arts era: Charles T. Davis and Larry Neal.

I have been fortunate in succeeding years to have come along in a generation of African-American literary scholars rich with innovative perception and inspiring verve. A number of these folk have been superbly generous with me for many years, offering an unchecked flow of insight and stimulation from which I've drawn at every phase of this project. To these "righteous bombers" I am continuously grateful: Bill Andrews, Michael Awkward, Houston Baker, Herman Beavers, Marcellous Blount, Rudolph Byrd, John Callahan, Hazel Carby, Skip Gates, Michael Harper, Mae Henderson, Vera Kutzinski, Deborah McDowell, Nellie McKay, Ted Mason, Bob O'Meally, Arnold Ramparsad, Charles Rowell, Kalamu Ya Salaam, Hortense Spillers, Bob Stepto, Claudia Tate, Gordon Thompson, Eleanor Traylor, Cheryl Wall, Mary Helen Washington, and Cornel West.

As this project swung into full gear, I was fortunate to share many intensely splendid moments with my local crew, the Racial Theory Group, comprising Raphael Allen, Eddie Glaude, Paul Jefferson, Wahneema Lubiano, Lou Outlaw, Fasaha Traylor, and Howard Winant, who substantially deepened my approach to the complex material and rhetorical contexts of the Black Arts Movement, while reminding me whenever necessary to "subject myself to some serious criticism." At a time when I might well have lagged or flagged in this work, no more spirited cohort could have been desired to provide encouraging support.

During this period, I have likewise been blessed in my institutional life, which has included the wonderful members of an English department marked by uncommon sanity and supportiveness. Over the years, they have sustained for me an ideal teaching environment while encouraging my research with a perfect blend of trust and candor. Thanks, then, to Julia Epstein, Steve Finley, Elaine Hansen, Joanne Hutchinson, Maud McInerney, Raji Mohan, Jim Ransom, Debora Sherman, Gus Stadler, Theresa Tensuan, Martha Wintner, and Tina Zwarg, as well as the marvelous staff of Dorcas Allen, Violet Brown, Carol Henry, Sharon Nangle, and Carol Wilkinson. Haverford College, with its traditions of rigorous, respectful exchange across all structural borders, has proven an exceptional place to pursue interdisciplinary study of the sort attempted in this book. The many humane colleagues across the disciplines who have helped shape my thinking over the years are too numerous to catalogue, and so with all of them in mind I'd like to thank especially participants in the recent Faculty Humanities Seminars on narrative, cultural memory, and performance: Kofi Anyinefa, Israel Burshatin, Roberto Castillo-Sandoval, Doug Davis, David Dawson, Steve Finley, Richard Freedman, Ashok Gangadean, Maris Boyd Gillette, Laurie Hart, Paul Jefferson, Rebekah Kowal, Aryeh Kosman, Jim Krippner-Martinez, Anne McGuire, Jim Ransom, Deborah Roberts, Ulrich Schönherr, Michael Sells, Debora Sherman, Sara Shumer, Kathleen Wright, and Tina Zwarg. And ultimately, anyone's work at Haverford College bears the positive stamp of its vibrant student body, to which I am grateful not only for their intellectual keenness but for their concern to vitalize knowledge through an active quest for social justice. I'd especially like to thank students from English 218, 261, 361, and 389 for sharing with me the exciting challenges posed by many of the works discussed in the following pages.

All of these people are very much part of the "family" to which this book is dedicated. But to the more immediate wellspring from which I've drawn sustenance "all the years" I owe special gratitude. My parents, George and Alice Benston, and my parents-in-law Myron and Madeleine Greengold, have been intellectual and moral exemplars; with grace, they have moreover actually believed me when I told them I was "almost done" with this endeavor. The closer sharers of my daily rounds, Sue, Shawna, and Cliff, have often known better, but have graciously cheered on my efforts, even when those labors came at their expense. By the same token, as the old academic lament has it, I might have finished somewhat earlier had it not been for the lure of their ever-joyous presence; but it is even truer that this work matters to me especially because of them. Yoy.

Finally, I'd like to thank those folk at Routledge who helped bring this book to fruition. The scholars who read the manuscript for Routledge were charitable in their judgments, but equally kind in their suggestions and criticisms, which I have tried to heed; if I have done so with uneven success, it has not been for lack of clarity or astuteness on their part. Talia Rodgers and her assistants Sophie Powell, Rosie Waters and Kate Trench surely have the patience of saints, but they also possess the command of savants, and know how to just plain get the job done: thanks for everything.

A last, but important, note: work on this book was greatly facilitated by an NEH Fellowship and a Whitehead Faculty Grant.

Kim Benston
Haverford, Pennsylvania

Portions of this book have appeared in different form in the following venues: Parts of Chapter 1 as "The Aesthetic of Modern Black Drama," in *Modern Black Drama*, ed. Errol Hill (Prentice-Hall, 1980), pp. 61–88; parts of Chapter 4 in "Performing Blackness: Re/Placing Afro-American Poetry," in *Black Literature in the 1990s*, eds. Houston A. Baker, Jr. and Patricia Redmon (University of Chicago Press, 1989), pp. 164–85; and parts of Chapter 6 in "Locating Adrienne Kennedy," in *Reconsidering Adrienne Kennedy*, eds. Robert Jackson and Lois Overbeck (Minnesota University Press, 1993), pp. 113–30. I am also grateful to audiences at the following places who have heard and through their comments improved sections of the manuscript: Beaver College, Emory University, Hamline University, Harvard University, the University of Michigan, the University of Pennsylvania, Princeton University, the University of Virginia, Wesleyan University, and Williams College.

Note on the text

I have employed a typographical convention that may need brief explanation. Single quotation marks have been used to denote paraphrase, cliché, and popular proverb, as distinguished from direct quotation (for which the standard double quotation marks are used).

Prologue
Performing blackness

Brothers and sisters, my text this morning is the Blackness of Blackness
. . . Black will make you . . . or black will unmake you.
                                                      Ralph Ellison, *Invisible Man*[1]

Brown is not brown except when used as an intimate description of personal
phenomenological fields. . . . that is, we need ahem, a meta-language . . .
something not included here.
                                                      Amiri Baraka, *The Slave*[2]

I

The Postal Official was taken aback: he was on a routine inspection of a
sorting office on Chicago's Southside, but what he saw was definitely *not*
routine. Off to one side, without ostentation or fanfare, a young worker
was sorting his pieces as if he were Michael Jordan giving a clinic: around
the back – *shump!*, into the box; through the legs – *swish!*, into the bag;
and so on. The Official couldn't forbear: "Young man," he intoned, "that's
truly amazing!" "Aw, man," the worker shot back, flipping another piece
over his head neatly into a slot, "This ain't nuthin . . . you just wait 'til I
can *read* this jive!"

I first heard this Dick Gregory tale when growing up in Chicago in the
1960s. Now, Gregory told the story to our predominantly black high school
audience with an undertone of sardonic bitterness at its implicit dichotomy
of blackness and literacy. At the same time – and no doubt Gregory had
this too in mind – we recognized humor in the delicious irony of style's
triumph over the alienating technology of officialdom: the trickster over
the chump, the hipster over the Man. With perhaps too little appreciation
of Gregory's cautionary tone (or of his appended maxim: "Get from the
playground to the proving-ground") the tale made the sandlot rounds for
many months, and even if we used to speak of Earl-the-Pearl and Chet
Walker instead of Michael Jordan, it answered exultantly to some rebellious
need we all felt as we crawled our way through the labyrinthine nightmare

of urban educational decay. We imagined that its strategies of indirection and displacement were designed to create alternative expressive possibilities to those proferred by the master('s) texts: its hyperbolic and parodic adherence to institutional order suggested how the wit and irony of performance could supplant the classifying norms of sanctioned writing.

Little did I suspect that the story could be redeemed years later as an allegory of my professional life – not, thank goodness, as a postal clerk, but, in one of its more perverse variations, a literary critic – a critic specifically of African-American expressive tradition. For at the time I was first encountering Gregory's little fable as a schoolboy in Chicago, the state of African-American literary interpretation was well reflected by the tale: obscured by the shadow of a hermeneutical technology produced as much to confine as to illuminate black expression, pieces of African-American literature were casually, if elegantly, sorted into categories (of period, genre, and "sensibility") – but few were actually being read as a dynamic activity capable of transfiguring both reader and the textual event of meaning. Since then, a veritable explosion in interpretive activity and acumen has taken place, so that we find ourselves on the threshold of an entire revaluation of the very image and import of African-American literary and cultural tradition.

A key ingredient of this critical revolution, indeed its enabling condition and interior rationale, was the vigorous debate taking place among black artists and intellectuals about the function of literary expression in the wider contexts of black liberation and evolutionary black consciousness. On the one hand, literature was seen as both an inadequate defense against the harshness of African-American experience ("ain't seen no poem stop a '38" – Haki Madhubuti[3]) and as an exile into the "dead letter office" of an alienating, duplicitous, and oppressive medium ("so many words, but none of them are mine" – Amiri Baraka[4]). On the other hand, writing, properly reconceived and directed as utterance and as act, was advanced as a signal instrument of cultural liberation. But, for this revolutionary alignment of voice and purpose to be achieved, the "new breed" (Peter Labrie, after James Brown)[5] of black artists would need to fashion a dynamic new poetics: expression would become preeminently theatrical ("the poet must become a performer" – Larry Neal),[6] performance would become transitive and transformative ("Art is change . . . poetry and writing . . . must move (swing) . . . this is what makes black culture go" – James T. Stewart),[7] and, finally, the artist would herself become an exemplary performance ("Don L. Lee/Is a poem . . ." – Marvin X).[8]

This book offers a preliminary exploration of the performative ethos informing African-American modernism, where "black modernism" designates that politico-aesthetic ferment arising with the black consciousness movement of the 1960s, a still-living moment in which a sustained effort to transform representation into presentation became the hallmark of a fresh chapter in the history of African-American cultural expression.

Though in my concluding chapter I will argue that this modernist upheaval's lengthening shadows continue to tinge today's critical and creative scene, my chief concern will be the era known, after Larry Neal, as The Black Arts Movement, the period extending somewhat beyond the defining decade of 1964 (the year of Malcolm X's rupture with the Nation of Islam) to 1974 (the year of Baraka's renunciation of absolute black nationalism), during which the category of "blackness" served as the dominant sign of African-American cultural activity. Such a description might well join hands with the satiric demythologization propounded by "*New Black Artists*" like Trey Ellis – whose thumbnail 'history' of the Movement catalogues such items as Eddie Murphy's angrier-than-thou poem of 'pure' blackness, "Cill [sic] my landlord," and Reginald Hudlin's 'people's ads' for a commodified Afro-Power militancy (one item: a combination spatula-backscratcher-toilet bowl brush, all with black clenched-fist handle-ends)[9] – in portraying the Black Arts Movement as a dangerously closed system of doctrines and fashions, and, in particular, as a self-deceived discourse declaring itself unambiguously to be a mode of authentic being unprecedented in African-American history. And yet the profound reorientation of energy and vision which took place among African-American thinkers, writers, performers, and their audiences during this period, centering on consideration of an intentional, autonomous understanding of the black self, took place through dynamically varied experiments concerning the provenance, nature, and teleology of the sign of blackness. Freed from slavish adherence to both the proclamations of its most ardent partisans and the caricatures of its more antic detractors, we can see the Black Arts Movement, not as creed or even as method, but rather as a continuously shifting field of struggle and revision in which the relations among politics, representation, history, and revolution are productively revalued.

In order best to move within this field with corresponding openness, I have chosen to discuss the polymorphic movements of "blackness" within a number of genres and artists: from drama and vernacular sermons to Ed Bullins and Sonia Sanchez, from New Wave jazz and autobiography to Ntozake Shange and Rev. C. L. Franklin. A more precise sketch of the design housing these explorations follows near the end of this Prologue, but in keeping with the need to read the Black Arts Movement *vis-à-vis* the suppleness of its inquiries rather than through predetermining frameworks I'd like first to outline the complex relation of blackness to performance that informs my approach. *Blackness*, in fact, emerges from close scrutiny of the movement's leading theorists – Malcolm X, Baraka, and Neal chief among them – as a term of multiple, often conflicting, implications which, taken together, signal black America's effort to articulate its own conditions of possibility. At one moment, blackness may signify a reified essence posited as the end of a revolutionary "metalanguage" projecting the community toward "something not included here"; at another moment, blackness may indicate a self-interpreting

process which simultaneously "makes and unmakes" black identity in the
ceaseless flux of historical change. Several animating tensions proliferate
from this abiding debate on blackness: Is the self of blackness an empirical
presence, a goal, or a necessary fiction to be ultimately discarded in the
higher interests of communality? Is there a language cognate with this
black selfhood, one capable of legitimating its most daring political and
psychic desires – and, if so, does this language exist prior to the intended
rupture with the past or is it an effect of that intention? On the other
hand, is traditional language, encrusted with the legacy of alienation, an
imprisoning mechanism or evasive lure? And if a meta-language can be
forged – for example, in the performative idioms of music, polemic, or
rebellion – can its styles of emancipation, didacticism, disruption, and celebration be reconciled in a coherent expressive discourse?

No doubt these are questions haunting the entire history of African-
American culture, and particularly those of earlier collective aesthetic
movements such as the Renaissance of the 1920s and the less-often
discussed bebop modernism of the 1940s. What gives such issues signal
emphasis during the period of the Black Arts Movement – and, in turn,
what makes investigation of the Movement's modernist impulse valuable
for an increased understanding of the larger history in which it is embedded
– is the way in which various socio-political and cultural perturbations
lent to the categories of change and difference an inherent, not merely a
strategic or historical, value. On the one hand, the modernism stirred by
Black Arts experiments must be studied as an adversary culture cultivating
styles of dissonance and refusal in an effort to resist the closures of all
received narratives and codes. In this spirit of calculated disorder, the
Black Arts descend, sometimes quite directly, from the dissonant fury of
the bebop generation.[10] On the other hand, seemingly anarchic negation
is deployed by African-American modernists in the interests of discovering
a space of redeemed value; in this quest for meaning and plenitude, modern
black art echoes the romantic metaphysics of the Renaissance.[11] But the
conjoined impulse toward rebellion without *ressentiment*, for a revisionary
violence which somehow both subverts and recuperates the past, delineates
the distinctive rhetorical field of Black Arts speculations on tradition. And
any critical appraisal of the Movement's effects must account for its
animating tensions in terms which reduce neither their contradictory nor
productive character.

In particular, we must negotiate the division that persists between our
appreciation of the era's expressions as text and our awareness of them
as performance – a gap which may fortuitously reflect the works' resistance
to totalization, to critical recuperation and ideological closure. Those critical narratives that do aspire to a synoptic assessment of modern black
expression evince a polar opposition: on the one hand, the work is measured
against a privileged notion of "blackness" which is posited as external to
both the Euro-American "mainstream" and, in a political sense, to the

work itself; on the other hand, the work is tested for conformity to a universally applicable norm of "the literary" (a trope of cultural value in general) which is supposed to exist both in and outside any notion of "blackness." I would argue that these views share a basic philosophic supposition – that the work's meaning may be located in some standard both prior and external to the expressive act itself – a supposition rooted in a common political implication: that the audience's role is to discriminate the "proper" from the "failed" or foolish, the correct from the deviant.

Let me quickly illustrate by contrasting two justly well-known appraisals of modern African-American poetry. Haki Madhubuti's (Don L. Lee's) *Dynamite Voices* may be taken as a representative of what I will term the "hermeneutics of blackness": for him, black poetry ranges on either side of the great divide of the Black Arts Movement, which created, in his view, the first thoroughly "Black" African-American poetry. While acknowledging the influence of earlier periods, especially the Harlem Renaissance, upon the new black poet's sense of purpose and seriousness, Madhubuti measures the "unique" status of the contemporary, originary black poem by a standard of didactic commitment, "concrete" subject-matter, and orality, a standard which no earlier poetry had fully realized. Against Madhubuti, we may place a representative of what I would call the "hermeneutics of recuperation," a reader such as Blyden Jackson, who, in his contribution to *Black Poetry in America* (co-written with Louis D. Rubin), sees likewise in the modern black poem a "world of blackness" where every utterance "sounds alike," a plainness which Jackson sees as threatening the reduction of the poetic to "a cartoon quality."[12] However, where Madhubuti sees in the modern discourse of blackness a salutary disjunction, Jackson offers to reassimilate the era's disharmonious outcries to the presumed continuity of a "synthetically American" tradition, allowing us to "think of recent black poetry at least as much in the context of poetry as of propoganda."

In a sense, Madhubuti and Jackson share a crucial presupposition for the interpretation of modern African-American expression: that the audience's role was radically reshaped or threatened by the emerging poetic of contemporary practitioners, a poetic which asserted that the peculiar power of black art was its refusal of difficulty and the accompanying need for professional exegesis or 'translation,' and, concomitantly, that the writer-performer, in questioning the authority of tradition, conceived his or her work as not merely experimental but as an exploration of radically alternative cultural constructs.

Curiously, both critical camps I have been outlining respond to this potential subversion of the uses and reception – indeed, of the very category – of black expression by reaffirming the rather traditional assumption that literature is an inevitable consequence of being, and that its "natural" role is to mime an experience whose authenticity is guaranteed by being enacted independently of any reflection upon it. Both Madhubuti and Jackson thus accept the opposition of expression-as-structure and expression-as-event, and each undertakes the task of maintaining the purity of one notion against the iniquity of the other. Behind this opposition stand a host of other, rather familiar, dualities which permeate both interpretive fields: assimilationism versus nationalism, language versus self, form versus content, oral versus written, craft versus politics (as in Jackson's dichotomy of "poetry" and "propaganda"), etc. It is the burden of my argument that unless we change place from a criticism erected on such contraries, locating our discussions at the challenging juncture of ideological and aesthetic concerns, we will be doomed to retrace the conceptual do-si-do marked out by the secret partners of recent years, the Schools of Absolute Blackness and Chastened Universality – and, further, we will fail to perceive or experience the era's own bracing lesson: that "blackness" is not an inevitable object, but rather a motivated, constructed, corrosive, and productive process.

Having said this much, I feel myself to be at a crucial methodological crossroads – for many of us, the next move has inevitably been either to take up one side or the other in revisionist fashion, or, in cursing both houses, piously or defensively to adopt some version of the (post-)structuralist/New Critical bromide about meanings, whether rhetorical or discursive, being "in the works themselves." The choice so constructed has been misconceived, and I would propose two alternative responses to the critical polarization in studies of African-American modernism that I have been outlining. First, the argument between Madhubuti and Jackson concerns the historical and ideological issue that, I am hinting, we as critics are as much challenged by today as are the artists of whom we dare speak; that is: What is the continuing meaning of the Black Arts Movement, on what terms shall we calculate its aims, achievements, and legacy? For our current disputes over, on the one hand, the propriety of extra-textual criteria, and, on the other hand, the political motivations of various neo-formalisms, should be seen as displacements or extensions of the essential inquisition of expressivity as a valid category of value, a questioning to which writers such as Madhubuti and Jackson were alike responding. The positions represented by Madhubuti and Jackson can be read as variant responses to the claims of rupture and resistance which were at the core of the "black aesthetic" – claims which, whatever their absolute philosophic and material validity, fundamentally altered the framework (conceptual and institutional) in which we operate today. Thus, one lesson of the fracturing of commentary into the poles I have described is that the tactics we employ in decoding and recoding modern black art still turn in some measure on our interpretation of the artistic revolution whose origins stand now at a generation's remove, on our attitude toward the programmatic declarations and practical performances which carry the Black Arts Movement's freight of aesthetic, ontological, and political visions.[13]

Relatedly, we must grasp with more particularity how this argument derives from African-American modernism's own struggle for self-definition.

Indeed, I would suggest that the two critical positions outlined above – one stressing the Black Arts' most vociferous ideological claims for an autonomous black poetics; the other seeking to situate black poetics within a larger, more continuous, and more textured field of expressive desire – echo an argument taking place among practitioners themselves about the nature of blackness, performance, and the modern African-American subject. To establish a paradigm for this discourse – which we shall see emerge throughout this study in the disparate arenas of theater, music, poetry, preaching, and criticism itself – I'd like briefly to contrast two passages which offer brilliantly compressed reflections of the key issues involved: the sermon on the "blackness of blackness" in the Prologue of Ellison's *Invisible Man* and Clay's climactic speech in Baraka's *Dutchman*. Each text privileges the relation of blackness to performance as a vision of African-American identity, grouping around that topos a complex of problems integral to any discussion of modern African-American expression (problems concerning the relations of history to tradition, revolution to repetition, textuality to orality); but they also do so in order to figure quite distinct theories of both black selfhood and its formation by and in the "play" of a renovated language of black identity.

II

This grid, ideal,
intersecting squares,
system, thought,
western wall,
migrating phoenix,
death to all.

Michael Harper, "Apollo Vision:
The Nature of the Grid"[14]

Let us begin with Ellison's passage:

I not only entered the music but descended, like Dante, into its depths. And *beneath the swiftness of the hot tempo there was a slower tempo and a cave and I entered it and looked around and heard an old woman singing a spiritual as full of Weltschmerz as flamenco, and beneath that lay a still lower level on which I saw a beautiful girl the color of ivory pleading in a voice like my mother's as she stood before a group of slaveowners who bid for her naked body, and below that I found a lower level and a more rapid tempo and I heard someone shout*:

"Brothers and sisters, my text this morning is the 'Blackness of of Blackness.'"

And a congregation of voices answered: "That blackness is most black brother, most black . . ."

"In the beginning . . ."

"At the very start," they cried.

". . . there was blackness . . ."

"Preach it . . ."

". . . and the sun . . ."

"The sun, Lawd . . ."

". . . was bloody red . . ."

"Red . . ."

"Now black is . . ." the preacher shouted.

"Bloody . . ."

"I said black is . . ."

"Preach it, brother . . ."

". . . an' black ain't . . ."

"Red, Lawd, red: He said it's red!"

"Amen, brother . . ."

"Black will git you . . ."

"Yes, it will . . ."

"Yes, it will . . ."

". . . an' black won't . . ."

"Naw, it won't!"

"It do . . ."

". . . an' it don't."

"Halleluiah . . ."

". . . It'll put you, glory, glory, Oh my Lawd, in the WHALE'S BELLY. . . ."

"Black will make you . . ."

"Black . . ."

". . . or black will un-make you."

(Ralph Ellison, *Invisible Man*, 8–10)

As if deliberately reversing the illusionary, dematerializing movement of humanist metaphysics – that movement of cancellation and concealment by which an irreducible expressive openness is emptied out into an essential propriety – Ellison ironically displaces "white mythology's" fable of the origin with a story of the beginning-as-blackness. At that beginning, the passage suggests, we find enacted a series of complex differences and dislocations, first imaged here as a "descending" through cultural realms (hence Dante, flamenco, and yiddishkeit are invoked even as the "spiritual" world of African-American descent is evoked). In what the novel will later teach us to call a Rineheartean questioning of the fluid world beneath any textual field, Ellison's hero plunges toward a site where language, in the crucible of national and family romance, has both the impulse to summon a presence and the power to declare its own absence, to proffer a story of the past while thematizing the performative or fictional character of all such telling. In the performance of the preacher, Ellison thus stages the strategy of the topos of beginning as an interrogation of received cultural abstractions asserting an absolute place of origination, those privileged allegories of Foundation by which historicism (*à la* Brother Jack, the neo-Hegelian political theorist of the Brotherhood) and mythography (*à la* Homer A. Barbee, the blind poet of the College's Moses legend) alike declare their mastery. By thus de-naturalizing "history" as an essential, teleological display of a preconstituted being-as-blackness, the passage forces us to consider blackness as a mediated, socially constructed *practice*, a process and not a product of discursive conditions of struggle.

The generative energy of the passage thus emanates from a dialogic site-ing (in the root sense of *sermo*): the preacher's public speech on blackness. But in noting Ellison's effort to expose the impossibility of a pristine narrative of beginnings which could stand beyond any revisionary performance, we might well observe that the passage is itself a critical repetition, a slyly belated quotation, of another 'primordial' sermonic beginning in American literature: the "blackness of darkness" briefly heard and quickly shunned by Melville's Ishmael at what "seemed the great Black Parliament sitting in Tophet" (*vide* "The Carpet-Bag" chapter of *Moby Dick*).[15] The blackness of Melville's preacher is an outcry of utter negation, a cacophony of "weeping and wailing and teeth-gnashing" which must be at once glimpsed and then escaped as the enabling, "stumbling" prelude to the more thunderous preachments of authorized whalers. For Melville's privileged figures, be they questers or questioners of the Primal Name, "blackness" remains "profound" and "aweful" but always chthonian, while the more resonant ambiguities of "fluid identity" are ascribed to the "grand hooded phantom" of a "whiteness-of-whiteness." Accepting the ambiguity of his own beginning, Ellison at once cites Melville's text as an inescapable element of the American scene and appropriates its authority over that scene by reshaping it toward a new "end." Ellison, in effect, forces Ishmael (and, with him, the quintessential American reader Ishmael implicitly mirrors from the moment of *his* inaugural "calling") to re-enter the arena of the preacher's dark pronouncement, and then suggests that the text of blackness is precisely about the internal contradictions, necessary repetitions, and transgressive revisions of any beginning *per se*. But further, Ellison's text thematizes the problematic of beginning as performed repetition by declaring its own divided status as expression.

"Black will make you . . . and unmake you": understanding its existence as irreducibly heterogeneous, blackness establishes and yet also destabilizes the very ground of its own figuration, thus simultaneously asserting and dislocating its own privileged status as arch-signifier of African-American expression. Embracing the "is" and "ain't" of the being-of-blackness, announcing a kind of dark Law of Contradiction *in place of* the dominant representations of black discourse, this topos presents the possibility of a differential principle of identity which refuses any effacement of the dissimilar by a totalizing theory of African-American existence (as in Ishmael's hurried critique of the "negro preacher's" sermon as "Wretched entertainment"). Thus, the sermon works by differential tensions, defining the ever-shifting 'scene' of African-American language as dialectical: "In the beginning" was the sign of the End, the bloody sun of *Revelations* (cf. *Rev.* 6:12); black will and it won't; love enfolds hate; laughter echoes moan – a doubleness experienced both rhetorically (won't/don't) and dramatically (the "ivory" whiteness-of-whiteness calls for the preacher's "black" response). Primordial blackness is thus not a node of absolute essence but, rather, the (re)discovery of the subversive ambiguity of any expressive act, its inceptive entanglement in a culture of veiled beginnings and benighted closures. It is the endlessly enigmatic name for a ceaselessly elusive agency, that which puts the reluctant prophet into the dark cave of the WHALE'S BELLY as the precondition of his deliverance through and for testifying.

This theory of blackness clearly has profound implications for performative and interpretive practice alike. But let us explore such possibilities in concert with a Barakan vision of blackness. Here is an excerpt from Clay's angry, and ultimately fatal, disputation with his "ivory" antagonist, Lula:

> Just shut up. You don't know what you're talking about. You don't know anything. So just keep your stupid mouth closed . . . and let me talk. . . . The belly rub? You wanted me to do the belly rub? Shit, you don't even know how. You don't know how. . . . Belly rub is not Queens. Belly rub is dark places, with big hats and overcoats held up with one arm. Belly rub hates you . . . They [whites] say, "I love Bessie Smith." And don't even understand that Bessie Smith is saying "Kiss my ass, kiss my black unruly ass." Before love, suffering, desire, anything you can explain, she's saying, and very plainly, "Kiss my black ass." . . . Charlie Parker? Bird . . . would've played not a note of music if he just walked up East Sixty-seventh Street and killed the first ten white people he saw. Not a note! . . . You don't know anything except what's there for you to see. An act. Lies. Device. Not the pure heart, the pure pumping black heart. . . . You understand? No. I guess not. If Bessie Smith had killed some white people she wouldn't have

needed that music. She would have talked very straight and plain
about the world. No metaphors. No grunts. No wiggles in the dark
of her soul. . . . all it needs is that simple act. . . . Ahh Shit. But who
needs it? I'd rather be a fool. Insane. Safe with my words, and no
deaths, and clean, hard thoughts, urging me to new conquests.

(Amiri Baraka, Dutchman, 34–45)

A vision of blackness in relation to being and performance, Clay's speech
is like the preacher's sermon in constituting an ideological and epistemological theory of signification. But if in Ellison we see the unmasking of
myths of idealized presence and the disclosure of a diacritical dispersal
of linguistic force, in Baraka we feel a counter-movement from the impure
to the essential, a deliberate and violent reversal of Ellison's descent which
points beyond the realm of figure to its corrected meaning in a "proper"
form. For Baraka, the expressions of language and the body of blackness
are diametrically opposed; discourse and being are not, as for Ellison,
thoroughly intertwined, and the possibility of "knowing" begins with an
emphatic refusal of eloquence's prestige. Blackness, far from being inextricable from the paradoxes of its articulation, finally transcends
representation. If it is the always present yet always coded subject of
African-American cultural expression, the appearances of that culture do
not themselves constitute blackness – African-American cultural expression
is not, in fact, the *thing-in-itself* of the blackness which its pronouncements
would invoke.

Clay's blackness "hates" the representational realm of *as if* in which he, as
a mere preacher of the Word, remains enclosed in a spurious "safety." It
longs for incarnation as literal presence, for the singular revolutionary
act that would "murder" self-difference and heal the breach between black
identity and discourse which the original violence of whiteness opened. The
effusions of a "pumping" blackness would replace Ellison's projection of
black performance as irresolvably mediate, positing a "pure" center around
which would gather an essential, empowered meaning to African-American
being. This center becomes the authentic "heart" of performance, redeem-
ing black expression from its condition as diasporic, alienated, and even
burdensome "device."

Clay's polemic against the "lie" of "metaphor" would shatter the
Ellisonian scene of textual construction, a scene which Clay's vision sees
as *itself* (and not simply the hidden white master) imposing the "mask" of
blackness-as-being: Ellisonian discourse, Clay seems to propose, points to the
self-repeating act of signifying (cf. the play's subway train in its mock-heroic
quests of endless return) rather than to the longed-for signified. Thus, the
image of destruction, of smashing the idols of the tribe, yields not silence but
"plain talk," the sacramental violence in which desire is at last fulfilled, not
deferred, in which speech is deployed not deferred to, in which the act of the
present cancels the emptiness of performances heard as ends in themselves.

We may, in fact, note that where Ellison is concerned with the twisting of ends into their "possibilities" as beginnings, Baraka more apocalyptically would deliver black speech from the cycle of servile reiterations we call African-American tradition, yielding a radically de-sublimated perspective utterly beyond the reach of a textuality suffused by pathos and limitation. Thus, though both authors stage their visions of African-American identity as a performative response to the historical condition of blackness-as-exile, their conceptions of that performance and the terms of its interpretation are instructively divergent. Where Ellison's questioning of origins gives to language a productive capacity accomplished only in its performance, Baraka's interpellation of a longed-for end envisions play as either a prerevolutionary diversion or, more radically, a postemancipatory sacrament in which the coded meaning of historical black expression would become "very straight and plain." Performative activities, in *this* world in which we perforce have our beginning, are at best only approximations of the continuous ideal of lived experience; as deflections of genuine revolutionary feeling, they are still more distanced from the continuous essence of truly free action. In the vision of a "simple act" of liberatory violence, Baraka's hero in fact assigns a signal role to the pure gestures of performance. But the authenticity of those gestures is realized only through a termination of the self-questioning (or, to fully accept Baraka's polemic against Ellison in this drama, self-falsifying) theatricality of the subterranean preacher. Performance is not, then, inescapably dissonant and aporetic. But until it is directed to invocation of an indivisible (not invisible!) kernel of blackness, becoming both the site and mechanism of a revolutionary transubstantiation, performance can only be a mockingly faint shadow of a more 'real' expression (Clay's speech, after all, understands itself to be yet another 'text' of African-American literary tradition, and its citation of Ellison's preacher, unlike the preacher's revision of Melville's Ishmael, reinscribes a sign of self-enslavement, not self-enablement). Thus, the prophecy of revolutionary blackness must supersede the Ellisonian story of performed blackness as necessary fiction, displacing the reductive "conquests" of self-reflexive play by the revelation of a de-metaphorized 'darkness of Soul-ness.'

III

i'm
gonna spread out
over America
       intrude
my proud blackness
all

    over the place

Mari Evans, "*Vive Noir!*"[16]

The Ellison/Baraka argument over the nature and telos of performed blackness brings us back to the question of interpretive strategies with which we began this more-than-Ellisonian deferral. Ellison's view of blackness as endless beginning suggests that its meaning does not inhere in any ultimate referent but is renewed in the rhythmic process of multiplication and substitution generated from performance to performance. This is not in the least to say that Ellisonian performance is arbitrary or empty, just as it is not abstracted or objectified. Rather, it is a construct of desire, mobilized at a site of struggle against various forms of ideological closure. As interpretive respondents to its performative call, we are asked to acknowledge the perpetually unsatisfying and contradictory character of its enunciations. As compensation, we are offered a notion of the black text as a dynamic producer of richly differing signifying perspectives – a fashioner, in fact, of a world (as the hero puts it near the end of *Invisible Man*) "seething with possibilities."

Baraka's vision, by contrast, asks us to negate the effects of such temporizing displacements, to materialize the presence dissimulated in performance by moving *through* the text to the truth of blackness beyond it (one might say, to *literally* per-form!). The dance of blackness here is, to those who embody it, spectacularly unconcealed: it possesses a sense and sensuality which precedes "anything you can explain." In a sense, Baraka's blackness stands beyond the need for exegesis as such; Clay's sermon is ironically directed to an auditor (i.e., Lula) who, *ipso facto*, can't "understand" it, while his longing is for a manifest, nonfigural "plainness" which precludes any need for elucidatory discovery. Indeed, until the "simple act" of revolution provides a transparent epistemology of black presence displacing the partial performances that inadequately prefigure it, we may surmise that it is the *audience* (here imagined to be more like Clay than like Lula) rather than the performance which requires scrutiny, and that the preacher's task is visionary annunciation of the *is*, not dialectical hermeneutic engagement of the *is and ain't*, of blackness. For Baraka, the Ellisonian play of language's doubleness is a duplicitous discord that screams the burden of black modernism, that imprisonment or delay of diasporic wandering where "multiplicity" is only a scattering of being-as-blackness and "play" is a hurtfully necessary postponement of murderous redemption. And in a curious sense, representation is finally not problematic for Baraka as it is irresolvably for Ellison, because it can never quite erase blackness so as to mark in repetition its absence. Instead, representation temporarily, if hurtfully, hides or encodes blackness, allowing the possibility of its becoming present as a history which would not be a fiction, as a wholeness which would no longer enact its own fragmentation.

We are finally in a position to return to the contrast of interpretive modes, exemplified by Haki Madhubuti and Blyden Jackson, to which Baraka and Ellison might at first blush seem to correspond. After all, Madhubuti, like Baraka, invokes the extralinguistic standard of "correct" blackness in erecting a vision of the poetic canon, while Jackson, *à la* Ellison, would refocus attention on the verbal medium in which a rather more eclectic or "synthetic" vision of blackness evolves from generation to generation. But Ellison and Baraka are alike in just the crucial respect which sets them apart from Madhubuti and Jackson: both their accounts of the topos of performed blackness begin by asserting that African-American signification arises through rupture, loss, and the consequent desire for restored plenitude – and if they disagree about the destination of desire's projects, they together differ from Madhubuti and Jackson in seeing no immediately available cultural authority which could *stabilize* blackness's performances. In this sense, the Ellison-Baraka contrast offers us a mechanism – an enabling allegory, if you will – for resituating the critical opposition of "blackness" and "universality" onto a ground internal to African-American discourse itself – i.e., in Ellison and Baraka, we are offered models of the black performative 'text' which imply that such an opposition is itself constituent of African-American modernism, which in turn suggests that criticism might make that opposition its own subject.

What might this look like in practice? At this point I'd like to turn back to the contemporary criticism of black poetic practice, and admit that I have neglected one global analysis which offers insight into this critical dilemma/opportunity – that is, Stephen Henderson's "Introduction" to *Understanding the New Black Poetry*[17] – a work whose foundational value for cultural criticism has been richly explored by Houston Baker in *Blues, Ideology, and Afro-American Literature*,[18] and which I now take up as a complex and rare instance of theoretical praxis attuned to black modernism's performative ethos. In its amalgam of conceptual and practical reflection, this work generates a series of tensions and juxtapositions which are at once fruitful and, I think, in need of further exploration. I am particularly interested in the apposition of Henderson's strategy for decoding the work's performative enunciations (the structural investigation of music as "poetic reference") – a strategy which opens up expression as a potentially infinite realm of play – with his concept of "saturation" – which seems to operate simultaneously as a goal and limit of the interpreter's own performance. Allowing for a range of technical, thematic, and conceptual implications, Henderson's observations on the uses of music as compositional device collectively suggest that expressive form, through the topos of performance, has become an arena of possibilities rather than a fixed datum. The language of blackness thus becomes a practice of open-ended signifying, so that the category of "structure" which contains these remarks implicitly yields a more complex idea of structuration, that power to continuously rethink and revoice centers of cultural vision celebrated by Ellison's preacher and his congregation. Here the motility of the signifier and the materiality of the signified play across each other in a copious display of invention.

At the same time, however, the very tabulation of tactics and devices begins to formulate a mechanical or instrumental mode of reading, hinting at an impulse to reify intention and agency through codification of written forms and oral formulae. Thus, as if answering the objection that artistic performance cannot be reduced to a category of precise structural explanation, Henderson proceeds to his theory of "saturation," that arena of a blackness which texts somehow "manifest" and proper readers somehow "simply know." It seems to me that a potentially self-disabling theory is at work here: the black artist is "saturated" by that which he demonstrates, asking his audience to identify with what they already are. The artist becomes thereby a curiously reactionary figure, for the work's performative activity is denied any transformative force, be it didactic or subversive. Thus, the energies unleashed by performance are finally neutralized or contained by the privilege of a mutually "saturated" subject, the artist/audience who merge into the stabilizing order of *a priori*, external, reified "blackness." "Saturation," it seems, becomes suspended in the space of its own tautology, allowing only the choice between a hypertrophied (*sated*) and an empty (*satired*) blackness: the blacker you are . . . the blacker you are.

What are we to make of this apparent division in Henderson's critical project, this double perspective on performed blackness as both energized by its processual nature and confined by an extrinsic, if impressionistic, touchstone? In fact, there are other issues at work in Henderson's critique which might illuminate this tension. Throughout the essay, Henderson takes pains to orient analysis of the work's logical structure in ideological terms, continually observing that interpretive acts are never merely aesthetic, never free from the desire for power and cultural authority. Most importantly, he notes that this authority is not given but constructed and contested, although it secures its prestige precisely by presenting itself as inevitable. In some sense, it seems to me, the tension between structuration and saturation is a product of this ideological critique, expressing as it does a bifurcated evasion or subversion of "western" critical authority: on the one hand, we are given a guide to a *science* of interpretation which would withstand the assault of arbitrary dismissal; on the other hand, we are given a mode of *engaged* interpretation which authenticates the black reader's very cultural being as the enabling condition of his/her activity. Thus, Henderson would simultaneously concretize a canon for "understanding" the textual practices of African-American modernism (which would create a formal barrier to culturally inspecific, historically relativizing, or other reductive appropriations of visionary black expression) and re-idealize these forms as residing among "things unknown" (thereby creating a spiritual barrier to imperialistic or depoliticized parsings of black textuality).

This balance of objectives is, I believe, unsettled, but it is also unsettling in a very useful manner. The danger it courts is that of dismantling one metaphysical/ideological system by erecting another, thus recapitulating the political structure underlying textualist-idealist aesthetics. At this point we might have recourse to historical explanation, noting that the uncertainty of this double proposition arose in part from the circumstances of an institutional critical voice seeking to negotiate a register somewhere between the ignorant hostility of mainstream standards and the sometimes equally hostile anti-academicism of the performers themselves. Such a discussion is no doubt still needed – and my final chapter seeks to address similar performative cruces in contemporary black critical practices – though in admitting it we should be wary of being ultimately dismissive of the ingenuity of Henderson's vision. For we may also see in its inner dynamic a productive yoking of Ellisonian and Barakan perspectives, which acknowledges the endless reverberations of black language while imagining the proximity to this open performance of a meta-linguistic realm of ineffable amplitude. Moreover, in his attentive scrutiny of the works themselves for manifestations of performance and blackness alike, Henderson points the way past the criticism with which we began, which followed a procedure at once mimetic and normative, at once spuriously demystifying (in its claim to lay bare a "true" black poetics) and blandly remystifying (in its confident avowal of a guiding poetic ethics). By contrast, Henderson brings us back to the expressive itself as a realm of *theoretical* as well as aesthetic/political activity, while reminding us that determination of performance's construction in a diversified network of choices and constraints, not bland reiteration of received ontology or iconicity, impels aesthetic and critical practice alike.

IV

> Proper evaluation of words and letters
> In their phonetic and associated sense
> Can bring the peoples of earth
> Into the clear light of pure Cosmic Wisdom.
>
> Sun Ra, "To the Peoples of Earth"[19]

This insight returns us to Gregory's postal anecdote, which provides a refined gloss on the performative-theoretical inspiration of African-American modernism. The black worker, we recall, finds himself enmeshed in the delivery system of written records, where documents assert power to encapsulate complex movements of social and personal life. Assuming easy correspondence between word and event and among those assigned authority to determine their meanings' destinations, the institution of letters depends upon fundamental, undisturbed rules of intelligibility, as well as upon the generally unseen labor of its proper 'sorting.' The entire process of correspondence – from inscription to collection to provisional classification to dissemination and consumption – remains invisible and unquestioned, a tidy ideological circuit of transmission and retrieval. But Gregory's mail clerk deftly unhinges this machinery of documentary self-extension, interrupting the redundant relay of pages written and read. He does so not by any overt refusal or blunt sabotage, but rather by an insouciant ironizing of the system's assumed integrity. Far from inevitable, stable, and guaranteed, the official delivery of writing is exposed here as vulnerable to disruption all along the way, but especially in the concealed zones where the actual tasks of disposition and distribution take place. And it is made to seem all the more precariously contingent by the worker's *style* of subversion, an elegant cunning that doubles (and thereby slyly ruffles) the appearance of conformity, undermining rigid classificatory norms by seeming to fulfill them with such spirited devotion.

The following chapters engage works that, above all, exemplify the range of intentions and effects that such disruptive performances entail. They explore disparate but interlocking figures whose work not only collectively images the traits that most distinguish the period's activity – a valorization of critique and change, privileging enactment and improvisation over particular artifacts, positions, or achievements; an aversion to discrete conventions and genres, leading to an incorporative logic of bricolage and narrative experiment; a critical engagement with tradition through acts of mimetic displacement, appearing by turns demystifying, corrective, absorptive, and remystifying – but which, moreover, implicitly asserts the interdisciplinary nature of African-American modernism's theory and practice. By thus interpreting modern African-American performance through several of its most distinctive works, practices, and practitioners, I hope to demonstrate the semiotic and practical interdiscursivity operating across cultural idioms in the Black Arts era's struggle for a synthetic vision of black identity.

We begin with exploration of the period's principal media of performance activity and speculation, drama and music. Focusing on the evolution of dramatic form as vehicle of ideological inquiry, Part I discusses the new black theater movement both as ideological projection and self-consciously evolutionary practice; Part II, extrapolating the musical ideal subtending contemporary black drama, centers first on the jazz innovations of John Coltrane and then upon the poetic practice inspired by his experimental ferocity and untimely death. Developing the abiding tension within musical and dramatic expression between personal and collective voice, Part III shifts to the scene of two profoundly influential and distinctive efforts to redefine black agency as an askesis of self-enactment: first, we will 'sound' the passages of Baraka's self-transgressive quest for revolutionary voice; second, we shall shift tone radically in pursuing Adrienne Kennedy's haunting project of self-staging, a project that inventively pressures the effervescent idealism of Baraka's "postwestern" poetics. Finally, in Part IV we confront the most intricate nexus of performative and speculative energy to emerge from the Black Arts Movement's assertions of visionary blackness, the call of vernacular creativity and the response of critical theory. Through consideration, first, of the modern chant-sermon, which presents a literally moving meditation on the (re)making of black historical consciousness, and then of the autobiographical (and vernacular) dynamic of contemporary black criticism, we will encounter more directly the figure who is, in fact, the central player in African-American modernism's drama of transformative consciousness: the audience. Conceived, as we shall see in our opening discussion of theater manifestos, as precisely those concerned to join the artist in revising ideas of blackness through a synthesis of vernacular awareness and revolutionary aspiration, the audience is enjoined to bring its energies of perception toward transfiguration in the present tense of enactment, thereby affirming itself as telos and co-creator of the modern black artist's expression, be it dramatic, musical, poetic, or sermonic.

It's only fair to note that a slightly more conventional approach might be to discuss the vernacular first in this study, as "background" and "vehicle" of contemporary experimentation – and, indeed, we shall see throughout the first six chapters that vernacular modalities enrich Black Arts visions to an extent many explicators of the period would find surprising, contradicting as it does constructions of the Movement as utterly repudiating tradition. However, I believe that this permeating, central presence of vernacular inflections will be reduced to an instrumental role if treated merely as introduction to our critical narrative. Therefore I have waited for the final section to focus on vernacular performance in detail, hoping that it will be seen as itself a vibrant element of black modernist practice, not merely a funding source of tales, tropes, and tricks from which "real art" draws its inspiration.

In each chapter, though in decidedly different languages and domains, we witness variants of the Black Arts Movement's defining effort to become a self-interpreting entity – a concern that the first chapter on modern black drama seeks to elucidate through a reading of the movement's theater manifestos. But we will find it necessary upon occasion to interrupt our own mimesis of this concentration upon black modernist production, specfically to take stock of echoes and differences between the matrix of African-American performance and the Euro-American avant-garde. For certainly the assault upon representation and interrogation of metaphysical presumption to which Gregory's mail clerk introduced us as harbinger of Black Arts praxis is as marked in the experimental theatricality of the modern West. Yet that radical repudiation of conventional dramaturgy, a repudiation founded in the conjunction of Artaudian "cruelty" and Brechtian "alienation," often sets the deconstructive instruments of performance *against* apprehending consciousness. Even when consciousness is to be intensified by its immersion in an idealized *mise-en-scène* (Grotowski; the Living Theatre), we find it set in opposition to the intricate burdens of history and the sinuous responsibilities of remembrance.

Because our comparative discussions of African-American and Euro-American performance will be generally local and concise,[20] we might do

well here, before setting forth on our journey through Black Arts speculations and practices, to sketch a more synoptic account of the encompassing
frame of reference within which contemporary African-American performance and its criticism takes shape. The very prestige of the term
"performance" in contemporary culture can be traced to modernity's recession from the Real.[21] Specifically, performance acquires significant theoretical capital once secular revisions of a theocentric tradition have begun to
struggle toward new idioms of knowledge, history, and value. With the
Cartesian and Kantian objectification of self and world, respectively,
modernity arrives as a "science of man" claiming subjectivity as a privileged
panopticon immune to the histrionics of rhetoric, social commerce, and
political context. In one sense, the advent of modernity constitutes a new
chapter in the West's narrative of self-scrutiny, establishing meaning
through provisional interpretations, rather than by faithful transcriptions of
a transcendent verity. Yet by seeking to recuperate the European subject as
reliable center of meaning, modernity also participates in an ongoing effort
within western discourse to contain the disruptive energies latent in unau-
thorized concepts of performance. Thus, modernity as Enlightenment, however much a break from medieval structures of thought, can also be seen as
the apogee of a western tradition of occidental "antitheatricalism" that,
as Jonas Barish and David Marshall have demonstrated, sought to banish
the discursive and ontological "subversiveness" of all mere appearance in
order to secure a transparent representational order.[22] Wherever the performative had previously connoted impulses transgressing logic (be they the
agitations of desire, dream, ideology, rebellion, or any other site of intertextual transaction), it was to be replaced by a notion of performance as a
closed mimetic economy, guaranteed by absolute visibility and accountability, in the interests of a stable continuum of subject, knowledge, and
– not incidentally – state.

But whereas in the antitheatricalism characteristic of premodernity the
disruptive potential of performance was acknowledged as all too actual a
threat (hence the specular hyperbole noted by Barish in antitheatrical tracts
from Plato to Prynne), in modernity performance's destabilizing energy is
negated as a semiotic phantasm and logical error. No longer lurking at the
edges of the proper as a kind of impish, licensed Vice figure, performance
is emptied of any affective or intentional power, becoming instead, rather
like Macbeth's dagger, a deception whose threat lies in its ability to per-
suade the subject of its illusory agency, rather than in any direct impact on
(and within) the subject herself. Thus depleting performance of any uncanny
potentiality, modernity adopts what we may term ab-scene vision.

It seems to me no coincidence – and of signal import to the Black Arts
Movement's fascination with vernacular-inspired insurgency – that the
Enlightenment's evisceration of the performative sphere should occur
alongside a pervasive concern with otherness and a compensatory fetishization of writing as foundation of authentic selfhood. Challenges to European

culture, whether internal or colonial, were frequently transformed into confrontations between nature and imagination, provoking twin genres that betrayed the Enlightenment's occult obsession with antithetical spectacle: the sublime and ethnography. For what characterizes discourses on both "natural" and cultural monstrosities is the unpresentability of their putative objects, which remain immeasurable or impenetrable "others" to epistemological and ethnological perception. The uncanny, be it mountain or native, is ultimately factitious, for what the sublime and ethnography stage is not so much alterity itself as the interpretive hubris by which difference is apprehended. The object is defined as external to the viewer's mastery, not in genuine recognition of its otherness but only to legitimate the observer's own "anthropological" primacy.

Thus, as we shall further observe in Chapter 7's exploration of modern vernacular performance, the development of an ethnological strategy for neutralizing invisible and recalcitrant performances through offstage commentary occurs exactly when European culture is itself 'othered,' facing its own disappearance as mythic center in a Ptolemaic cultural design. So, too, conjuration of natural wonders restages a threatened fiction of mastery, reflecting modernity's characteristic doubleness as a putatively original and yet suddenly belated mode of self-presentation. The re-emergence of a more transgressive idea of performance within modern western culture must be seen as an internal resistance to this legacy of Enlightenment's sublimated, ethnocentric antitheatricalism.

Metaphors of performance proliferate, unsurprisingly, in those discourses that, however derivative of Enlightenment, begin by questioning its hierarchical relation between the observer and the scene of knowledge. Such revisionists as Freud, Nietzsche, Darwin, Marx, and Saussure decenter mythologies of the subject, logic, hermeneutics, the state, and the sentence with self-staging discourses of desire, rhetoricity, chance, ideology, and signification. And in the theatre itself Büchner, Strindberg, Pirandello, Artaud, and Brecht drive from the boards a classical paradigm of dramatic presentation, with its fixed distance between authoritative text and *mise-en-scène*, by defamiliarizing theatrical narrative, character, authorship, acting, and reception.

Nevertheless, this clearly subversive modernist valorization of performance over the meaning that would dominate it has not failed also to recapitulate modernity's imperialistic grasp for authority over the event. Intent on displacing the subject as an effect of language, psychic apparatus, episteme, or some other structure, diverse strands of Euro-American modernism converge in hurling agency into a "crisis" that menaces individual will and fractures communality. Above all, these modes of ironic disturbance have not produced a vision or methodology of audience identification sufficient to transform mimetic designs into what we shall term in the context of African-American theatrical experiments "methexic," or participatory and collective, practices. I suggest, then, that in the background of Black Arts speculations we keep in view Euro-American modernist performance as a double gesture: on the one hand, an impulse of revolt that would transcend modernity by acknowledging the failure of hegemony to eradicate difference, be it "indigenous" or "foreign"; on the other hand, a submission to modernity's metaphysical logic, allowing evasion of historical imperatives that remain either beyond its conceptual reach or outside its practical understanding.

As we shall note at opportune moments, African-American modernism, by contrast, augurs a sacramentalized performative present in order to redeem, not deny, the promissory notes of historicized subjectivity. The freedom it seeks dwells within, not beyond, collective resources of memory and desire. Developing parameters suggested by the Ellison/Baraka dialogue, performers in the era of the Black Arts Movement variously pursue a syntax of enactment capable of mobilizing spectatorship as a simultaneously sensate and sense-altering body, capable at once of unruly critique and revolutionary revision. Avatars of those silenced and abjected by modernity and western modernism alike, they comprehend diasporic consciousness not merely as conceit but as material condition. And so their experiments in dramatic, musical, poetic, vernacular, and critical form must at every moment negotiate momentous questions of sacrifice, sedition, and self-realization – but always with style, always with guile: ***shump!***, *into the box; through the legs* – ***swish!,*** *into the bag; and so on* . . .

Part I

Will the circle be unbroken?

Drama and the quest for communality

> And it is time now
> It is time
> It is time
> It is time
> Now
>
> Naomi Long Madgett, "The Twenty Grand
> (Saturday Night on the Block)"

1 Sighting blackness

Mimesis and methexis in Black
Arts theatrical theory

I

> The Revolutionary Theatre must take dreams and give them a reality.
> Amiri Baraka, "The Revolutionary Theatre"[1]

Modern African-American drama – the beginnings of which we might heuristically locate in 1964, with the first performances in New York of Baraka's bracingly experimental plays *Dutchman* and *The Slave* and the writing alongside them of his explosive theatrical manifesto, "The Revolutionary Theatre"[2] – arises in the fluid space between dream and reality, measuring their distance as a mode of historical critique while seeking their reconciliation as a means of cultural realization. At once resistant to prescriptions of social circumstance – the *is* of experience as confirmed by inherited conventions of "truth" – and eager to refashion stage representation as a vehicle for insurgent desires – the *must* of a reconfigured dramatic praxis – the African-American theater movement that emerges under the aegis of Black Arts innovation vividly embodies the double economy that we have sketched in the contrast between Ellisonian and Barakan figurations of performative blackness. For modern black drama seethes with impulses both radical and recuperative, visionary and strategic, iconoclastic and redemptive. Such vectors of de- and re-constructive energy are, I hope to show, only seemingly contradictory, determining as they do a matrix of theatrical exploration that sets thematic passion – the "dream" of a liberated blackness – and formal purpose – the agency of a refashioned "reality" – into dynamic, dialectical partnership.

The increasing visibility and influence of drama among the African-American arts during the Black Arts Movement has a clearer etiology than is usual in aesthetic evolution. During a period of expanding black (self-) consciousness, historical awareness, and public assertiveness – a time in which the rhetoric of collective identity and aspiration was quickly translated into stunning, often violent action – the African-American artist naturally sought a mode imbued with the structure of communal, and efficaciously political, activity. Hence, in modern black poetry (of which, as we shall see in Chapter 4, the Coltrane Poem is exemplary) we find a subtle yet unmistakable shift from valorization of the written word as signature of an achieved liberty, from what Robert Stepto has called "the Afro-American pregeneric myth of freedom and literacy,"[3] to privileging of the voice as both musical and oratorical instrument of rebellion. Hence, too, the appearance in African-American literary theory of overt ideological struggle and of the "black aesthetic" school with its emphasis on "extra-literary" values and opposition to the perceived formalism of academic criticism. Cognate with the emergence in African-American philosophy of what Lucius Outlaw terms an "antifoundationalist" quest for specifically "black theorizing" that is "itself a form of social praxis,"[4] black aesthetic and expressive inquiry made purpose the measure of speculative insight, real-ization the touchstone of reflexivity. In such an atmosphere, the rapid devel-opment of theater, an extremely political, because preeminently social medium, was inevitable.

As black artists soon recognized, the very essence of theater is its imma-nently collective experience, and in very practical terms, its affirmation or challenge of the audience's codes of conduct, their mechanisms of survival, their shared necessity, outrage, and vision. Theater can tap and redis-tribute custom and ceremony; it can generate violent energy (the French Revolution is sometimes said to have really begun when the opening night audience of Beaumarchais' *Marriage of Figaro* reacted angrily to the depic-tion of aristocratic life) or neutralize the impulse toward action. In political terms, then, theater can, when skillfully employed, become a powerful weapon for regulation of communal values, or, conversely, for radical change. Unlike written literature, it makes no demands of literacy or privacy; as the impulse toward agitprop street events and the proliferation of community-center/theaters during the era of the Black Arts attests (The Black Arts Repertory Theater/School [BART/S] of Harlem; The National Black Theatre, or Sun People's Theatre, also of Harlem; Concept East of Detroit; East Cleveland Community Theater; La Mont Zeno Community Theater of Chicago; Watts Repertory Company of Los Angeles, to name but a few), theater may become an enlivened synecdoche and galvanizing site of the self-defining national culture envisioned by its practitioners.

The emergence of a dynamic, articulate, and prolific African-American theater movement during the mid-1960s has been duly and variously noted by many scholars. Apart from sharply focused comments on individual play-wrights, this criticism has tended to be concerned with the drama's nation-alist values[5] or with the evolution and continuity of its moral and narrative ideas.[6] As a consequence, some comprehensive, insightful images of modern black drama have begun to take shape: we now glimpse clearly its messianic, didactic, and mythical lineaments. If, in the critical pursuit of thematic understanding, the drama has been too often subject to facile schematization or even distorting reduction, there yet exist now viable formulations of the black theater movement's basic ideological suppositions and effects.

Nevertheless, it is striking that – as has too often been true in interpretation of black literature generally – so little regard has been paid to
the structural dimension of the playwrights' interrogation of ideology's
implication in performative style and decision. It is its detractors who most
consistently call attention to the drama's form; by them, it has been
made to appear 'instinctive' or 'audacious' in the most reductive sense
– unshaped, fragmented, unreflexive, and indulgently improvisational,
centered only by reliance upon stereotyped action and tendentious narrative.[7] Sympathetic observers have, until recently, done very little to correct
this image, for they, too, seem to believe that modern black drama is
something that, formally, simply *happens*, oblivious or perhaps deliberately
antithetical to shaping concerns of aesthetic and imaginative design, as
befits its antipathy to oppressive systems and reified structures.

This inattention to the crossing of iconoclasm and formal experiment
is indeed ironic for, as is the case with African-American music, the self-
conscious development of organizing principles in black drama is the very
essence of its visionary quest. Such undervaluing of structural factors may
be understandable when one considers that exegesis of black drama, even
more than that of black poetry and fiction, has been forged in a climate
of polemical strife, marked by immediate demands of elucidation or affirmation, and hence has too frequently limited itself to a narrow conception
of ideological issues.[8] But beyond pressures of occasion, most particularly
the drama's intrinsic exposure to instantaneous public scrutiny,[9] modern
black drama's disavowal of conventional theater's disposition to aesthetic
distance – a resistance that, we shall see, is constitutive, yet various and
supple – has understandably evoked in its readers a corresponding resistance to formalist inquiry that isolates the subject in space, removing it
from historical context. Following the drama's own rebuke to alienated,
or disinterested, observation (the choice of Marxist or Kantian terms being
itself a matter of perspective upon varieties of Eurocentric estrangement
from engaged enactment), criticism has perhaps confused empathetic
involvement with a call to interpretation governed by thematic, characteriological, or propositional concerns. Scrutiny of the playwrights' own
struggle to define terms for the new drama, however, reveals a continuous, complex effort to imagine theatrical forms capable of containing
"revolutionary" content, to clear ground for a topos of performance that
dissolves stark distinctions of vehicle and tenor, modality and meaning.

Abiodun Jeyifous, in an historical, fundamentally thematic, critique of
black writings on African-American drama conducted in the twilight of the
Black Arts Movement, acutely defined the change in the modern (post-1963)
era as a shift from the commentary of "Negro Sensibility" – a blend of "western bourgeois esthetic criteria and a sentimental racial awareness" – to the
advocation of black "consciousness" – an avowed synthesis of dramaturgical
and ideological presuppositions.[10] As Jeyifous suggests, this desire to unite
a radical theatrical idiom with a new political vision caused the modern

playwrights to direct their theoretical as well as their practical efforts toward developing what Amiri Baraka first termed a "postwestern *form*." It is into this still comparatively untravelled and uncharted territory of theoretical form – what might be accurately termed the "self-staging of black theatrical consciousness" – that we must travel in our exploration of black theater during the Black Arts era, for an analysis of the modern black theater movement's major speculative documents will reveal just how intimately (and necessarily) intertwined have been ideological and formal innovation in the drama's search for a revolutionary mode of collective enactment.

Such scrutiny of disquisitions by theatre practitioners on the nexus of concept and medium serves not just as prologue to the next chapter's exploration of the era's staging of philosophic and political vision in three singular yet representative dramas – Ed Bullins's *Clara's Ole Man*, Adrienne Kennedy's *The Owl Answers*, and Ntozake Shange's *for colored girls who have considered suicide/when the rainbow is enuf.* It is itself a way of attending to the dialogic and contestatory enactment of that vision, as these treatises themselves constitute one of modern black art's most effective performance genres. For the Black Arts theater manifesto employs strategies of voice, characterization, and rhetorical presentation that self-consciously *dramatize* alternative aesthetic and political positions. Particularly in their shifting constructions of audience and styles of address, these texts – by turns meditative and exhortatory, descriptive and lyrical, prescriptive and celebratory – conjure the performance dynamic that they champion, evoking the adversarial and participatory possibilities central to the envisioned drama's *mise-en-scène.* By becoming themselves crucibles of cultural postures that inflect alternative theatrical values, modern black theatre manifestos seek deliberately to compel a response of repudiation or embrace that makes readerly performance not merely an effect but the essential aim of their tactics. As such, these texts stage their general conceptual ambition of enfolding theory and praxis through the generative agency of performative meaning.

I should make clear from the outset that these documents together describe an arc of development that, as the focus of our exploration, belies descriptions of the Black Arts Movement as a static, homogenous, and monologic formation. Restive and textured, black theater manifestos comprise diverse images of dramatic intention that cohere as a dialogue on presence and mediation, authenticity and signification. Specifically, the path of modern black drama's self-staging describes a curve which moves dialectically from quasi-naturalism and a defining obsession with Euro-American institutions toward the shaping of uniquely African-American mythologies and symbolisms, flexibility of dramatic form, and participatory theater *within* the black community. Spiritually and technically, this movement is one from mimesis, or representation (whether of a condition, ideology, or character), to methexis, or communal "helping-out" of the action by all assembled. It is a process that could be alternatively described as a shift from display, the spectacle observed, to rite, the event which dissolves traditional divisions between actor and spectator, self and other, enacted text and material context. And through this process, the black beholder has been theoretically transformed from a detached individual whose private consciousness the playwright sought to reform, to a participatory member of communal ceremony which affirms a shared vision.

At the same time, these contrasts of mimesis and methexis, exposition and ritual, can function only as strategems for denoting relative emphases and provisional directions within the movement's self-articulation. For modern black theater, considered as a collective endeavor, seeks ultimately not to jettison but to transmute mimesis, liberating it from its association with coercive reproduction – what Derrida terms the "mimetologism" anchored to a Platonic regime of the "proper" that is stabilized by refusal of revisionary play[11] – and redeploying its potential to organize a Scene of Instruction from which supplementary, even insurgent, images of 'the real' can be fashioned. In one sense, this 'thinking through' of mimesis, posited as the basis for dramatic representation from Aristotle to Benjamin, signals a kind of 'end to theater' as conventionally understood: where mimetic modes of action and perception founded that theater's purchase upon presence and consequence at the price of submission to an 'originary' (thus offstage) *autho*rity, modern black drama would rupture this metaphysical closure to forge transformative mechanisms of identification and meaning-production. Like the feminist "mimétisme" explored by Elin Diamond,[12] it seeks to displace white mythology's "scene of representation" by piercing its normative boundaries with alternative instruments of legitimation.

In this regard, modern black theater shadows antimimetic urges familiar in Euro-American dramatic (post)modernism, which likewise threaten to dissolve stage traditions in the interests of a broadly emancipatory protest. Yet where antithetical veins of enactment within Euro-American drama (be it Artaudian, Absurdist, or even Brechtian in inspiration) represent a discursive struggle within western canons that often pits defamiliarization against custom, culture against freedom, along lines dictated by the self-disabling logic of the avant-garde,[13] African-American modernist performance works to align disruptive play with cultural reconstruction, resituating rather than deconstructing the subject as an agent of historical ferment. Most particularly through an effort the renovate vernacular expression as a mechanism of ideological critique and communal revaluation – but not least in its insistence that annulment of the distance between stage and audience serve reconception not abrogation of the project of culture – modern black theater diverges from its Euro-American counterpart in retaining commitment to remembrance and history even as it annuls inherited mechanisms of social reproduction. Its refiguraton of mimesis, and the concomitant espousal of postnaturalist presentational techniques, seeks not an exit from history but a means of remaking historical consciousness: the urgency of that revisionary demand in turn yields novel images of theatrical space, expression, and perception. In effect, modern black drama asks whether mimesis cannot be reconsistuted *outside* the closures of mimetologism, such that its passage toward strategies of methexis can be seen as a quest for a reformed mimesis.

Considering the long-observed *will to self-enactment* embedded in African-American life and traditional art – the "poise for drama"[14] displayed in minstrelsy, the dozens, toasts, the call-and-response pattern of musical and religious performance, and the signifying improvisations of the street – we might have expected an untroubled flowering of dramatic innovation set in motion by contemporary political exigencies. However, given the need to articulate a radical contemporary vision of ideal-become-practice, the problem of form for the black dramatist is not so simple, the translation of dissident idea to dramatic action not immune from the sometimes ironic pressures of mediation. Though freer than the prose writer from the restrictions imposed on black vocality by the silent finality of a fixed text, the playwright must still face the task of creating a black theatrical idiom with the materials proffered by various dramatic conventions, each of which retains sedimented histories of stylistic and thematic implication. The modern black drama movement emerges, even in the space of specifically African-American theater, as an intricate encounter, by turns appropriative and antagonistic, with an inherited theatrical tradition in which audience and performer are kept distinct, narrative develops with sequential clarity, and character is explored as either exemplification or mockery of an historic investment in individual destiny. Such drama, whether it be that of a neoAristotelian liberalism (*vide* Hansberry) or its emblematic mirror in what Geneviève Fabre terms "the theater of experience"[15] (*vide* Hughes or Baldwin), assumes an apparently objective perspective on the "organic" evolution of personality and social structure, and understands randomness, disorder, anarchy, and simultaneity in experience as either threateningly unnatural or redemptively demonic. Its affirmation (as in the American tragic tradition from O'Neill to Miller to which it owes a fundamental allegiance) is of a painfully earned autonomy; its revolt (as in Expressionist or Absurdist drama, which it occasionally emulates or echoes in the pageant dramas of Hughes, the blues scenes of Baldwin or Childress, the elliptical fantasies of Edgar White, and the phantasmagoric eruptions of Hansberry's late plays) is a self-deprecating gesture of alienation, at base another form of willed isolation. Long fueled by the energy of revolt,[16] mid-century African-American drama remained uncertain how to proceed from dislocation to rearticulation, from exploration of incoherence within traditional paradigms of dramatic experience to restoration or institution of what Yeats called "the ritual of a lost faith." We might say that the modern black playwrights, recasting their predecessors' instinct to transpose available theater conventions into recognizably African-American circumstances, committed themselves to thorough reconsideration of the limits, costs, and even pleasures of such adaptive methods, prioritizing discovery of a language of shared symbolic struggle and thus, ultimately, of material liberaton over the requirements of dramatic propriety as defined by canons of personal determination. Most especially, their stance *vis-à-vis* received form was guided by a search for an idiom of the communal self that is both prior and consequent to individual expression, a ritual of faith not lost (as Yeats supposed) but suppressed, burdened, and variously displaced.

II

> America needs a killing.
> America needs a killing.
> *Survivors will be human.*
>
> Michael Harper, "Deathwatch"[17]

Inevitably, then, contemporary African-American theater's iconographic, thematic, and narrative (historical) concerns have led to inquiries into the nature of the dramatic experience itself. It is the continuity of dramatic *theory*, in fact, which allows us to see the apparently contrasting genres of the movement (didacticism, naturalism, various kinds of allegory, serious and comical rites, and, especially, numerous hybrid reconfigurations and attempted syntheses of these) as necessary and interdependent elements in a general reform. It is perhaps fitting, in light of the growing scepticism before received modes (including writing itself), that the first significant (and still most influential) manifesto was written by a figure with an already established reputation as poet, novelist, and essayist. Baraka's "The Revolutionary Theatre" self-consciously enunciated the guiding principles for a renegade, insurrectionist drama. Its tone, in typically Barakan fashion, is at once prophetic, apocalyptic, and hortatory. While foreseeing a theater "peopled with new kinds of heroes," the essay principally advertises the revolutionary theater as a "theater of Victims" which, despite superficially echoing the pathos of his forerunners' dramas of individual ruin and bafflement, will force upon the black onlooker images that kindle revelatory anger and liberating violence:

> The Revolutionary Theatre must EXPOSE! . . . It should stagger through our universe correcting, insulting, preaching . . . [it] must Accuse and Attack anything that can be accused and attacked. It looks at the sky with the victims' eyes, and moves the victims to look at the strength in their minds and their bodies.
>
> (Amiri Baraka, "The Revolutionary Theatre," 210–11)

Baraka's call is for a theater of uncompromising "assault" upon all that appears inimical to realization of black power. Doubling and troping Artaud's "theater of cruelty," which passionately rejects "our artistic dallying with forms, instead of being like victims burnt at the stake, signalling through the flames,"[18] the "revolutionary theatre" strips accretions of learned and imposed obligation to bare the essential gesture of "authentic" blackness. Evoking an Artaudian concentration of historical energy upon the present-ness of rigorous spectacle ("We are preaching virtue again, but by that to mean NOW ... [in] this consciousness epic, what's happening" – 210, 212), Baraka seeks to reverse the longstanding relation of theater and catharsis in black drama, purging the theater itself of tragic residues. Indeed, the envisioned theater, propelled through the essay by a series of forceful transitive verbs – *crack, kill, stagger, force, flush, reshape, move* – becomes itself the Artaudian actor, the living, priestly instrument by which culture is vitalized in a rite of purification that retrieves the root violence of the *sacred*. Or, more exactly, it is to be a theater without actors as such, propelled by forces that erase imprisoning outlines of personality, deconstructing individuals into attestations of mutual fatalities: "Our theatre will show victims so that their brothers in the audience will be better able to understand that they are the brothers of victims" (213). Thus, the aim of its aggressive exhibition is to "expose" the audience's own complicity with "artistic dallying with forms" that render them conventional "actors," miming sterile formulae of official scripts rather than forging identifications that elide the difference between witness and participant.

Like the Artaudian vision, then, the "revolutionary theatre" seeks to discredit habits of presentation and spectatorship that merely image but fail to promote cultural upheaval and revolution ("The Revolutionary Theatre should force change; it should be change," reads the manifesto's first incendiary pronouncement – 210). In its insistence on welding response to responsibility ("ethics and aesthetics are one" – 212), and in its urge to "reshape the world" as a specifically "social" praxis (212), "the revolutionary theatre" departs from the "disinterested" rigors of Artaudian gesture.[19] No less concerned than Artaud to "cleanse" stage space and theatrical perception of its oppressive opacity in the cause of a repotentialized and possibly postdramatic ceremony of collective release (210, 215), Baraka nevertheless projects a mode of performance that requires narrative clarity and precision, a succession of harsh representational moments, as it seeks to identify the exact institutional causes and effects of present conditions: "The Revolutionary Theatre is shaped by the world, and moves to reshape the world ... It is a social theatre ... we will change the drawing rooms into places where real things can be said about a real world" (212). The violence it would display and inflame is a product of uncompromising distinctions between the "reality" of black desire and the fantasms of "tired white lives" (213) that negotiate the gap between staged and "actual explosions" (214), collapsing "victim" and "brother" into a pluralized agent (an initial "they" being transmuted into the essay's insistent "we") through the critical depiction of "what we are." The theater

Baraka here envisions – notwithstanding its alchemical affectivity ("turned into the lights [of Revolutionary Theatre's] black nigger magic, . . . if the beautiful see themselves, they will love themselves" – 210) – is therefore a drama of the corrective, homeopathic, and pedagogical *word*.

At the heart of the revolutionary theater is the programmatic, and pragmatic, thrust of the then uncanonized "black aesthetic":

> . . . what we show must cause the blood to rush, so that pre-revolutionary temperaments will be bathed in this blood, and it will cause their deepest souls to move, and they will find themselves tensed and clenched, even ready to die, at what the soul has been taught. We will scream and cry, murder, run through the streets in agony, if it means some soul will be moved.
>
> (213)

The Barakan word, implicitly aimed toward creation of a unified black audience from the disparate fragments of "pre-revolutionary temperaments," is visceral and muscular, not introspective or disembodied (his "new kind of heroes" are not to be "the weak Hamlets" – 214). An intrinsically corporeal language, his dramatic idiom will implicitly model freedom from the tyranny of preexisting 'scripts' by its immediate concreteness. Seeking to heal the division between utterance and expression, between the materiality of speech-effect and the anteriority of 'authoritative' writing, the revolutionary theater correspondingly reimagines 'character' by communicating directly with the audience's anatomy. The heroes of his theater, like the African-Americans who are to observe them, are to be galvanized, not immobilized, by their materialization as "victims" whose redemption lies in shocked recognition of their own privation and potentiality: "Possibility is what moves us" (213).

Thus, Baraka ostensibly abjures the mournful tonalities inherent in the notion of an aggrieved heroism, the amoral pathos of inescapable and intolerable personal catastrophe. Having set in motion the bloody spectacle of victimization, Baraka recoils from the possibility of our stressing emotional commitment to the character who dies at the expense of attention to the action in which he struggles. He fears the establishment of a rhythm of *tragic* identification in which the ceremony of sacrifice is drowned more in pity than in blood. He fears, that is, the dissolution of revolutionary theater into the melodrama of liberal metaphysics and the recuperative economy of Aristotelian (dis)closure. And so the revolutionary hero (and the protagonists of Baraka's own early plays, *Dutchman* and *The Slave*, are striking instances) ultimately appears in "The Revolutionary Theatre" under a precariously double aspect: the sense of wasted individuality is to be dispelled by a joyful, if ruthless celebration of freshly conceived values. The hero is simultaneously forged and consumed by the sacrificial dynamic that defines the revolutionary theater's refusal of the very psychic structures it is designed to "expose." In turn, self and group converge, but do not quite coincide or cohere; the latter's ethos survives as implicit compensation for destruction of the former. Thus, while the essay is by implication a summons to unification, its admonitory "moving" of the black "victim" finally produces – or, at least, cannot fully forswear – a structural and emotional distance between the "theater of assault" and its supposed beneficiaries.

This problematic view of the hero and his audience is accompanied by a subtle, but definitive, dualism with regard to form. Baraka clearly desires a didactic and visionary theater that renounces the tepid naturalism of fourth wall ("drawing room") modernism, yet he is also committed to a kind of social realism, to a "preciseness [of] method" and a "social theatre . . . where *real things* can be said about a *real world*" (my emphases). An antifoundational polemicist with a distinctly Hegelian tinge ("This should be a theatre of World Spirit" – 212), he dreams of fusing "history and desire" (212) as physic for a continuing DuBoisean double consciousness, and proposes for his dream a violent test: subjective passion and concrete realism are the twin poles of his imagination. Baraka seems to sense here that the more intense the desire for heightened vision the more one must be pulled back to confrontation with the tangible, material world that appears doubly as essence and illusion. The key to this ambiguous realism (and its faint undertone of ambivalence in both provoking and mistrusting identification) is Baraka's recognition that what is at stake in revolutionary action is precisely the power to define "the real" itself: in the Barakan calculus, what one seeks is "*the* real world," antidote to the stifling "appearances" (codes) of "*this* 'real' world." Accordingly, "The Revolutionary Theatre" envisions landscapes of the "consciousness epic" which are yet contiguous with the agony-and-blood-drenched streets of its heroes. When act and art – "ethics and aesthetics" – are indeed "one," the fracture in "the real" will have been mended: "We are witch doctors and assassins, but we will open a place for the true scientists to expand our consciousness." (215).

As we will see when we revisit the visionary realism of Baraka's temper in Chapter 5, "The Revolutionary Theatre" played a critical role in the evolution of Baraka's own performative ethos; for our purposes here, it is enough to note that the treatise (and the drama he wrote contemporaneously – especially *Dutchman*, *The Slave*, and *The Toilet*)[20] has had profound effects upon subsequent theories. Of these, Ed Bullins's "The So-called Western Avant-garde Drama"[21] and K. William Kgositsile's "Towards Our Theater: A Definitive Act"[22] are closest both chronologically and conceptually to Baraka's piece. Even in their titles, one discerns traces of yet another subtle birfucation in "The Revolutionary Theatre"'s project: on the one hand, a dominating emphasis on quickening the African-American audience as instrument of its own deliverance; on the other hand, a continually resurfacing concern with Euro-American contexts of enactment (the new theater's enemies, Baraka's manifesto concludes, are "most of you who are reading this" – 215). Baraka, of course, was notorious both for the audacity with which he severed allegiance to his white ("downtown") artistic fraternity, moving uptown to found the BART/S, and the lingering impulse to cast final looks back in anger even as he was polishing the prophetic style of his black nationalist appeal. Taken together, Bullins's and Kgositsile's manifestos suggest that this divided attention is only partly a manifestation of double consciousness, and might rather be understood as elemental to allied necessities of critique and divination subtending the new drama's revisionary agenda.

Bullins's essay illuminates the mounting preoccupation in the final pages of "The Revolutionary Theatre" with mainstream culture's reaction to the new black drama, expanding upon Baraka's caustic espectation that "Americans will hate the Revolutionary Theatre because it is out to destroy them and whatever they believe is real" (214) and offering extended comparisons between Euro-American and African-American "worldviews." Bullins castigates modern Euro-American theater for its concentration on Freudian and existential dilemmas that, he contends, hold a mirror up to its own tortured psyche but not to the world of significant actions. Their "reality" is, as Baraka had implied, no reality at all; it is a frightening projection of "disbelief" and, ultimately, of despair. This squandering of meaningful experience, Bullins asserts, has resulted in the drama's loss of "plot and story and character," by which he means a naturalism that supersedes the anxieties of self-alienation. Bullins's essay thus calls attention to the threat to subjectivity posed by modernism's interest in identity as an aggregate of conflicting drives, a disruption of narrative logic that bespeaks a general cultural disorder in the aftermath of world war and the collapsing ironies of imperial ambition.

On this view, Euro-American art is, above all, belated, an art in which a strange, dissipated action (or its mere memory) has supplanted the vital, if sometimes disturbing investigation of shared presuppositions that made the appearance of "character" possible. Bullins is thus essentially determined to preserve the primacy of African-American theatrical narrative in an era of global performance experimentation that augurs displacement of revolutionary change by a fetishizing of psychic deconstruction. The tactile ferocity with which he concludes his essay conveys his desire for a new black theater that rejects the pervasive cultural decay implicit in western theater's flight from its own origins and promotes a black-oriented "realism" that remains visionary as an agent of moral legitimation:

> To paraphrase Brother LeRoi Jones [Baraka]: It is a post-American form of Black theater we Black Artists should be seeking. It is Black Art that is like a dagger pointed at the vitals of America, and through the rips "we" (US) can enter the New Epoch.
>
> (Ed Bullins, "The So-called Western Avant-garde Drama," 145–6)

Kgositsile's "Towards Our Theater," which foregrounds from the gitgo the collective pronoun that Bullins's manifesto ultimately invokes, represents a significant departure from the concern with Euro-American values and mainstream response: its sentiments concern black people only. Yet, like Baraka's, Kgositsile's program for black theater is based on a stringent critique of black culture as presently constituted:

> The desired and desirable will be seen through elegant image and symbol abstracted from life. The undesirable, the corrupting, the destructive, will be portrayed in a grotesque manner, its sinister qualities driving us to the mercy killing of the villain.
>
> (K. William Kgositsile, "Towards
> Our Theater: A Definitive Act," 147)

This discourse, as announced by the essay's first word – *TESTIFYING* – is the homiletic exercise of a righteous preacher, one whose text is dictated by focused nationalist principles and the imperatives of a cultural jihad. Though Kgositsile speaks briefly of a "theater of poetry" that combines "image, rhythm, and symbol," he clearly desires a sharply sententious, if sternly didactic, drama that confronts the audience with appropriately idealized or demonized figures instead of soothing it with theatrical illusion or complex ("poetic") representation. Kgositsile seeks ultimately a morality-play presentation devoid of "decadent" lyricism and driven by a programmatic firmness that castigates, worships, alienates, or affirms in unequivocal fashion. And, indeed, a good deal of black drama contemporary with "Towards Our Theater" is much as such a manifesto would establish: polemically, if impatiently, narrative, characteriologically reductive, and politically emblematic.[23]

Thematically Manichean, "Towards Our Theater" nevertheless courts hybridity in form even as it would secure new dramatic norms through an abjection of anything excessive to a "desired" blackness. And this vibration within the formal embodiment of well-policed content suggests how even in the most ardent nationalist theory determination of authenticating procedures cannot be divorced from often overdetermined exigencies of signifying practices. As Bullins's rejection of western experimentation involves reclamation of a classic representational logic, uneasily welding a potentially passifying naturalism to a putatively activating inspiration (a tension we shall see at work later in Bullins's tragi-visionary play, *Clara's Ole Man*), so Kgositsile's amalgam of grace and carnage compels the black dramatist to entertain dramatic means that must be themselves objects of murderous intent. In these tracts, then, we perceive an anxiety underlying the evident embrace of bold presentational tactics: a clearly felt (if uncertainly expressed) fear of dependence on the materialism inherent in pure realism. For in realism the hero's milieu takes a preponderant part in shaping his destiny; all actions, decisions, and feelings are enveloped by an awareness of extraneous determination, all sense of freedom is hedged and devalued. The hero (like Baraka's Clay) might declare the madness of reality, but reality must finally stand, little affected, above his "plight." The paradoxically didactic "realism" of Bullins and Kgositsile, like that of Baraka's more complex overture, is clearly not a concentration of events so much as a movement of the (revolutionary) psyche. Moreover, it is not the activity of an individual but a more general action which all share by analogy. It is a realism that absorbs, and narrates, the literal only to transfigure and ostensibly transcend it.

This theater, which seems to master the African-American audience even as it elevates it, to dominate it with sententious images of "a real world" even as it distills it as the singular focus of theatrical theory, is truly the dramatists' objective correlative to a deeply subjective vision in which the antithetical call to liberating violence pressures, and is pressured by, concrete ideas of "form." Indeed, as suggested by the invocations of disconcertingly incongruous genres (naturalism, allegory, symbolism), these early manifestos cohere precisely in the common tension between their passionate proclamation of the primacy of content over form and their incessant drive toward a just accommodation of meaning and technique. Their purchase on reality, the means by which they sought to depict a subject-matter more "truthful" than that of either the conventional or avant-garde mainstream, was that of moral concern. That was both their strength and limitation. For such "realism," quite apart from any restriction of heroic action, could not advance its claims very far as long as it simply replaced superficial topicalities with an instructional seriousness. What was needed beyond thematic clarification and a rejection of available notions of form was a more complex realization of the structural implications of the new revolt. Hence, the didactic element had to be textured, which meant not that it had to be eliminated but that it had to become more reflexively responsive to the need to unpack contradictions in black theater's evolving attitude toward representational praxis, specifically toward the abiding conflict – and potential alliance – of mimesis and desire. Nevertheless, the effect of the early modern, predominantly "destructive" theory was overwhelming: by destroying complacent dependence on current ideas of dramatic structure, and by thus opening up a vast new field of subject-matter, these advocates of what we might call "moral mimesis" opened the floodgates for a spate of new formal, as well as thematic, possibilities.

Not long after Bullins's and Kgositsile's declarations were published, several tracts appeared which began a shift toward this more complex concept of black theater. At the core of this crucial phase of development in modern black theatrical theory was a willingness to turn contradiction into a constituent element of a revised mimesis. Disturbing the assumption that dramatic resolution must take place only either inside or outside the theater itself, theorists pressed an alliance of perception and play that began to change the very construct of theater as a space apart from community. If this was already a conceptual ideal of "The Revolutionary Theatre," later manifestos began to sketch its palpable and visible features, carrying the generative uncertainties of mimesis forward to the empowering engagements of methexis.

In one sense, this sophistication about theater as a material web of aesthetic and social intentions was achieved by severe delimitation of purpose: following Kgositsile's lead, theorists of the black theater began to address themselves exclusively to the need for a drama of, about, and within the emergent "black nation." Ron Milner, a leading playwright in the movement, struck an influential chord with his plea for black theater to "go home" to the black community both psychically and physically:

> This new theater must be housed in, sustained and judged by, and be a useable projection of, and to, a black community! The community itself will be the theater, and the black artist's house of drama like a weirdly fixed and pointed looking-glass, a light-prism casting warnings, directions, fruitful memories and marvelous imaginings on the walls of the doomed, or soon to be recreated buildings.
>
> (Ron Milner, "Black Theater – Go Home!")[24]

In language no less urgent and vivid than Baraka's, Milner here challenges the black playwright to draw her material from the people to whom she, in turn, communicates intensified and organized perceptions. Milner's black theater assumes a unified black consciousness as audience. A theater for the oppressed, it is yet no longer a "theater of victims" but an expressive and reflective instrument of a "community" immanently present in and *as* its "house of drama." In terms that amplify Barakan divination in tangible and implicitly tactical ways, "Black Theater – Go Home!" enjoins modern black drama to disavow any autonomous site of performance activity. Conventional scenic mimesis, the imitative décor of the auditorium set aside for discrete viewing experiences, is abolished in favor of a spatial conception that refuses any separation of aesthetic and social function: no stage in such a community of performance can ever be silent or empty, for such demarcations of civic and theatrical locale blur as traditional notions of dramatic *action* converge on eruptive visions of cultural *activity*. "What happens" is thus no longer the secondary image of an 'original' idea, obedient to laws of universal applicability in the Aristotelian manner, but is, rather, the immediate, contingent, temporalized discharge of multiple energies capable of transforming governing axioms of structure and event. And this theatricalizing of expressive environment becomes elemental to the manifesto's own performative style: the hyper-prepositional torque of the essay's opening injunction, for example, reverberates with the excitement of thus enfolding every element of dramatic process – construction, enactment, perception – into a single cause of theatrical realization.

Just as in this creative interaction each element achieves identity and purpose in ever-evolving *relation* to the others, so the "community itself," the "Real" of African-American historical aspiration, issues from the kaleidoscopic montage of commemorative, critical, and oracular projections. The envisioned theater asserts its freedom from generic requirements and the expectations they support, remaining free to improvise new formations, images, and gestures. Though still announcing a drama of "warnings" and "directions," Milner now speaks of "marvelous imaginings," those Imaginary anticipations of communal liberation that would free black theater from the bonds of realism, "assault," and didactic exhortation. Appropriating Plato's cave as a scrim for enlightening refigurations and liberating enchantments, black theater is now no longer seen as a discrete institution addressing itself to a fragmented audience; nor is it simply within its chosen community: it and its congregants are entwined synergically in mutually defining union. Here we verge on the transformation of drama into ritual; for Milner's theater could not, like the theater of assault, be the formalization of ideology into narrative or emblem. It would have to do with essences, fatalities, and completed acts in which the destinies of self and group are indissoluble. It would, above all, move toward the simultaneous creation and expression of collectivity.

But how could such a ritualized theater avoid the trap of anthropological performance theory (as per Erving Goffman and Victor Turner),[25] which merely displaces narrative containment from the sphere of dramatic emplotment to the frame of enactment *per se*? What models or methods of collective "imagining" could rupture the closed system of structural anthropology's account of performance as symbolic repetition, with its preclusion of unruly and unpredictable resistances, while retaining the productive force of shared values? Larry Neal, in a series of reflections, critiques, and manifestos on the burgeoning black theater movement – "Cultural Nationalism and Black Theatre/Two on Cruse: The View of the Black Intellectual"; "Toward a Relevant Black Theatre"; "New Space: The Growth of Black Consciousness in the Sixties"; and especially "The Black Arts Movement" (with Baraka's "The Revolutionary Theatre" the most influential commentary on modern black drama)[26] – captured the crux and formulated means for its solution by expounding the nexus of revolutionary politics and vernacular expression. In particular, "The Black Arts Movement," which combines theory with one of the best critical summaries of the pre-1968 revolutionary drama, itself demonstrates the interaction of continuity and revision, for it self-consciously resonates with the idioms and passions of its predecessors even as it carefully transplants the debate to fresh terrain. In "The Black Arts Movement" Neal joins Milner in affirming "the integral relationship between Black Art and Black people" (31); indeed, Neal's manifesto opens with the declaration that "the Black Arts Movement is radically opposed to any concept of the artist that alienates him from his community" (29). Recalling Bullins's rebuke of white avant-garde drama, "The Black Arts Movement" disparages the "cultural emptiness" of Euro-American theater, excoriating its "[refusal] to confront concrete reality" (33). Echoing Baraka's ongoing criticism of black literature as a whole,[27] Neal emphasizes throughout his essay the need for an autonomous "symbolism, mythology, . . . and iconology" to facilitate the construction of a black drama wedded to the history and desires of Afro-America (29). But by linking the initiating tropes of alienation and critique to the visionary discourse of symbolic production, Neal was among the first theorists to perceive the need for the black theater to develop *specific* technologies and idioms linking "new" political convictions to distinctively "black" historical conditions.

Milner, too, had perceived the formal requirements of a black-oriented theater, but in notably vague terms:

> I won't go into the demand for a new dynamics, for a new intensity of language and form, that the material and the desired atmosphere will make of you; except to say that the further you go home, the more startling, new and black the techniques become.
>
> (Ron Milner, "Black Theater – Go Home!" 291)

To Milner's nascent awareness of structural demands Neal added concrete suggestions for a formally viable "black aesthetic." In varying patterns of reference and emphasis, Neal's essays directed the playwright's attention to the cultural traditions of African-American and African societies, formulating one of the earliest links between the radical Black Arts and vernacular expression.[28] "Spirit worship," whether embodied in African orishas, New World voodoo, or Afro-Christianity, could provide, Neal suggested, a source of emotive energy: jubilees, blues, spirituals, and dance would allow for rhythmic and lyric expressiveness; shamans, preachers, musicians, hustlers, conjurers, poets, and various other "survivors" would stock a theater with a complex amalgam of heroes and moral forces; and a radically historicized folk consciousness in general – radical because no longer composed of nostalgic and pietistic *memoriae loci* testifying quaintly to an inert past, instead reclaimed in connection to contemporary pan-African liberation praxis – would offer a plethora of responses to and refabrications of diasporic black life. In a manner that complements vernacular expressions of the sort we will encounter with the modern chant-preacher (Chapter 7), this integration of idiomatic and revolutionary expression effects a kind of anti-ethnological operation, dislodging folk modalities from purely sentimentalized or aestheticized classifications and restoring them as transgressive elements of cultural self-legitimation. No longer granted status and function according to external criteria (as in the decontextualizing expropriations of mainstream 'crossover' art or the depoliticizing antiquarianism of folkloristic appreciation), the vernacular performance idioms will speak in Neal's modern black theater to the desired coordination of perseverance and transformation precisely by epitomizing a tradition of perpetual revisionary resistance. It is just this recognition, via a kind a vernacular-inspired insurgency, that styles of memorial figuration do not exclude but, indeed, enable creative reinterpretation which allows Neal to proclaim modern African-American theater an auspicious site for enacting a distinctively black *consciousness*.[29]

Thus elaborating Milner's intuition, Neal discerned that if black drama was to become a truly "autonomous" vehicle of black values, it had to be shaped into new forms which are yet rooted in historically tested expressions of the black nation it vitalizes and serves. What began, then, with Baraka as a sweeping revolt against established conventions became through Neal's situation of the vernacular lexicon as element and exemplar of black theatrical practice a revolutionary rediscovery of convention on a deeper level. The early iconoclastic suspicion of structure thereby metamorphosed into a gritty, detailed discussion of the possibility of form. Through Neal's successive interventions, the focus of theoretical exploration shifted from the emphatically thematic (which, after all, gave the initial impetus to African-American dramatic experimentation) to the nucleus of the artistic transaction where ideology (content) and its performative embodiment (process) find their mutual determination. He gave to the Black Arts Movement not just its defining name (itself a generative act of summation and summons) but its titular momentum as an environment for progressive theatrical engagement.

The 1960s, then, saw a development in treatises on black theater from abstract, essentially distrustful concern with existing institutions to an affirmation of unified black strength and a fresh, more particularized dedication to constructing new conventions and formal arrangements by reworking the most enduring and critically insightful of the old. The contradictory status of mimesis that emerged from early manifestos – their simultaneous impatience with available modes of mediation and insistence on regulating the play of signifiers in adequate representations of 'authentic' blackness – evolves in their successors toward a transfigured presentational strategy guided by vernacular surrogations[30] capable of provoking a participatory identification in the black spectator. Since the early 1970s, several theorists have offered blueprints for a distinctively black theatrical event capable of propelling this postrealist, postdeconstructive mimesis toward a mode of affective synthesis, where meaning and being can coincide in the moment and space of enactment. Whatever their specific proposals, these writers share the belief that, as Clayton Riley expressed it, black theater would be "structured to take people away from basics, from fundamentals, into a special kind of chapel atmosphere for rituals."[31] While "ritual" supplanted "message" as the key word in the theorists' rhetoric, religiosity, emotiveness, and style overtook edification and exorcism as defining elements of black drama's *mise-en-scène*. And, quite naturally, the processes of performance, with all its messy contingencies and dynamic possibilities, replaced the particularities of text as the theorists' focal point.

Once again, Amiri Baraka initiated this change in tenor from critique to reconstruction with a call for plays which would show "how we triumphed,"[32] evoking in generalized terms the image of achieved action as theater's principle concern. Milner, however, was one of the first writers to outline the specific features and methods which might characterize such a theater of actualization. He had already hinted at these in "Black Theater – Go Home!" by asserting that "musicians are pointing out to us" the inevitability of innovative techniques in a distinctively black art (291). Eight years later the music is promoted from exemplar to essence:

> Everything is music. My whole basis for art – the only criteria or model I have. . . . If you listen to the good lines in a show, and the show is moving right, it's moving like a piece of music, and it has to hit like a piece of music. . . . If it doesn't do that, it just sits there and it's just a play.
>
> (Ron Milner quoted in
> Smitherman, "We Are the Music," 4)[33]

Just a play – Milner, claiming black music as vanguard inspiration, envisions a performative matrix that supplants the classic account of conventional dramatic narrative, shape, and meaning as inscription, the secondary effect of performance being its embodied supplement or imitative fulfillment.[34] As with music, black drama is to be materially embedded in the conditions of its making and thus become itself the "movement" that it provokes. Echoing Neal's location of spiritual sustenance in contemporary jazz innovators, whose experimental explorations blend historic and living vernacular resonances – "we should want to have . . . in our work the kind of energy that informs the music of John Coltrane, Cecil Taylor, Albert Ayler, and Sun Ra: the modern equivalent of the ancient ritual energy"[35] – Milner presses the relation of playwright to musician nearly to the point of identity. The essence of music, for Milner, is its affective quality, its ability to initiate the listener into its special cosmos. The call-and-response pattern characteristic of African-American music is a legacy of the Africanicity embedded in what Neal calls "the ancient ritual energy,"[36] that functional locus of communal legitimation that Milner too identifies as the ur-theater of black culture. Thus, Milner's African-American theater will be a synthesis of African-rooted spirituality and African-American musical form, a secularized structuring of tribal ceremony:

> Black theater is moving to the point where we've taken the ritual, passion, drama, and intensity of the church and put it into secular music so it can be a functional kind of thing; so you can use your catharsis, your collective energy and collective prayer in your everyday life. When Black theater has incorporated those three ingredients

– the church, the rock 'n' roll music dynamic and the drama – then
it will be total and full.

(Smitherman, "We Are the Music," 6)

Reimagining catharsis as a ceaselessly circulating datum of social presence
rather than a contained effect of circumscribed dramatic representation,
Milner deliberately braids "functional" contingency with affective
"totality." Drama does not achieve carthartic energy as a residue of narrative presentation but appropriates and augments its ongoing capacity to
motivate an affective dynamic of collective exchange. Cartharsis is not the
'final cause' of drama, but its source, a continuously regenerated power
of a culturally honed aptitude for the antihierarchical commerce of call-
and-response. In such a theater, there can be no authorial mastery of
mise-en-scène from beyond the site of enactment, because there is no
contoured distinction between a textual 'inside' and generating 'outside,'
and hence no concept of textuality as a privileged, closed, and autonomous
structure. Correspondingly, there can be no distinction of spectatorial
enrichment apart from theatrical experience itself, no securing of significance from the intentions and productions of performance through a
process of objectifying disengagement.

In the reciprocal dynamic of call-and-response expression that Neal and
Milner bring to theoretical center stage, 'performer' and 'auditor' designate
ever-shifting, ever-available positions, each speaker or player being also a
listener, each listener being always ready to reply. Such interactions arise
from the concrete situation of social relations, from a scene of utterance
that is simultaneously imaged and, in its presentation, altered, readying it
again for a continuing activity of meaningful transmission. Thus, too, no
single utterance or gesture can be isolated from the shared historical condition that enables it, the 'language' of communal consciousness from which
it arises and which it inflects with a transformative difference. In the
dialogic encounter of call-and-response, each participant is forced into
critical awareness of his or her customary behaviors and expectations, so
that role and reception are cognate with, not prior to, performance. Drama-
as-exchange thereby interrogates and amends beliefs that instigate and
circulate through it, distantiating perceptual habits and so instituting new
codes of understanding. Moreover, this rhythm of defamiliarization and
revision converts alienation to a kind of working-through of collective identity, as the different or distant is always already elemental to the self.

Constituting significance as a dispersal of signifying enunciations across
multiple, but related, subject positions, Milner's theater of call-and-response
thus "houses" an expressive economy that escapes enclosure within various
representational categories to which a classic aesthetic would confine it.
At the same time, it renders internal to the ethos of performative blacknesss the preservation of difference without ceding the will-to-fullness:
transgression and recognition are two aspects of the same disposition. In

theatrical terms, this theater resists narrative essentialization and finality without suspending the quest for defining form . . . or, in terms of Milner's earlier formulations, it emancipates the metamorphic fluidity of a black Imaginary while maintaining the rigor of symbolic negotiation.

Milner's musical-ritual vision of black theater, and the expressive strategies of vernacular realization it advances for encoding blackness-as-performance, found practical realization in several notable plays of the era, particularly Baraka's *Slave Ship* (1967) and Milner's own *Seasons' Reasons: Just a Natural Change* (1975). Like African ceremony, this African-American theater of music and dance fuses purpose and meaning, method and event. At once visionary and functional – functional, in fact, *because* visionary – it conflates passion and creation and (tapping only seemingly contradictory sources of 'collective energy') equates improvisatory invention with social significance. Exploiting the preestablished symbiosis between black audience and black musician, Milner's thesis seeks to free the African-American theater from the shackles of written narrative, translating its commission from mere communication to manifestation. Re-presenting condensed modes of thinking inscribed into a written script gives way here to expressive innovation by body and voice. The perspectival relation (and barrier) between seer and seen essential to traditional drama (be it realistic, expressionistic, or symbolic) is dissolved into the im-mediacy of ritual flux: placed in the middle of the action, the spectator is engulfed and physically affected by it, and, more, is 'called' upon to 'respond' in unconstrained tones of re-petition. The dramatic event thus posited is one in which black people do not so much discern, or even discover, as determine communal identity and solidarity during the theatrical happening itself.

III

> Sometimes I feel that the condition of the Afro-American writer in this country is so strange that one has to go to the supernatural for an analogy. . . . The Afro-American artist is similar to the Necromancer.
>
> Ishmael Reed, *19 Necromancers from Now*[37]

This, then, is the point from which succeeding African-American dramatic theorists have begun: How can the audience's activation, its sense of affective participation, become the central feature of theatrical realization and significance, the core of its transvaluation of all cultural values? How can its experience – whether "experience" be understood as a literally embodied act and/or as a movement of sensibility – become the basis of a reconstituted image of 'the real'? For "realism," as a kind of metaphor of concrete aspiration (more than as a specific generic marker), maintains its force even as the formal dialectic swings away from the pole of narrative transparency and strictly iterative representation of social circumstance. Freed from narrow didactic demands and aesthetic proscriptions by virtue of a more rigorous commitment to the generative ideal of communal liberation, theorists and playwrights together appropriately seized upon the form in which African-American conservatism and rebellion alike are rooted: religious ceremony. In the process, a new convenant with mimesis was forged, one wholly committed to translating the grammar of stage representation into the grammatological[38] methexis of presentational movement.

Though religious in its implication of ritual celebration, Milner's theater stresses its secular form as shaped by the rhythmic interactions of music, dance, tale, and poetry. Black ritual theater as espoused by such artists as Barbara Ann Teer, Carlton Molette II, and Paul Carter Harrison utilizes these vernacular materials in a more overtly sacramental framework. Molette, in stark contrast to the mid-1960s' playwright's assault against the "Old Spirituality,"[39] heralded the dynamic ceremonies of the Afro-Christian church as the basis for a spiritually invigorated communal drama.[40] As in the earliest manifestos of the movement, Molette's model performer is the preacher. Yet, for Molette, the essence of the preacher's sermon "is not what he says . . . it is the way he says it" ("Afro-American Ritual Drama," 7). Molette is not eschewing verbal communication *per se*; rather, he is asserting the formative role of stylistic enunciation in determining meaning, while recognizing the traditional African-American fusion of oratory and active response. In this "house of drama" (to appropriate Milner's phrase, with its embedded reference to African-American sites of spiritual convocation), the Apollonian compression of character is loosened by a Dionysian effusion of common passions, motives, and moments. Molette's model is the Afro-Christian chanted-sermon in which the biblical text is gradually subsumed into a communal ecstasy centered in spontaneous song, shout, and dance. In this "order of service," the preacher's use of oral techniques – repetition, rhythmic emphasis, variety of pitch – bends the relatively arbitrary textual content to the primary intention of "heightening emotional intensity" (10). Church ceremony thereby creates, as Molette says, "a total spiritual involvement . . . an affirmation of a sense of community" (10). For the ritual-minded playwright, no longer embroiled in a confrontation with mainstream drama as were Baraka, Bullins, and Kgositsile, the chanting-preacher is a more viable exemplar than the typical dramatist: through his agency (call), the "audience"/congregation encounters (responds to and realizes) the Other but is not other; it believes rather than appreciates; it creates through time yet abolishes the prisonhouse of normative temporality (the condition of true freedom); it is efficacious, not entertained.

The modernist revolt of Baraka's evangelical exhortations now joins Neal's call for idiomatic complexity in a reconfigured mode of vernacular performance, suggesting the need to see modern black performance and African-American expressive culture as mutually entangled, not antithetical, vectors of the Black Arts adventure . . . notwithstanding certain inclinations of post-Black Arts Movement literary criticism.[41] In a later chapter, we will probe the chant-sermon's own contributions to this blending of critique and ritual affirmation in the spiritual politics of African-American modernism. Our concern now remains the service performed by such vernacular modalities for the production of a fresh vehicle of black dramatic energy. The religious basis of Paul Carter Harrison's ritual theater, while incorporating elements of Afro-Christian rites, expands upon this vernacular impulse toward somewhat different ends than Molette's, since being primarily African in influence its emphasis is upon a cultural anthropology that is relatively archeological and philosophical in character. Harrison's writings, the last to be considered in this exposition of modern black theater theories, constitute the most intricately articulated dissertation on black drama yet recorded. His vision begins in a critique of the agitprop drama of the 1960s, which, in Harrison's view, is condescending and doomed to failure for a self-absorption that befuddles both the neo-realism and emblematic thrust of its project. Though ostensibly designed to communicate with the black masses, black theater which places dogmatic conceptions above the imaginative flexibility of the audience is, Harrison avers, squandering the community's constitutive immersion in 'engaged' action:

> The embattled brutha on the block finds it burdensome to wade through the heavy polemical prolixity . . . which tends to inhibit the necessary catharsis while whetting the radical palates of the white bourgeois intelligentsia. . . . Street plays . . . tend to have an ephemeral effect on the brutha who eschews the realistic detailing of his immediate surroundings and which urge him to action that has consequences he is only too familiar with and which he is unwilling to be glib about.
>   (Paul Carter Harrison, *The Drama of Nommo*, 203)[42]

Troping Baraka's "scream . . . through the streets," Harrison contextualizes the production of cartharsis "on the block," the pun locating the "brother's" double circumstance of rootedness and endangerment. Situating catharsis within a matrix of cause-and-effect that is the shared property of play and audience, Harrison, quite unlike the Baraka of "The Revolutionary Theatre," assumes that the black spectator is well aware of the injury to which s/he is daily subjected. What he seeks, therefore, is not a theater of violent indoctrination but a mode of "spiritual release." He urges the black dramatist to "move beyond material objectivity to form a nexus with our spiritual experiences" (204). To this end he shares with Milner an advocacy of "cultural continuity" or, more specifically, a veneration of African-American musical and religious conventions as appropriate vehicles of black theater ritual. At the same time, he shares with Molette a persistent emphasis upon spiritual models as foundation for secular assertion and affirmation. But he departs from both Milner and Molette in finding within all potential elements of the African-American theater dynamic an essential manifestation (or "memory") of an ancestral (African) ethos.

Following Janheinz Jahn's analysis of traditional African and neo-African cultures,[43] Harrison outlines a theater based on the specific terminology of Bantu cosmology. According to Bantu logic, Muntu, or all intelligible life including man, Kinto, or all objective phenomena, and Hantu, or the intersecting dimensions of time and space, cohere as a single reality under the aegis of NTU, or Pure Being. Kuntu, or the modality and contextual origin of an image, and Nommo, or the image (Word) itself, are the forces by which man as Muntu brings himself into harmony with other enveloping forces. The precise emanations of these forces and their mutually sustaining relationships are exactingly elaborated within Jahn's account of the Bantu cosmography, and even Harrison – seeking to put "Nommo on the block" in *The Drama of Nommo* – has little use for the more esoteric aspects of the Bantu system. His citation of Bantu theosophic speculation is, in fact, a calculated rhetorical device by which he undermines the more "practical" and prosaic systems of nationalist ideologues, strategically replacing them with a flexible (hence ultimately *anti*systematic) lexicon of physical and philosophical dicta. Black theater, according to Harrison, should be measured, not by a standard of realism or polemicism, but by its ability to "invoke the force of our ancestral spirits" (xxiii). Thus, the Baptist preacher, the bluesman, the modern jazz artist, the poet, and "even the Pimp, peacocking in his colorful threads" (xxiii) are not simply historically interesting heroes but common purveyors of the Bantu traditions. And just as the various elements of the Bantu "force field" form a synthetic whole, so the ultimate task of black theater ritual – the "Kuntu drama"[44] – is affirmation of collective consciousness, a shared and traditional sensibility nurtured by spiritual vitality.

The shift from a discourse of stage dialogue – that "language [which] was designed to reinforce the objectification of stage imagery . . . oftentimes contradict[ing] the physical action" (211) – to a dialect of Nommo entails more than a substitution in privileged reference and practical resource; it signals a primary concern to forge an absolute theatrical idiom fusing body and utterance, space and narrative. Modelled on the somatic intensities of black religious ceremony, Harrison's Kuntu drama seeks to rescue the uniqueness of dramatic enactment from the structures of artifice and "secondary" realization that divide it from its own intuition of "ecstatic freedom" (195–7). Thus, one finds throughout Harrison's neo-anthropological translations of African cosmology into African-American theatrical *style* a stress upon the physicality of Nommo, signifying that in black theater images and declarations must be treated, not as otherwise empty vessels of meaning, but as concrete 'episodes' in their own right: the tangibility of inflection will proclaim and sanction the "force" of ritual presence. The aim of this expressive materialization is not elevation of image over communication, but rather their combination into a sinuous instrument capable of communicating directly, with and through the anatomies of the audience. Ancestral memory, too, will be evoked not as trace or echo, but as immediate manifestation, making theatricalized Nommo a salient mediation of genealogical and revolutionary impulses.

Unlike the avant-garde Euro-American theater contemporaneous with Harrison's investigations (e.g., the experimental phenomenology of Richard Foreman's Ontological-Hysteric Theater, Robert Wilson's extravagant epic productions, or Edward Albee's continuing adventures in absurdist deconstruction) – to which Harrison makes frequent, often penetrating allusion – Kuntu drama bends the spatio-temporal coordinates of habitual thought to achieve an "expansion of consciousness" (198) that reorganizes and redirects, rather than disperses, historical perception. Thus, his quarrel with realism entails not simply its inability to frame the "chaos" of modern experience – a trope that, in any case, serves Harrison differently than his counterparts in the Euro-American avant-garde, figuring as it does for him the sassy complexity of the Street rather than what Eliot termed "the ruins" of post-Enlightenment cultural crisis. Rather, Harrison's critique is ideological and conceptual, bearing on the formal articulation of alternative structures of possibility: "realism is at the heart of the problem: it deters the fullest excavation of hidden meanings by locking images into fixed relationships with the surfaces of social life. The mode becomes static" (24). Because there is no plasticity in the relations among performer, role, narration, and spectator, realism can only be a catalogue of images, not an active challenge to perceived circumstances and values. Socially – but not spiritually – ritualized, the performer is no risk to the context of his acting, merely displaying its content as inscribed on his body. It is perhaps this interrogation of realism as a mystification of 'reality' that leads Harrison to defend his theory against insinuations of "mysticism," resolutely aligning sacramental performance with political commitment as inextricably interwoven principles of African-American experience ("there is nothing mystical about any of this: a black man's total sense of spiritual being is like a built-in survival kit" – xiii). It illuminates, as well, Harrison's effort to break beyond the form-content prison ("discussion on which comes first in artistic expression . . . is unnecessary" – 207) by adumbrating a "modal" concept of dramatic construction, in which the "real" is not a preestablished datum to be passively inspected via imitative display but a fluid continuum of positions, constantly subject to the mutations of recontextualization:

> African thought has not tried to force reality into fixed limits so that it can be recognized as *real*. Forms must be active rather than constant . . . Content is the totality of any given mode, and how that mode is activated or focused will determine the shape of the form.
>
> (Paul Carter Harrison, *The Drama of Nommo*, 207–8)

Articulating the need for a norm of embodiment that is responsive to specifically performative, or "activated," imperatives (and perhaps intimating resistance to the more cramped injunctions of his peers), Harrison posits black theater as an ongoing dialogue with itself, an autocritical and perpetually reinvented quest for the vinculum of gesture and belief. The 'script' of modal theater must inhere in the evolving perception of the narrative and corporeal action as it unfolds, so that its achieved inter-sections of recognition (cf. 'realism') and identification (cf. 'ritual') *are* its formal realization. Or, put differently, theatrical form must now be not a medium of thought and desire, a transcription of purpose and passion; it must itself *be* the movement of consciousness that it brings to "focus."

Reconceiving theater as the site of incessant invention, Harrison's drama thus transfigures every element of enactment, from protocols of impersona-tion and scenographic design to relations among linguistic, gestural, and imagistic signifiers of dramatic intention. Centrally, the Kuntu drama espoused by Harrison cultivates an audience whose members, "owing to African continuity, are not spectators by nature."[45] Harrison here extends his critique of the detachment of social realism by suggesting that intrinsic to modal Africanicity is the embedding of meaning in a reflexivity that reconciles modernity and historicity. The distinctive aspect of this drama is a nonparadoxical fealty to transformative resolution, in regard to both performance technique and to the depth of lyrical-metaphysical "content" which it actualizes. As in Barbara Ann Teer's Harlem-based National Black Theater Company (a vital functional model for Harrison's concepts), there are no actors or spectators in Harrison's drama, but instead "acti-vators" (Teer employs the more adulatory term "liberators") and "participants." The improvisational spirituality of the theatrical event – kindled by invocation of traditional motifs, sounds, or sayings (Nommo) – becomes, as we have seen, virtual yet self-transgressive content in Kuntu drama. Resisting the desubjectifying methods of the Happening to which it bears superficial resemblance, Harrison's Kuntu theater admits black folk as collaborators rather than consumers of the performance occasion, so that 'indeterminacy' is not a melodramatic groping toward Rousseauist 'originality' but an index of collective revision.

The end toward which each such occasion should move is destruction of any sense of theater as spectacle and inclusion of the whole "congre-gation" in the activity of methexis – in a way, what the spectator at first watches s/he must ultimately become. Yet inclusion and participation are not mere metaphors; they are acts of consciousness and, often, of body. The audience must be permitted to mold the locus of enactment, actually to feel that it is their space just as the activators' images are, by ancestral right (and rite), the community's. Time and space are shaped modally, arising equally within performance and within the audience's perception of that performance, while conventions of episodic succession, singularity of location, and individuality of intention are dispersed into an expansive, recursive exploration. This is no small part of the reaction against the fragmentation and illusory linearity of Hansberry's "socio-realist drama"

(200–2), whose physical space, like the events within it, is compartmentalized and strictly contained – an accurate metaphor of the conceptual demarcations that give such theater its "meaning." By contrast, many African-American community theaters erected during the late-1960s and early/mid-1970s (Detroit's Concept East being a lively and pertinent example, having been sculpted within the edifice of a neighborhood church) exemplified a resistance to the predeterminations of the proscenium and "round" architecture: often allowing the particular rite and its participants to define the playing space, these theaters became by formal design psychic, material, and political extensions of local constituencies. Thus, as Harrison says (echoing Milner's dismissal of traditional dramaturgy and Baraka's disparagement of Hamletean [in]action), "Rather than the play, the *event* is the thing, the total impact of environmental rhythms . . . the *event* becomes the context of reality, a forcefield of phenomena which is ritualized".[46]

The performance thereby rises to meet the audience, develops through both open and closed audience permission, and finally flows into the communal will. Bringing to "focus" the entelechy of modern black drama as a transitive intervention, a material effect in a specific locus that is yet, as "event," unbounded by any assumed form of the "real," Harrison points to a reconciliation of Barakan antitheatricality and Ellisonian play, revolutionary critique and improvisatonal commemoration. It is, finally, this rhythm of dialectical stimulation and response that Harrison feels can fulfill the initiatory and still essential aim of modern black theater:

> We depend upon the theater artist, the *activator*, to achieve a balance between disciplined innovations and subtle channels for spontaneity. His task is not to report daily life, but to elevate the symbols of that life in a manner that avoids offending the sense with prosaic reassessments of *natural* life that induce the temporary sensation of sentimentality. Melodrama is a nuisance! A vehicle should be sought that allows the experience to be confirmed by the intuition of the *participators*, be it un-huh, a finger-pop, or a muted howl, so as to achieve totality.
>
> (Paul Carter Harrison, *The Drama of Nommo*, 199)

*

Theoretical concepts within the contemporary black drama movement, then, have clearly been various yet oriented toward unification of ideological, emotional, and aesthetic impulses. Baraka was perhaps the most prophetic and cogent critic of the new movement when he opened his pioneering manifesto with the declaration that "the revolutionary theatre" should not just produce but should *be* "change," a cause that would be always its own effect.

On one level, the evolutionary path dictated by the theorists' ever-changing perspectives has led from an emphasis on naturalism and dogmatic pedagogy to an equally passionate desire for ritual evocation of a common ethos. The primary aim of the black theater event has thus altered radically in the development of modern black drama from "educating the people" to embracing the audience in collective affirmation of certain values, styles, and goals. If narrowly didactic gestures were in the process curtailed, the theater became no less political, for the newer forms could not function without direct reference to the society in which they were embedded. Whether recalling the past or restructuring the present, Harrison's ritual performance, like Baraka's "revolutionary" realism, is essentially a prediction for a reordered future. No less than "the revolutionary theatre," Kuntu drama deconstructs social practices into conflictual perspectives, "exposing" them as historical practices; but it simultaneously reconstructs positionality as a "modal" manifestation of distinctively black expressive resistance, figuring style as substantive effort to seize and amend conditions of "reality."

On another level, modern black drama theory has refigured, and hence reclaimed, mimesis as an intersection of quality and process by which collective aspiration can be realized in theatrical experience itself. Dramatic narration has been thereby not dispatched but displaced into collective improvisation: it emerges from the cauldron of unblinking if self-limiting naturalism as a self-interrogating activity that spurns authorial mastery for the provisional legitimations of call-and-response. As a modal dialectic of mimesis and methexis, the envisioned performance event claims the "force" to confront, combat, and even subvert prevailing knowledges, categories, and rules of formation, while continuously articulating the sanctioned logic of a sanctified blackness.

In the period of theorization that we have traced, black theater itself creatively emulated its philosophical guides – indeed, theory and practice have rarely been as sensitive to each other as in the Black Arts Movement. The large body of theoretical criticism generated by the movement proved fundamentally necessary to its practical evolution, though in no way does it simply dictate its interests or predict its formal and conceptual range. The energy of the theory's initial revolt from inherited idioms was the moving power; and its intelligence ensured that it would pass, almost immediately, into construction and into creative development.

Most notably, playwrights during the period recognized that the problem of communicability – the keynote of all the manifestos – is, in fact, the problem of convention, and the revolt of their art against established social orders became a dazzling investigation and testing of formal possibility. At every point in its evolution, modern black drama pits an awareness of contingency against an assertion of control. The result has been not defamiliarizing irony, or deconstructive cruelty, but the invigorating innovations of what Bullins has termed *black dialectics*: "the dialectic of change and the dialectic of experience."[47] It is a dialectic pressing the dual claims of completion and renewal, seeking the image of Afro-America "surviving yet not surviving but being" (Sonia Sanchez).[48]

The history of their theater – a chronicle not yet fully told – would thus be a tale of radical experiment and reconstruction, innovation and affirmation. Whatever shape such an exploration may take, it must be sure to locate the formal junctures of ideological prescription and poetic energy, and to discern their dialectical relation in the black dramatist's search for a theater of communality. As an effort to adumbrate this chronicle, our next chapter will examine three exemplary texts – Bullins's *Clara's Ole Man*, Adrienne Kennedy's *The Owl Answers*, and Ntozake Shange's *for colored girls who have considered suicide/when the rainbow is enuf* – which 'collectively,' so to speak, suggest the material steps black theater has taken in its journey to the defining crossroads of mimesis and methexis.

2 Site-ing blackness

Abjection and affirmation in modern black drama

I

> My mother has been going to the theater, and not because she's my mother.
> She is straightout working-class, but she and her friends go to plays in search
> of some kind of fundamental understanding about the texture of life: her
> life, and life in general. . . . The new acceptance of art [echoing that of]
> singers and jazz musicians has had an important effect on consciousness, on
> attitudes toward oneself, and, above all, on that level of aspiration which is
> necessary for any ideology of change. When you present a horizon, you can
> show the need for change, and build a model for what change should be.
> Larry Neal, "Into Nationalism, Out of Parochialism"[1]

At the height of the Black Arts Movement, Larry Neal delineated for
theater practitioners the subtle circuitry of production and reception
through which a viable new theater practice could flow. Theater was now
felt capable of moving audiences on the scale of music and oratory because
it tapped the affective reservoir of vernacular culture, while audience
responsiveness to fresh images and forms of dramatic realization fueled a
politics of change for which theater became a vanguard exemplar. Neal's
visionary "aspiration" is thus rooted in a decidedly historical grasp of
theater's own "horizon," stressing as it does the contingency of its success
as an event within the "life texture" of very particular, very rooted commu-
nities, their needs and expectations.

Neal thus envisions modern black theater as a dialectical encounter that
puts itself into question as much as the issues and images that serve as its
content. Play and audience are thereby engaged in a constant process of
negotiation, and dramatic interpretation is dislodged from any assumed
institutional frame and delivered to the 'living' immediacy of collective
judgment. As such, the evolution of its specific forms will necessarily be a
story of ceaseless revision, guided however by visible threads of concern
that stretch across the footlights from one gathering to another in the *mise-
en-scène* of African-American theatrical performance.

Modern black theater has progressed, accordingly, precisely in openness
to its constituency, which it has at the same time sought both to reclaim

and to renovate, to open to the "change" that its own explorations in blackness have made possible. At the core of this experimental process, as Neal's reflection hints, is a dialogue between legitimacy and authorization that is triangulated among play, audience, and 'world,' by which I mean the referential illusion that is as often demystified by the dramas will we soon engage. I think it no accident that Neal cites his mother while sketching key terms of this dialogue, for, as we shall see, both male and female playwrights have grappled with looming and often excessive forms of origin, sacrifice, and transmission in crafting fresh modalities of performative authority, often situating these dramatic (re)figurations at the site of familial, especially feminine, crisis. Whether with Ed Bullins's "ole man" (where we begin) or Ntozake Shange's "colored girls" (where our horizon beckons), we shall find that the revisionary staging of blackness returns, like Ellison's descending hero, to a "voice like my mother's" in order to undertake its mission of revolutionary change.

Through close study of three representatively precise and reflexive plays, we will discover, then, that the restless energies of modern black drama set it against ideologies of regulation that seem inimical to collective "consciousness" but not necessarily against all received avowals and meanings. The freedom it seeks – notwithstanding a defining urge for critical and improvisatory immediacy – is not one unconditionally disengaged from others' claims but, precisely, one open to perpetual realignments of self and other, including elements of otherness within the self. As its protagonists discover in myriad ways, both frightening and stirring, blackness is not just a product but a medium of this realization, an ever-shifting site of radical exchange in which all, including its authorizing audience, are enjoined to participate in its quest to supplant sacrificial abjection with covenantal affirmation.

II

> What I can use madam . . .
> What I can use. I move now
> trying to be certain of that.
>
> Walker in *The Slave*[2]

Ed Bullins is easily the most prolific black American playwright in history. Author of some 40 plays, the vast majority of which explore the daily struggles and enduring desires of the destitute, the distressed, the broken, and the untamed in urban black America, Bullins is, with Baraka and Shange, the prime mover of modern African-American theater. Reading or viewing a Bullins play, one is struck especially by three features: the spare and idiomatically fluent language; the tendency for feeling to be focused in short scenes of sudden illumination and great poignancy; and a general mood of disillusion and futility, relieved by specially highlighted moments of tenderness and assertiveness. Bullins's discourse is strong and supple dialogue prose, very near to the spoken everyday argot of the urban street, brutally hard and keen, but often yielding to visionary intuition and touched with vivid poetic images. The scenes that impress one most are nearly all quite brief, intensely evocative of terror, despair, or anguish, and in consequence disturbing and moving. The general mood of tormented existential struggle includes feelings ranging from a coarse and comic cynicism to a more dignified tragic protest. Bullin's drama is, in other words, a physicalized *blues lament*, born of injury and injustice, yet capable of sustaining transcendent vision.

The starting-point of the typical Bullins play is a precisely realized situation with the most clearly observed, even hyper-naturalistic speech. In his self-styled "theatre of reality,"[3] the element of phantasy, when it does appear, is thus identifiable as the outward projection, the concretization, of Bullins's sharply etched characters' dreams and anxieties. With Baraka, Bullins initiated the modern black drama movement by taking the 'well-made play' as his basic form but subjecting it to social and symbolic pressures that exposed its conceptual underpinnings (especially, the congruency of familial reintegration and theatrical mimesis) and opened it to a fresh realization. The apparent realism of Baldwin and Hansberry with its half-hearted concern for an appearance of vraisemblance became in Bullins penetrating study. Manners and mores were no longer simply ornamental trappings which clothed theatrical moments: they became the drama's chief concern, the medium of conflictual confrontations between official (often hidden) power and marginal (often equivocal) alternatives. Expropriating realism as an optic of socio-linguistic inquiry but rupturing it as a seamless illusion of ahistorical verity, Bullins infused borrowed forms with a counter-hegemonic intelligence.

Bullins's impulse is for a kind of supra-realism which can offer a vision of black life in its ambiguous and contemporaneous entirety, a theatrical hypothesis for an audience to scrutinize in which all the "facts" are presented but never pre-judged. The Bullins actor thus presents his or her character both by externalizing an examined bundle of motivations and drives and by exuding a series of social *gests* (to borrow the Brechtian term) that figure the historically-conditioned and relational structure of black identity. A Bullins character emerges from (and, thus, too, in some sense disappears into) the web of circumstance that s/he seeks both to voice and to affect, with often frustrating and even explosive consequences. The shaping realism of Bullins's dramatic narrative must likewise be read as a contextual mimesis of estrangement and adjustment, susceptible to reproduction of dominant ideologies even as it bares them for critical scrutiny. Making visible – or, more often, audible – veiled processes of economic, psychic, and cultural (mal)formation, the Bullins play thus moves toward a dubious convergence of recognition and revelation that, in its precarious finality, both sustains and suspends the ideological, if also affective, implications of (dis)closure.

None of his plays illustrates the complexities of this procedure, or the divided mimesis that it evinces, better than *Clara's Ole Man*.[4] The entire one-act drama takes place in the kitchen of a South Philadelphia slum apartment whose every detail, from pots to oatmeal boxes, is meticulously delineated in Bullins's stage-directions. Clara, a pretty teenaged girl, shares the apartment with Big Girl, a stocky, loquacious and bodacious woman "of indeterminable age ... anywhere from 25 to 40," and Big Girl's "mentally retarded teenaged sister," Baby Girl. Jack, a young ex-Marine attending college-prep, has returned to the neighborhood of his rearing to romance Clara while her "ole man" is out at work. The characters sit, drink cheap wine, accept visits from drunken neighbors and local gang members, and, led by Big Girl's irrepressible authority, talk of "everything," in a seemingly random concatenation, from Big Girl's rescue of Clara from abuse and imminent prostitution (culminating in the loss of her child and abandonment by the "little punk" who would have pimped her) to the gang's recent escapades. Finally, as the group prepares to leave for a special outing to the local theater, Jack casually inquires about the whereabouts of Clara's ole man. When Big Girl (who has impulsively taken the day off from work) indignantly declares, "Clara's ole man is home now" (170), Jack "becomes sick" at the revelation of homosexuality. As Clara and Big Girl exit, Big Girl, despite the protests of her young mate, orders the gang to trounce the intruder for his witless vulgarity. After a drunk (Miss Famie) briefly reappears, Baby Girl is seen screaming her mad curses to the accompaniment of Jack's beating. Stoogie, the gang's leader, downs a last gulp of wine, "then saunters outside" to the scene of Jack's 'punishment,' and the play ends with "a single spot on Baby Girl's head, turned wistfully toward the yard" (171).

The surprise that climaxes *Clara's Ole Man* lies not only in the sudden declaration of an implied yet unconfirmed reality, but also in a turn in human relationships supported by a careful expositon of the social and personal environment. In contrast to the passionate overt violence and savage internal warfare of Baraka's early quasi-naturalistic drama, Bullins's play investigates the outward desperation of souls contending with their own felt inadequacies and imperfect yearnings. Though faithful to concretely representational method, Bullins pits character against character in an attempt to describe what Raymond Williams would call a "structure of feeling," an intersection between the "realism" of his drama and the "reality" of the world from which that drama is abstracted. In Bullins's characteristic manner, *Clara's Ole Man* develops the tension between idiomatically opposed figures who triangulate the quest for authenticity and dominion; here, Jack, the 'neo-Ivy League,' middle-class 'fool' (an avatar of Baraka's Clay) contrasts with both the "vulgar" lesbian Big Girl and the streetwise hoodlum Stoogie, enacting a conflict not only between styles of subjective assertion but between disparate vernacular expressive values and their attempted transumption by alienated desire.

The characters' public strife, initiated by Big Girl from the play's beginning, is paralleled by Clara's private conflict of allegiances which her very invitation to Jack has evoked. Jack, the only grown male in a play rife with figures of liminal determination (adult "girls," infantile toughs), lacks the strength or self-knowledge that might 'save' Clara from the chaotic alliance which clearly saddens and effectively silences her ("I wanted to talk to somebody," she cries near the end; "I don't have anybody to talk to . . ." – 170), even as he provides a singular source of alternative vision and potential escape. Ironically, as Lance Jeffers points out, "in the midst of this world of winos and hoodlumism and irrational[ity], Big Girl herself is a symbol of order."[5]

The thrashing of Jack that concludes the action, though audibily physical, is resonantly 'symbolic' of Big Girl's significant triumph, which is linguistic. Always, in Bullins's world, personal impotence expresses itself in an inability to engage and employ verbal resources as decorum and circumstance demand. In *Clara's Ole Man*, the failure to communicate, and especially to articulate in a flexible and persuasive intonation, is felt by Jack as a mark of inferiority; that is why he tends to dwell, with near comic effect, upon his aresenal of pointedly "educated" diction:

Jack:	Yes, it does seem a problem. But with proper guidance she'll more than likely be conditioned out of it when she gets into a learning situation among her peer group.
Big Girl:	BULLSHIT! . . .
Jack:	I beg your pardon . . . I didn't exactly say that. I said when . . .
B. G.:	*cuts him off.* Don't tell me what you said, boy. I got ears. I know all them big horseshit doctor words . . .

(Ed Bullins, Clara's Ole Man, 161)

Power – ultimately, the power over body as well as social authority – derives from the ability to make one's antagonist accept one's own lexicon and the discursive and moral system it upholds. Jack's introduction of refined terminology is, Big Girl early perceives, an act of invasion in this environment charged with verbal display, censure, and defense; it constitutes an aggressive effort to appropriate the domestic milieu as scene of instruction, desire, and mastery. Much of the drama unfolds as a series of agons over terms (terms that often subliminally underscore themes of legitimacy, ownership, and mobility), so that even seemingly random concatenations of dialogue bear on the struggle for expressive legitimation and command:

Stoogie:	What kind of boat were you on, man?
Jack:	A ship.
Big Girl:	A boat!
Jack:	No, a ship.

Stoogie: *rising, Bama and Hoss surrounding Jack.* Yeah, man, dat's what she
              said . . . a boat!

(169)

Linguistic possession and physical violence coil around each other as the
play spirals toward the double violation of the climax. Impotence – which
one encounters everywhere, but especially among those who will not (Clara)
or cannot (Baby Girl) speak save in imitative and reductive forms, imprisoning themselves alternatively in expressions of submission, denial, or
denunciation ("NO! NO! SHIT! DAMN! SHIT!," Baby Girl exclaims more
than once) – is not a simple condition of economic circumstance, for it
exists in a complicated relationship to the play's idioms of subjugation,
which are at the same time subjugations of idiomatic assertion: madness,
confinement, intoxication, repression, and, finally, expulsion.

The play accordingly portrays Jack's increasingly desperate attempts, on
the one hand, to establish intellectual and social superiority by controlling
the operative interpretive registers, and his equally futile efforts, on the
other, to extricate himself from presentational traps set by his antagonists'
interruptive critique:

Stoogie: *to Jack.* What did you do in the Army, man?
Jack: *feigns a dialect.* Ohhh, man. I told you already I was in the Marines!
             . . .
Stoogie: What'cha do now, man?
Jack: Ohhh . . . I'm goin' to college-prep on the G. I. Bill now . . . and
             workin' a little.
Stoogie: Is that why you sound like you got a load of shit in your mouth?
Jack: What do you mean?
Stoogie: I thought you talked like you had shit in your mouth because
             you had been ta college, man.
Jack: I don't understand what you're tryin' to say, man.
Stoogie: It's nothin', man.

(169–70)

Bullins's discourse here is gestural – that is, the syntax and rhythm of
each sentence alone forces the actor into making appropriate signs and
movements. Jack's speech, for example, demands an impotent swaggering
gesture, where Big Girl's vigorous style of speech dictates a constant panton-
imical titanism. Thus, taking up where such plays as Baldwin's *The Amen
Corner* (1967) and Baraka's *The Toilet* (1967)[6] left off, Bullins reworked,
reduced, and stylized the idiosyncrasies of African-American street dialect
to an idiomatic instrument that has almost totally lost its sententious, melodramatic element and has fully merged into dramatic action. In a way
that links Bullins to Harrison across the realism/ritual divide in effect if
not in method, what this offers is at once the attachment to ordinary life

and a covert valuation of "tribal" men and women not masked and changing, but in ordinary clothes, speaking prosaic words – a frail spiritual connection now domesticated in the veiled rituals of daily life.

Thus, too, Bullins's use of language here is that of a social *gestus*, thematic as well as narrative, tropological as well as presentational. In effect, exposition, crisis, and dénouement are driven by a rhetorical conflict that entwines naturalistic exchange with verbal theatricality. Eloquence is given political and psychic value, but is also contextualized, rendered conditional, by the relative nimbleness and reflexivity of its claimants. Just when the conversation seems ready to slide into the byways of random speech, the dialogue strikes quite another key, evoking codes that possibly exceed the speaker's intention but certainly expand the moment by establishing patterns of significance through echo and implication. Indeed, the play's formative rhythm is composed of continuous, sometimes sudden, modulations from neo-naturalistic to more hybrid and evocative modes of heightened expression, achieving a fusion of the spontaneous and the symbolic, the casual and the compelling.

Upon close inspection of Bullins's dialogue, then, one finds that behind the apparently aimless or merely imitative rendering of colloquial vernacular there lies a rigorous economy of means. Each word is, in fact, essential to the total structure and decisively contributes to the overall effect of desire menaced by an opacity unintended by its user. Indeed, Bullins's dramatic writing has the density and texture of an oral poetry that enacts a kind of incantational mimesis, an iterative emphasis on the quotidian whose repetitions suggest a lurking, if disquieting, metaphysical aspiration. Thus, although Bullins is not primarily an allegorical or philosophical writer concerned with emblematic structures, even as carefully naturalistic a piece as *Clara's Ole Man* creates an aura of symbolic suggestivity, most especially in its crossing of denotation and epiphany.

This divided mimetic urge speaks through every major character: Clara, with her abrupt illumination of erotic repression by a professed inability to speak; Baby Girl, with her impulsive repudiations erupting through a masquerade of mimetic desire (throughout the play she is "made up" in the manner of Clara, miming her hairdo and cosmetic embellishments); Jack, with his self-ironizing skids from one "feigned" dialect to another; and even Stoogie and his crew, whose gangster prowess is demonstrated not by the immediacy or profit of the "action" but by the comic glee of its Falstaffian reenactment (167–8). But this doubleness of representational and stylized, eruptive meaning circulates to most dramatic effect through Big Girl, who presides over the *mise-en-scène* with a directorial hauteur that is part Prosperian (teaching Baby Girl to "curse" [162] and commanding the final "show" of discovery and distributed justice [170–1]), part Calibanesque ("It's all part of my master plan, baby. Don't you worry none . . . Big Girl knows what she's doin'. You better believe that" – 160), and part Arielan ("Ya see, when I was a little runt of a kid my mother found out she couldn't keep me . . . so I got shipped out . . . I spent 12 years with those people" – 163). Yet her sovereignty cannot exempt her from a confessional discharge that is as much self-revelation as it is naturalistic commentary: and so Big Girl, who is employed as a "technician" in a state mental institution, is compelled, through a gradual, invisible, thread of conversation, to speak with a laden eloquence of the lessons she learns from the inmates' wild outbursts:

> Ya see, workin' in the hospital with all the nuts and fruits and crazies and weirdos I get ideas 'bout things. I saw how when they get these kids in who have cracked up and even with older people who come in out of their skulls they all mostly cuss. . . . Mostly all of them, all the time they out their heads . . . and boy do some of them really get into it and let out all of that filthy shit that's been stored up all them years. But when the docs start shockin' them . . . [they] think they're gettin' better, but really they ain't. They're just learn'n like before to hold it in . . . just like before, that's one reason most of them come back or are always on the verge afterwards of goin' psycho again.
>
> (162)

Big Girl does not draw explicit parallels between the lives of madmen and those of her own world's denizens, which simply renders the analogy more emphatically an image of mimetic displacement than any facile, melodramatic interpretation interior to the drama itself would have allowed. The pointed rhythm, the repetition and balance, extrapolate from naturalistic syntax a layered emphasis on a world become topsy-turvy, distinctions of position and authority blurring even as the pronouns do. But what is the destination of this disruptive symbology? How does it affect the audience's apprehension of scenic image and narrative meaning; and, in turn, how does the dénouement of exhibition and sequence affect estimation of Bullins's overall dramatic purpose?

On the one hand, we have the implication of a pervasive, levelling 'insanity,' made dramatically concrete by Baby Girl, whose incoherent babble, violent protests, and fantasies of pregnant cats constitute the most articulate plea for liberation in the play. The metaphor of society as hellish madhouse[7] whose saner members shriek from the pains of unwanted knowledge is furthermore unself-consciously evoked by the cursing, humorous, yet finally tyrannous Big Girl herself, whose own confessional outburst stops short of improbable self-revelation:

> You want to know how I got this way and been this way most of my life and would be worse off if I didn't let off some steam drinkin' this rotgut and speakin' my mind?
>
> (162)

Marked by ambiguous formulations of release ("let out all of that filthy shit"; "let off steam"), this perspective shades *Clara's Ole Man* into the exuberant and dangerous territory of the carnivalesque, with its distur-bance of official institutions and mockery of elite poses and attitudes. And, indeed, just beneath the play's naturalistic veneer are all the lineaments of a riotous festival of misrule: intemperate banqueting and drinking; riotous laughter (Big Girl's speeches are frequently punctuated by the "HAW HAW HAW" and "hee hee hee" of her "hard" cackling); macabre and deflationary parody of suffocating manners and pretentious decorum; indulgent obscenity, climaxing in excremental excess (*Baby Girl*: "SHIT! SHIT! SHIT! DAMN! SHIT!" – 169); raucous dancing (*Stoogie*: "DO THE SLIDE, MAN! SLIDE!" – 168); and bellicose exhibition of what Bakhtin called the "grotesque body," both corporeal and social.[8] Effervescent and irrepressible, carnivalesque participators privilege "madness" as an eman-cipatory urge, exalting the repressed, the indecent, the noncanonical as a means of *dis*figuring hegemonic constraints and refiguring collective power as transgressive cultural practice. Rejecting any idea of "allowed discharge" (as per Jack's interpretation of Big Girl's asylum anecdote: "Wow, I never thought of that! That ritual action of purging . . . can open up new avenues in therapy and in learning theory and conditioning subjects" – 162), the carnivalesque celebrates the unbounded freedom of continual cartharsis.

Cognate with this subversive descent into the illicit is the central element of lesbian identity, which integrates carnal and political trespass. The black female body thus eludes the signifying system that fastens orthodox mimesis to phallocentric power, asserting a different destiny for the corpo*real* of black desire. This ought not to be considered simply as an attack but rather as a *signifyin'* upon patriarchal Law, potentially clearing ground for radical resignification. Reversing norms of the social symbolic, for example, Big Girl claims to have rescued Clara from the hetereosexual abject ("When I met you you didn't even know how to take a douche" – 163). The domestic arrangement through which Big Girl asserts her mastery – having retrieved Clara from the failure of a conventional "christian" upbringing and having survived the breakup of her own "normal" household[9] – is clarified for us at the moment of dramatic climax, thus sabotaging the imbrication of family, patriarchy, and narrative enshrined by classic realist theater. Foregrounding anti-Oedipal resolution (alongside the pre-Oedipal or "hysterical" ejaculations of Baby Girl: "CAT! CAT! CAT! CAT! . . . NO! NO! NO!" – 171), the play signals a menacing demystification of "drawing room" realism's veiled ideological processes.

On this view, pulsating under the narrative surface of *Clara's Ole Man*'s naturalism is a denaturing resistance to the very codes through which the play's persuasive verisimilitude makes its appearance. And yet the uncer-tain tone and imagery of its closure suggest other possibilities of symbolic resonance within the prevailing aura of release, abjection, and sacrifice. For the punishment of Jack – the drama's antifestive *alazon* (or "mister smart and proper," as Big Girl jeeringly dubs him – 161) – reverberates with the discordant 'cruelty' of sacrifical expulsion by which, to apply René Girard's account of anthropological mimesis, the community secures its presence and continuity.[10] As the "victim" of a potentially "revolutionary theatre" of anti-Oedipal assertion (Big Girl, recall, names the final event a "show," having performed a number of preparatory exorcisms of Jack through various "mockeries" and "pretences" [cf. 163–4, for example]), Jack mirrors its own undecidable or liminal status: both active and passive, necessary and erased, the victim and community emerge from and threaten each other equally at play's end. For what, after all, is Jack but a sacrifical "substitute," a bad actor who must be released from his contract? The homeboy enacting an incomplete return to the 'hood, he exudes a power of attraction and repulsion that figures the community's own incomplete passage from hurtfully imposed to triumphantly reclaimed identity:

Stoogie, to Jack:	Where you from, man?
Jack:	Oh, I live over in West Philly now, but I come from up around Master.
Stoogie:	Oh? Do you know Hector?
Jack:	*trying to capture an old voice and mannerism* Yeah, man, I know that cat.
Stoogie:	What's your name, man?

(169)

Having left the place of self-designated 'mastery,' the victim obscurely embodies an equation of creation and catastrophe, here linking reclamation with unnaming. Lacking a principle of coherence, split and vacillating among a repetoire of viewpoints and needs, Jack reflects the community that throttles and banishes him in being made aware of his entrapment, his tormenting and imperfect self-knowledge. Carnivalesque liberation thus appears as what Girard calls "sacrificial crisis," for there is no definitive elimination of inverted "madness" or pompous "propriety," an indeterminacy that mirrors the victim's failure to achieve social reintegration. Where before we entertained the promise of mimesis transformed to methexic deliverance, we now might see the play and its principal figures as remaining in the grip of that form of unresolved mimesis that demands a scapegoat (actor) for its incomplete project of "real"-ization: after all, Big Girl, who was "shipped out somewheres" while Baby Girl was "shipped out somewheres else," and Clara, whose "folks had kicked her out" (163), likewise bear the marks of expulsion as formative elements of their diasporic 'asylum.' The community of *Clara's Ole Man* retains its initial status as a site of conflict and difference, hinting that its liberational subtext might only be a structural illusion of its divided representational method.

This tension between emancipatory and sacrificial symbolizations with a mimesis that is itself ambiguously naturalistic and rhetorical places the drama's audience in a suggestively uncertain position. The evidently naturalistic psychology allows it to empathize with, perhaps even enter into, the characters' dilemmas, until, meeting the limits of identification, spectator and character come to share most profoundly the irredeemable abyss within and between subjectivities. If the overtly comedic and implicitly festive activities of the play encourage affective pleasure, the explicit and suggested patterns of stasis and violence suggest a disheartening failure of affective movement, both inside and beyond the dramatic continuum. Each party – dramatis and spectatorial personae – remains isolated and incomplete, forced to acknowledge the inability of mediation to transform experiential lacunae into inspiriting presence. Will such estrangement lead, as in Brechtian theory, to a recognition of social contingency that opens a space for a different future? Or are we locked in a scene of emotional transaction, articulated as the mirroring of social reality by theatrical display, that seduces us to accept its coordinates as those of an inalterable cultural "present"?

From one point of view, insisted upon by the characters' own biting humor and flair for mimicry, this world of uninhibited, inebriated ('spirited'?!), dozens-playing homeys surrounded by frightening anxieties is grotesque and comic; from another angle, provoked by the invitation to identifications with figures whose abjection and violence cannot fully sustain empathetic response, it appears noble and tragic. Through the shaping of what Craig Werner terms (following Bullins's lead) a theater of black dialectics,[11] Bullins brings to life the commonplace call-and-response of black life and its subtext of heroism and terror, an effect achieved by the combined deadly precision and indefinite resonance of representation. There is inherent in *Clara's Ole Man* a quite traditional moral judgment recognizing that the clashes of its characters produce despotism and destructiveness even at the site of exuberant communitas (*Big Girl*: "I want you to dance, Clara . . . DO LIKE I SAY! DO LIKE BIG WANTS!" – 168–9), though no facile recipes for amelioration are offered. Clara's final plea to Big Girl – "I only wanted to talk, B. G. . . . I don't have anyone . . ." – trails off, unacknowledged, into piteable silence; and Miss Famie's concluding line – "See ya tomorrow" – affirms the repetitive continuity of her world's discord. Although Bullins presents a view of what the African-American "is," he never judges his illustrative figures. He suggests no simplistic alternative to their actions, just as he denies them realization of their full human potential. Yet the best of them – Big Girl, Clara, Baby Girl, even Stoogie – achieve a kind of heroism, even glimpse the limits of being possible to the human spirit. Their creator's naturalistic eye, it seems, is turned upon them, *à la* Baby Girl, in wistful admiration.

III

Is the total black, being spoken
From the earth's inside.

There are many kinds of open.
How a diamond comes into a knot of flame
How a sound comes into a word, colored
By who pays for what speaking.

Audre Lorde, "Coal"[12]

Bullins subtitled *Clara's Ole Man* "A Play of Lost Innocence," betraying (perhaps self-consciously) modern black drama's initiating impulse to subject presiding images of African-American aspiration (bourgeois, integrationist, and unassuming) to mordant demystification. In itself, the phrase evokes mingled sympathy and reproach, but it is driven by a combative purposiveness that smacks at once of apostasy and defensiveness. That formulation surfaced again, in all its enigmatic instability, when Bullins found himself at the center of what proved to be the central *scandale de théâtre* of the Black Arts Movement: the outcry surrounding the staging at Robert Macbeth's New Lafayette Theatre (where Bullins served as playwright-in-residence) of his play *We Righteous Bombers*,[13] which was revealed by Larry Neal to be substantially plagiarized from Camus' *The Just Assassins*. In a lively and influential symposium on the ensuing controversy conducted under the auspices of the New Lafayette-sponsored journal, *Black Theatre*, several leading theorists and practitioners in the movement (Neal, Baraka, Macbeth, Askia Muhammad Touré, Marvin X, and Ernie Mkalimoto) discussed the play's merits in the shadows of the author's transgression, debating most vociferously its exposition of the (im)proper stance of the "revolutionary black artist." Despite his defense of the play during the forum as a valuable provocation to reconsiderations of the role of form in the production of revolutionary vision, Neal, in his preface to the panel's transcript, "Toward a Relevant Black Theatre," theatricalizes Bullins's "hoax" as a "bad scene" at which "we have all lost something" – a call to collective self-assessment that the "editor" (i.e., "Ed." Bullins himself) responsively footnotes as "Our innocence."[14]

Appropriately enough, Bullins authored *We Righteous Bombers* under a pseudonym, "Kingsley B. Bass, Jr.," a mask tinged with oscillating associations of buffoonery and tricksterism (with its evocations of Garveyesque grandiosity and the labile minstrelsy of Amos "N" Andy – King(be)*fish*). A purported martyr of the Detroit uprising of 1967, "Kingsley B. Bass, Jr." exudes the sacrificial residue of *Clara's Ole Man*, encapsulating the emergence of sovereign legitimacy from the divided identity of the community/victim (king/animal). Circulating on both sides of the fourth wall of Bullins's drama, then, is the *general* economy of scandal through which secular (nationalist) culture arrogates and disseminates the founding violence of sacred authority (righteous bombing), bringing with it the double bind of fascination and repulsion, the efficacious and endlessly reiterated bonding of religious enactment (*re-ligare*). As a spectacle of (dis)possession and ambivalent identification, the conjuncture of (lost) innocence and plagiarism is an apt signifier of modern black drama's own equivocal relation to theatrical representation. For if theater is to be reverenced as a site of self-definition (activated by the "revolutionary artist's" capacity for realistic description implying alternately the need for demonic exorcism and communal reconstruction), it is also a 'prison-house' of substitution which can only defer the *jouissance* of liberation into a masque of symbolizations, suggestions, and other forms of supplementation.

This matrix of representation, sanction, and realization implicates the divided mimesis of Bullins's drama in a confrontation of politics and judgment that poses, as Neal suggested, "fundamental questions concerning the role and the direction of the Black Arts Movement" in its early development.[15] At one extreme, the theorists' call for theater adequate to the "reality" of black experience employs a rhetoric of immediacy, a figure (so to speak) of figural effacement through which an "authentic" blackness can generate a transformative dialectic of performance and perception. This assumption of a prediscursive real, this trope of an absent rhetoricity, locates the justice and authenticity of revolutionary blackness in an origin external to theatrical mediation itself, while positing the possibility of smooth exchange between the empirical and the imaginary, the political and fictional. The apparent insouciance – certainly the expansive audacity – of Bullins's "theft/expropriation" of Camus affirms the easy translation of elementary description into authoritative prescription that follows from this distinction of the political 'real' from its representational inflection. And yet, of course, from another viewpoint such usurpation does just the reverse, disturbing the order of "original" and "copy" upon which the "law" of "proper" mimesis depends. Bullins's impudent plagiarism, and the loss of innocence that it flaunts, can be read as a calculated attack on the regime of "truth" that upholds other forms of hegemonic entitlement. By piercing the western tradition's self-enclosed totality in an act of plunder and mimicry, Bullins's play declares its own "righteous" violence against scripted mastery – mastery *as* (pre)scripted – linking injustice to anchored (non-metaphorical) language in the name of unbounded deviation.

The doubleness and even hesitation of Bullins's relation to mimetic regulation (well after the imposture was exposed, he continued to publish *We Righteous Bombers* under the signature of his *nom de plume*) suggests the conflictual trajectory of modern black drama's quest for an expressive mode capable at once of critique and reconstruction. Subtending that uncertain adventure are those disturbing valences of abjection, victimization, and commodification against *but also through* which elements of Black Arts speculation sought to secure a normative black subjectivity inflected by both political agency and visionary ethics. The ethos of authentication attendant to this difficult process of de- and re-construction produces an anxiety for stabilized meaning, rooted in a myth of originary presence, that mistrusts the very play of difference through which its insurrectionist idealism is generated. The struggle against alien constructs of black humanity becomes itself the search for a corrective Image or Voice of blackness, even as the "revolutionary black artist" inserts himself into a field of multiple inscriptions and competing positions.

But, granted the divination and proclamation of such a Voice, *who is it that speaks*, to whom and for whom does it proliferate its new-found image of a blackness proper to unconstrained identification? At the end of the previous paragraph, I employed the masculine pronoun alone advisedly, for thus driven to exhume the possibility of a performative ideal scourged of ghostly traces of unresolved difference, excess, or otherness, Black Arts theory in the moment of its overt pursuit of a "relevant theatre" threatened at times to become an exclusively masculine affair, a spectacle of Symbolic purification intent (with varying degrees of explicitness) on defining its aims of origination in terms that excluded or severely demarcated black female participation. At some level, one might say that the New Lafayette symposium on *We Righteous Bombers* was *about* this (en)gendering of black theater theory, not simply because of the combative bravado and studied virile swagger with which the participants comported themselves –

Touré: I think that this crushes our spirit. And I definitely raise the –
Neal: My spirit ain't crushed, man.
Touré: Also, another thing –
Neal: Let me interrupt you a minute. Is anybody's spirit crushed because of this play?
    (*Voices*: No. No. No.)
Neal: I mean, really. Go ahead. Finish reading.
Touré: I'm not reading.
Neal: I mean speaking. I'm sorry.
Touré: Also, someone – I think Robert Macbeth –
Neal: I just had to explode. I'm sorry.
Touré: Yeah.
Neal: I got the spirit, right there.

(New Lafayette Symposium,
"Reaction to *We Righteous Bombers*," 23)

but, more suggestively, because the central argument concerned whether history should be seen as fully guided by the "priestly" wisdom of a prophetic "nation builder" (as Touré and Mkalimoto held in their condemnation of Bullins's play for displaying what the symposium termed "counter-revolutionary images" – 16–17, 22–4) or whether history should be embraced in all its turbulence and potential for rupture (as Baraka and, principally, Neal maintained by asserting that even revolutionary drama remained framed by contingencies which render perception partial and history "hurtful" – 18). This conflict between visions of history as governed by a univocal figure of mastery and as entered in awareness of the hetero-

geneity that is intrinsic to history's dialectical agency arises through a
contrast of styles (the upright and uptight, but sometimes self-surpassing
solemnity of Touré and Mkalimoto, versus the shake-n-bake, but sometimes self-satisfied interrogations of Neal and Baraka) that plays out
throughout the symposium as an agon for audience enthusiasm. That is
to say, gender proved elemental to the *mise-en-scène* of Black Arts theory
not just (or even, I would assert, primarily) as a problem of what Eldridge
Cleaver called "hyper-masculine" mythography, but as a crisis *within* male-
focused discourse itself, an enigma of nationalist speculation that caused
an illuminating, if comic, moment of impasse in the panelists' unfolding
exhibition of "revolutionary" disputation:

Touré:	At this point, too, I would like to make a suggestion to Mr. Chairman, like in terms of this panel. Since in this play two sisters are main characters, I ask that we be truly revolutionary and ask some of the sisters to come sit up on the panel. (Applause) We got (like) Sister April Spriggs, Helba Kgositsile in the audience.
Macbeth:	I think that we would have enough to talk about at this point. I – (Laughter) I – with all due respect to the sisters – think that we five brothers have a great deal to talk about right now. The sisters are our friends, but let's try to get to what we've got to talk about right now, and then we can go home. Okay?
Marvin X:	We have a panel –
Touré:	Yeah, brother, but maybe the sisters might want to sit on the panel. What's wrong with that? (Applause; banging of gavel) . . . (Break in continuity of tape) (Macbeth gets two extra chairs and places them at the table. There is a wait. When no sisters come up to take the seats Touré continues.) . . .

(17)

What is at stake here is not so much proportional representation in the
production of modern black drama (this is indeed an issue of legitimate
concern – after all, the sisters are still at a 3:1 disadvantage, having been
offered at best two seats to the brothers' six! – though the still-undervalued
activities of such figures as Barbara Ann Teer, Sonia Sanchez, Jayne
Cortez, and Salimu attest to the empirical presence of black women in
the building of Black Arts theater). Rather, what opens through this
momentary interruption in the panel's official enterprise is the politics of
theatrical representation itself, the wider stakes of 'taking the stage' in the

name of revolutionary blackness. Difference – here the difference of gender – is always already at work, "at this point . . . now," in the determination of the drama's insurgent discursive 'truth,' always already an enabling ingredient of its performative ambition. In seeking redistribution of power and meaning through a new conceptual dispensation, the drama cannot help but rearrange the furniture of its own house, discovering within its own ideological mission an open-ended relation between structural value and revisionary displacement: as the theater itself had demanded, there could be no safe zone at "home" untouched by the uprisings 'in the world' outside.

Were we to hold back the Chairman's gavel an instant, distending the indeterminate suspension in masculine theory and entering the "break" in its "continuity" rather than tolling again the law of its unchallenged resumption, I'd like to imagine that two sisters would indeed arise and make the "wait" worthwhile, two sisters named Adrienne Kennedy and Ntozake Shange. But it would be self-contradictory and historically misleading to summon the sisters either as "main characters" in the Black Arts' more flamboyant ideological dramas or as diametrical rivals to its phallologo-centric nationalism. In relation to the evolving ethos of modern black drama, their work cannot be construed either as filling a "lack" in black masculine discourse, refuting and replacing male images of potency with rites of feminine presence, or as offering a wholly alternative diagnosis of African-American cultural desire and theater's role in its therapeutic fulfillment. Instead, Kennedy and Shange offer representatively urgent experiments with dramatic form that explore the entanglements of authenticity and mediation, originality and historicity, knowledge and performance, identity and identification, that we have seen erupt from within the project of their masculine peers. In their works, gender and sexuality do not simply occupy the place of the "self" or the "Other," but join race and class as shifting sites of repetition and difference where the struggle for a nuanced, efficacious black performative can be progressively engaged. By resituating their plays as vital elements of, not antidotes or affronts to, the Black Arts Movement, we can more accurately gauge the Movement as a self-interrogating search for a mode of blackness where meaning and its performative legitimation coincide.[16]

At the point to which Bullins's yearning style of mimetic realization brought modern black theater, this exploration needed to become not just self-questioning but self-transgressive, and no contemporary works were better designed to rethink the consequences of mimesis for the staging of black consciousness than those of Adrienne Kennedy. In her fragmented, aleatory, disruptively lyrical drama, Kennedy makes central to fabrication of character, dialogue, narrative, and scenic continuum that very ambivalence of affect and understanding which we found bubbling beneath the nervous realism of *Clara's Ole Man*. By thus constructing what Elin Diamond, in a series of incisive readings of Kennedy's oeuvre, has termed a "theater of identification,"[17] Kennedy foregrounds the sacrificial crisis of black subjectivity nascent but unfocused in Bullins's work, making the conjunctions of self and collective, history and ritual, the very thematic and formal crux of her project.

As we shall see, a crucial effect of thus centralizing the relational paradoxes of identification is a significant shift in modern black drama's mimetic paradigm, specifically an increased concern with the process of composition that presses theater toward methexis by demanding the audience's active participation in the shaping of dramatic meaning. Problematizing even the simplest depiction of phenomenal reality, Kennedy's plays urgently incorporate into theatrical presentation the dislocating uncertainties of portrayal itself: for her directors, actors, charactors, and audiences, the sheer act of reproducing the world as word and image exposes and troubles precisely those conventions meant to objectify representation. We see, too, not simply the intersection of circumstance and idea that constitute a cultural identity, but the dispersion of that identity in the evasions, misprisions, and resistances sedimented in those very circumstances and ideas. If in viewing Bullins's characters we are asked to read through the densities of their vocalized texts to the verities of their psychic constitutions, in Kennedy we are challenged to heed discontinuities of motive and abysmal layerings of simulation and dissimulation: in hearing the eloquent perorations of Big Girl, or even the paratactic rants of Baby Girl, for example, we can assume that language belongs to character – our task is to determine expression's meaning; but in attending to Kennedy's personae, we find that "character" is semiotized, becoming an effect of discourse that shapes personality as an hallucinatory palimpsest – our task is to track the conditions of meaningfulness. This distressing deconstruction of personality into fragmented personification and imperfect impersonation does not abandon ideological critique for a nihilistic political despair but reorients it as a disruptive weapon against unconscious complicity with hegemonic stratagems of reduction, reification, and fetishization. Calling into question conventionally accepted meanings for blackness by excavating from apparent identities contradictory possibilities, Kennedy's drama highlights the conflictual dynamics that occur as language, convention, intention, tradition, and desire converge in a space ill-equipped to negotiate clarity or decision among their jumbled differences. The result is a theater that places unbearable – hence altering – pressure on forms of embodiment while obliging its audience to do more than solve the riddle of blackness whose solution already shines through a transparent display.

Full appreciation of Kennedy's challenge to what we have called the crisis of divided mimesis in 1960s Black Arts drama requires further elucidation of that drama's formal bearings. The neonaturalism of which *Clara's Ole Man* is exemplary seems to be satisfied, more or less, with the forms it finds in "life": prosaic interchange; non-figurative language; an illusion of non-selected events; a "natural" sense of emphasis; and a non-musical (not necessarily cacophonous) sound. The most distinctive attribute of this form is its guiding sociological and materialistic conception of consciousness. Social energies, be they conservative or critical, are contained within an order of significant form that gathers even the most exorbitant fragment of self-expression into a coherent (usually narrative) structure. Thus, organized by what Leo Bersani has called the "temporal myth of real beginnings and definitive endings,"[18] naturalism presents itself as an enclosing structure (however "tragic" its content) that ultimately domesticates (one might as easily say "redeems") seemingly unintelligible (or untamed) impulses into a readable "plot" of intention and effect.

Naturalism might be accounted, then, the secret sharer of melodrama, which, as Peter Brooks has demonstrated,[19] resolves antithetical instincts into a balanced design affirming an abiding epistemological ecology. It takes the subject to be a part and function of its environment and depicts it as a being who, instead of controlling concrete reality, is itself controlled and absorbed by it. Human acts – whatever their intent, outline, or incidental effect – contain an element of the determined, something that does not originate in consciousness and that makes the subject seem the unalterable product of an unmotivated and structural "reality." So long as African-American drama maintained naturalism as its dominant mode, then, it could do little more than express the "plight" of black people. Its heroes might declare the "madness" of reality but reality inevitably declared its ascendancy over them.

In its search for a more triumphant vision than naturalism affords, modern black theater has produced a number of agitprop and simplistically allegorical plays. In works such as Baraka's *Experimental Death Unit #1* and Salimu's *Growin' Into Blackness*,[20] one feels the drama, in its effort to surpass the sceptical irresolution of works like *Clara's Ole Man*, mirroring naturalism's austerity but with inverted emphasis in being stripped to its essential grounding in a thematic of value: to a pattern of abstract actions, of moral relationships, that has the simple intensity of melodramatic (because proscribed) normative conflict. Such plays were at once powerful and, in both effect and influence, ephemeral. For, as Harrison trenchantly observed, a dramatically communicable vision could not make itself present in African-American theater as an avowed progression from stark realism merely by hypertrophying ethical certainty at the expense of a subtler analysis of social, psychic, and even ethical issues. Some other theatrical grounding to the evolving vision of African-American modernism was needed, and this, it emerged, was provided by poetic experimentation – both linguistic and visual – the rising prestige of which was due to the growing emphasis on spirituality, the development of increasingly complex accounts of black selfhood, and deepening attention to black musical innovators like John Coltrane (the subject of our next chapter).

For the programmatic vector of the Black Arts Movement, Baraka's *Four Black Revolutionary Plays* showed the way to putting new life into sterile

forms, and even though the salient feature of these works is their plati-
tudinous satire, stirrings of a more profound insight were evident. Yet
more quietly, enjoying a more delayed if lasting influence, Kennedy's
cryptic, surrealistic plays had already taken the first steps toward a radical
departure from naturalism. The pervasive aura of her oeuvre in the period
from *Funnyhouse of a Negro* (1964) to *A Movie Star Has to Star in Black and
White* (1976)[21] was one of mystery, mythic fantasy, and poetic ambiguity,
and the steadily increasing interest in and appreciation of her work among
African-American artists during this period, culminating with Harrison's
adulatory comparison of her drama's "intricate polyrhythms" to those of
intrepid jazz explorers like Coltrane,[22] attests to the era's growing interest
in expressionistic models of theatrical innovation. Kennedy's contribution
to this changing orientation of modern black drama is singular and
profound. Rather than seeking to produce an essential image of blackness,
her work consists of an obstinate struggle with the very question of
black identity, and specifically with the historically conditioned distance
between the longing *for* that essential image of self and the discourses that
frustrate while sustaining such aspiration. Drama, as a vexed medium of
self-presentation, is thus itself subjected to keen scrutiny, and is thereby
moved with its characters and audience to acknowledge that the attempt
to transcend structures of power can often subtly reinstate them in other,
less recognizable shapes. The 'figurative' element of Kennedy's plays is
registered exactly in the fissures that consequently open between desire
and history, the self's voice and the voiced subject. By thus relocating
drama's structural gap between page and stage to the affective and imagistic disparities displayed by performance itself, Kennedy's peculiar style
of poetic theater advanced the Black Arts' quest for a reflexive enactment
of psycho-historical inquiry.

The uncanny theatricality that results from this mutual inhabitation and
displacement of 'self' (i.e, the uncertain intersection of voice and body that
orbits the libidinal urge for agency and presence) and 'other' (i.e., natural,
social, familial, and historical conditions of this craving) pervades
Kennedy's sensibility with such intensity as to eventually define the very
possibility of her writing as performative 'signature' – this is the focus for
our pursuit of her exorbitant self-stagings in Chapter 6. Our concern here
is the particular effect of an exemplary play, *The Owl Answers*,[23] upon an
evolutionary understanding of modern black drama. One of Kennedy's
most complex and lyrically beautiful pieces, *The Owl Answers* is an illuminating example of her dramaturgy and vision, representing an ambitious
attempt to refract contemporary struggles by plumbing dangerous inter-
sections of body, language, and event. The play stages the central Black
Arts question of black identity around a specific cluster of themes (sexuality,
family/tribal structure, death) and images (animals, light/dark motifs,
musical accompaniments, and innumerable fragmented and phantasmagoric objects of all kinds). But her aim is not to so much to disclose

the veiled truth of her protagonists or even to offer them as exemplars of a quest for discovery as it is to lay bare the network of relations in which they're caught, and to suggest the subversive potential of their efforts to resist reproduction of dissociating mechanisms while staring down their mimetic submissions to the violence of alien(ating) economies of meaning.

The Owl Answers is what Harrison would call a "Hantu" form; that is, its structure turns upon a fluid time/space relationship which eschews linear presentations of episodes in favor of a more imagistic and symbolic design. Thus, the multiple personalities of the characters and their various environments change rapidly, often obscurely, and together form an intricate matrix of associations which alone defines the totality of their world. As in *Dutchman*, "the scene is a New York subway" but, as Kennedy's note for the set continues to tell us without punctuation or any other indication of differentiation, it also "is the Tower of London is a Harlem hotel room is St. Peter's" (171). Realism's informational signs thus share space with an array of locales implying a palimpsest of historical, linguistic, and cultural strata. Bullins's *Clara's Ole Man* makes no special demands on a theatrical imagination, for it accepts the realistic stage much as Bullins found it. Its setting, for example, displays a photographic sensibility for reproducing on the stage every detail of a typical 'ghetto' kitchen and the street life that intrudes upon it. Kennedy's setting, by contrast, is a mixture of real and surreal which reinforces the play's thematic ambiguities. Tellingly, Kennedy includes with her text a "costume plot" and elaborate set design, thereby emphasizing the counterplot of visual elements in the total meaning of her work.

In effect, setting gives way in *The Owl Answers* to spacing,[24] so that the actors do not so much step upon a stage as enter a performative arena where the very idea of space is elemental to the unfolding sequence of events. Or perhaps in *The Owl Answers* one might better speak of a tense dialogue between setting and spacing, in which gestures are simultaneously lodged within the claustral zones of specific enclosures (rooms, subway cars, altar spaces) and sent floating into indeterminate regions of impression and evocation. Setting character in motion within these shifting environments of architectural definition, *The Owl Answers* both highlights and distantiates narrative's shibboleths of causation and motivation. This elasticity of time and space as structural determinants of narrative meaning creates a particularly theatrical anguish, framing at once the impulse to root gesture in recognizable structures and the contingent, even illusory, quality of that urge for lucidity and agency.

The result of such an assembling and decentering of symbolic landscapes is to add a function to action itself. Instead of treating a plot that explores human relations in their moral aspect, *The Owl Answers* makes action into another signature of emotion. It is not a limited vector, stemming from and dependent on what we naturalistically call 'character,' but invokes instead the intimacies, ecstasies, and anguish of what Harrison terms the African-American's "soul-life." In Kennedy's plays relations between people matter less than the struggle of such a soul with an all-enveloping spiritual mystery. The coherent action-sequence that illustrates the moral nature of black life in the naturalism of Hansberry or the neonaturalism of Baldwin and Bullins gives place to a complex pattern communicating a numinous insight. In this pattern action is sometimes, it is true, bound up with the life of human relations; more often it is an element of the unseen life of desire and of spiritual power, presented through anthropomorphic images in a design of figurative theatricality.

Ambiguity of presence and event, then, haunts the play's very determination of character, for the protagonists' bodies are themselves the spaces in which sensations of solidity and vacancy drive through the voice with fragmenting intensity. Their bodies are presented not as determined entities but as kaleidoscopic sites where multiple languages and experiences compete for purchase: 'character' is itself the product of this uncertain struggle to sustain language within an identifiable bodily locus. Dramatic identity is consequently not finished but a continuous structural negotiation that is at once inter- and intrasubjective. The main figure is "She Who Is Clara Passmore who is The Virgin Mary who is The Bastard who is the Owl"; she has come from Georgia to London to mourn her Dead White Father who – no ironized patriarchal 'ole man,' he! – was once "Goddam Father who is the richest White Man in the Town" and who is also her stepfather, the black Reverend Passmore. SHE is held prisoner in the Tower of London by a chorus composed of Shakespeare, Chaucer, William the Conqueror, and Anne Boleyn (who is also both the Bastard's Black Mother – once a cook for Goddam Father – and the Reverend's wife). Immediately, we are made to share SHE's own recognition that she is being placed within – indeed, that she "is" – a series of repetitions and substitutions that fuel the machineries of cultural, familial, and personal desire, assigning her overdetermined places in an historical melodrama populated by alternately eminent (white) and generic (black) dramatis personae. SHE's very existence within this tragicomic processional dissolves identity anchored as a product of a functional identification into a set of tensions, mutations, or contradictions within a continual process of subject-ification. The birth of SHE from this structural displacement places her ever at the seam of competing orders of significance – white/black, male/female, dead/living, past/present, imaginary/real, human/animal, patrician/menial, mobility/imprisonment, longing/loathing: as a perpetual and unresolvable mediation among conflicting registers, hers is a decidedly liminal or *bastard* mode of being or becoming.

SHE's attempt to assume the white, English patrimony of the Dead Father by visiting his bier, which lies in St. Paul's, is the play's central 'action.'[25] SHE's claim is to the lineage of her blood ancestors, a claim made poignant by the juxtaposition of her love for English culture and her brutal rejection by the chorus of exemplary Anglo-Saxon heroes:

She: My father loved you William . . .
They: *interrupting*. If you are his ancestor why are you a Negro? . . .
She: Let me into the chapel. He is my blood father. I am almost white,
         am I not? . . . I am his daughter.

(172)

Speaking at the edge of supposedly sacral and spurious locations – not merely the boundary separating white and black cultures but the juridical delineation of racial identification itself – SHE suffers from the very inheritance that is denied her, being pinioned by Anglo culture's contradictory conflation of ancestral (socially constructed) and lineal (biologically determined) legitimation in the constitution of its own authority. But more importantly, speaking is itself a riven activity arising at the suture-line of SHE's abjection. Is she at the threshold of an objective cultural formation or does she encounter projections of figurations already sedimented within? *I am/am I not/I am*: what – and where – exactly is this "I" generated through an incessant chiasmal spasm of tentative assertion ("almost") and absymal negation? Certainly not the sovereign Idealist "I" that, distinguished from the content that it differentiates from itself, reigns as a transparent self-consciousness always 'at home' with itself. On the contrary, SHE's "I" openly concedes the anguish of standing outside the portals of full self-possession, suffering the wound of ex-centricity, exile, and homelessness, forever barred from itself.

But in being barred from itself, SHE's "I" is also denied absolute identification with the idealized form of her imagined satisfaction, which, because this icon of totality is necessarily other (paternal, white, fantasmatic) as well as similar (feminine, black, vital), intrinsically threatens any attempted self-constitution. In SHE, Kennedy suggests that the black subject's quest for authentic being consists in her endlessly fragmenting struggle to separate herself from what partially constitutes that being through an historical identification with it. The effort to enter the arena of authorized symbolic exchange – a privileged locus here ironized as one of ghastly stillness and permanent death – is thus revealed as the play's defining crux, as much enabling as disabling for being impossible. Following the paradigm of that 'white mythology' to which SHE seeks access, SHE attempts through much of the drama to embrace the paternal Law that would presumably overcome the vertiginous experience of self-dislocation, with its perspectival confusion of interior feeling (the signifier of 'identity') and external meaning (the signified of 'the real'). For SHE, the search for the father and the quest for self-coherence begin as one but subtly diverge in a moment of ambiguous combustion. As the play's episodes unfold, the individual roles of the father and mother remain unique and legible, each representative of a distinct and partially relevant aspect of SHE'S inheritance, while SHE's roles become increasingly atomized and estranged from a discursive core, either designated imperialistically by others or abruptly embraced in her desperate pursuits of autonomous and holistic being. THEY are cold, abstract, aloof; SHE moves among their apparitions desiring love in a lifeless world:

> DEAD FATHER *rises, goes to her, then dies again. Great clang.* BASTARD'S BLACK MOTHER *shakes a rattle at* SHE. SHE *screams at the* DEAD FATHER and the MOTHER.

She: You must know how it is to be filled with yearning.
They: *laugh.*

(179)

Filled with yearning, SHE is tormented by the fact that the language of realization is not hers, and the very effort to appropriate it returns her to a scene of endlessly repeated repression, mockery, and obliteration. Yet SHE's desire cannot be situated confidently in either the social or Imaginary spheres, accounted clearly as either intentional or unconscious in its mimetism. The laughter of her interlocutors suggests a refusal of recognition that locks her into the indeterminacies of a dialectic in which (ex-)slaves assert a violent mastery over those to whom they gave birth as avatars of their own unresolved aspiration. The black family it seems secures itself as community through a parodic form of sacrificial exorcism, expelling in her the difference that marks its own place within the wider cultural order of its own (unconsciously) splintered being. In spurning her, SHE's father and mother refuse what they have produced, consigning new forms of desire to nonsatisfaction. And with this bifurcation in the genealogical structure of African-American "yearning," blackness, on the Ellisonian model, is fractured at the junction of origination and reproduction.

Accordingly, SHE becomes a black ghost caught in the histrionic machine of the Euro-American Imaginary (that space where all 'other' supplications and identifications mirror its own claim to symbolic primacy), a spectral haint[26] of unsanctioned will destined to an itinerary of indirection, mediation, and repetition. All the objects she encounters – books, weapons, handkerchiefs, wigs, and, above all, bodies – are themselves reflections of this simulacrum of imitative assertions: each object in its own way figures another's desire, scripted from elsewhere in the dead space of otherwise empty signs that ceaselessly declare the imperial sanctity of whiteness. Whiteness in *The Owl Answers* indeed figures the prison (or elevated "Tower") of theater founded on a sacrificial logic of mimetic substitutions, the cost of which is amortized across the bodies of its subaltern participants. The shattering frustrations of SHE's confrontations on the shifting stages of that theater, then, ought not to be read as betraying Kennedy's political irresolution[27] but, to the contrary, as constituting a critique of a colonial ideology that invites its subjects to self-defeating projects of mimetic desire.

SHE must therefore be heard as neither an historical nor mythical figure, neither a colonized nor postcolonial subject, neither a psychological nor hallucinatory cipher. Rather, she is a figure navigating and disturbing these dualities in ways that illuminate the complicity of whiteness and silently aligned discourses of modern 'truth': ethnology; canon-formation; realism . . . all of which posit a unified, naturalized, inviolable identity defined against an inchoate, unruly, abjected 'other.' SHE's quest for the father modulates almost imperceptibly into a demand for *love* (179 and ff.), shifting the ground from underneath the drama of colonial identification and plunging SHE into a drama of overlapping positions that would annul and replace the specular economy of colonial power. Finally, a dark Negro Man, whom SHE calls "God," tries to supplant her vision of love with the sordid sexuality of a Harlem hotel:

Negro man: What is it? What is it? What is wrong? (*He tries to undress her. Underneath her body is black. He throws off the crown* SHE *has placed on him.*) . . . Are you sick?

She: (*smiles*) No. God. (SHE *is in a trance.*) No, I am not sick. I only have a dream of love. A dream.

(184)

Her dream-world bursts into flame as she and the Negro Man grapple in a space that is suddenly transformed from a hotel room to High Altar. SHE's once-calm demands upon the past give way to a final hysteria in which she strips through each available racial and sexual identity – Clara, the Negro child of Reverend Passmore; Mary, the martyred Virgin; Bastard, the Mulatto daughter of Dead White Father – until, inflamed and dripping in her suicidal mother's blood, she at last becomes the mysterious Owl. Is this the ruin or apotheosis of that *jouissance* which, refused by the succession of patriarchal figures from Dead White Father through Negro Man, relocates subaltern desire in the mother, the place of 'truth' beyond reach of the Father's prohibitive Law and (dis)empowering name? Does the tumult of SHE's transgressions signal the failure of misguided identification or, perhaps intead, the explosive translation of mimetic critique into revolutionary transformation? Through a gesture that transfigures patriarchal realism into a mode of subversive extravagance, has, in fact, the legislating *nom-du-père* been exchanged for the unnamed and unnaming resistance of an alternative praxis? At play's end, the owl, solitary, wise, dispassionate, cries out the question embedded within the name "SHE WHO IS" – *Whooo*. Denied the complex legacy of her 'blood ancestors,' surrounded by deception and death, SHE nearly answers by asserting an identity with the nocturnal creature. Yet this concluding statement is only a muted, seemingly painful, and ultimately enigmatic moan, haunting in its faint, self-mutilated echo of Bullins's Baby Girl: "Ow . . . ow" (187).

One of the most notable features of *The Owl Answers* in the context of modern black drama's evolution is this convergence of formal and psycho-political investigation. Kennedy so integrates the construction and deconstruction of time, space, speech, image, and gesture as to render historical analysis and theatrical experiment two sides of a fundamental endeavor. Particularly significant is the addition to Bullinsesque natural-istic psychological torment of symbolic overtones that actually alter the character's psyche as they resonate at climactic moments, so that, as the play progresses, character becomes symbol in a way that doesn't merely avoid but implicitly critiques the covert affiliation of realism and melo-drama. The reflexivity of this process not only affects a deployment of space and narrative that proves excessive to the mimetic means that it none the less exploits but necessarily alters the actors' styles of represen-tation. Kennedy's actors cannot reflect the 'natural' expression of identity expected of a Bullins troupe, but must instead inflect precisely the agency of performance as an historical and affective *problem* always at work in the production of 'character.' Just as identification is the subject, not the unquestioned assumption, of SHE's presentation, so must the actor develop her protean peregrinations in a manner that challenges the audience's instinct to bond with such a protagonist *without*, however, falling into a totally Brechtian style of *Verfremdung*. Not self-revelation but self-signification is the task of Kennedy's actors. Confining gestures and intonation to spare measures against the grain of their exclamatory energies, the actors must exceed the formal imperatives of naturalistic transparency to register the simultaneity of presence and absence, referentiality and fantasm, instinct and textuality in their composition. Thus, "ghosting" themselves,[28] Kennedy's actors become agents of the perception that her 'characters' are not threatened by anything more than the stage itself, by the imbrication of theatrical supplementation with sacrificial oppression.

Likewise, *The Owl Answers* radically alters its audience's mode of expe-riencing black theater's fusion of spectacle and narrative, requiring of it specific sensitivity to these shifts in presentational emphasis – some slight, some abrupt, some daring – and especially to those moments of symbolic expansion when the characters lunge forward, thrusting their significance at the beholder in excess of narrative expectation. At such moments, the audience becomes pointedly conscious that it *is* an audience, that it is acti-vated as a mutable spectatorial body exactly as the characters are pressed forward in their unsettled expressivity. Spectatorship, too, becomes an uneasy and self-conscious activity of loss and appropriation. The feeling of dislocation that the audience experiences as the drama moves between the realistic psychological mode and the symbolic one involves it in a constant, conscious process of readjustment to the fictional world: the audi-ence, like the stage, becomes a site of constant redescription where memory and resistance commingle to uncertain ends. And if the play itself has become an ensemble of citations that disperse desire into a repertoire of critical images, postures, and episodes, then the audience becomes, finally, the main locus of Kennedy's effort to render modern African-American drama's nurturance of black consciousness a vehicle for more incisive collaborations of epistemological critique and ontological innovation.

This reorientation of mimesis from the axis of stage/world to that of stage/audience also accounts, in considerable part, for the sense of threat that pervades Kennedy's work, a menace that centers on identities captured in the flux of translation (rather than, as with Bullins, on selves caught in a state of pre-translational arrest). But it is the terror of meaning and its impossibility, of horrible or blinding revelation, more than the eruption of literal violence, that lies at the root of this menace. It is the fear that what lurks in the inner self and the collective past will emerge still-born, grotesque, or useless, so that represented events won't explain their historical etiology or suggest their future redemption but will simply generate sterile and corrosive reiterations of a single repressive paradigm. The stammering and incantatory repetitions of Kennedy's diction dramatize this dreaded conflict between development and stasis. All assertion in *The Owl Answers* threatens to become mere rehearsal – *répétition*, as the French would have it – an effectively mute restaging of colonialism's scene of origination. And yet the play's incessant visual and aural doublings suggest a strategic hyperbolization of mimesis, a kind of grievous mimicry, that exposes the ideological fastening of meaning to form. The result is that when the audience begins to hear and piece out the play's symbolic resonances it also begins to feel the special frightening unease characteristic of them. For that sense of menace is intimately related to a paradoxical phenomenon: the further the play moves into the realm of defamiliarized motive and blurred causality, the nearer it comes, through the echoic process of ritualized self-citation, to the world of the audience itself.

In a work like *The Owl Answers*, Kennedy is pioneering for black theater a subjective-critical mode that constitutes a disturbingly innovative dramatic response to the visionary aspect of the Black Arts Movement. In the mingling of elements of seen and unseen, of the 'natural' and the 'fantastic' in a vortex of ideology and resistance, action comes to have the force of symbol, and conversely symbol assumes the quality of a praxis. Kennedy thus opened the way for black writers to become poetic dramatists rather than simply dramatic poets, reimagining the stage as a venue for metamorphic challenges to 'reality.' Yet in the interest of fully appreciating the disconcerting provocation of her theatrical experiment, the vernacular substratum of her drama should also be emphasized: borrowing from distinctive traditions of masking such as minstrelsy, hoodoo tales, and African rites, *The Owl Answers* crashes the barriers of realism by establishing a lyric metaphysical emphasis in context of a trenchant assault upon the spuriously naturalized racial ideology of Anglo-American patriarchy. Thus, the "white pallor" that paints the characters' visages can be stripped to reveal the "black flesh" beneath. At the intersection of narrative and theatricalization, then, this excruciating tension between white masks and black skin offers a neo-Fanonian demystification of Euro-American culture's production of racial identity at the site of social, psychic, and physical 'castration.'[29] But what is crucial in Kennedy's conception of this dynamic of (de)composition is the multivalence of its performative character. The "pallid" visage is as likely to reside beneath the "black face" as the reverse (174), and so no preordained relation of canon and deviation, and no hierarchized relation of perception and expression, can be fixed within the scene of Kennedy's address to the sources and crises of blackness.

Moving away from the less supple Black Arts practitioners' discrimination of 'positive' and 'negative' images to investigation of the process of subjectification, Kennedy's theater opens fresh possibilities for interrogating and reformulating African-American self-performance. Aptly, the final impression left by *The Owl Answers* is that of an exhilarating disturbance. Though Kennedy's heroine is caught in webs of congenital horror, a product of both the history of race and the psychic condition it shrouds, she still passes through crisis to epiphany, shattering though this process may be. Moreover, a more particularized, yet also visionary, emphasis is discernible in the play: SHE is exalted in her irremediable distance from the patriarchal origins of her divided voice, hinting that in her very ghost-liness lies a latent potentiality for re-embodied agency. The menacing quality of her unfulfilled and cryptic quest for Dead Father (or is it for the father's death?) is perhaps less a reflection of authorial nihilism than a warning to those who look on – although we will see in Chapter 6 that the autobiographical element of Kennedy's spectral theatricality positions her as audience to her own 'rehearsal' of self-realization through interiorized otherness. Kennedy furnishes her play with a reality of motives and inclinations, but her world is like a beachhead on the edge of a darkness teeming with a host of spirits, ambiguously inimical to a reborn consciousness they yet somehow conjure. *The Owl Answers*, like Kennedy's theater generally, leaves an impression of restlessness and an unresolved longing to believe, thereby infusing an insistent, if enigmatic, spiritual impulse into black theater. Thus far, it has been left to others to evolve in this spiritual mode from search to celebration.

IV

And what love had to do with it
    stuttered, bit its tongue.
Bided our time, said only wait,
              we'd see.

. . . Cramped egg we might work our
way out of,   caress reaching in
    to the bones underneath.

                                                        Not even
        looking. Even so, see
                        thru.

        Watery light we tried in vain
              to pull away from.   Painted
                                              face,
              disembodied voice. Dramas we
                    wooed, invited in but got
        scared of.   Song so black it
                                        burnt
              my lip . . .   Tore my throat as I
              walked up Real Street. Raw beginner,
                                                green
                    attempt to sing the blues . . .

        Tilted sky, turned earth. Bent wheel, burnt
                                              we.
              Bound I. Insubordinate
                              us

                                    Nathaniel Mackey, "Song of the
                                    Andoumboulou: 12"[30]

The Owl Answers is enacted in scenes of strange power, achieved by
Kennedy's departures in method: the breakdown of autonomous 'characters'; the elaboration of a pattern of verbal themes that resists absorption
into discursive continuities and logics; and alteration of the representational stage into a traumatic dreamscape of expressionistic scenes. Most
crucial is the way in which an order of symbols and motifs, usually
concretized by objects or masked figures, joins with spectacular and super-
natural effects to create an aura of lyric otherworldliness and a conciseness
of dramatic statement that aches for that singular gesture capable of
crystallizing a meaning toward which the drama fatefully gropes.
    Among the more striking linkages of figure and object in *The Owl Answers*
is that between SHE and a collection of notebooks into which she has
attempted to inscribe her effort to "communicate" with, rescue, and, in
effect, 'bind' her father in the all-encompassing "thesis" (184) of her desire.
Kennedy's stage directions indicate that these loosely bound volumes will
fall from her grasp throughout the play and that "SHE will pick them up,
glance frenziedly at a page from a notebook, be distracted, place the notebooks in a disorderly pile, drop them again, etc." (171). SHE appears both
terrorized and distracted in the effort to gather these scripts into a totality,
as though their pretense of narrative control and canonical accumulation
both supplements and ironizes her claim to own a voice in the great
western story of geneaological transmission. Her fragile compilations
are constantly subjected to the harassing interruption of action, as though
their attempts to fix history, meaning, and language in a singular "order"

of intentional expression are intrinsically doomed by being immersed in the unpredictable medium of enactment. The dependence on pre-existing systems of sense is thereby hurled into unpredictable scatterings of engagement.

Like the leaves of SHE's notebooks strewn across the stage, identity in *The Owl Answers* is seemingly dispersed and disordered, blown into incoherent heaps that mock the outward image of clear (Clara) and immaculate (Virgin Mary) self-production. Kennedy's insight into the conditional status of autobiographical knowledge – and, in particular, the distressing marginality of black women in discourses of the public sphere, wherein they may appear only to ensure that they will disappear – thus takes the shape of a tragi-travesty of conventional dramatic hierarchy, in which the actor/character's assumed freedom is undermined by her enslavement to a script or Book that hollows the asserted autonomy of gesture, motivation, speech, and action.

And yet these vignettes of SHE's fumbled papers complicate the relation of structural containment and phenomenological expression that they appear simply to expose with such oddly burlesque poignancy. On the one hand, they seem to emblemize SHE's willful participation in what Derrida has called the "theological stage" of whiteness,[31] with its deferral of self-realization under the watchful eye of an absent (dead and deadly) patriarchal authority. On this reading, every effort by SHE to assert the self against all that would constrain and wither it merely reinforces the inhibiting structure of power. Dissidence is already another form of obedience, as the drama of desire (under)writes an imperative of reiteration that erases rather than marks the subject's freedom. On the other hand, the notebooks' slippery, dispersive qualities mitigate, even redirect the pathos of SHE's trying to wield the very technology and to occupy the very position that provide means and justification for the forces that would hack her to pieces (along with her precious notebooks). For the Book's collapse figures, too, the absence of any meta-language or transcendental certainty that can anchor what is 'real' in racial experience. This de-signification of any structural 'master' suggests the possibility of SHE's entering another model of discourse, one free from a closed system of representational relations for its foundation or purpose. Rather than pursuing history as an already inscribed, prelimited arrangement of episodes and commentaries, those scraps of unbound textuality beckon to SHE's nascent instinct to *aggravate and expropriate* history as a medium of unpredictable risks, transactions, and subversions.

The fragmented notebooks of *The Owl Answers* thus operate as a double image of Kennedy's theatrical project, its predicament and challenge: on the one hand, a Theater Book, the tome-as-tomb, whose stature as monumental sepulcher of all knowledge and expectation dominates a frightening scene of self-limitation; on the other hand, the endlessly disseminative Performance, the tomb-become-womb, encrypting not the final word of colonial violence but the potential transfiguration of the victim into a figure free to move outside the field of regulated differences that constitute the oppressor's paternal language. This liberational praxis can only be parabolically insinuated by *The Owl Answers*, because it remains itself a repetition of a script determined elsewhere, and so can only thematize performative self-sufficiency as the "dream" of an eruptive force – "love" – that imagines some other, some future production in/different to that in which SHE remains captive. The movement from Book to Performance, which Kennedy's drama augurs but does not itself accomplish, cannot on the other hand be undertaken as a simplistic substitution of spontaneous 'scene of presence' for finished 'scene of writing': merely fetishizing physical or prelinguistic immediacy cannot provide a revolutionary critique of history and consciousness, but becomes itself another (possibly more insidious) form of dissimulation. In order to imagine Kennedy's deconstruction of the theatricality of race and gender in another, reconstructive key, black playwrights had first to fully embrace the subversive paradoxes of mediation and difference unveiled by her theater; but they needed to do so, too, in such a way that textuality and performance were made to repeat and displace each other in ways that improvise bold new orchestrations of power and desire, history and psyche, experience and expression.

Kennedy's drama already intimates that at the heart of such fresh visions we should find a vigorous confrontation with the stage as a slippery, unmappable surface upon which is conducted a sacrificial exchange of aspiration for realization, and, in turn, of image for aspiration. Any progressive mutation in black performance practice would therefore need to locate that intersection of being and becoming, representation and invention, that could retain (rather than barter) desire within revolutionary experience. More precisely, modern black theater required a distinctive choreography of *body* (in all its signifying ontology and signifyin' nuance) and *mask* (in all its simulative cogency) within a refashioned performative *space* (shaped by rather than delimiting the movements of desire, resistance, and change) . . . and no play assumed this (com)positional task with more tact, grit, or innovative consequence than Ntozake Shange's *for colored girls who have considered suicide/when the rainbow is enuf*.[32]

for colored girls succeeds in exactly those areas where *The Owl Answers* remains tentative or incompletely realized. Most particularly, Shange's play coordinates performance and perception in a collaborative design, rather than entangling them in distinctive, if daringly parallel, frameworks. Kennedy's drama provides the Black Arts perhaps its most provocative stimulus to spectatorial reflexivity. Yet her development of expressionist and symbolist techniques and the addition thereto of a language which seeks to penetrate beyond surface meaning have not always produced events during which the playwright and audience are in recognizable accord. This incongruity – indicative, certainly, of her plays' capacity for disquieting challenges to racial and sexual mythographies – partly derives from the density of her iconology. But it is more a function of the very form through which her experimental metapsychology is given material expression. Her plays allow the spectator to close the gap between herself and the spectacle by an act of nervous decoding, albeit, to be sure, an interpretive movement that engages emotive response. In that sense the play invades the spectator's mind, putting her in intimate contact with the inner visions she and the playwright share. Yet she is denied a means for authentication of interpretation and, in addition, is offered no heuristic image of her own participation, or even implicaton, in the event itself.

Embracing a translucent spirituality and a reconciliation of private and collective history that transforms Kennedy's melancholic repetitions to (post)elegiac resignifications, *for colored girls* by contrast with *The Owl Answers* achieves the integration of vision and community envisioned by contemporary theories of black drama. As with earlier turning-points in the development of black theater, this advance is achieved dramaturgically, not merely thematically or polemically; but in both the idea and history of its realization, Shange's play links this dramaturgical experimentation to a vigorous rethinking of authenticity, authorship, and production that alters the landscape of Black Arts theatrical practice.

To fully appreciate this revisionary ethos, we must begin with a close look at *for colored girls*'s Preface, an exuberant and intricately layered account of the play's history from pre-conception in the years of Shange's fledgling artistry in San Francisco to post-production in the aftermath of extraordinary success in the sophisticated theater culture of New York. Along with Baraka's "The Revolutionary Theatre" and Neal's "The Black Arts Movement," Shange's Preface emerges as one of the most textured theater manifestos of the era, surely its most dazzling synthesis of historical, political, affective, and pragmatic criteria for a revolutionary mode of African-American dramatic performance. In its narrative of the play's generation, evolution, embodiment, and reception we can discern a consistent indifference, at once cavalier and calculated, to sanctified notions of how experience is to be organized into drama's formal patterns. Shange's Preface purports to be a history of the dramatic 'text,' but it becomes truly a fresh dramatization of how performance itself ceaselessly rearranges relations between textuality and history, along with its assumed cognates: understanding and experience, space and time, consciousness and body. As such, it offers modern black theater a new *paideia* or Scene of Instruction in which the work's material enactment becomes both medium and meaning for a dynamically cultural vision of black agency.

Shange presents the journey of *for colored girls* from idea to production as itself a continuous, synecdochic enactment of the play's central insight that the process of creation is always already a practice of historical struggle. Throughout the Preface, *for colored girls* is shown developing its identity within contrasting milieux of memory, consumption, exchange, and contestation: the early women's studies programs and poetry centers, where the excavation of silenced lineage took specific linguistic and intellectual form (x; xiii); the bars and coffee houses, where Shange and her feminist peers battled to be heard within a robust, combative, mostly masculine scene of verbal invention (ix, xii f.); the dance studios, where the body was reclaimed as expressive instrument and testimonial site of ritual and vernacular knowledges (xi, xiv). However much this story shadows that well-worn genre of high culture, the personal memoir recounting a work's generation, the Preface insists at every turn on the play's fabrication as a social and institutional event rather than celebrating the autonomous creation of an individual mind. Thus, textual revision becomes inextricable from material conditions and social location: the play's individual segments, or choreographed poems, are rooted first in Shange's fortuitous encounters with other Third-World women artists and intellectuals, so that they are from the beginning part of a shared effort to "direct our energies toward clarifying our lives" – the lives, moreover, not merely of themselves but of an enveloping structure of generative kinship, "the lives of our mothers, daughters, & grandmothers" (x); learning women's history among pioneer scholars and African-American dance among a "troupe of five to six black women" allows the works to issue further from a nexus of technique and common passion (x, xii); the earliest pieces are performed not in theaters but in "the space I knew," so that a given performance's material, duration, and tone would be dictated not by the text's fixed parameters but in dialogue with the audience's "mood" (xiii); and so on. New political, pedagogical, and performative circumstances shape the activity of revision, as the poems that move toward what Shange came to call *for colored girls* (chosen as a trope of this experiential process of conception and enactment itself – xii) remain open to emendation by multiple audiences as well as fellow actors, dancers, and writers. *for colored girls*, then, issues from a dialectic of forces that are elemental to a changing cultural consciousness, and thus not only thematizes (as we will see) but concretizes a playful interchange of position and composition, petition and repetition.

Fundamental to this tale of compositional genesis within the socio-economic matrices of heady cultural commerce is the play's quest for community within nontheatrical spaces. As the poems' mixed brew of music, word, and dance begins to determine its own imperatives, like Topsy "growing to take space of its own" (xiii), the performances assume the personalities of the locales in which they're presented: raucous and gutsy like the bar scene; intimate and savvy like the coffee houses; angry and lyrical like the voiced-poetry venues. Shaped in such environments, *for colored girls* embodies the concept of "modal" composition espoused by Harrison, in which form, function, and content turn upon nonnaturalistic imperatives of realization, eschewing exposition in the exploration of events that collapse distinctions between sociality and spirituality, materiality and figuration, temporality and topography. *for colored girls* is thus placed not so much in a setting as in a spatial dialogue between undifferentiated and provisionally marked positions. If *The Owl Answers* fractures setting into an undecidable juxtaposition of cubist layerings, *for colored girls* moves even further from mimetic illusion to a fluid spatiality that serves both to interrogate competing social locations (as we shall see, for example, in the "sechita" episode) and to project shifting arenas of self-exploration (as we shall see in the play's final sequences). As a disavowal of specifically theatrical institutions of scenic mimesis, the 'stage' thereby offers itself less as a copy than as a site of life events, though such events are precisely those in which 'meanings' are determined in an active exchange between performing and perceiving bodies.

The physical restrictions of such locations, as well as the economic limitations of these early performances (the actors received drinks as often as dollars for their labor), pressed the drama further toward a vision of space and its properties as forms of 'symbolic capital' to be expended as ingredients of a politically inflected visionary ethos. Thus, once lights were finally affordable to Shange and her dancers they are used sparingly and in expressive fashion: rather than defining 'realistic' decor with floodlights and footlights, Shange employs localized or 'motivated' spotlights to frame postures of distress, arrival, or departure, and to sketch a chiaroscuric interplay of emotive gestures (e.g., 3, 16, 33). Light does not function in *for colored girls* to indicate space, but rather participates in its discovery and (re)formation. By implication, the boundaries of theatrical space are blurred, the staccato play of light and shadow rendering indistinct the difference between 'positive' (onstage) and 'negative' (offstage) location. Performance space is no longer a static given for the viewer to stand over against or outside. The division between 'fictional' and 'real' space, and its attendant ideological implications, is therefore disturbed, transforming what the spectators 'actually' see into a prism of social and psychic enactments that they must themselves delineate for 'meaning' to occur. It is not that verisimilitude or, on the other hand, rapport cannot be felt by the audience, but either must arise through the collaboration of its imaginative intervention and the performing bodies before it.

The Preface teaches us, then, that in *for colored girls* performance is simultaneously, and indistinguishably, representation and being. The material ingredients of performance, its spatial, social, physical, and economic premises and modes of transaction, both embody and challenge the mimetic dimensions of the play's narrative(s). In this way, the play as performance radically temporalizes those elements of signification (image; myth; story; reference) that conventionally claim to secure legitimacy for theater's ephemerality. Space becomes itself characteriological: open and subject to change in all the ways that we associate with mortal bodies. Indeed, Shange's focused use of light and near elimination of stage properties – along with the characters' costuming in a spectrum of colors expressive of light passed through a prism (as though their bodies are, in great measure, exactly what gives form to light, which, as Adolphe Appia observed, "must light *something* . . . encounter obstacles")[33] – suggests Shange's interest in figuring space between characters as purposive and intentional, at times ironizing desire (by widening or freezing distances), at times promoting its consummation (by telescoping toward the moment of touch). This is not to say that space is itself any more free of those intersecting operations of power than are the bodies with which it inter- acts, but it is likewise effective, not passive or abstract.

Itself a body, Shange's performance space is, too, the domain of the body's exploration, the central mode of which is dance. The Preface tells us that dance infiltrates and inspirits *for colored girls* intially as a medium of historical discovery and vernacular self-apprehension. Having studied under the African-American choreographers and dance masters Raymond Sawyer, Ed Mock, and Halifu, Shange finds a new conjunction of imagination, language, and body. "With dance I discovered my body more intimately than I had imagined possible. With the acceptance of the ethnicity of my thighs & back- side, came a clearer understanding of my voice" (xi). The voice is inextrica- bly bound to the body, not just the speaker's somatic medium but the tangible datum of racial identity and its language. Resonant in Shange's reclamation of the black body as site of knowledge and expression is the his- torical violence of what Iris Young, employing Kristeva, terms "horror" in the western construction of black bodies.[34] As Young argues, the oppositional structure through which a relatively stable enunciative position is secured for the authorized occidental identity (in its most effective guise, a white, male, heterosexual, propertied, and Protestant subject) necessitates the disavowal, or exclusion, of the black other, specifically by marking its corporeality as grotesque, disordered, and unclean. In other words, the sacrificial drama through which whiteness becomes the standard of mimetic legitimacy precisely locates blackness outside the sphere of expression *per se*. This "abjection" of the sensible, in all its pleasures and pains, cyclic processes and temporal movements, codes blackness as a nonsignifying entity, wholly sen- sible but incapable of making sense. However impossible theoretically, such a drama of abjection, when introjected by its victims, sets voice against body in a tormenting maelstrom of self-fragmentation. Shange's embrace of her body through dance as prelude to assuming a systemic expressive control thus constitutes a kind of abjection of abjection itself, not only jettisoning the implied uncertainty of "ethnic" identification but smashing the idol of mas- tery that subtends the western Imaginary. Such a ground-clearing expropri- ation prepares for dance's capacity to unfold for Shange an encyclopedic grasp of "irony and control" as responses to diasporic experience, lending her the expressive technology to "pull ancient trampled spirits out of present tense Afro-American Dance" (xi). Dance becomes what Pierre Nora terms a *milieu de la mémoire*, a commemorative site or mnemonic methodology of cultural survival, retention, and transmission.[35] But further, Shange locates in dance a *will to remember* that inscribes living traces of ancestral wisdom, insurgency, and self-understanding in the stylized improvisational movements of African-American thighs, backsides, etc. – that is, in just those viciously stigmatized (minstrelized) features of the black abject. Dance thus is not just a personal impulse but a cultural imperative, for only in its performance can dance realize its power as remembrance, epistemology, instruction, critique, avowal, and confirmation.

In many traditional African societies to which Shange implicitly alludes (cf. xii), dance is the essential form of aesthetic and religious expression, a guarantor of meaning within a constantly shifting universe. To cite A. M. Opoku of the School of Dance and Music in the Institute of African Studies (Legon), "to us, Life with its rhythms and cycles is Dance, and Dance is Life."[36] But for Shange, dance might better be seen as a reflexive vehicle for inquiring into meaning's possibility, a polemical, if passionate, means of foregrounding the body's presence as it inscribes itself within and against an already highly-semiotized space. It is true that her characters share the Preface's ebullient antigravitational instinct, the urge to soar through the moment's messy uncertainties to a possibly idealized origin of Africanicity. But such impulses are everywhere checked by a refusal to detach spiritual achievement from material insight, affective generality from concrete reference:

> The freedom to move in space, to demand of my own sweat a perfection that could continually be approached, though never known, waz poem to me . . . dance . . . insisted that everything African, everything halfway colloquial, a grimace, a strut, an arched back over a yawn, waz mine. I moved what waz my unconscious knowledge of being in a colored woman's body to my known everydayness.
>
> (xi)

Through movement, Shange's body reacquaints itself with space as a function of time, thus historicizing the place of enactment while focusing the present tense as a locus of an unpredictable event. In this way, Shange glances against Euro-American modern dance's concern to locate a gestural vocabulary adequate to the altered temporality of contemporary experience,[37] but avoids its hesitancy in coupling motion with emotion, its fear of 'feminine' excess against the 'masculine' contours of formal precision.[38] Most distinctive in relation to the canons of modernist dance is Shange's sensuous, cerebral, and political amalgamation of word, movement, gesture, and music, which insists on a modal relation between private and public expression. Shange insists not merely on dancing the ethnic body but on "strutting" it in a social arena that is rife with multiple vernacular habits, attitudes, and sonorities. That is to say, dance in *for colored girls* is a deliberate encounter of diachronic legacies and synchronic desires, objective analyses and "the mechanics of self-production" (xii).

Such commitment to dance as a whirl of displacements and repositionings reshapes the mimetic lure of bodily presence to visionary ambitions, with notable consequences for the drama's acting protocols, generic strategies, compositional ethics, and spectatorial responsibilities. Shange's actor must approach the playtext as much as a score as a script, a kind of musical chart enabling improvisatory and not simply imitative response. Her body must accordingly be mastered as a technically complex instrument of expression that issues from identification with vernacular motives lodged in the memorial yet continuously renovated discourse of African-American gestural inflection. She can neither lose the critical perspective submerged within the Stanislavskian project of affective immersion nor absent herself from the role's emotive kernel in the manner of Brechtian defamiliarization. Framed by expressive lights and flowing, brightly hued costumes that both liberate the body's movements and dissolve its contours in a blur of coloristic propulsion, Shange's actors must inhabit their characters as both persons and personae, challenging preconceptions of subjective presence in being both exposed and masked configurations of mobile expression. Mimesis and motivation are therefore grounded in neither naturalist nor (post)modernist tactics, yet both must be working in Shange's actor so that she achieves a transformative discharge within an evolving compositional structure. Especially because any given actress will be called upon in *for colored girls* to embody several different figures – her "colored" identity taken literally as a trope or *coloring* of a variety of subjective tonalities – this task of quicksilver mediation instills a sense of terror and exhilaration (as actresses like Renée Raymond and Kabeera McCorkle who have played *for colored girls* have often told me), a freedom that derives from a constant search for the nexus of local circumstance and unconfined implication.

The text is thus a *pre*text for a realization that 'writes' itself through the breathing dynamic of performance; in turn, 'character' must be felt to emerge from enactment itself, rather than to exist in some representational antechamber awaiting an activating cue. In a sense, then, Shange's actor must realize character as a kind of intertextual, or rather, in Shange's own terms, "interdisciplinary" figure, a junction of rhetorical suggestion and kinetic *orature*.[39] "We are an interdisciplinary culture [which] must use everything we've got," Shange has commented,[40] and, appropriately enough, *for colored girls* is constructed as a kind of interdisciplinary adventure that, as James Brown would shout it, uses what it's got – dance, verse, storytelling, light, dress, and music (in the manifold New World styles of jazz, rhythm-and-blues, soul, funk, salsa) – to get what it wants, indeed to probe "want" (lack, desire) as itself a function of the acculturative forces of hybridity and translation. As a potpourri of voices, memories, and perspectives, *for colored girls* rejects the process of abjection at the formal level that it critiques in western metaphysics and racist discourse. In so far as the actor's body becomes the crucible of this expressive gumbo, it takes charge of the dialogue between the ideality of abstract forms (music, gesture) and the specificity of discursive forms (poetry, storytelling) that we normally think of as an authorial privilege. No longer a slave to a sacrosanct textual master, the actor shapes character by intermingling personation and as participation, modelling in turn the audience's active function in engaging the spectacle simultaneously as an insistent theatrical event and as a mediation of historically forged experience. Shange's "choreopoem" (her designation for the form's interdisciplinary modality) thereby decenters drama as a wax medium for the author's impressions, a "pure" vehicle of her version of blackness. The Preface makes clear that the play cannot be grasped as a pure text comprised only of those elements 'original' to a single creative consciousness, excluding in principle any idiom that cannot be reconciled with a primal interest or design. Rather than conceiving *for colored girls* as this kind of closed domain, the Preface takes great pains to suggest that the entire enveloping social milieu – including those audiences that happened to "show up" as the piece evolved (xiii, xiv) – should be seen as the 'author' or source of performance that develops through a ritualized combination of commentary, contribution, and endorsement. Play production thus becomes in itself a model for a vision of revolutionary blackness as collective revision: openly acknowledging its establishment within a network of material, philosophical, and discursive relations, it distributes the authority normally reserved to the author across a field of competing and cooperative positions.

Accordingly, Shange sees the critical turning-point for the play as being the moment when she yielded her place of mastery to others: "The most prescient change in the concept of the work waz that I gave up directorial powers to Oz Scott" (xiv). This gesture accomplishes many things, and it does so through a paradoxical process of abnegation: yielding the writer's primacy, it opens the play to multiple possibilities for amendation; yielding artistic mastery, it infuses fresh interpretive energy into the work's creative process; yielding the right to police the play's production, it cedes to the work a continuous afterlife beyond conception and first articulation. No longer is the play's performance a sign of what was originally 'meant' by its writer; rather, it becomes an active, and temporally open, translation from any number of perspectives, including those of reception. By thus defetishizing authorial control, Shange liberates her work from that suffocating sense of prescription that silently (re)turns 'play' into 'text': "By doing this," she continues, "I acknowledged that the poems & the dance worked on their own to do & be what they were" (xiv).

Shange's Preface bears witness, then, not to her playwrighting but to her collaboration within the vibrantly "interdisciplinary" arena of African-American expressive culture in the moment of the emergent Black Arts (notably inclusive in its sense of national space, being a bicoastal saga). The Preface marks *for colored girls* as a *practice* any textual image of which (such as the book that lies inert on my desk, ready to be activated in my imaginative vision alongside those productions I have witnessed and still others that have been described to me) must be seen not so much as the record of its occurrence as an invitation to its improvisational extension. In this comes liberation, both for the play as image of collectivity healed and named after uncertain existence in "pieces" – "I came to understand these twenty-odd poems as a single statement, a choreopoem" (xiv) – and for the problematic posture of authorial identity itself – "*i am on the other side of the rainbow/picking up the pieces of days spent waiting for the poem to be heard/while you listen/i have other work to do*" (xvi). Rejecting the paradigm of playwright as exterior, presiding Cause, Shange is free to be elsewhere, including the play itself, but now as an element dispersed into its communal fabric: appearing in early productions as the lady in orange, and encrypted in the poem "somebody almost walked off wid all my stuff" ("this is mine/ntozake 'her own things'/that's my name/now give me my stuff" – 50), she locates achieved agency – the intersection of voice and body that is the authentic "stuff" of self-possession – in the *event*, which is provisional yet provident, rightly grasped.

Such is the condition of the play itself, understood as embodiment rather than commodity, as practice rather than prescription. If, for the writer, the work's completion becomes a moment of liberating de-composition, for the work representation dissolves into the post-textual futurity of performance: both gestures suggest, in the figure of the rainbow to which we shall return, a space of realization beyond imaginative closure, based on a perpetual "dance" of departure and relocation. Its wager is that of collective revision, a process of working through (rather than simply acting out) initiating circumstances of trauma, abjection, and paralysis. Following the intricacies of the Preface's tale of realization, *for colored girls* presents a world ungoverned by plot yet shaped, through the counterpoint of isolated and shared acts of vocalization (chant, outcry, storytelling), by contrasting rhythms of constraint and deliverance, discovery and disenchantment, dispossession and recovery. Through the interlacing of its 20 texts and the thematically-linked choreographic textures that are placed among the poems, *for colored girls* graphs a communal labor of elegiac recuperation that simultaneously mourns and reconstructs the occasion of hurt, a wound to psychic and somatic wholeness that takes forms various as the multi-tinted heroines themselves. In the process of depicting these bereavements, the characters grasp what is no longer theirs, redressing the anguish of personal displacement (rape, theft, child-loss, betrayal) by a gradual *recognition and enactment* of a common fatality.

The seven nameless characters in the drama appear in their common guise as "colored girls": lady in brown, lady in yellow, lady in purple, etc. Much is afoot here, as Shange clearly revises both the tradition's obsessive attention to solitary *black boys* and nameless *invisible men*: her characters are female and plural, and they tinge blackness with multifarious colorations, sounds, and shapes. What they share, initially, is a state of deprivation: negotiating the urges of The Life against the chaos of death in a sinuous blend of gritty acceptance and mythopoetic faith, they rehearse a devastating range of losses – loss of virginity ("graduation nite": 7–10); loss of trust (as smiling friends turn into "latent rapists": 17–21); loss of nascent life ("abortion cycle #1": 22–3); loss of ennobling fantasy ("toussaint": 25–30); loss of "sparkle" ("one": 31–5); loss of physical and imaginative space ("i used to live in the world": 36–9); loss of "stuff" ("somebody almost walked off wid alla my stuff": 49–51); loss of children ("a nite with beau willie brown": 55–60). But these narrative encounters with ruin are literally prefigured by the body's struggle within a scene of dis-ease, bewilderment, and even hostility:

> *The stage is in darkness. Harsh music is heard . . . One after another, seven women run onto the stage from each of the exits. They all freeze in postures of distress.*
>
> (3)

This arrest of the body, in its metonymic intensification of frozen gestures at the expense of flowing motion, presages the language of impairment that haunts the play's opening. Yet it figures, too, the intensity of the women's desire for presence, their urge to *be there*, which one can feel is interrupted but not fully corrupted or nullified. The figures are cast both as ghostly and as solid, seized before fulfillment and statuesque in determination. Right away, we are asked to focus upon an image of yearning immediacy compromised in some uncertain way by forces that obstruct realization. Do they arrive too early or too late? Are they frozen out of history, or captured within it at a moment of obscure torment? As in the Coltrane Poem that we will discuss in Chapter 4, the entire work begins not merely in but *as* crisis, potentially *still*born, a staging of calamity prematurely deadened without evident means for quickening deliverance. Should we ever move forward, we will retain the effect of this tableau as a lesson in attentiveness, for here time becomes not just the unobserved medium but the palpable subject of theatrical experience: duration signals an incalculable mixture of fearful dubiety and hopeful alertness. Only the dialectical interplay of this spectacle with light (as an agency of time) and word (as the essential will-to-signify against absence and constraint) can jolt us beyond this instant of potentially permanent immobility:

> *The follow spot picks up the lady in brown. She comes to life and looks around at the other ladies. All of the others are still. She walks over to the lady in red and calls to her. The lady in red makes no response.*
>
> (3)

The drama's development from static iconicity to exploratory exchange must begin at this juncture of failed interaction: Shange signals that the specifically African-American performance modality of call-and-response is itself the desired and denied communion that the women will be seeking in their polyglot amalgams of movement and narrative. From here, then, the possibilities of narration can emerge. By turns epic and autobiographical, nostalgic and revolutionary, the women's tales commence within a vortex of violence, perplexity, and melancholy that recalls Bullins's brutal undercurrents and Kennedy's savage imagery, though always modulated by cross-rhythms of fierce expectancy. Immediately, we are thrust by the lady in brown into confrontation with the loss of innocence in a mélange of discordant, grotesque, and ghostly fragments:

> dark phrases of womanhood
> of never havin been a girl
> half-notes scattered
> without rhythm/no tune
> distraught laughter fallin [. . .]
> it's funny/it's hysterical
> the melody-less-ness of her dance
> don't tell nobody don't tell a soul
> she's dancin on beer cans & shingles
>
> this must be the spook house
> another song with no singers
> lyrics/no voices
> & interrupted solos
> unseen performances
>
> are we ghouls?
> children of horror? [. . .]
> don't tell nobody don't tell a soul
> are we animals? have we gone crazy?
>
> i can't hear anythin
> but maddening screams
> & the soft strains of death
> & you promised me
> you promised me . . .

(3–4)

for colored girls thus opens within a landscape of negation ("never/ without/no/don't/nobody/no/no . . ."), where the "darkness" of black "womanhood" signifies an 'otherness' excluded from communicative, performative value. Sliding into the animalistic, insane, or supernaturally forbidding, the women endure disjunctions between expression and intention or affirmation (songs without singers, performances without auditors). *Double entendres* indicate not rich polysemy but mocking confusion of boundaries, which undercuts the self-sufficiency of voice and the 'per-version' of self-authentication. In a halting, self-violating syntax and prosody (with phrases like "melody-less-ness" miming the jagged rhythm and dissonance they thematize), the ladies suffer the sparagmos or "scattering" of consciousness among literally abjected or 'thrown away' cultural debris: not only the "beer cans and shingles" (shards from what broken festivals or homes?), but the fertile womb of "womanhood" itself, called out of its name as "hysterical," the wandering *hystera* of neurotic excess. The black female subject is thus posited – thrown into the world – as the underside of symbolic authority, always already related to animality, pollution, and death.

And yet latent within this discourse of "horror" are terms for reconstruction and recognition, the materials for fashioning a counter-memory, an alternative configuration of those "notes" broken in mid-articulation. The Orpheus myth – so crucial, as we shall see, to the transfigurative imagination of modern black jazz and poetry – in which music fills the void of pure mourning, is here evoked in the neo-Ellisonian "spook" sonata of molestation and invisibility. The "always playing" (5) music of lamentation, fused in the choreopoem with dance idioms, addresses grief from the impudent posture of errancy and the unsaid. One awakens perhaps to cacophony and defilement, but this is not the only possible scene of self-apprehension. In particular, alertness to the presence of other timbres and rhythms within the voice refurbishes echoic "righteousness" as an instrument of collective assertion, realigning voice not with the forces of its suppression ("don't tell nobody don't tell a soul") but with its indwelling potential for regeneration:

> sing her sighs
> sing the song of her possibilities
> sing a righteous gospel
> the makin of a melody
> let her be born
> let her be born
> & handled warmly.
>
> (5)

To make time, touch, and communality possible (again) by expression, to transmute "half-notes" of 'animal' sound into the voice of human consciousness, memory, understanding, and affection – such is the orphic ideal enjoined by this grammatically textured summons, which hails us in nuanced moods of hope (optative), provocation (imperative), and proclamation (declarative). The verse's structure encodes the basic paradigm of dialectical process by which this transformation is achieved in Shange's choreopoem: a primal expressive urge – *sing, sing, sing* – links to release and acceptance – *let, let* – through the mediation of euphonious *poiesis* – *makin' of melody* – confirmed by sensate intimacy – *& handled warmly*. But the path leading to completion of this design is often arduous, often torturous, indeed. And, ultimately, this journey is as much the audience's task as the characters', as the injunction to "sing" theatricalizes us with its reminder that, rather than enjoying the complacency of standing in mastery beyond the stage, we are elemental to the scene's ongoing reconstruction as a drama of expressive decisions.

In the play's opening, then, enunciation is ghostly, liminal – neither granted full-blooded legitimacy nor utterly buried beyond the reach of defiant desire. If the "ghoul" of blackness is already subject to the expulsions of sacrificial violence, it yet maintains the strategic capacities of trickster resistance, flowing easily across borders erected to cage its craving for post-elegiac sustenance. Deviation and excess, the terms of blackness's abjection, can be reincorporated by a different musical aesthetic into a political expressivity that makes 'proper'/ty a site of struggle, not an assumed instrument of regulation. What is at stake, then, in these opening moments is the authority of framing through which signs and bodies are summoned, arranged, and interpreted. On the one hand, the spectacle of "distress" connotes a mechanism of exclusion through which any achieved identity will attain its coherence by refusal of what has been deemed marginal – the ungovernable wildness of protest ("screams"), materiality, and, paradoxically, the aspiration for wholeness itself. The disorderly itself is felt to injure the framework of intelligibility, denying blackness subjectivity and meaning. But against this implication (which covertly serves the interests of mimetic power) is the undertow of irony, tenderness, and sass that hints at a reframing of identity *through* embrace of all that is labeled aberrant or exterior to 'normality.' The opening movement thus completes itself with an ambiguous positioning of the ladies "outside" the domains of modern urban experience, suggesting that the place of exile might be appropriated as the locus of exultation:

> *lady in brown*
> I'm outside chicago
>
> *lady in yellow*
> I'm outside detroit
>
> *lady in purple*
> I'm outside houston . . ., [etc.]
>
> *lady in brown*
> & this is for colored girls who have considered suicide
> but moved to the ends of their own rainbows.

(5–6)

Throughout its succeeding sequences, *for colored girls* traverses the double track implied by this chant of shared exteriority: on the one hand, locating various ways in which representational and physical violence repeatedly positions black women at the fringe of communal experience, placing them in a disturbing relation to their own speech and bodies; while on the other hand moving almost imperceptibly toward the possibility that it is at the edge – the threshold of darkness and light's chromatic return – that new sites of collective commemoration and even triumph can be rooted.

Remembrance is the medium of progression: the garland of poems exists as an act of re-collection. Notwithstanding the awkward isolation of the play's still-life beginning, and in contrast to the often gruesome loneliness that suffuses each tale, reminiscence is a shared activity. After establishing a backbeat of primal vocality with the slavesong "mama's little baby likes shortnin bread" and the childhood ditty "little sally walker" (juvenilia of race and gender), the colored ladies freeze in a game of tag to determine she who will remember first (6). Martha and the Vandellas's "Dancing in the Streets" is heard (with its litany of urban spaces *within* which folks "gather" to "music, sweet music"), and – who could resist?! – "all of the ladies start to dance" (8–9). The lady in yellow then offers the first story, the saga of "graduation nite" when, giddy with the excitement of "moving from mama to what ever waz out there," she loses her virginity in a rite of passage that mingles "hot" soul rhythms of the Dells with the heat of newly welcomed bodily movements:

> doin nasty ol tricks i'd been thinkin since may
> cuz graduation nite had to be hot
> & i waz the only virgin
> so I hadda make like my hips waz inta some business
> that way everybody thot whoever was gettin it
> was a older man cdnt run the streets wit youngsters
> martin slipped his leg round my thigh
> the dells bumped "stay"
> up & down – up & down the new carver homes
> WE WAZ GROWN   WE WAZ FINALLY GROWN
>
> (9)

Shange immediately challenges her audience with a presentation of the black female body not as an object of masculine desire or hegemonic derision, but as a self-determining figure capable of *jouissance* on its own terms. Those who have lambasted the play for its supposed antimasculine calumny would be well advised to observe that the drama's first storytelling act presents this burgeoning female desire not as opposed to masculinity but simply as engendered and authorized beyond its controlling terms.[41] In contrast to the discordant "phrases" of the opening's frightfully aborted girlhood, Shange establishes here a playfully intentional and consciously theatricalized space of self-enactment where a frisky 'nastiness' potentially redeems the loathing, fear, and sadism that haunts the black female subject. In place of the burden of corporeal convulsion and psychic division that weighs upon the opening song, the lady in yellow proposes here a piquant, if tactical, movement within the prevailing logic of sexual assertion that allows participation in a common ritual of transition and self-realization. But, indeed, the possibility of thus defining this little episode of advancement, of *owning* its implications, seemingly depends upon another vantage than hers alone, one that introduces a specular economy alongside the tactile measure of meaning:

> bobby started lookin' at me
> yeah
> he started looking at me real strange
> like i waz a woman or somethin/
> started talkin real soft
> in the backseat of that ol buick
> WOW
> by daybreak
> i just cdnt stop grinnin.

(10)

Here, I think, the male look joins rather than jolts the achievement of transfiguration, becoming part of a mutual 'softening' that breaks out in a new day's irrepressible joy. But the faint trace of a surrender of the moment's significance to another's point of view is hard to completely deny under the pressure of subsequent stories of rape, abandonment, and deception by those (not always male) who likewise offer first only the friendliest of aspects. What is crucial in these harsher tales (e.g. "no assistance," "latent rapists," and "pyramid") is the persistent connection of violation and estrangement with a penetrative or alienating gaze. The "latent rapist" is the treacherous *non*stranger with "pin-ups attached to the insides of his lapels" and "ticket stubs from porno flicks in his pocket" (17, 18); the terrifying pain of abortion is felt as "eyes crawling up on me/eyes rollin in my thighs" (22); the tightening constriction of Harlem gathers "round midnite," leaving the lady in blue "praying wont no young man/think i'm pretty in a dark mornin" (37). Theater seems to be the emblem of ruin for the black woman, making her a witness to her own degradation as damaged image in a sordid spectacle of commodification, assault, and self-sacrifice. "Suicide" – refracted through the silencing, the private humiliation and public erasure, that accompanies each abortion, rape, betrayal, or act of terror ("pressin charges will be as hard/as keepin yr legs closed" – 18; "i cdnt have people/lookin at me . . . /and i didn't say a thing/not a sigh/or a fast scream" – 22) – is already submission to this mutilating, duplicitous theatricality. Against it, the women initially can only assert the pure performative gesture of dance without language in the hopes of ridding the stage of a phallic theatricality, privileging the auditory and gestural over the visual and narrative:

lady in orange
i don't wanna write
in english or spanish
i wanna sing   make you dance
like the bata   dance   scream
twitch hips wit me cuz
i done forgot all abt words
aint got no definitions
i wanna whirl
           with you [. . .]
and i can't   i can't
talk withcu no more

                                 (14–15)

Here a blues-tinged orphism seeks to impose itself against the distancing mechanisms of image (both linguistic and dramatic), replacing textuality with a tangible insistence on dancing the abyss between one mentality and another. Musical presentation is to fill the chasm opened in expression itself. Shange, who portrayed the lady in orange in the compelling manner that Tejumola Olaniyan aptly terms "combat breathing,"[42] embodies here a passionate alternative performative modality to that of the scopic prison that freezes her sisters in postures of anger and self-abasement: fluid, improvisational, seductive, its manner is unashamedly 'feminine' in just those terms that have historically inflamed the stern arbiters of the "antitheatrical tradition."[43] Flaunting what the scopic theater flagellates – the body in all its overflowing urgency, vulnerability, and generosity – this sumptuous performativity would void spectatorial violence by dissolving all witnesses into participants, and as such figures an ideal that will only be reimagined fully at the play's end.

For now, such an invitation to an emancipating forgetfulness remains fragile, even in its own terms, for in disengaging movement from narration the lady in orange's restive Tanztheatre figures an Imaginary that cannot openly combat the symbolic violence from which it offers shelter. It becomes in its own way another kind of mirror scene, hopeful in seeking to absorb all images of self and other in a singular Image of graceful abandon, yet stutteringly ineffectual (i cant i cant) as an intervention responsive to a world of hostile "definitions." There is, again, something of sacrifice in this splendid offer of hip-twitching mutuality, an undertone of repression-in-creation that later is imaged as a burial of "treasure" which must be exhumed for the rainbow to be fully navigated.

In this juxtaposition of performative modalities, then, we find the essential venture of the play, the underlying charge of its quest to redeem the broken "promise" of the "black girl's song." As the women are plunged back into the process of telling history from which pure dance would absolve them, the plangent call for continuity – "we gotta dance to keep from cryin/ . . . we gotta dance to keep from dyin/so come on/come on/come on . . ." (15–16) – habitually shatters into a helplessness in the face of actions suffered in dark concealment: "nobody came/cuz nobody knew/once i waz pregnant & shamed of myself" (23). Being filled with self brings remorse not joy; and at their nadir, the women cannot utter even the "fast scream" of the Barakan Victim. In such moments, Shange's play edges toward a threat of arrest more lethal than that of the opening segment: abandoning dance in search of a narrative voice that is unsparingly honest, they often mime in their own damaged self-regard the very regime of specular entrapment they protest; seeking a fresh alignment of word and anatomy, they often find themselves 'learning to curse' rather than fashioning 'things unknown'; assuming guises that hyperbolize the 'excessive' cultural productions of blackness and womanhood, they often foreground but cannot undermine the construction of historical discourses and identities.

Most important in the choreopoem's evolution, therefore, are those characters who transform the oppressive instruments of self-staging, among whom none exerts upon the drama's trajectory a more evocative force than sechita. Perhaps *for colored girls*'s most individuated voice, sechita introduces a vision of the divided performative self whose veiled presentations serve as a cryptic antidote to an abusive theatricality. She enters, indeed, as melodious name ("soft deep music is heard, voices calling 'Sechita' come from the wings and volms") and as story, offered to us in "liquid toned" epic-elegiac strophes by the lady in purple:

> once there were quadroon balls/elegance in st. louis/laced
> mulattoes/gamblin down the mississippi/to memphis/new
> orleans n okra crepes near the bayou/where the poor white trash
> wd sing/moanin/strange/liquid tones/thru the swamps
>
> sechita had heard these things/she moved
> as if she'd known them/the silver n high-toned laughin/
> the violins n marble floors/sechita pushed the clingin
> delta dust wit painted toes/the patch-work tent waz
> poka-dotted/stale lights snatched at the shadows/creole
> carnival waz playin natchez in ten minutes/her splendid
> red garters/gin-stained n itchy on her thigh/blk-diamond
> stockings darned wit yellow threads/an ol starched taffeta
> can-can fell abundantly orange/from her waist round the
> splinterin chair [. . .]
>
> (23–4)

Like sechita's carnival frippery, Shange's language gathers around its subject in a sinuous, glittery stream of coloristic profusion and textural complexity, blending contradictory sounds (moanin/laughin/violins), images (elegance/trash; gin-stained/diamond), temporalities (once/wd sing/had heard/in ten minutes), territories (st. louis/bayou), arenas (balls/carnival), and conditions (silver n high-toned/delta dust). Her typography – and the rhythm of breathing that it notates for the performer – effect a kind of rite of invocation that stages words themselves in a "dance" of complex implication (Shange has spoken, in fact, of her desire to forge an idiom that is mobile at the root level of language, the letter: "I like the idea that letters dance, not just that words dance").[44] Through the release of phrasing from the conventional maneuvers of metrics, syntax, and orthographic arrangement, language itself becomes, too, a mythic and performative subject, at once masked and intensely physical, not the work of a single consciousness but of contestatory cultural spaces, histories, and assertions. Within the phrase – which, more than the line or the stanza, is the key unit of Shange's verse – words appear and disappear, trapped at caesuras, released by surprising enjambments, withdrawn or prolonged in a manner that betokens a bluesy bending of notes, responsive to some inner principle of writerly mobility as much as to dictates of any presiding 'sense.' Typographical nonconformity and metrical surprise help indicate a fracture between voice and image that is thematically crucial to sechita's condition as a dancer in the sleazy Southern sideshow, but not one whose value or fate can be calculated in advance of experiencing the dance itself. That is to say, Shange activates sechita as an assemblage of verbal events such that *style* becomes itself a cultural activity, the import of which must be grasped in the oxymoronic stale luminescence of its constituent elements.

"Choreopoetic" composition here attains reflexive significance: just as classic choreographic notation borrows from linguistics (positions are "vowels"; steps are "words"; sequences "phrases"; and so on), so Shange here "laces" body and discourse such that they meet in the elaborate tropes (or 'turns') of sechita's entrance and ensuing performance. Accordingly, sechita appears as a body already enmeshed in a hazy aura of (dis)figurations: if Shange's letters dance, her dancer likewise 'composes' herself in the ambiguous diction and grammar of a "carnivalesque" that shares the stage with countervailing mythic evocations:

> sechita/egyptian/goddess of creativity/
> 2nd millennium/threw her heavy hair in a coil over her neck/
> sechita/goddess/the recordin of history/spread crimson oil
> on her cheeks/waxed her eyebrows [. . .]
>   the broken mirror she
> used to decorate her face/made her forehead tilt backwards [. . .]
> [she] had learned to make allowances for the distortions/
> but the heavy dust of the delta/left a tinge of grit n
> darkness/on every one of her dresses [. . .]
>   (24)

With mythic African splendor "coiled" around "history," the contingencies of carnival are given the shape of a sacral event. "Distorted" self-reflection, ambiguous (re)inscription of the past's patterns on one's own face, the ironic mastery of self-composition in foreign domains – these are the diachronic resonances that reverberate in the present under the patchwork tent. Preceding the imposition of colonialist expectations, before initiation of self-image into the domain of the Law and the Gaze, there pulses another cultural syntax. And yet, of course, after Middle Passage, after slavery, and still after the incomplete reconstructions of emancipation, the black subject articulates herself through an interaction of disparate spheres. Only the eruption of Africanicity into the musty light of the circus of white supremacy can quicken alternative meaning, inserting subversive difference into the signs sechita arranges on her showgirl veneer. Mundane time is both suffered and suspended, a trick perhaps of angled light and (eye)shadow but none the less suggestive of a constant process of remaking through which sechita becomes visible. Will her performance be a 'creative' repetition of a long-suppressed, numinous grandeur, or an illusory seduction, of herself as much as of her carnie audience? Painting herself *as* appearance, does sechita thereby penetrate the veil of modernity to a hidden source of racial and sexual iconography, or does she succumb to the machinery of power in misrecognition of her image's origin? In the double-edge of the fetish that sechita not so much is (as her audience must assume) but presents herself as, her preparations make her both more and less visible, heightened as construction but possibly elusive not merely as masked visage but as mythical reconstruction. Self-as-image is thus divided along the faultline of agency; it implies not one but two modalities of the Imaginary, two inflections of plenitude and origination: one prepared for her audience, one allusive to a transgressive (and culturally exiled) template of apotheosis. The oil that spreads across her, readying this layered 'foundation,' erases as it enables (we could, of course, as easily reverse these terms), making way for evidence of contrasting knowledges, technologies, ontologies. sechita will certainly not secure identity by overcoming contradiction. Hers is inalterably the sphere of the abject: the triangular, sexually-charged "delta" of fertile dust and dirt whose "tinge of grit" resonates with the duality of humiliation and resolve.

In what sense, then, can the gig she plays be a scene of truth, a reflection of something other than the image that the audience anticipates, indeed commands? Her "broken mirror" already indicates the dilemma of her performance, which solicits mimetic appreciation through a practice that simultaneously occludes and preserves identity, repossesses and suppresses ghostly traces of primal blackness. Along its cracked surface operates the logic of sechita's visage-as-mask, which signifies by virtue of belonging to double orders of transformation: the plastic signifiers of present appearances and the indexical signifiers of historical/mythic racial experience. The carnie dance is thus, too, a double gesture of enticement and transmission, soliciting attention to two different, antithetical orders of desire. And so sechita is an ungraspable subject, perhaps, precisely because she is transforming, not simply occupying or anchoring, the 'real':

> [sechita] made her face
> immobile/she made her face like nefertiti/approachin her
> own tomb/she suddenly threw/her leg full-force/thru the
> canvas curtain/a deceptive glass stone/sparkled/malignant
> on her ankle/her calf waz tauntin in the brazen carnie
> lights/the full moon/sechita goddess of love/egypt/
> 2nd millennium/performin the rites/the conjurin of men/
> conjurin the spirit/in natchez/ [. . .]
> sechita's legs slashed
> furiously thru the cracker nite/and gold pieces hittin the
> makeshift stage/her thighs/they were aimin coins tween her
> thighs/sechita/egypt/goddess/harmony/kicked viciously
> thru the nite/catchin stars tween her toes.
>
> (24–5)

One is reminded that the rise of theater in ancient Greece was accompanied by three other signal innovations in the symbolic economy of western power: rhetoric; monetary exchange; and tyranny, all mechanisms of dissimulation and expropriation that stage an undecidable shadow-play of truth and betrayal. Money functions like light and the signs it illuminates, suggesting – brazenly – a redeemable relation between the seen and the absent; together, they remit legitimacy to the tyranny of a masterful Gaze, by which is meant not merely the individual glances of the theater's patrons but the whole system of controlled differences upon which a rigged exchange of looks depends. Under the tattered tent of this commodified theatricality, gold and eyes thrust toward sechita in phallic gestures of scopic possession. If, as Laura Mulvey has suggested, sadism demands a story,[45] then aggressive voyeurism likewise demands a body at a remove just close enough to be penetrated by its unbridled declarations of ownership. sechita's furious effort to "strike thru" this insidious complex of economic, discursive, and histrionic entrapments refracts key features of an all-too familiar scenario. She is framed within, but also responds from, the margins of spectacle, and so crafts an improvisatory 'breaking' of its repressive scripts by seizing and redirecting its own discourse (not merely evading it, as the ladies earlier seek to do with their idealization of pure dance): "carnie lights" are stripped of their ideological glare in the "full moon" of her crazed resistance; the defilement of crackers "conjurin" black bodies becomes the ceremonial righteousness of a goddess "conjurin the spirit"; the dirty flash and tinny sound of gold pieces "hittin the makeshift stage" becomes the "harmony" of a cosmically rearranged canvas, coins turned to stars in a Hurstonesque image of earthy, somatic metaphysics.

No revisionary improvisation is more crucial than that which sechita works upon herself. Beginning as the to-be-looked-at spectacle shackled to exhibitionary servitude, sechita quickly shifts attention from repeated arche-type to created posture: "[she] made her face immobile/she made/her face like nefertiti/approachin her own tomb." The reiterated "made" (hovering hopefully over the text since its introduction in the Preface through a burst of anaphoric creativity: "With as much space as a small studio [we women poets] proceeded to make poems, make music, make a woman's theater . . .," – ix) gathers momentum toward a poetics of self-construction that, by its connection with venerable pageants of black female sovereignty ("nefer-titi/approachin her own tomb" evoking other "goddesses" of "egyptian" self-display, such as Cleopatra), establishes sechita as a griot of a tradition of talismanic self-realization. Alignment with nefertiti allows sechita to retrieve agency for the black female subject at the intersection of two opposed histories, styles of self-display, and norms of spectatorial consump-tion. "Performin rites" rather than "recordin history," Sechita asserts an enigmatically disjunctive presence which scuttles the organizing temporal-ity that seemingly imprisons her. If in psychoanalytic theory, the mirror is the place where the subject discovers her constitutively divided aspect, sechita's 'splintered' reflections suggest a tactical duplicity. Performance is a "deceptive glass" whose 'sparkling malignancy' hurts two ways, a *diss*-simulation that operates not only as the masquerade charming salacious white eyes for the "trash" of subsistence but as what Homi Bhabha has termed an anticolonial "mimicry" that strikes "thru" the "curtain" of mastery's despotic carnival, exposing its funhouse distortions.[46]

As with various kinds of double-voiced vernacular impersonations, then, sechita's ambiguous and ambivalent carnival striptease is a masking ritual whose invisible history must, as Eleanor Traylor has elegantly observed of minstrelsy, be "re-visualized like a ruin . . . of an *ecstatic* performance."[47] The effects of this subversive mimetism are complex and, instructively, impenetrable. The implicit rhetorical opposition at work in it is not that between mask and self but between kinds of masks and their modes of presentation to the world. On the one hand, sechita is trapped on a stage that requires her to produce herself as an image easily consumed by the rash lust of a white-patriarchal gaze, and so her excessive miming of that expectation "immobilizes" the ideological certainty of her audience, unmasking its effort to naturalize her condition as commodity by tearing her passion to tatters. On the other hand, sechita displays the fetish spec-tacle in order to play with it, distending and remaking it with that "irony and control" (not unmixed with keen rage) that Shange attributes to the heritage of jazz dance in the Preface. This simultaneous (over)doing and undoing of the minstrelized black body renders in dance performance the Penelopean craft of un/weaving implied in her "darned" stockings and the "poka-dotted patch-work tent" under which she strikes the pose of enigmatic (im)mobility.

Taken together, these specular performative gestures craft a parodic/celebratory imitation of a past that may or may not return through her. Her action of 'making herself up' in a vivid and tactile (re)framing of performative transcendence insinuates a subliminal relation to the vernacular "stuff" of imaginative endurance, linking her to the motherwit of a crazyquilt survival achieved by mending and joining shards of inherited, found, or 'sampled' cultural material. Thus, stitching character from the image-repertoires of evidently alienated practices, sechita dramatizes the possibility of fabricating blackness neither wholly inside nor outside the field of the Gaze but across the multiple positions that arise both within and beyond its restricted sightlines.

sechita's tale thereby restages the discourses of authenticity, mimesis, and revolutionary difference that stoke modern black theater's progressive dialogue on innovation and renovation. We might ask, whose body is present here, whose image does the audience perceive, and whose agency is thereby plumed? The contrast between sechita's unmoving face and thrashing body incarnates a duality in the spectacle's rationale, that rhythm of subjugation and negation that would bring her closer while keeping her at the distance of a coin's throw. But it also figures a tension in her own presentation between surface (which denies any revelation of essence, either as occult substance or as licentious projection) and depth (the possibility of significance beneath or beyond dissembling, confirming either cracker fantasy or an altogether different legacy of desire). By foregrounding the performativity of her very appearance (clothes are costumes; possessions are props; gestures are poses), sechita's story itself appears as a shadow-play of concealment and disclosure whose challenge is not that of narrative (de)coding but of theatrical perspective. sechita's erotic and signifying power is both 'there' and 'elsewhere,' focused locally for a specific audience and deferred, indefinable, irreducible to the visible scene of enactment. As called for, she engenders an act of seduction, but she does so by producing a spectacle in which she is absent as well as present, deflecting as well as enchanting the white audience's vision through a "distortion" of overt "definitions" and a veiling of covert possibilities. The craft that shapes her also shrouds her, and perhaps further, reshapes her within that very disguise. Through this spiral of mimetic excess, disidentification, and resignification, sehicita devises gestures that simultaneously mold a politics of confrontation ("kick[ing] viciously thru the nite") and limn an alternative space of cultural enactment ("catchin stars tween her toes").

Crucially, this double relation to audience perception is given specific form by the totality of what we might call the "sechita episode." For the drama of exhibitionism and voyeurism exploited within the carnival is supported by Shange at another level as well – that of dance. The split mechanism of mimicry/masquerade through which sechita's story is projected as narrative (the tale we've been following) is repeated in the total *mise-en-scène* of Shange's text with the presence of the lady in green, who "dances out sechita's life" as it is narrated by the lady in purple.

Shange's presentational strategy calls attention to itself as a palimpsest of masked figurations, as the audience is reminded of the tension between fiction and performance, imagination and impersonation, in the double vision of "sechita"'s staging. Literally, she is present to us as inextricable from and outside the 'textuality' of her narrative, and this duality (really a mimed duality, since one must admit the performative quality of the narration as well as the discursive implications of the pantomime) suggests both the inevitability of our participation in sechita's fabrication and the propensities, the choices, that motivate that participation. We are situated not merely at a distance from the performance but indeed within it, as we, too, must sift among identifications and disavowals (most obviously *vis-à-vis* our relation to the cracker audience, but equally with regard to sechita herself) and must generally acknowledge the performance space as a site of alternative positions that encode our own necessary involvement.

At every level, then, the sechita episode emblemizes Shange's theater as a process of unbounded exchange in which no one agent can transcend the conflict of positions that constitutes the core drama of splintered, restitched, and relocated identity. The seductive dance and glance of sechita teaches us, in other words, that there is no place of privileged neutrality from which judgments of her or her kin can be established: her mask, it so turns out, is ours, as well – we are likewise caught within the gaze of theater, within representation, as its ambiguous object and agent. Through the torn curtain floods awareness that theater is now not a peephole for viewing the Victim's sacrifice but a volatile arena of decision, rivalry, and affiliation. And just as we are made to see that there are many modes of perception available within our supposedly singular look – and hence that our perception is as much the drama's subject as any other narrative of violation and recuperation, that the structure of looking is constitutive of our own subjectivities and values – so *for colored girls* becomes after the "sechita episode" a series of opportunities to choose between one kind of play and another, to practice the politics of identification with which sechita struggles within her own abysmal Scene of Instruction.

The carnivalesque *dédoublement* of the carnie audience, through the split images of pantomime dance and revoiced narration, thus presents a challenge to the choreopoem's spectators that only *for colored girls*'s full progression of elegiac refiguration can bring to meaningful (dis)closure. At their most affective, the remaining tales loop to the opening sequences by inflecting the sacrificial crisis of childhood, variously reimagining the onto-genetic 'nefertiti' of each woman's soul, threatened by distortion or prematurely killed. In "toussaint," for example, the poem that immediately follows "sechita," we are given a story that charmingly resituates sechita's enigmatic assertion amidst a layering of historical and mythical facsimiles. The lady in brown tells of her discovery, loss, and displaced rediscovery of the revolutionary hero Toussaint L'Ouverture whom she 'encountered' by crossing the boundary of childhood and 'real' maturity separating her from the library's ADULT READING ROOM. Denied the comfort of his written image when authorities refuse her access to the "adult" domain, she makes the pugnacious decision to roam beyond the claustrophobic textual chamber and seek her hero of freedom in his homeland, Haiti, comically literalizing the traditional quest for rebellious black art. Whom does she meet? A "silly ol boy" whom she sasses:

> 'ya bettah leave me alone
> or TOUSSAINT'S gonna get yer ass'
> de silly ol boy came round de corner laughin all in my face
> 'yellah gal
> ya sure must be somebody to know my name so quick . . .
> looka heah girl
> i am TOUSSAINT JONES
> & i'm right heah lookin at ya
> & i dont take no stuff from no white folks . . .'
>
> (29–30)

Recalling the magical conversions of "graduation nite," "toussaint" forges a quest romance through the movements of discovery, disenchantment, and substitution which concludes with the young girl accepting replacement of projected image by immediate presence of a young male partner and his steady, embracing regard. As with "sechita," two plays vie for attention and loyalty, one 'mythic,' one 'historical,' welded by a name of iconic potence. Their harmonious exchange yields a different dance of possibility in the lady in brown's St. Louis than that which sechita endured:

> touissant jones waz awright wit me
> no tellin what all spirits we cd move
> down by the river
> st louis 1955
>
> (30)

But in the next poem, "one," the double drama of being framed by and slashing through the spectacle entangles the protagonist in a melancholic cycle of deceit, revenge, and despair. Adorning herself like sechita in the eye-catching spangles of feminine allure, the lady in red casts men in a drama of reversal, baiting them with her body and turning their wanton gaze into an instrument of their own entrapment:

> she wuz sullen
> & the rhinestones etchin the corners of her mouth
> suggested tears [. . .]
> she always wore her stomach out
> lined with small irridescent feathers

the hairs round her navel seemed to dance . . .
    she waz hot
    a deliberate coquette [. . .]
& she wanted to be unforgettable
she wanted to be a memory
a wound   to every man
arragant enough to want her
    she waz the wrath
       of women in windows

                                    (32)

The lady willingly makes herself available to violation by sight, as the verse itself opens with the "wound" to desire that she both suffers and plans. In mimetic vengeance for a legacy of "women in windows" stared into subjection, she orchestrates a "dance" of seduction that participates in the illusion it fosters, or at least enwraps itself in a mystifying confusion of appetite and deceit. As her story unfolds, the spectacle of fetishistic enticement, which equates the lady in red's desire with her desirability, becomes a paradoxical effort to hoist scopic 'arrogance' on its own petard, to explode its possessive coercion by a whiplash of excessive accommodation and unyielding repudiaton:

    so she glittered honestly
    delighted she waz desired
    & allowed those especially
    schemin/tactful suitors
    to experience her body & spirit [. . .]
    & now she stood a
    reglar colored girl
    fulla the same malice
    livid indifference as a sistah
    worn from supportin a wd be hornplayer
    or waitin by the window.
                  & they knew
                  & left in a hurry

                                (33, 35)

Two dramas, one a masque of shimmering imposture, the other of "reglar colored" candor, form the lady in red's narrative, though whether guileful or unvarnished both finally comprise a tale of anguished self-deception:

    she wd gather her tinsel &
    jewels from the tub
    & laugh gayly or vengeful [. . .]
    & when she finished writin

the account of her exploit in a diary
embroidered with lilies & moonstones
she placed the rose behind her ear
& cried herself to sleep.

(35)

Without the hostile Gaze, there is for the lady in red no landscape of
seduction, no accoutrements of fascination; within it there is nothing but
the perpetuation of a hostile logic of trappings and entrapments. "Schemin"
and "delight" become so braided as to cancel each other, while the possibilities of a feminine mode of self-inscription (the diary adorned by weaving,
flowers, and lunar jewels) collapse into that flat "recordin of history" against
which sechita danced with such enigmatic abandon. As the play gathers
momentum toward a climactic valuation of self-enactment, "one"
poignantly suggests the limits of a purely adversarial aesthetics, which
cannot alter the modes of representation, address, and identification that
impede effective theatrical revision.

After "one," that achievement seems immanent in the choreopoem's
gradual shedding of specular and spectral entanglements for fearless self-
acceptance ("i dont wanna/dance wit ghosts/ . . . lemme love you just like
i am/a colored girl" – 44). Tales of betrayal and bereavement are increasingly mitigated by sassy command and collective movement, and the
women openly prepare for a ceremony of collective acknowledgement that
yields a sacramentalized corrective to carnival distortion:

> *everyone (but started by the lady in purple)*
> oh sanctified
> oh sanctified
> oh sanctified
>
> *everyone (but started by the lady in blue)*
> magic
> magic
> magic . . .
>
> *everyone (but started by the lady in red)*
> and complicated
> and complicated
> and complicated . . .
>> *The dance reaches a climax and all
>> of the ladies fall out tired, but full
>> of life and togetherness.*

(48–9)

The penultimate poem, "a nite with beau willie brown," both delays
and more deeply prepares this ritual climax through the play's most severe

confrontation with misrecognition and the catastrophe of destroyed child-hood. The shocking termination toward which this piece moves, when the heroine, crystal, stands mute and immobile as her estranged husband, beau willie, dangles, then drops their children from a tenement window, focuses the annihilation of voice and body that interruptions to choreographic self-realization threaten. One of *for colored girls*'s most controversial pieces, "a night with beau willie brown" narrates the bitter confusions that grip a poor young black couple not because of beau willie's craven masculine narcis-sism, but because of the overarching system of power and indifference that contains them both as people of color in the New World.[48] Undereducated and unemployed, beau willie is a Vietnam Vet crazed by the command to kill other people of color: "there waznt nothin wrong/with him/he kept tellin crystal/any niggah wanna kill vietnamese children more n stay home/& raise his own is sicker than a rabid dog" (55). But it is the equally undernourished crystal who is left to rear the children, trapped in a cold-water flat and an undying need for beau willie's companionship that will not, however, yield to his threatening pleas "to take him back/& let him be a man in the house" (57). Each of them both seeks to control their position in a ruined family structure and reproduces their position as narrative pawns within an unseen scheme of social control, that hovering, invisible Gaze of white authority figured partially by the poem's unique representation in the third person. As this gripping piece moves to its shattering end, the lady in red, who has served as a pure vessel for the story and its clashing voices, steps from the objectifying third person to the intimate first person, sharing crystal's agony at the moment of unspeakable sacrifice:

> as soon as crystal let the baby outta her arms [. . .]
> he kicked the screen outta the window/& held the kids
> offa the sill/you gonna marry me/yeh, i'll marry ya/
> anything/but bring the children back in the house [. . .]
>
> i stood by beau in the window/with naomi reachin
> for me/& kwame screamin mommy mommy from the fifth
> story/but i cd only whisper/& he dropped em
>
> (59, 60)

   The violence of unutterable loss is cognate with a leap of hazardous iden-tification, a risky shift of performative mode that merges narration with enactment in a painful community of shared astonishment and grief. As actress Kate Malin has told me about playing this role, "I felt broken at this point and sought to remove myself to a safer place, at a distance from the story . . . but to be able to get through the end, I (as the lady in red) had to allow crystal to finish it herself."[49] Closing the double drama of mask and face, face and body, body and spectacle, into a truly purgative "one," crys-tal's story converts semantic setting (from which the actor and audience alike can imagine themselves absolved in their distant regard) to ontological space (within which all parties share responsibility for the pain/pleasure of enactment). In doing so, it also prepares a radical vision of tragic release, which identifies the social causes of suffering, its rootedness in a regime of imperialism and racism, without suggesting that suffering must be gaped upon without resistance: crystal's paralysis is contrasted with, and (we shall soon see) ultimately redressed by, the lady in red's intervention, and performative identification becomes a form of psycho-political excess that overwhelms the reactionary function of conventional catharsis.

Considered theatrically, then, "a nite with beau willie" prepares for the play's closural segment by insisting doubly on the dynamics of engagement, both with the network of social relations against which colored people struggle for legitimacy, sustenance, and love, and with the play's own quest for a performative means of such collective action.[50] Fittingly, it is the lady in red who utters the final chapter of the women's evolving tale of ruin and reparation, no longer fixed in the place of crystal's mute victimhood, but "swingin rose light everywhere":

> I waz missin [somethin]
> i wanted to jump up outta my bones
> & be done wit myself [. . .]
> it waz too much
> i fell into a numbness
> til the only tree i cd see
> took me up in her branches
> held me in the breeze
> made me dawn dew
> that chill at daybreak
> the sun wrapped me up swingin rose light everywhere
> the sky laid over me like a million men
> i waz cold/i was burnin up/a child
> & endlessly weavin garments for the moon
> wit my tears

(63)

It is this figure of pellucid (crystal) refabrication that initiates the final movement toward communal affirmation, as the lady in red strikes the choric refrain, "i found god in myself & i loved her/i loved her fiercely" (63). Each private history finally flows into the general theme, which is fully internalized and solidified in this last scene of the choreopoem. Entitled "a laying on of hands," this episode stresses the grave yet regenerative necessity of shared suffering through ritual acknowledgement – not the thanatic gestures of ambivalent subterfuge and counter-violence seen in poems like "one," but the "fierce" participation of body and spirit in resistance to all that hollows the communal self. Devaluation is turned to a kind of revolutionary mourning in which each player "locates god in [her]self" by giving it to the others without reserve or compromise.

"A laying on of hands," with its overtones of vernacular religiosity, evokes an achieved *caritas* under the aegis of a holy ghost (not 'spooky ghoul') that returns us to the opening segment with revisionary emphasis. The initial discord of despair haunting "interrupted solos" becomes a unifying "song of joy" (63), as the broken "you promised me" of the black girl's 'birth,' the call to "bring her out/to know herself" (2), is at last realized as the "promised . . . holiness of myself released" (61, 62). Fragmentation become (w)holiness, private tale become communal meaning, stillborn terror become ecstatic revery, broken voice become choreopoem – these developments form the thematic substrate of a trans-formation stamped as the dramaturgical shift from separate entrances and frozen poses to collective song and circling dance:

> *All of the ladies repeat to them-*
> *selves softly the lines 'i found god*
> *in myself and loved her.' It soon*
> *becomes a song of joy, started by*
> *the lady in blue. The ladies sing*
> *first to each other, then gradually*
> *to the audience. After the song*
> *peaks the ladies enter into a closed*
> *tight circle.*

(63–4)

Having practiced choreopoetics in myriad permutations of longing and distress – as therapy; as exorcism; as dissimulation; as memory; as apotropaic defense – they return to it as gift, offering a different image of the removed moon-child, of nefertiti decomposed into a new logic of carnival. Enjoining "the audience" to perform the ritual of "common love" (65), the many girls become one familial, covenantal rainbow of fluid color. What had appeared to be didactic (if existentialized) psychosexual drama is swiftly transmuted into an integral ritual of triumph involving the entire theater ensemble. Thus, the emotion generated by the actors is socialized, felt communally, intensified and rendered "real" for the assembled collec-tive, which has often been moved to join the onstage choric movement of the colored girls' triumphal "tight circle."[51]

The dénouement of *for colored girls* thus temporalizes mythic form, fore-grounding the ritual culmination as an accomplishment of the present tense. Aptly, in its final lines we hear intoned an echo of the prologial dedication – "& this is for colored girls who have considered suicide/but *moved* to the ends of their own rainbows" (6) – significantly amended to admit an active, open temporality to the implied "promise" of self-possession: "& this is for colored girls who have considered suicide/but *are movin* to the ends of their own rainbows" (64; my emphases). The play has come to inhabit, not just invoke, the legacy of the rainbow, which appears as a cosmic reconciliation of spirit and flesh, mediating absolute light and contingent sight, arching between sky and earth with no definitive origin or certain end. Shange's signature image is now a fully adequate figural seal of the drama's blend of hitherto conflictive modal forms, its struggle for a new mimesis capable of generating and effectively directing methexic energy. The 'authentic' is forged within, not against, difference, as individual voice, extended to the relation between actor and spectator, is made consubstantial with collective realization. The closural rite is thus instrumental as well as expressive, indeed instrumental *as* expressive of the need to specify the relation between performance and knowledge, to merge strategic and formal acts of discovery and decision. The rhythm of extending from and gathering into the circle – an event affirmed by what the old spiritual calls "the rainbow sign" – works simultaneously as a propositional, mnemonic, and performative gesture, becoming the meaning that it declares. It is an achievement that takes place in and through its enunciation, not a "recordin" or belated image of some external comprehension.

Of special importance to this generalized convergence of ritual and historical consciousness is the breathing rhythm of the circle itself, which is both a closed structure betokening common resolve (cf. the spiritual "Will the Circle Be Unbroken?") and open organism signalling the work's status as a subject-in-process. My students, having only the text before them, have often viewed the performers' turn inward to the circle as a refusal of others, and there is perhaps an important insight in that reaction: certainly that physical phrasing indicates a repudiation of the specular regime against which so many of the colored ladies struggled (e.g., in "abortion cycle," "sechita," "toussaint," and "one"). But the play's performance history, and the interior logic of its thematic and formal evolution, suggest we read this gesture as instructing us to shed voyeuristic impulses, indeed the whole economy of seer and seen, before joining the welcoming embrace of communal festivity. By thus modelling for us the effacement of theatrical divisions, of objects displayed for privileged viewers who, as it were, toss gold in return for an ephemeral scopic satisfaction, the figures assembled in the choric (rather than circus) ring establish a mode of self-presence that refuses any mimetic sacrifice, any residue of potentially abjected difference, as the price for a revolutionary vision of refulgent "color."

In confronting the audience with an intelligible myth of African-American survival from an unimaginable process of loss, treachery, and grief, Shange revives their sense of participation in that process and provokes them into casting off everyday, alienated masks to partake in a common, "reglar" experience. Specifically, Shange's motif of communally inspired emancipation from the pains of isolation is taken up by the audience because she has called upon the community's shared ethos: the elaboration of improvisatory self-composition from the politics of remembrance. As a result, the spectators face the opportunity to resituate themselves through the changing energies of identification, redefining the 'spectacle' of collective enactment. No longer detached judges of a confused welter of paradoxical images, they are afforded the opportunity to join (and thereby extend) the encircling affirmation of the choreopoetic climax. The self-consciously performative collectivity of ritual has thereby resituated the elegiac individuation of drama: modern black drama – released from the "spook house" of stark mimesis – has come to celebrate whatever is "enuf."

*

The revolutionary dramaturgy of *for colored girls* reveals how, in the critical praxis of black modernist performance, naming is always also unnaming and renaming, omission is always also opportune spacing, the body is at once the thing itself (registering a spectrum of pains, needs, and joys) and a representation (never purely a space from which consciousness can hide or into which the mind can release itself from historical imperatives), and our own capacity for meaningful response is always an instrinsic element of the artist's project of redefinition and renewal. In its quest for a perfectly "full note" of communalized blackness, modern black drama in general proves a highly self-conscious amalgam of inscription and elusive movement, a complex play between visual and aural modes seeking the desired nexus of recognition and reconstruction. Such recuperation is never undertaken as purely event or structure, but, instead, as a dynamic interfusion or dialectic between them – a dialectic for which the black musician is taken as exemplary guide and instance. It is to the music itself, then, as epitomized by the breath and inspiration of John Coltrane, that we now turn, in continuance of this journey along the "rainbow" of African-American modernism's visionary performances.

Part II

Blow into the freezing night

Expressive agency in Coltrane and the Coltrane Poem

dig the cosmic Trane
dig be
dig be
dig be
spirit lives in sound
dig be
sound lives in spirit
dig be
yeah! ! !
spirit lives
spirit lives
spirit lives
SPIRIT ! ! !
SWHEEEEEEEEEEEEEEEETTT! ! !

take it again
this time from the top

Larry Neal, "Don't Say
Goodbye to the Porkpie Hat"

3 Innovating blackness

Praxis and passion in (late)
Coltrane

coltrane is off with a hoot
directed supine
nowhere in generalness
into the din and the death

David Henderson, "Elvin Jones Gretsch
Freak (Coltrane at the Half-Note)"[1]

I

into the sixties
a trane
came/out of the
fifties with a golden boxcar
riding the rails
of novation.
     blowing
     a-melodics
     screeching,
     screaming,
     blasting – [. . .]
music that ached.
murdered our minds (we reborn)
born into a neoteric aberration.

Haki Madhubuti, "Don't Cry, Scream"[2]

Modern black culture, in its insistently revisionary quest for an authoritative voice, wants to remake that fundamental activity of mind we call "art". At the same time, whether revisionary or revolutionary, resurrective or iconoclast, it has come to realize that all real transformations in the form of expression, especially when envisioned as integral to fundamental shifts in the structure of collective consciousness, can take place only within a transfiguration of the idea of expression itself. "Art" names the political and cultural aspiration of black modernism when it becomes the scene of reinscription, a critical intervention within inherited practices that may well appear first as a shattering of convention but sustains its subversive energy as a perpetual interrogation of the world as "given." Thus, while the new "black aesthetic" turns inside-out all the pieties of life and art, speaking 'outlandishly' against the grain of normative African-American aesthetic discourse, it still speaks for the life and increase presumably afforded by a new syntax of desire. That it has dared to do so in such assertive tones is certainly attributable to the startling innovations of contemporary jazz musicians, chief among these John Coltrane.

In the agitprop journals that fueled the aesthetic politics of the Black Arts (e.g., *Negro Digest*, *The Journal of Black Poetry*, *Liberator Magazine*, *Amistad*, and *Umbra*), in the prefaces to anthologies of the 'New Black' writing (e.g., Addison Gayle's *The Black Aesthetic*),[3] and, most notably, in the pages of the movement's manifesto centerpiece, the self-consciously avant-gardist and combative anthology *Black Fire*[4] (edited by Baraka and Neal), we find on nearly every page the evocation of music as preeminent medium and vanguard exemplar of the era's devotion to restless experimentation, disruptive discovery, and the immediate translation of vision into act. Elevating expressive energy over achieved artistic production, and often evoking an African ethos of artistic use-value as opposed to the purported 'autonomous' abstraction of Euro-American aesthetics, writers such as A. B. Spellman, Lindsay Barrett, Peter Labrie, and James T. Stewart joined Neal and Baraka in their insistence that music epitomized a 'black ethos' of transformative assertion through a ceaseless dialectic of dissolution and reformation – a dialectic at once formal and thematic as structures of meaning are subjected to the force of new social and emotional conditions. Stewart's encomium to black musical creativity crystallizes its putative freedom from crass contingencies and fashions, its distinguishing production of an autonomous language arising in the space of its own self-authenticating power, and its peculiarly historicized essentiality:

> Whatever constitutes a Black Aesthetic has and will rest on the musician. The black musician is ahead of everyone in the expression of true black sensibility. For him, negritude or soul or blackness has never been a matter for soapbox articulation. The musician has not expressed his self through the power of speech or an African wardrobe. More than any other kind of black artist, the musician creates his own and his people's soul essence, his own negritude.
>
> (James T. Stewart, "The Development of the Black Revolutionary Artist," 7)[5]

Penetrating superficialities of ornament and fortuities of received discourse, the black musician on Stewart's view confronts directly the struggle for legitimation spurring African-American modernism's quest for freedom and power. Like Harrison's modal playwright eschewing the ephemeral agitprop oration for movements of collective anamnesis, Stewart's black musician directly affects – indeed produces – his people's consciousness by locating that place where "the power of speech" gives way to a more "essential" expressivity, the guarantee of which is its distinctively stamped mode of self-possession. Black music is thus made to take up what we might call the *ordeal of authority and meaning* at the heart of modern black performance, forging from its opposition or contrast to symbolic norms a fresh semiotic force. Precisely because it breaches the system of signs through which black writers struggle to assert significance against the grain of dominant idioms, black music becomes itself the arch sign of a will-to-revolutionary "articulation" that is at once excessive practice and authentic being, disruptive critique and constructive vision, subjective experience and objective truth. As we shall see, Coltrane's extraordinary musical speculations bear special scrutiny for their exploration, and not mere exemplification, of this challenge to those logical antinomies that have habitually beset linguistic practitioners, leading them to privilege music as black modernism's herald and host.

Baraka's *Blues People* (1963),[6] the movement's most systematic exposition of this musical ethos, set the tone for the era's treatment of African-American music as the harbinger of other black idioms. In Baraka's account, African-American music models for all manner of writing, exhibition, and public speech a progressive narrative from "root" forms of black inner life (such as blues or bebop) through popular debasement (swing, cool) to eventual reappearance of the essential energy in a more insurgent form (modern experimental jazz). The detailing of this process is not, however, primarily the record of a sustained, evolutionary tradition; it is rather a vigorous exploration of the effects of psychological crisis on a culture, and the possibilities of artistic response to such crisis. Not so much historicizing the endurance of African-American artistic ingenuity as appropriating black music as emblem of a revolutionary praxis, Baraka's imagination and critical sense are involved most in *Blues People* by the outbreak of spontaneous gestures in response to an altered political and spiritual condition (thus bebop is examined as a product of a particular quality of African-American urban alienation), or by detection of an altered attitude behind the facade of traditional forms (thus rhythm-and-blues is viewed as exploiting a variety of preestablished techniques to effect a more subversive, 'underground' utterance). With a keen sense of dramatic peripety that catches with vivid eagerness that historical moment when an art form must choose between continuation or rupture of inherited assumptions, Baraka's narrative arrives at the current moment of jazz's "neoteric aberrations" suffused by an aura of millenarian exultation:

> The implications of this music are extraordinarily profound, and the music itself, deeply and wildly exciting. Music and musician have been brought, in a manner of speaking, face to face, without the strict and

often grim hindrances of overused western musical concepts [. . .] It
is [. . .] a terrifying freedom.

(Amiri Baraka, *Blues People*, 227)

Face-to-face: In this double figuration, evocative at once of ineffable
sublimity and irreducible materiality, we find the core of Coltrane's
centrality to the black aesthetic's privileged trope of musical authority. For
in their radical tactics of defamiliarization, in their dissection of mainstream, jazz, and vernacular vocabularies in search of the purest tissue of
musical being, in their relentless quest for what Trane called "something
that hasn't been played before,"[7] Coltrane's compositions and improvisations marked black music simultaneously as a realm of imminent
potentiality and immanent particularity. In his playing, black performance
seemed to commune directly with itself, becoming more than mere
discourse yet losing nothing in transformative reflexivity for that liberation, conducting an interior yet communally accessible dialogue on the
efficacious juncture of expression, action, expectation, and celebration.
Constantly aware of its own place in this conversation yet always seeking
another scene for its enunciation, Coltrane's music became the "Moses"
latent in Baraka's testamental formulation to an entire generation of innovators searching for the Promised Land of an ultimate, if searing, revelation
beyond the darkling plain of diasporic experience.

And indeed, the music to which Baraka refers – the sounds of Coltrane,
Ornette Coleman, Sonny Rollins, Sun Ra, Cecil Taylor, Albert Ayler,
Archie Shepp, Pharoah Sanders, and their fellow travelers – unfolded
before the black aesthetician and writer a new kingdom, a world which
refuses the systematized expectations of received wisdom, a realm in
which one subdues private passions in order to discover within oneself an
uncertain but shared longing. The "New Wave" jazz – having extended
and mastered the contribution of bebop – opened the floodgates of passion,
anger, pain, and love, and aroused that fury for liberty which is the essence
of the new black art. It joined itself to earlier, major epochs of black music
by elaborating the creative union between the improvising soloist and the
total musical collective. But it also forged a new role for music in the hierarchy of black expressions – that of guide rather than mere analogue to
other communicative modes.

The root of the black writer's elevation of music to a position of
supremacy among the arts lies in the music's aversion for fixed structures.
By the very fact of its 'otherworldliness,' of its independence of values
derived from alien experiences, it enters the African-American's consciousness on its own, necessarily general, terms. Establishing idiosyncratic logics
of rhythm, duration, intonation, and integrity, black music thus linked the
twin impulses of sedition and realization that lend modern black performance its urgency, but also its anxiety of achievement. Tapping an ancient
ambivalence surrounding music as both perfected form and unconstrained

novelty, Black Arts theorists grasp the music's exploratory character as source of a subversive instinct sanctioning the deepest necessities of traditional imagination. And because of their distinctive, often dissonant, differences from familiar, 'western' idioms, these terms represent for the new artists the energies of black aspiration with an absoluteness and an immediacy denied to other creative media. But if such a notion is already familiar in the aesthetics of Romanticism and its heirs, African-American speculation departs from western theory's Saussurian emphasis on the musical sign's referential 'emptiness' in its insistence on the *signifying potential* of the new music's supra-mimetic phenomenology.

The thought of giving to words and prosody values equivalent to music is an ancient one, in African as well as western culture.[8] But with modern black literature, it assumes the force of a specific idea: the notion that black language leads *toward* music, that it passes into music when it attains the maximal pitch of its being. "If you listen," Shange intones in the suggestively titled polemic "takin a solo/a poetic possibility/a poetic imperative", "you cd imagine us like music & make us yrs."[9] This belief contains the powerful suggestion that music is the ultimate lexicon, that language, when truly apprehended, arrives at (and doesn't merely aspire to) the condition of music and is brought, by the poet's articulation of black vocality, to the experience of that condition. Imagined, as Shange enjoins us, through the chiasmal sympathies of expressive player and attentive auditor (who, hearing the poet as one would the musician, hears the poet *as* musician – *imagine us like music*), such language possesses experience in the intimacy of shared presence rather than the distance of re-presentation. Thus, in the verse of Sonia Sanchez, Lance Jeffers, A. B. Spellman, Larry Neal, Carolyn Rodgers, Calvin Hernton, Jayne Cortez, David Henderson, Michael Harper, and countless others, the poem, by a gradual transcendence of its own forms, often strives to escape from the linear, logically determined bonds of denotative speech into what the poet imagines as the spontaneities and freedoms of musical form. Black poetry unabashedly seeks the unfettered lyricism of "actual music" (Haki Madhubuti) for it is in music that the poet hopes to achieve both the individual creation – the *call* bearing the shape of his own spirit – and communal solidarity – the *response* of infinite renewal.

From Henry Dumas's Probe ("Will the Circle be Unbroken?") to Ishmael Reed's Loop Garoo Kid (*Yellow Back Radio Broke-Down*), the artist-hero in modern African-American writing is, typically, a musician (especially, like Coltrane, a hornplayer – or, perhaps, as Shange's lady in red would have it, a wd be hornplayer!); for it is only in music, the literature seems to say, that renovated aesthetic conventions can touch upon both the pure energy and improvisational wit deemed necessary for survival in the black diaspora. The modern African-American writer posits the hypostatization of music as the perfect metaphor for black life; s/he has collapsed the distinctions between musical and other black expressions to such an extent that black music is seen as black life itself, pressed to its purest essence. The musician is, therefore, imaged not only as a contributer of "sorrow songs" and a legacy of endurance; increasingly, s/he assumes an evangelical role, and "the music" is embraced as manifestation of radical interrogation and transgressive innovation.

The fullest and most self-reflexive statements of this aesthetic, of this merging of the word with the musical idea in a vision of black modernist revolt, can be found in the myriad poems directly inspired by Coltrane. The "Coltrane Poem" has, in fact, become an unmistakable genre of contemporary black poetry to which a host of accomplished black poets have contributed – Ebon, David Henderson, Haki Madhubuti, Sharon Bourke, Sonia Sanchez, Jerry Ward, Jayne Cortez, Carolyn Rodgers, A. B. Spellman, and Michael Harper, to list but a few – and it is in this genre that the notion of music as the quintessential idiom, and of the word as its annunciator, is carried to its technical and philosophic apex. Yet beyond this specifically aesthetic concern there exists in these works a more subtle dynamic: a productive tension born of the recognition that such poetic interest demands a larger awareness of death and the consequent struggle for spiritual and communal resurrection. For Coltrane, like Charlie (Bird) Parker, Robert Johnson, and countless kin before him, died young, and so he provides the archetype of the threat to (as well as the potential for) expression. Thus, Harper's "Dear John, Dear Coltrane," for example, in the brooding intensity of its incantatory lyricism, turns upon a metaphor of cosmic, and searing, musicality. It images the black man's spirit, Coltrane's essence, as a resolve to play the elemental notes despite the rending of generative power:

> there is no substitute for pain:
> genitals gone or going . . .
> > You pick up the horn
>
> with some will and blow
> into the freezing night:
> *a love supreme, a love supreme.*
>
> > (Michael Harper, "Dear John,
> > Dear Coltrane")[10]

All the poets, like Harper, felt in Coltrane's music the self-commitment to an exalted state, the "will" to pass beyond apparent limits of material existence or mere method. Listening to Coltrane – whose revolutionary approach to bebop and the blues changed the nature of the African-American musical lexicon – they sensed that a fresh, renovated art no longer derived from the dictates of an inherited tradition but reflected instead the spiritual unity of sacrifice innate to African-American vision. Since this vision was inimical to existing structures, the traditional artistic forms would not be entirely adequate to contain it, and new forms, expressing the radical approach to the old, would necessarily arise. They did arise. And Trane's was the most magical of formal revolutions – to hear the poets, and especially to grasp their encounter with Trane as a collective improvisation on history, innovation, and performative self-revision, we must first hear him.

II

> His head is
> at the window. The only
> part
>   that sings.
>
> Baraka, "A Poem for Willie Best,"[11]

> One hears and sees
>   heard and saw
> One feels and feeling
>   felt and feels [...]
> And no one feels and feeling
>   felt and feels
> And no one hearing holding
>   the and the
>   to never know and scream
>
> Frederick J. Bryant, Jr.,
"Black Orpheus"[12]

For the black aesthetic of which Coltrane was a prime mover, fury envisions apocalpyse as the artist engages Euro-American culture in an increasingly agonistic relationship. This apocalypse is something more than the destruction conceived by the oppressed as retribution against their enemies. Implied in it is a nearly total reimagining of western history and metaphysical presumption. The revolt of the African-American artist against specific literary or social conventions is, at bottom, a rebellion against authority and the memory of imposed systems. As trumpeter Clifford Thornton (alumnus of the fabulous Sun Ra cabal) declared, true revolution of consciousness begins by a radical "unlearning" of existent modes, stripping the order of expressibility to trouble meanings that entrenched discourse seems automatically to assume or confer. Such is the ethical and political imperative of the new art's torrid formal experimentation. It is not an improvement of available techniques that African-American modernist rebellion requests; rather, its call is for an entirely fresh grammar, what Baraka called a "postwestern form."

Set apart from the enveloping society, the black modernist sets out on a fresh journey into unmapped spaces of the self. S/he courts the dismembering anger of the herd by risking a liberating psychic descent, paradoxically undertaken on behalf of the community's own concealed identity. Coltrane partook of this vatic fury, a metaphysical revolt without metaphysical surrender, a dialectic of violence and renewal in which Being itself is put on trial. For if the riven voice that sings on is a response to history's chaos, it is also an appeal to the specific forms of collective experience to which only its participants can give witness. It thus invokes a reordering of life by an alteration of consciousness; it summons apocalypse in its original sense of revelation by penetrating the moment's perplexities to the heart of awareness in a gesture that clarifies rather than dissolves history's wounds: "One hears and sees/heard and saw." Fury and Apocalypse: these are the obsessions of the modernist 'Black Orphic' imagination, the vital and dangerous necessities of its existence.

Music can be privileged over conceptual or imagistic formulations of this fervent program because its intensity belies the tropic nature of its assertions. But the turn to music acknowledges that it is not annihilation of expressive form that is sought but rather a kind of paradoxical destructive restructuration that rearranges the field of understanding and possibility. Such restructuration implicates music, too, in the rhetoricity of its own habits, norms, and procedures; it touches upon a 'primordial' ontology only through epistemological inquiry that works as an intervention into musical discourse even as it signals a recuperation of transcendental authority. The "meta" realm of music, that is to say, is itself a mode of notation, and music already belongs to the conversational matrix of metaphor, narrative, and interpretation even as the poets emblemize it as a signifier of natural force. (It should not surprise us that even as the poets embrace musical tropes to exert a pressure against the limits of verbal expression, the musicians resort to linguistic terminology to define their own aims of precision; thus, for example, trumpeter Tommy Turrentine on improvising "linear or melodic" motifs: "It's like writing a sentence. The commas, the periods, and the exclamation points have to be very *pronounced*,"[13] the final word here cunningly merging writerly and oral-performative kinds of emphasis.) When we look at the music itself, then, we find that its evasion of conventional grammars entails a "method" that at one and the same time suspends and intensifies method, that makes method itself the vehicle of vision, confirming vision's fundamentally rhetorical design.

This complex tension is strongly felt behind the technical ingenuities of Coltrane's music. The passionate focus of its formal investigation claims a distinctive place in the history of African-American music, being more self-conscious and self-transgressive than even its bebop predecessor. It rethinks the very idea of form, in the process forcing new considerations of jazz composition as medium of a specifically performative inquiry. After Coltrane, no concept of arrangement or improvisation, solo or ensemble, tone or mode can be ever approached in quite the same way again. In its search for the quintessential nexus of pitch, rhythm, and timbre, for what Coltrane termed (speaking of the astounding late composition "Om") the "first vibration – that sound, that spirit which set everything else into being,"[14] Coltrane's music constantly demanded disruptions of the very decorums that supported its reflexive investigation. The movement from phase to phase in his career, and indeed from phrase to phrase within individual pieces, seemed driven by an inexorable metamorphic imperative marked by violence and excess, as notes tumbled over the rhythmic barriers of the measure and stylistic norms (often recently achieved and still labile with unsettled possibility) gave way to their critical supplements, elaborations, or outright displacements.

The signature of the Coltrane sound was always an irrepressible dislocating of the 'standard' (be that the specific familiar tune or general musical principle), a depositioning of morphic limitation from within the contours of known structure itself. What was recognizable in his 'style,' therefore, was a quality of discontinuous repetition, an insistence on breaking the very patterns that he discovered in the evident interest of finding their unfathomed resonance or unprobed relation to more intricate arrangements of meaning, and thus what unified his oeuvre was a process of repeated discontinuity that seemed patterned in its very disturbance. From the standpoint of any prior experience, even experience of Coltrane's own work, the listener of a fresh Coltrane performance often felt the shock of a kind of aural *Verfremdungseffekt* that demystified assumptions about order and chaos through which even the relative disturbance of bop transmitted its meanings. With Coltrane, jazz became a music played at the limits of musical systemizing and comprehension, and hence seemed to put music as a mode of articulation and even of consciousness on trial.

By thus seeming to place the uncertainties of relentless questioning and uncompromising freedom above the symmetries of charted statement and accomplished edifice, Coltrane's music appeared to threaten jazz as an institutional formation, or at least to shift its disciplinary logic from one of stepwise (and periodically consolidated) progression to that of incessant change. Aptly enough, his antagonists in the controversy that swirled about him from the time of the earliest innovations gathered under the banner "anti-jazz,"[15] a term that, if nothing else, crystallized the sense of high-stakes provocation that his music provided those invested in the medium as a vehicle not only of musical but of cultural expression. Violating every procedure of melodic, harmonic, and tonal organization that dictated unity as the measure of jazz energy's heterogeneity, Trane's musical journey intimated that the way to the self-transcendence of that "first vibration" was the *via negativa* of radical divergence, disjunction, even dissolution.

Coltrane's music thus constitutes a kind of negative dialectics that sought to rescue the remainder, the particular, the ephemeral latent within the regularizing patterns of even the most dissonant bop adventures. Its spell works by a disenchantment of familiar musical elements (the jaunty 4/4 and bouncy swing eighth-note rhythms common to jazz expression; the outlines of distinctive melodies; the ordering structure and temporal requirements of statement-elaboration-restatement; etc.) that redirects attention exactly to just these compositional elements, as opposed to the customary disappearance of musical particularity in the course of a piece's overall exposition. In this way, Coltrane liberates the individual note (and all its neighbors that roil about it in a vortex of endlessly forming and deforming clusters and sequences, the stuff of melody and ornamentation), suggesting that music not only moves forward but can go astray . . . moves forward precisely by a process of restless nomadism. Played with unexampled agility and alacrity, Coltrane's notes seem at once a revelation of the subatomic richness of a given phrase or scale and a declaration of their inassimilability to even the limited totalities upon which musical narrative conventionally depends. In the peculiar combination of their piercing definiteness and whirlpooled engorgement, they seem to be *about* the question of where the specific note ends and the phrase begins, that is, about the epistemological relation of detail and narrative, or the ethical relation of individual and collective. In its verve and speed, the Coltrane note-sequence is, paradoxically, a plea to think through the propriety of associative selection wherein difference is submerged in the interests of (re)stating an *a priori* idea. It is an invitation, as it were, to return to the moment before the beginning of musical narration – that is, to a true beginning, before the 'end' implicit in any dominating phraseology or motif (however much it might be elaborated in accordance with governing principles of the given musical genre). Coltrane's notes, that is to say, plead the case of their ontology apart from contextual requirements, and it is for this reason that they seem, for all their layered intricacy, like some elemental cry of desire for unfettered identity.

It is this refusal to allow prescriptions of melody or harmony to dominate the note that gives Coltrane's music its extraordinary quality of risk, its alarming and fearsome bearing, for it nurtures the unsystematic, overflowing shards that music habitually recuperates in the interests of perceptible form. The freedom of its improvisations thus seem quite unlike those of conventional jazz: not so much a matter of swing as a vertiginous, inconclusive, unlocalized, and rhythmically unpredictable insistence. Where improvisation before Trane reworked units that retained marks of their relation to the prevailing narrative statement, his riffs worked increasingly over the course of his career to *un*bind these figures from any enveloping referential obligation in order to free more energy latent within them. This shift of emphasis from what we might think of as a metaphorical to a metonymical mode of improvisation (though, as we shall see, any such radical division would be ultimately misleading in accounting for the production of meaning in Coltrane's work) has profound implications for the temporality of musical statement, as it intensifies rather than resolves the conflict between theme and riff, or at least works to postpone, and thereby reconceive, resolution. Of course, Coltrane always was playing a tune – you can hear it in "Om" as much as in "My Favorite Things" – and the charge made against the music that it didn't swing was, in fact, a sign of inattentiveness to his passionate interest in rhythmic diversity, but he never took the tune to be identical with the playing: his was a playing against "music" in the interests of discovering the root of "that sound . . . which set everything else into being."

The resistance in Coltrane's music to conventional terms of musical narrative suggests a disavowal of symbolic registers. Rather like the "pulsing" drives and "semiotic" rhythms of Kristeva's abject, his distended improvisations and, so to speak, un-barred phrasing evoke something before or outside articulation as commonly understood (Baraka writes movingly of one Trane performance as being like "watching a grown man learning to speak"[16]). Yet, having emphasized Coltrane's challenge to convention, it is necessary now to emphasize – particularly in view of the misleading impression left by many of Coltrane's critics and admirers alike that his work is an effort to remove rather than remake musical configuration *per se* – that the supersession of established formal principles did not lead to formlessness, to an irreparable splintering of the black orphic 'ax.' The dynamic power that Coltrane and his "new breed" brethren unleashed seemed to shatter the very possibility of clarity and form – such was the force of the new content that was being freshly conceived. But there is a rigorous inner logic at the root of these works which, upon scrutiny, disposes of the view that they were 'amorphous,' 'random,' or simply shucking, as critics claim.[17] As Trane's evocation of the primal Om suggests, the aim of his negations is, ultimately, affirmation, but it is driven by realization that negation and errancy can be of greater practical importance than the protocols of commonplace presentation. It is the interplay of negation and affirmation, denial and avowal – too jagged, really, to be termed dialectical, but none the less fundamentally dialectical in playing against musical expectation without, however, abandoning the idea of music itself – that lends Coltrane's music its peculiar sensation of transgressive revelation, its simultaneous capacity for deconstruction and revision. Its achievement thus lies in the manner of its performance, the density of its textures and sonorities, the value it places on praxis as itself the medium of conceptualization so that consciousness and its substantive creations are grasped as one and the same. Before the "everything else" of the sounds we hear lies the "first vibration," Coltrane tells us, thus capturing the basic paradox of his work: that music is itself the instrument for recovering a primal intonation, a musical ideal that is essential only in the sense that it already re-sounds a relation of assertion and echo. Like Clay's pumping black heart, it is original and natural; like Ellison's blackness-of-blackness, it is re-petitional and temporal.

Returning to the basic structure of the note within improvisation, we can observe in Coltrane's work a compositional pattern that explicates this abiding tension between deformation and reformation. In increasingly complex gestures of reiteration, inversion, and distension, Trane reworks a small (usually three- or five-note) phrase or cell in order to deduce all the possible instances that such clusters might articulate. The process requires that the "topic" of improvisation initiates, as if within the logic of its own cellular structure, a movement which necessarily bears the piece further and further away from that theme. It thus seems as if the piece is fueled by an imperative that drives the note toward a vortex of energy unshaped by the theme's pull toward a containing order, relocating its commitments in a self-undoing centrifugality. Yet Coltrane always reminds us of the theme, even if in new and surprising guises, because it is the heuristic postulate of his own argument, the spur to his compositional journey. Each sequence of improvisational extension is joined to the others, not necessarily by the conventional "bridges" established by chordal changes or melodic recall, but by the guiding principle of elaboration through which the improvisational matrix as a whole is conducted. Adopting Frank Kermode's narratological distinction between sequence – the metaphorical axis of achieved meaning and narrative (dis)closure – and secrecy – the metonymical encrypting of occult detail resistant to assimilation into interpretive "connexity"[18] – we might hear the Coltrane solo as speaking for a clandestine, scenic, fragmentary uncertainty about meaning, for the displacement of answer by the inchoate, even groping openness of question. It thus can seem an effort to empty meaning by frustating our assumptions about intelligibility and blocking our habituated interpretive moves that make a set of sounds the ever-present assurance of "harmony" as a piece advances. But it ought rather be heard as an implacable probing of musical signification, a suspension (rather than emptying) of presuppositions that effectively harden hearing by foreclosing its "secretive" potentiality.

The Coltrane improvisation, then, can be thought of as a destructuring quest for fresh intimations of order and understanding. Its attack against form is carried out in a most rigorous fashion, and each lick is itself a prodigy of controlled astonishment, born of that mastery that can afford to *let be* (to turn upon the Hamletean element of one of Trane's more wondrous late explorations in uncharted territory, "To Be"). Its movement is thus lissome and protean (even in the modal and pantonic compositions), by turns ironic and prophetic, as though Trane is always both in and out of the place where he is speaking, "always looking off somwhere," as Freddie Hubbard once remarked (serendipitously evoking the famous photo-portrait on the "Love Supreme" album cover of a Coltrane glancing fiercely outside the viewer's plane), "like he's thinking of the next note he's going to play."[19] Quick imaginative reflexes are required by both fellow band members and listeners (as indeed, by Coltrane himself) to sustain this adventurous activity, which at times seems driven by the absolute impulse to assay singular patterns of statement and counter-statement, treating each momentary coagulation of musical "sense" as a strategic invitation to a new metamorphic leap. But it is this very move-ment of assertion, scrutiny, and revision that constitutes a method that transcends yet always depends upon each of its discrete units, such that far from being formless, Coltrane's music can be seen as a resolute inquiry into the potentiality of structuration within the musical afflatus that the axman "blows into the freezing night."

Coltrane's oeuvre, which traverses an encyclopedic range of jazz, blues, balladic, sacred, and even cross-cultural frameworks, thus constitutes a bracingly self-reflexive investigation of the nature, limits, and unheard pos-sibilities of his art. This is, at the same time, a decidedly political and his-torical inquiry precisely because of its heightened awareness of the contingency of any given convention and the necessity – both burden and blessing – of operating *within* those contingencies even as the search for the foundational Sound persists. In some sense, Coltrane's career unfolded as a fundamentally contradictory, or perhaps ambivalent, enterprise, a kind of sceptical idealism: in the quest for a sound that can be reached only through its imperfect reverberations, Coltrane's playing must use and abuse, quote and misprize, establish and destabilize the formulae, genres, instruments, and other performative conditions at its disposal. With progressive empha-sis, each Coltrane piece finds a way to point out its animating conflicts, becoming along the way a critical rereading of its own 'motives' (in the double sense of intentional and melodic development). Each piece thus marks the provisionality equally of conventions and of its own improvisa-tions upon them, suggesting the ongoing implication of Coltrane's music in that which it seeks relentlessly to remake. Its dauntless challenge to received modes is never greater than its courage to differ with its own assumptions. It is this honesty, and the incessant upheaval of self-transformation that it demanded, that folks felt most deeply about Trane during his lifetime, that lies at the root of the poets' versification of his sacrificial legacy, and that stamped the general lineaments of his oeuvre's development, making sense of the defining relations between disturbance and reparation, particularity and universality, change and continuity that we must now seek to graph more exactly within the evolving notes themselves.

The late (post-1962) pieces present the greatest task for a structural and thematic explanation of Coltrane's career, and so will form the core of our examination – they are in every way the summit of his challenge to his poetic peers (Elvin Jones was said to have remarked, with a mixture of admiration and exasperation, of Coltrane's late forays when he departed the band in early 1966: "Only poets can understand it"[20]). But, even in such a focused exposition of Coltrane's stylistic experiment as this will be, there is a path to be traced before one reaches that expanded space of imaginative transfiguration. After an apprenticeship in the Philadelphia milieu of rhythm and blues with such band leaders as Joe Webb (featuring the powerful blues singer Big Maybelle), the high-honker King Kolax, and the hard-driving bluesman Eddie (Cleanhead) Vinson, Trane came on the jazz scene during the mid to late flowering of bebop, establishing his presence under the tutelage of bop legends Dizzy Gillespie, Thelonious Monk, and Miles Davis. Until its first crucial turn in the early 1960s, his style was a meticulous, impassioned development of Charlie Parker's vertical (harmonic) experimentation with melody and the chord. Perhaps reflecting his experience in the rough-and-tumble dancehall world of the blues bands, Coltrane brought a jagged and robust texture to his interpretation of bop's chordal expansions, an almost importunate accent stamped by his peculiar sense of earnest purposiveness. Coltrane's challenge to harmonic patterns bore, too, the influence of the great vertical stylist Coleman Hawkins (with whom Trane played in Monk's band), for like Bean he threaded melody through energetic arpeggios, giving them a characteristic lift and graceful power. But as he was already showing during his too-little appreciated period with Monk, from whom he learned to seize his instrument as a vehicle of constant experimentation and self-extension ("Monk was one of the first to show me how to make two or three notes at one time on tenor . . . he also got me into the habit of playing long solos, playing the same piece for a long time to find new conceptions for solos"[21]), Coltrane had from the beginning a distinctive focus on something elusive within the smallest element of chordal statement. Harmonic changes became almost an end in themselves, so that inside the spaces Monk carved out with incomparable delicacy and foresight Coltrane began to plumb vigorously fresh possibilities within chords themselves as if, like an early particle physicist, searching their unseen substructures: "The harmonies got to be an obsession with me," he once confessed; "sometimes I was making music through the wrong end of the magnifying glass."[22] Eventually, by accepting Monk's challenge to work within his preternaturally wide intervals, maintaining contact with melody while pursuing the accelerated harmonic variations, Coltrane began to work toward the mode of on-site self-examination that became a hallmark of his second stint with Miles Davis in the late 1950s (for example, in the extraordinary *Milestones* album of 1958). Once he set out with his own ensemble, on a piece like "Giant Steps" (1959) one hears emerging from Trane's tenor what Zita Carno aptly called the "hard drive"[23] of a style that was becoming something more than a working out of bop's implications,[24] indeed was an uncompromising shearing of residual bop clichés as all facets of the bop lexicon, including his own "pet phrases" (in Carno's argot), were subjected to exacting scrutiny. On this signature piece – and others of the period such as "Countdown" and "Cousin Mary" – a prismatic layering of chordal cross-sections, played with unexampled fluency and precision, joined sharp juxtapositions of asymmetric rhythmic bursts to produce the 'driving' momentum that remained a hallmark of Coltrane's method. "I found," he remarked, "that there were a certain number of chord progressions to play in a given time, and sometimes what I played didn't work out in eighth notes, sixteenth notes, or triplets. I had to put the notes in uneven groups like fives and sevens in order to fit them all in."[25] Rather like Big Daddy Lipscombe's self-professed approach to football tackling – "I just gather 'em all up, then peel 'em all off one-by-one 'til I find the one with the ball" – Coltrane played *everything* in searching for the *one* holding the purest sound. (Cannonball Adderly once only-half-jokingly wondered after a Trane solo flew through every imaginable register, skipping across all the accents and dashing across all the bars, "what do I play now that he's played it all"![26]) If that sound *per se* eluded him, propelling him to further experimental investigations of harmony and rhythm, by 1960 Trane had mastered his impulse toward (chordal) progression, moving through arpeggios and three- or four-note scale fragments with remarkable velocity and dexterity, declaring adamantly that the technical facility to achieve "giant steps" to spaces unknown was fully in reach.

Those spaces opened first through Trane's elaboration of Miles's discoveries in modal composition, most dramatically exemplified on the classic *Kind of Blue* suite of 1959. With bop reaching its logical fulfillment, and with the tremors of what was to arise as the Black Power and Black Arts movements being clearly felt in the clubs, lofts, and studios, the watchword in the jazz avant-garde was *freedom*: freedom, as Sonny Rollins declared in making the epochal *Freedom Suite* with Max Roach, to imagine a new spontaneity within established forms adequate to the changing climate of African-American assertion;[27] freedom, as Ornette Coleman asserted, for new metrical variations that changed the time of the player's thinking, even of his breathing;[28] freedom, as Coltrane put it, reflecting on his gains and divergences from Miles Davis, to pursue simultaneously vertical and horizontal axes of development, thus fundamentally altering the field of improvisational invention.[29] As Coleman undertook his swerve from bebop by discarding vertical for horizontal (melodic, thematic) improvisation, Coltrane began to undermine the chordal approach from within, by a systematic dissection, multiplication, and scattering of the individual chord. Rather than employing the intervals within or around the chord, Coltrane began to utilize the chromatic scale implied by the chord. If Bird had shown that by moving past, or stretching, the chords' roots the improviser could force melody into his/her own design rather than succumb to thematic prescription, Trane liberated harmony, the relation of chords, from rigid tonal progressions with a more jolting insistence. Thus establishing an infinite variety of stepwise relations to the chord, the playing of many chords upon or within a single implied chord, Coltrane did something more than the pyrotechnical feat of making the sax do what only a stringed instrument should achieve, thus generating the famous *glissando* of his "sheets of sound."[30] He established the chord as the space within which a new *temporality* of improvisation could be enacted, for one might dwell (with furious intensity) within the many kaleidoscopic facets of the chord itself, or, free to unwind motivic elaborations without waiting for the changes to intervene, extend the improvisation to a length limited only by imaginative capacity. By the time of such Coltrane standards as "My Favorite Things" (first recorded in 1960), "Chasin' the Trane" (1961), "Africa" (1961), and "Afro-Blue" (1963), the rapid and free movement through various pitches and registers left him fairly bursting at what the modal guru George Russell called "the chord barrier."[31] As a result, melody was achieved through polyrhythmic attack, 4/4, 6/8, and 3/4 being utilized as the moment dictated, flexibility not the measure or bar-sign being the guiding rule. Coltrane was discovering that "these implied rhythms give variety"[32] and that emancipation from chords provided vast room for creative expansion. The near-frantic, yet ever-controlled flights through the register (sometimes Trane soared a whole octave at once, as Joshua Redmon once marvelled), from the growling lower to the screeching upper regions (toward which Coltrane's scalar runs, ever-aspiring, seemed always to be reaching), were exultant shouts of this newfound freedom.

In some ways, the contrast of Coleman's and Coltrane's departures from bop encodes a fascinating lesson on styles of black modernism, for where Coleman's innovation was, in its nearly absolute liberty from harmonics, stepping altogether outside even the more radical inherited terms of chordal expression, Coltrane was striving for new room *within* those terms, seeking to press through its forms to some occult root of intonation, following a seemingly asymptotic arc along the linked pathway of chord and tune. Both pioneers were ex-centric, and the enormous effect of Coleman's "spread rhythm" and boundless melodic ingenuity on both contemporaries (including Coltrane) and successors ought not be denigrated or fatuously measured against Trane's on some mythical scale of heroic radicality.[33] More importantly, Coltrane's approach, by contrast with Coleman's, suggests the effort to speak to the historical discourse of jazz improvisation from inside its formations, following through the inner, if as-yet incompletely deciphered, logic latent within its unfolding dialectic. This effort to shift the discourse without being recuperated by it has important consequences for the relation of Coltrane's modernist stance to tradition, a concern to which we shall shortly return in assessing his final pieces, and which portends crucial implications for the poets' embrace of Coltrane as model for their own revolutionary praxis.

No piece better illustrates the principles of citation, displacement, and reinvention that spurred Coltrane's mode of modernist intervention than "My Favorite Things," which proved not only Coltrane's entrée into wider public esteem after its introduction in the fall of 1960 but a template for performative revision throughout his career. Enlarging the modal basis of improvisation gleaned from the Davis years, Coltrane appropriates Richard Rodgers's lilting waltz melody in such a way that wide spaces opened within the showtune for a fresh style of solo and group creation. Working alternately within both the E-minor and E-major figures of Rodgers's theme, Coltrane was able to play off the tones at will by shifting pitch at the scale's end, in effect denying the mode's 'natural' closures, freeing the soloist to pursue phrasing in a variety of patterns. Pianist McKoy Tyner's pedal-point vamps and Steve Davis's or Jimmy Garrison's throbbing bass-line provided a textured regularity that allowed the soloist to move without harmonic constriction, while the familiar three-note clusters and scaleruns of the tune provided opportune touchstones for communication among the musicians. Swirling through scale-patches with aching lyricism, incantational concentration, and confident exuberance (all the while exploiting the mystical twang of the soprano's timbre), Coltrane took the piece through a complex series of sharp melodic and rhythmic cadenzas that constantly turned aside the imminent endings implied in them (on some later recorded versions, moreover, the piece doesn't conventionally 'end,' but is instead taken out by engineering fade). Thus, Coltrane's riffs took on their own multiforms, achieving an extraordinary mesh of intricacy and lucidity, for even the modal norm was often breached if an idea demanded notes from outside its parameters, and subtle shifts in rhythm (frequently in dialogue with Elvin Jones's complementary experiments in polymeter) likewise kept alive difference within the layers of repetition extending from the two basic scales and governing motifs. The traditional solo trajectory from simplicity to complexity, with its investment in 'narrative' ideas of emphasis, augmentation, and recapitulation, gave way to a strategy that could assert, withdraw, or modify intensity at the drop of a chord, so to speak. The solo no longer described a predelineated progressive mold, but was liberated to express any mood or untangle any thought whenever and wherever the player's spirit deemed necessary. Always touching base with but never compelled by the simple melodic statements, the solo could double, or even triple notes in intriguing formations that kept the piece at once hypnotically focused and ever vivid. Repetition was not so much indulged or employed as thematized, declaring only self-satisfaction out of bounds, making surprise the rule, each headlong utterance seeming inevitable once played, but only then.

In a sense, therefore, the piece became a commentary on Hammerstein's lyrics, as well, for by producing an improvisatory mechanism capable of potentially endless and multiply-configured processes of statement, alteration, return, and reelaboration, processes at once tightly organized yet driven by a profusion of spontaneously generated ideas, Coltrane's version of Rodgers's song suggested that unchecked expressive inquiry – the *articulation* of the moment's disposition, desire, and intuition – was the "favorite thing" of Coltrane's New Thang. By subtly unfolding its motifs as a series of nonlinear and multidirectional self-translations, thus suggesting a temporality no longer governed by causal and hierarchical imperatives, Coltrane's version of the tune explicitly compels us to ask how we should measure the authority of 'rendition' as against 'original,' and by way of that question, how construe the relation of interpretation to invention. On its face, appreciative response to the piece has itself been divided between those who see Coltrane as "murdering" (Baraka's term) mainstream fustian and those who hear rather a clever form of adoption, clarification, or perhaps redemption of unexploited potential within the popular.[34] The argument itself illuminates, indeed reflects, the double leap of Coltrane's achievement, its inhabitation of the prior as a ghost of revision and its occupation of new terrain as a harbinger of momentous perception. In Coltrane's method and vision, the instant of deconstruction was already also self-presentational: structural critique was immediately phenomenological inflection. As known melody blurs into riffing discovery, one principle of intelligibility (deployed with a kind of nonchalant élan by Rodgers) becomes vulnerable to its distantiation by another that has mastered and transgressed its terms, and begins to split open under the force of a new kind of representational idiom, revealing a new dispensation wherein meaning is not coined once and recirculated for a requisite number of choruses but slides from turn to turn in an interminable display of *signifyin(g) as possibility*. For what Coltrane sought was not merely a disruption of the governing system but a shaking down to the roots of musical language itself where the possibility of meaning itself might reside. His approach to recontextualizing received material, and the critical argument that flowed around the re/composition that resulted, bespeaks a conflict *within* Coltrane's project between representational and presentational instincts, or perhaps one might better say a dialogue between mediated and incarnational expression that lies at the core of his instinct for self-revision.

For Coltrane, the transformation of meaning always involved a transposition of convention – "I've found you've got to look back at the old things and see them in a new light"[35] – and thus the very system he wished to transform could only be superseded by working through its underlying assumptions to a fresh insight. But the hearty continuities celebrated by adherents of insouciant transmission between 'tradition and individual talent' give way in his work to a procedure more severe than that accountable to a discourse of citation and rearticulation, putting a stress on strategies of appropriation and dissemination, incorporation and reinscription, that productively confuse quotation with erasure, re-turn with effacement. This pressure against the referent makes the 'original' phrases of Rodgers's tune seem to give way to a sound that *precedes* their sprightly but predictable intonation, as if the soprano's improvisations have stripped down to the "object" or Image from which "My Favorite Things" itself arises. It is almost as though Coltrane effects a metaleptic reversal of Rodgers's figures, making himself the 'originary' in the manner of Harold Bloom's Satan transuming Homeric lances and shields;[36] but we would not, on the other hand, ascribe to Coltrane the Miltonic lust for priority, for what he dis-covers in the 'borrowed' material is the metaphoricity of its 'originality,' the latency within it of a field of expressive energy that infinitely multiplies the luminous details of imaginative power. That is, Coltrane's blazing figurations upon Rodgers's base-line suggest not so much a refutation of that simple waltz motive as the release of suppressed, possibly devalorized, utterances trapped within and silently orbiting around it. Interpretation thus serves not as either assassination or acknowledgement of the prior but as an agitative intervention that propels a dazzling movement of substitutions. Like the horn's play upon a vamp's modal foundation, Coltrane's improvisatory translation both reiterates and disperses Rodgers's figures, making room for a conception that then is itself both center and excess.

As exemplified by "My Favorite Things," Coltrane's stance in relation to mainstream expression is one of bricolage, which first recontextualizes and then reactivates elements so that they acquire unexpected implications. While seemingly acknowledging the propriety of received codes within the workings of present conceptions, this critical resituation at the same time unwrites the proprietary assertion of precedence by treating the 'borrowed' material as though it imposes no constraints on new arrangements, flaunting a capacity for performance to meltdown sedimented codes into the flux of current imagination. Through this procedure of collage and montage, "original" material is reassembled and redeployed within a new framework: in particular, melody is not destroyed or abandoned but disseminated into open, echoic networks of refiguration, disappearing and reissuing in eddies of dissolved and recombined patterns severed from any determined order of origin or end. This bears especial emphasis given the conventional view of modal improvisation as non- or even anti-melodic: in fact, through the bricolage techniques of rupture and recapitulation, melody is treated as a departure for invention rather than a pre-resolved mandate of sense to which other expressive movements ultimately pay tribute. It is in this sense that mainstream material may be said to be 're-motivated' within a Coltrane composition such as "My Favorite Things," for it appropriates rather than terminates cited phrases, thus as it were producing their alterity as a new referential ground of his own statement. The core note-clusters of Rodgers's song thus are ever-more heard in quotation marks, reminding us that their 'sense' in its travel from context to context arises in their iterability across the fabric of a terrain now defined by Coltrane's augmentations. Coltrane's renderings interpolate rhythmically and tonally so many distinctive ideas through these super-impositions that repetition can be heard as agitated alternation, but it is the combination of rupturing detachment and meticulous attention to concealed potential that most exactly defines Coltrane's work upon Rodgers's notes.

Coltrane's version of Rodgers's song therefore can be said not to reproduce its sense and sensations but to penetrate and in some sense even to determine them: one hears the tune after Coltrane not with easy familiarity but with that shock of recognition peculiar to an event that is productive in its immediate moment. Like modern black drama in the long gesture of its evolution, a composition such as Trane's "My Favorite Things" disturbs

classical models of mimesis, refusing the secondary status of performance
and complicating normative assumptions of organic development, referentiality, and closure. Through the methexis of its interpretive reinventions,
Coltrane's playing refuses to reflect 'the real,' foregrounding the decisions
by which it seeks instead to reimagine, indeed to change and regenerate,
'the world' as conventionally scored. Performance thus operates in "My
Favorite Things" simultaneously as epistemology and ontology, historio-
graphical analysis and ideological challenge, a means of asking both *where
am I?* and *what is to be done where I am?* It is for this reason that it must be
heard equally as technical achievement and visionary stimulus: as pianist
Cecil Taylor aptly remarked when Coltrane stood at the threshold of independence as a bandleader, "his tone is beautiful because it is functional. In
other words, it is always involved in saying something."[37] In Coltrane's
approach, instrumentality and creativity are inextricable. For any particular note not only occupies a specific place in relation to others played around
it, it contains within itself the potential to operate elsewhere in new ways to
fresh effects. At any given moment, the product of such technique is thus
also only byproduct, for nothing is ever finished, the essence of the process
being the playing itself, not its thematic reiterations.

By thus exploring a tune in order to thematize the plurivocality of its
enunciation, Coltrane signaled that his project was not just that of
producing new meanings but of reopening the question of meaning's
production, all the while turning the musical idioms and systems within
which he operated toward new communicative directions. In this manner,
he refined and radically extended the process of citation and commentary
typical to effective jazz improvisation,[38] injecting it into every level of his
music's macro- and micro-development, making the music a crucible for
exchange between self and other, for the assiduous excavation of otherness within – or *as* – the self. The place of "My Favorite Things" in
Coltrane's repertoire encapsulates the *self*-interrogating momentum of this
focus, for it became over the remaining years of Trane's life a paradoxical 'standard' of transformation, interpreted through increasingly complex
harmonic textures and instrumentations, accommodating an ever-
expanding ensemble of players and styles, stretching the horizon of
improvisational adventure as it grew in its recorded versions from an initial
studio treatment of about fourteen minutes to nearly a full hour of live
performance (and indeed, Elvin Jones recalls with wry fondness having
played "My Favorite Things" under Trane's insistent leadership for nearly
12 hours before a final take was given approval, marvelling that "I was
never bored; each time was a new experience, and the last take was
probably the strongest that we did"[39]). Particularly with the addition of
other reed instruments, the piece's enlarged scope allowed the *interiorized*
call-and-response implicit in Coltrane's soprano licks to be communalized
in the dialogic play between his horn and, say, Pharoah Sanders's tenor
(dynamically displayed in the 1963 Village Vanguard recording) or, if the

other reeds layed out, generalized in increasingly intricate interchanges between saxophone and rhythmic counterparts of bass or drum.

It's at this point, as "My Favorite Things" asserts itself as an emblem of Coltrane's emergence and presence as a modern master, that one begins to see the instinct for self-transformation take residence at the heart of Coltrane's work, for what might have been seen as the perfecting of the era's idioms (first, the hardbop intensification of Bird's improvisational techniques, then, the palimpsestic deepening of Miles's modal textures) was clearly being employed as the starting point for fresh inquiries. In a *Down Beat* interview with Don DeMicheal, conducted the day after DeMicheal heard the Coltrane quintet (with Eric Dolphy on tenor) perform "My Favorite Things" with unprecedented stamina and vigor, Coltrane met the challenge of the "anti-jazz" critics by averring that "It's just recently that I've tried to become even more aware of . . . the life side of music. I feel I'm just beginning again. Which goes back to the group and what we're trying to do."[40] Re/composing was becoming for Coltrane an act of divination through inquiry, a method that we can see at once as utterly objective (since it is the notes themselves that contained values the player dis-covered by pursuing the full range of their inner logic, tirelessly regrouping their elements) and inescapably subjective (since this continual process of destabilization and reconfiguration could only proceed through the most ardent devotion to the task – and Coltrane's obsession with honing his chops through unremitting practice and the intensity of his in-performance concentration were equally legendary, encompassing many tales of playing through extreme pain to the limits of physical endurance – a sense of commitment that in context of group improvisation necessi-tated the utmost of intimacy, tact, and trust). Hence Coltrane's pieces became open to a kind of double hearing already implicit in the compo-sitional dynamic of "My Favorite Things": that of the phrase or line or movement as it redirects elements used otherwise than in his own and others' sources, the phrase *as* reinflected; and that of the same material as it announces itself as a discrete inspiration or event. In the mid-1960s, when Coltrane's music increasingly focuses the spiritual dimension of this stylistic *dédoublement*, each juncture of his development seems at once an end and a beginning, as each ensemble establishes its unique brand of collective articulation. "Every group of individuals assembled has a different feeling – a different swing," he told DeMicheal, answering a typical charge made by those startled at Trane's radical innovations in rhythmic emphasis.

And yet each late Coltrane piece, stamped with the singular authority of his restive, searching personality, can be said to swing always upward, in rising sequences of clustered fragments. The pulsating dynamics of *A Love Supreme* (1964) – to which we shall return in greater depth when exploring Harper's poetic response in "Dear John, Dear Coltrane" – are exemplary of new tactics of vehemently 'sprung rhythm' through which Coltrane's horn could be heard, as Bill Cole well described it, "reaching and always leading to the highest note he could play."[41] What he was reaching for, in gestures that inspired the scatting typographical and metrical innovations of contemporary black poets, was an expanse sufficient to contain unfettered expressiveness, "living space" (to borrow the title of one of Trane's most intrepid late explorations) for forms as yet unknown. The precept that, as he said to Valerie Wilmer, "there are so many things to be considered in making music" was one that he came to feel in the broadest sense.

> The whole question of life itself; *my* life in which there are many things on which I don't think I've reached a final conclusion; there are matters I don't think I've covered completely, and all these things have to be covered before you make your music sound any way. You have to grow to know.
>
> (Valerie Wilmer, "Conversation with Coltrane," 1962, 4)

Covering ground with the "giant steps" of a dauntless colossus, Coltrane's work changed shape so frequently in its final phases that theme and improvisation became nearly indistinguishable. The turbulence of this metamorphosis is felt so profoundly in late Trane partly because bare particles of musical form were made the crucibles of his explosive experimentation. Indeed, in the works of 1963 and after, form – as static or pure structure – feels content – as intensity of statement – straining its contours. Coltrane's music thereby performed the grand, simple gesture of opening the plasticity of form that makes content understandable, persuasive.

This quest for uninhibited musical freedom took several directions. Coltrane experimented with a variety of new instruments – bass clarinet; flute; and soprano saxophone – mastering the latter and thrusting it from relative oblivion (Johnny Hodges and especially Steve Lacy having played some impressive soprano sides, but having had restricted impact on the instrument's standing) to heights of lyric beauty comparable, perhaps, only to those achieved by Coltrane's avowed model, Sidney Bechet (both indebtedness and amplification are beautifully evident in Trane's tribute to his predecessor, "Blues to Bechet"). He worked with a plethora of groupings (especially after the marvelous quartet of Trane, McCoy Tyner [piano], Jimmy Garrison [bass], and Elvin Jones [drums] disbanded), adding some instruments (including those of Africa and the East), doubling others, and consequently creating (along with Sun Ra's Arkestra) the most meaningful large ensemble works since Basie and Ellington. But the major acquisitions of space were made within the realm of the notes themselves. Building from moments quoted from early experiments like "Chasin' the Trane" and "Impressions" (1961), the later works redirect Coltrane's characteristic swing from vertical progression to a pluridirectional unfurling of diverse tempos and tonalities, allowing him to "fit in" all his new visions. Influenced partly by nondiatonic aspects of Indian and African music, Trane moved completely away from both fixed tonality and strict verticality toward panmodal, chromatic articulation. Chords, whether singular or multi-layered, were boldly cut loose from any tonal center of gravity. In the fierce declamations of "Om," for example, motives that might in themselves seem assimilable to a pentatonic scale become dislodged from any certain tonal location as the piece becomes ultimately a virtual cyclone of tonal assertion, moving in and out of the original scale's values. Trane's characteristic overblowing techniques now serve more than as protest against the harmonic prison, expressing a need to pursue ideas beyond all established borders of structure and theme ("damn the rules," he would often say when questioned about transgressions of even his own customary patterns and sounds). As in all the late works, particularly those of the final period initiated by "Ascension" (1965), Coltrane here separates himself from the inner sphere of tones and becomes master of them. There ensues an electrifying vibration back and forth between one motif and another, producing a coruscating surface of shimmering timbre and pitch in which all things are continuously transformed in the tonal flux. In this manner, Coltrane achieved, like Bird and Louis Armstrong before him, the consummate act of generalization, of translating a private, obviously intolerable hurt into a code of public statement.

Too little remarked is the rhythmic emphasis of Coltrane's late explorations, indeed of his entire revolution in jazz improvisation, and, with that, a certain cultural and philosophic implication of his developing vocabulary. Though at times seemingly anti-lyrical, the long arc of his struggle against chordal and then tonal dictation can be seen as an attempt to liberate melody's essential imbrication in syncopated expression, to recenter tempo as the stream of musical consciousness. Among the most significant segments of his work from the *Giant Steps* album on are his duets with drummers, from the reverberative exchanges with Art Taylor's 36-bar double-time invitations on "Countdown" to the chase-and-run duels with Elvin Jones's furious polyaccentual excursions and, finally, to the nearly recondite conversations with Rashied Ali's underappreciated experiments in nonmetered, pitch-oriented percussion. Always fascinated by the intricate textures and inexhaustible vocabularies of African (especially West African) master drummers, Trane came to see the tubs as perhaps the quintessential dialogic voice within his always enlarging landscape of communal interlocutors. Of Ali, whose indifference to symmetrical meters allowed for a thick description of crossrhythms and percussional sonorities that approximates effects achieved by West African drum ensembles, Coltrane declared, "The way he plays allows the soloist maximum freedom. I can really choose just about any direction at just about any time in the confidence that it will be compatibile with what he's doing."[42]

One can grasp the full import of this release into space as marked out by the player's own temporal sensibility in the late session entitled *Interstellar*

Space (1967), an extended suite of six saxophone-drum duets that was among the last recordings Coltrane would make. Each composition is a remarkable realization of that integration of design and spontaneity that Coltrane had sought from the earliest rambles with Monk and Davis. "Keeping time" in distinctive but interlocking ways, the players together build the pieces upon what Lewis Porter suitably terms "musical events"[43] that both proclaim and disperse lines of motivic communication. As complex as Rashied Ali's rhythmic ground becomes, Coltrane never stammers, as tempo itself is delivered from the 'plot' of strictly vertical or diatonic playing and systematic metrical prognosis. Ali's traps, recalling the oral similitudes attained by West African drumming techniques, achieve melodic effects, even as Trane's ax carves out a throbbing pulsation of layered cadences within lines crafted by generously coloristic emanations.

Enriched by abstruse patterns of inverted and rotated phrases, these interwoven pieces gradually become a disquisition on memory and transposition. For just as the evocation of West African percussive tactics in *Interstellar Space* recalls the spiritual, purgative, and political resonance linking the African sacred drum to its diasporic displacement in slave strategies of rhythmic affirmation (ring shouts, handclapping, call-and-response, etc.)[44] – as, I would suggest, do many other Coltrane pieces of the later years, including the exceptional album *Meditations* (1965) on which Jones and Ali shared drumming responsibilities, a twinning that particularly echoes the distribution of rhythmic duties in the African drumming society – so the suite as a whole functions as a "deep memory" of Africanicity within a forcefully reimagined temporality.[45] Closing the final segment, "Saturn," with an affecting recollection of "Afro Blue" that never quite completes that composition's fundamental motive, Coltrane and Ali refigure Trane's hardbop dissonance as a mechanism for both concealing and revealing differing time structures, each phrase's present tense obscuring but not obliterating a mobile periodicity that suffuses the entire album. Each phrase, every 'now' of the dialogue, announces a peculiar facet of the playing consciousness, yet is revealed fully in connection with other instants that likewise seemed singular in their articulation. The present is thereby accorded unusual, and objective, autonomy, yet is suffused with the trace of a more primordial duration, which must be thought of in terms of a different movement of intervals than even modal improvisation afforded. In the most profoundly philosophic spirit of call-and-response, time is thus experienced in reference to its other, space, while the spatiality of the musical event is audible only in the unfolding of sequences that cannot be 'measured' in conventional terms. Through the cogency of their interchange, Coltrane and Ali assert a mode of self-communion that acknowledges its foundation in dialogue with a rhythmic other, continually translating the alterity of the beat, its devious irregularities, into a form of self-identity. Their conversation gradually implies discovery of a language 'before discourse' as such, that is, a language which closes yet also re-marks the fissure of time that, in some sense, is the diasporic self, making music the meeting point of exile and self-presence. Nothing could come closer to that aboriginal, yet always reinterpretable, "vibration" that Coltrane openly sought from the time of "Om."

This expropriation of temporality through tonal innovation and rhythmic speculation suggests that, for all their apparent affinities, Coltrane's revolution in jazz improvisation and contemporary experiments in Euro-American (post)modern music are essentially dissimilar. The music of the white avant-garde, in its revolt from the 'purposeful,' teological art of western culture, courts antitonality in order to expunge traces of intentionality and authorial control, becoming directionless, unkinetic, goalless. Its sytematic use of chance as a technique of composition is designed to create sounds without syntactical-grammatical relationships, sounds as individual, discrete, objective sensations. Thus, narrative is not diverted into a transformational 'rhetoric of temporality,' as with Coltrane's use of progressively varied recollections and disruptions of harmonic schemes, but is depleted by repetitive and random sounds that discard all functional and causal frameworks. Memory, likewise, is not renovated but jettisoned, as 'absolute sound' seeks to efface all signs of priority even as the listener is refused any role of interpretive or anticipatory assessment. The movement's foremost composer, John Cage, signals this post-phenomenological (yet also metaphysical) urge with his injunction to "let sounds be themselves rather than vehicles for man-made theories or expressions of human sentiments".[46] Hence the Euro-American modernists seek tones without specific implications, not to create more space for the mind's struggle toward redefinition, but to drain the will from the act and arena of interpretive intervention and intentional creation. In their work, as Ihab Hassan (the Gabriel of modern Euro-American orphism) points out, "forms define themselves by their absence, their felt omissions."[47] For them, the orphic mutilation is self-inflicted.

The music of Coltrane and his "free jazz" accomplices, as Frank Kofsky has observed, is *not* atonal.[48] They find themselves exhilarated not exhausted in the face of formal possibility, seeking to widen not confound consciousness, acknowledging contingency but not cultivating accident in the eruptive flux of performance. But the distinction between them and their Euro-American contemporaries runs deeper than the mechanics or even philosophy of form. For, to the African-American modernist in search of the black nation's potential, what could be more forbidding than the denial of human will? And what could be more troublesome than an assertion of pure, impersonal presence wholly *outside* the horizon of historical struggle? The musical challenge of African-American modernism cannot brush aside intentionality and duration as centripetal pressures of a communal enterprise. The sometimes gnarled, troubled syntax of its formulations betoken the vitality of concern and *caritas*, informed by enveloping cultural conditions and expressed within the evolving decorum of collective improvisation. As Harper saw, Trane's searching energy was always put in service of the subject's renewal, always striving for greater "manifestations" (Trane's word) of excellence. "Spirit and will . . . these are the things that I like to have up [on the bandstand]," Coltrane declared,[49] guarding against the sentimentality of surrendered agency (and its latent nostalgia for a plenitude *before* the "vibrations" of human presence) as a means of exiting the often frustrating labyrinth of representation. If, as Alice Coltrane, speaking for us as well as Trane, rightly observed, "he never stopped surprising himself,"[50] the violations of expectation characteristic of his inventive pursuits were carried out in the interests of a quickened and diversified, not anesthetized, imagination capable of fathoming the vicissitudes of shared experience.

If, in his capacity for surprise and his disciplined grappling with the erosions and potentialities of time, Coltrane probed the scope and sacramental ramification of a 'singular' sound, he also divined the plenum of silence. Pauses and silences are often the climaxes of his late works, the still centers of the prophetic storm, the nuclei of tension around which the whole movement is structured. The more one listens, the more those silences seem to be among the first causes of the overall effect. This is, again, partly a technical consideration. From pieces as early as the Monk/hard-bop works, Coltrane was leaving large rests within lines, delicately spacing bursts of triplets, in the effort to achieve rhythmic variation within given harmonic limits and to sculpt thematic plateaus that served as staging grounds for further expeditions.[51] When his playing became liberated from the centripetal force of insistent tonality, the distension of intervals became the product of more complex decisions, increased elasticity facilitating seemingly unbounded elongations within the ultimately temporal musical order. The authority of the silences are a direct consequence of the late pieces' density of texture: each note and each rest is part of an integrated design of utmost economy and vigor. The uncanny effect, to paraphrase Stewart's projection of a fundamental musical (re)generation, is that of a time that is no longer the time of life extended through linear consequence, but of a present so amplified as to enable unhurried, meditative reconsideration of narrative cause and consequence.

But this dialectic of sound and silence bespeaks more than just a technical refabrication of music's spatio-temporal categories. Coltrane's is the silence of orphic utterance momentarily stilled, of the voice that temporarily ceases singing in the face of mystery, only to embrace a new strain that will henceforward echo this silence, but *in song*. This silence presupposes the possibility of song and the relevance of expression to the life of the individual soul and the community. Coltrane, like his African forebears, was delving for the primal Sound that lends music its "magical" quality,[52] that is, its capacity to contain already that which must be expressed within it through time and which, once expressed, expands infinitely its contours of possibility. The very possibility of such discovery, he intuited, begins in the silence of the quest, what Kenneth Burke termed the hunter's "silence of purposiveness."[53] Thus, Coltrane felt, are power and knowledge conjoined with the enveloping significance of expressive desire: "Your true power . . . is to be part of all, and the only way you can be part of all is to understand it. And when there's something you don't understand, you have to go humbly to it. . . . You absorb. But you have to be quiet, you have to be still to do all this."[54]

Again, let us pause to distinguish this watchful silence of Coltrane from that of the Euro-American innovators. John Cage, once more, is the avant-garde's most eloquent and influential spokesman: "What we re-quire is silence. . . . Inherent silence is equivalent to denial of the will".[55] This is the silence of discontinuity and indeterminacy, the dumbness of an enervated will alienated from its aimless universe. Its project (if the word serves us here at all) is that of continuous self-negation that erodes (through the drone of an unmarked repetition) communicative process. By soliciting a mute surrender of memory and expressive intent, such silence betokens a gradual and inevitable dissolution of human possibility itself. It is, simply, silence that indicates retreat from the quest into the indistinguishable submissions of utopian ahistoricism and the death drive.

But if the hushed moments of Coltrane's late pieces indicate a hidden abundance, they still seem to issue out of the struggle and terror preludial to ecstatic fullness. In "Out of This World" (*Live in Seattle*, 1965), for example, one senses the occasional need to draw back completely from the horns' aching crescendo lest the vision be destroyed at the border of a new mode. In such passages Trane accelerates, sometimes lyrically, sometimes painfully, toward an intimation of that which lies beyond eloquence. And, in works such as "Evolution," "Cosmos" and "Out of This World" (all on *Live in Seattle*, 1965) and "Expression" (on the album of that name, 1967), one feels a refusal to transgress the bounds of known (even though recently discovered) discourse, and the furious quest is taken up again on the other side of the pause. There, silence is deceptive repose, like the stillness as one enters the eye of the hurricane.

Yet in other works – e.g., "Welcome," "Vigil," "Kulu Se Mama" (all on *Kulu Se Mama*, 1965), and "Ogunde" (*Expression*, 1967) – Coltrane relentlessly pursues the numinous, converging on the ineffable root of expression. On "Ogunde," the polyrhythms and mixed tempos gradually condense ballad-like lines into a single moment. Trane's fading tenor, so lyrical and playful and yet reverent until the final epiphany, plays cat-and-mouse with Alice Coltrane's piano, sculpting a deep and wide space in the line. As the notes grow fainter, in wider intervals, the silence aspires to an impossible concreteness and luminosity, as though resurrection could emanate from the quiet of the void. The piece ignores the expectations of closure aroused by the underlying ballad structure. Instead, as horn gives way to piano, which in turn strikes, in stillness, a tentative note in unresolved tonality, we are left with a chilling, thrilling whisper of the Black Orphic dream – the quest that leads, endlessly, to a music without notes, to a *tabula rasa* of "never know and scream."

Ultimately, the silences of Coltrane's last works ask a haunting question, imaged starkly by Baraka's "Willie Best": must not the head of the vates be severed so that he may continue to sing? Must not the self be destroyed before a new being can be born? The exquisitely poised moments of these pieces are the loci at which such reciprocal necessities of eradication and reconstitution coalesce. They suggest an intuition of being's hesitancy to reveal itself through utterance, so that silence must be also a means toward its appearance. Only through silence can the temporality of sound be grasped: as such, it figures, too, the necessity of negation, of death, to hardwon affirmations. Silence, we might say, incarnates the essential into the temporal, inscribing the 'no-longer' and the 'not-yet' into the persistent continuities of desire. Appropriately enough, this bracing recognition emerges with starkest clarity on what was perhaps Coltrane's final recorded composition, "To Be" (*Expression*, 1967), in which he plays the flute (that most essential of elegiac instruments) handed down to him from the hands of his dear, departed comrade, Eric Dolphy. While Alice Coltrane delineates a line hollowed by absent thirds, supplying around those gapped chords a rich texture of ornamented statements, Coltrane's flute engages in an anguished dialogue with Pharoah Sanders's piccolo in which "expression" (the album's bluntly alluring title) comprises a metrically untranscribable weave of lyrical susurration and haunting quietude. In the sinuous, distrait polyphony of the winds' counterpoint, stillness becomes indistinguisable from the murmur of presence. Itself an apparent stasis, silence generates the mobility that renders "To Be" something other than the static incantation of Euro-American postmodern atonalism. As implied by the urgent copula of its title, "To Be" works to transform the musical vocabulary into a materialization of the player's breath, an exhalation of intention into performative being. But like all breath, even that which achieved the extraordinarily extended trajectories of Coltrane's outpourings, it necessarily resides in the 'interval' between what was and what is yet to be. "To Be," that is, tells us that to be is to suffer what Paul de Man calls the predicament of temporality: this is what the will-to-blow *affirms*, which is why in the late pieces one cannot distinguish the passionate need for silence from the irrepressible imperative to expression. For it is not despite, before, or after performance that Coltrane seeks the "Om" of essential resonance, but through and in performance itself: the notes are the resolution they cannot quite achieve, the summons to being they can endorse only through commitment to mortal change. More than anything, they prepare the ground for Baraka's stunning appraisal of the Coltrane-led movement: "New Black Music is this: Find the self, then kill it."[56]

In his fierce reflection of Coltrane's dialectical askesis, Baraka, Trane's most spirited critic, was trying to express what so many new black artists sensed in the presence of a music more powerful, more anguished and celebratory than any in recent memory. But there is a source to this power, despite the blinding sparks of Coltrane's titanic assault on tradition (which, admittedly, are difficult not to foreground or even to stress somewhat tendentiously). What he actually did was to obey an often obscured but profound impulse to revolt against established conventions in order to rediscover convention on a deeper level, to question, as it were, what was played without saying in order to rehabilitate fundamental principles as a condition of change. It is this double imperative of reflexive revisitation that makes his art both an historicized and progressive discourse on the very nature of his medium, particularly on the vexed concepts of origi- nality and closure that makes the trope of jazz achievement such a complex temptation to modern black poets. An indefatigable student of jazz history, particularly the tradition of his instrument – "I'm very interested in the past, and even though there's a lot I don't know about it, I intend to go back and find out. I'm back to Sidney Bechet already"[57] – Coltrane under- stood that the jazz idiom was not a neutral discourse which was the private property of a current generation; it is a continuum saturated with codes and practices of articulation that remain available in each instant of fingering, each breathy utterance: "I listened to John Gilmore [saxophonist with the Sun Ra band] kind of closely before I made 'Chasin' the Trane' . . . But then I don't know who he was listening to."[58] This awareness of taking up the horn within a network of traces invisibly (but audibly) linking past and present suggests how historical consciousness within black modernism properly necessitates, rather than contradicts, a commitment to innovative process rather than to (the illusion of) finished forms. In turn, the more discerning of his peers heard the stirrings of a loquacious cultural tradition suffusing Trane's horn: "When you listen to John," fellow tenor trailblazer Archie Shepp declared, "he's talking about Negro life from early New Orleans to right now."[59]

In particular, Coltrane recalled, for himself and for his generation, the old cry and shout of the *blues*. This impulse can be felt throughout his career, and lies at the root of his experiments with chants (*A Love Supreme*; "Om") and other vocalic interpolations (as in the mapping of the speech rhythms of a eulogizing Martin Luther King onto the registral placements of "Alabama," Trane's searing elegy for four black girls killed in the KKK bombing of a Birmingham church). In his construction of melody, he always maintained a hint of the blues' folk scales, and the rough textures of his sound leapfrog bop's harmonically enriched blues lines, taking the listener back through his rhythm-and-blues apprenticeship to the edgy, sultry timbres of earlier blues vocalists. When, in the later works, the tonal centers were mixed and shifted in rapid succession, the blues did not dis- appear. On the contrary, they were asserted more energetically, more *fundamentally* in the sheer outpouring of shout, screech, wail and cry, in the uninhibited pitch and movement within the register. Listen to

"Transition" (*Transition*, 1965), to "The Father and the Son and the Holy Ghost" (*Meditations*, 1965), to "Manifestation" (*Cosmic Music*, 1966). There are long patches which are virtual encyclopedias of oral tradition, with grunt, scream, joke, and soothing speech all intended as confessions and calls to the people.

One feels the blues as naked vocality especially in recordings of Coltrane's *live* performances, which, as Cole has claimed, are the genuine hallmark of a feral immediacy no record ever quite captures.[60] Coltrane always sought to pull his audience into the "force-field" of his long, explosive solos. His ideal, like that of the dramatists, was one of collective creation, and he enjoined his listener to engage the music as a participatory activity. "When you know that somebody is maybe moved the same way you are," he once said, "its just like having another member in the group."[61] Again, the contrast with the avant-garde of Euro-American postmodern music is revealing. To the latter, demands for communication and involvement are not only irrelevant but disruptive of the fundamental rage for disorder, for an anti-teleologic recovery of chance and a zero degree of expressive intention. It seeks the dismemberment and defers any challenge to aleatoric incident by craft. For Coltrane, as for his fellow black artists, the community's involvement in a *ritual of restitution* is paramount. It is they who must ultimately – and continuously – re-member the total being of a visionary Black Orpheus.

Specifically, Coltrane's achievement of destructuring and reformulating jazz's very form became a model for the poets' effort to reinvent creative language where the pernicious and deadening grammar of received idioms reigned. The tirelessness of Coltrane's experimentalism, with its eventual price of premature death, became, in turn, a touchstone of the poets' embattled ideal of renovating a latent, collective spirit despite and even because of the perils of annihilation (both personal and cultural). Through nuanced response to the complex rhythms of his artistic and experiential call, the poets variously reimagine "Trane" as a flexible vehicle of their modernist irruption, the perpetual revolution of desire under the mobile sign of blackness. The result, as reflected in the Coltrane Poem, has been a crucial development in the intention and achievement of modern African-American poetics.

4 Renovating blackness

Remembrance and revolution in the Coltrane Poem

I

John Coltranes dead & some
of you
have yet to hear him play
How long how long has that Trane been gone
                              Jayne Cortez, "How Long
                              Has Trane Been Gone"[1]

To the African-American elegist, the death of Coltrane is not experienced merely as a withdrawal of Coltrane from the sphere of the living; it is an event that threatens what is left behind. It is an enforced rupture in the fabric of collective being, a ruin in the time of growing communal consciousness – and, hence, it is both metonymic instance of an alienated Afro-America and synecdochic type of the modern black poet's crisis of expression. The stilling of Coltrane's horn is taken as a representative assault on black voice as a shared instrument of perception and inspiration, its capacity for memory and its readiness for efficacious action. Coltrane's death registers a disturbance at the core of modern black culture's claim to performative power sufficient to exceed a history of containment, to transgress the systematic codes that have sought to reduce African-American culture to a vacant sign of futility. Does black expression, the poets wonder in the face of Coltrane's loss, meet its vanishing point exactly where it seemed (to cite Spellman's "Did John's Music Kill Him?") most "brilliant"?

The elegist's confrontation with deprivation and death, the 'others' of life, becomes inevitably the poet's meditation on chaos and silence, the 'others' of language. How, each asks, can the paralyzing pain of loss be transformed into collective progress and productive speech? For the elegist, the task is to find celebratory praise where only lamentation seems possible; for the poet, the quest is for song that dispels the suspensions of silence, for an incandescence of language that reclaims banished creativity and restores the eclipsed world. In turn, in a manner that shadows and sharpens (by virtue of its concentrated focus) the choreopoetic assertion of *for colored girls*, remembrance demands revision in order not simply to commemorate but to re-call the "not yet" of Cortez's moving Trane: the propelling recovery of an authentic self depends upon a reclamation of time, language, and finally, of Coltrane "himself." The dead must be transformed into an instrument of the living imagination whereby the poet and his people can assess their mission in a new way. The resultant metamorphosis of Coltrane into "Trane," of figure into figuration, tells a story central to the evolution of modern African-American poetics as it reshapes the values of culture, history, and poetry itself. The death of Coltrane ultimately becomes in modern black poetry an event not of communal recession but of cultural redefinition. But the reconstructive visionary begins as elegist, and for both the beginning is the grammatically (i.e., experientially) closed but colloquially (i.e., ontologically) moot question: "Where you done gone, brother?" (Madhubuti, "Don't Cry, Scream").

The question, appropriately evocative of the blues and its topoi of restless interrogation, of travel and travail, is orphic and elegiac in thematic, structural, and rhetorical ways. In orphism and elegy, negation is the turning-point in a narrative of desire, an antithetical juncture of disfiguration that must be confronted "face to face" for renewal to take place. As defined by Walter Strauss, the triadic "moments" of orphic experience – an original capacity for transfixing and transfiguring performance; descent (*katabasis*) and redoubled loss in the nether realm of death; and return to song despite dismemberment (*sparagmos*) – comprise a dual quest: one of *gnosis*, the pursuit of concealed knowledge essential to salvation; and one of *askesis*, a revisionary movement of self-discovery by way of self-purgation.[2] So, too, elegy encounters discontinuity in the dark, enclosed form of mirrored bereavements, the entombed other and the confounded self. The elegiac poet, like the Theocritus of the first and second *Idylls*, or his greatest successor, the Milton of "Lycidas," seeks to resolve emotional crisis by poetic transformation, progressing past painful silence in the face of acknowledged irrevocability to the consoling, restorative, and reordering power of what Milton cunningly termed a "melodious tear." The deaths of Orpheus and of the poet's piping comrade alike portend the death of song; for it is out of the hideous, dark, subterranean roar, out of the harsh, crude pain that knows no words, that the dismembered vates and grieving poet must fashion their melodies. The passionate questioning each deprivation engenders bears on the immediate project of lamentation itself, both hollowing and refurbishing expressive possibility. The Coltrane Poem is about that process, that orphic-elegiac struggle to articulate the inchoate pulse of agony, (re)forming it in a gesture that is not merely mournful but defiant.

Wide-ranging in its thematic interests – typically touching upon love, landscape, prophecy, politics, as well as death and poetry – elegy is personal and procedural, concerned with feeling (as Horace's dictum that elegy is the medium of *querimonia* or *voti sententia*, complaint or gratitude, suggests)[3] and thought. In assessing the relation of the Coltrane Poem to its entwined subjects of music and death one cannot agree with Helen Vendler, or, rather, with the Keats of "Ode to a Nightingale" of whom she keenly speaks in asserting that "questions of ideational content and of social and moral value . . . become very nearly unintelligible when posed with respect to instrumental music."[4] As Baraka was to say, reflecting on Coltrane several years after his death, "we heard [in his music] our own search and travails, our own reaching for new definition."[5] But if modern African-American poets thus championed Coltrane in repudiating Romantic distinctions between musical sensation and political thought, down what paths did they travel in riffing the ever-changing chart of his example? If the writers, as Baraka here intimates, recognize in the very form of Coltrane's art the genesis of modernist poetic discourse from contemporary musical innovation, they thereby acknowledge, too, the presence within representation of that which spurs the very claim to signify-with-a-difference that will be the hallmark of their own gestures of radical will. As such, their poetic responses to Coltrane will be often arranged around what we might call a "revolutionary moment," that is, a critical caesura facilitating transposition from one condition to another, a pause between the past and future that we might judge equally "the present" and "death." The difficulties of apprehending that suspended instant – often, indeed, experienced narratively in the poems as a moment of suspense – and somehow hurtling voice through catastrophe to futurity lend the Coltrane Poem its air of crisis and exhilaration, its rhythmic momentum and its constant obligation of choice. To seize, with Coltrane, that revolutionary moment is to wrestle from within the event of death what Giorgio Agamben describes as the "*negative* foundation of the human word," the word in its ethical bearing that grasps, through affirmation of language as such in the flash of agonal awareness, the logical necessity of free, articulate being.[6] The Coltrane Poem thus images its imaginative process as the double act of re-membering the shattered Trane and then responding to the mobilizations enabled by its own act of re-collection. Thus locating belief within desire and generating the poetic event from language's disappearance, the Coltrane Poem becomes a supreme fiction capable of converting negativity to being, wresting power from the encounter with self-consciousness demanded by the evident death of blackness emblemized in Trane's untimely departure.

For some of the poets, this assertion will be taken as powerful enough to resolve the underlying antinomies of exilic experience, leading to a hypostatic union of thought, language, reality, and expression through the (re)convened medium of Coltrane's authority. For others, this final merging of truth and presence remains a stimulus to continuous *poeisis* within the temporal destiny of black experience, an ongoing struggle to align history and language, materiality and consciousness, that becomes, eventually, a task too great for the poet or poem to bear alone. Each position inflects distinctive views of textuality, speech, body, meaning, and understanding, and each therefore defines a distinct role for the reader in determining its significance. One death, one common perception of revolutionary provocation, but divergent principles of intelligibility and response, making different kinds of poetic "sense" of the event along the mobius strip formed of incarnational passion and representational commitment. On such relational distinctions do the genre's cultural semiotics and visionary politics ultimately hinge.

So the Coltrane Poem – like the music of the figure whom it eulogizes, and like the modern African-American poetics of which it is a complex microcosm – traverses the regenerative itinerary of loss, outrage, and restitution through a theoretically infinite series of beginnings and forestallings of final resolution. This doubleness of momentary arrest is essential to the Coltrane Poem's orphic-elegiac procedure, which engages loss by revaluing the meaning of Coltrane, the meaning of death, the meaning of blackness, and the meaning of meaning (in its specific cultural determinations, as well as its general categorical configuration as that which enables interpretation and communication). Such engagement is a burden the poets accept in identification with the very spirit they seek, echoing modern black drama in tracing the performative arc from mimesis to methexis. As Coltrane himself said, there can be no retreat from the sometimes tortuous exertions of such expressive trials: "You just keep going all the way, as deep as you can. You keep trying to get right down to the crux"[7] – such, too, is the scream and whisper of Trane's poetic heirs: *they* are themselves the severed head of the *corpus civitatis* that re-members and sings on.

II

> Train is blowing all the colors in OM
> saying
> MOM HOME WOMB TOMB . . .
>
> Walter K. Dancy, "Jazz Coltrane Sings"[8]

Born alike in the didactic and ritual formulations of Greek scepticism,[9] elegy and orphism share the enabling motive of *peripeteia* (reversal) the aim of which is ultimately *anagnorisis*: revelation, discovery, manifestation. But disclosure courts again closure, and so recuperative impulse can quickly become reflexive hesitation, idealism threatening either to harden into monumentalism or to dissolve into nihilism. At one verge of this recognition within the Coltrane Poem genre we find those works that seek to pre-empt indecision by distilling the tempestuous energies swirling about the name of Trane into a final form, a self-sufficient shelter of meanings immune from death's shattering surprise. In Dancy's clever formulation, the chromatic totality ("all") of a prolonged "Om" spreads itself equally through the lethal t*o*mb and generative w*o*mb, eliding their difference, collapsing beginning and ending into a foundational circle of eternal return (to M*o*m, to h*o*me). Origin and destination are one, thus allowing movement – the dislocation of death as much as the musician's "blowing" articulations – without unpredictable or disruptive consequence.

The jazz Coltrane sings in Dancy's poem implies a closed economy of performance that benefits but does not alter or activate its audience:

> like he's paying dues for us all
> when he sings
>
> A LOVE SUPREME
> a love supreme
> a love supreme
>
> a love supreme
> (Walter K. Dancy, "Jazz Coltrane Sings")

Conscience, eloquence, commitment all suffuse the musician's exquisite devotion to the assemblage whose unity subtly authenticates the love bestowed upon it (note again "all," which floats through "Jazz Coltrane Sings" like a talisman of assumed collectivity). With a similarly preinstructed receptivity, Jayne Cortez's "How Long Has Trane Been Gone" organizes "Trane" into an even more rigorous design of propositional force, building from his example an impressive edifice of nationalist imperatives.* "Always/John Coltrane," the hero appears as arch signifier or Image of communal meanings rendered insecure only by a hypothetical forgetfulness that the poet dispels with preacherly admonishment:

> Tell me about the good things
> you clappin & laughin
> Will you remember
> or will you forget
> Forget about the good things
> like Blues & Jazz being black
> Yeah black music
> all about you.
>
> (Jayne Cortez, "How Long
> Has Trane Been Gone")

Under the blended sign of African-American music and blackness, all accident is gathered into essence, all experience is affirmed by intuition of a generalized 'goodness' that can be altered only by disregard. Cortez uses the discourse of analogy ("like Blues and Jazz . . .") only as a bridge

---

* See Appendix A (pp. 314–16) for full text.

to a comprehensive language of ontology ("all about you"), so that to be *like* the blacknesss stirred by black music is to *be part of it*. This enfolding of any particular predication into the embracing "being" of blackness is accomplished by steady patterns of metrically regularized repetition (ingeniously rephrasing Leroy Carr's classic "How Long Blues"), which work to close the distance between past and present: through the speaker's rhythmic emphasis of witness and encouragement, the initial interrogative tone gives way to an accomplished affirmation: "Yeah." The pluralizing effects of potential negations are thus never given particular, sensuous presence, but instead are gathered with spectacular immediacy into the poem's order of endorsements and syntheses.

To hear Coltrane, Cortez's poem "tells" us, is at once to discern and participate in a mimesis of an absolute condition which moves not so much in the text as through it. In effect, the poem establishes itself as a veil behind which the attentive reader can perceive an unchanging heroic essence, and it is therefore the reader, not the text, that is charged with the need of illumination by the expressive fullness of Coltrane's integrity:

> And how many Tranes will go
> before you understand your life
> John Coltrane who had the whole of
> life wrapped up in B flat.
>
> (Jayne Cortez, "How Long
> Has Trane Been Gone")

"Understanding" here subscribes to a hermeneutics of immanence and singularity: it arrives precisely in the cancellation of the signifier's infinite departures, its frustratingly endless polysemy, through attention to the already completed signification of Trane's all-containing note. Salvation comes not from continuous, provisional interpretation but from a "whole" embrace of the Proper Name that doubles "you," even as Coltrane's playing of B-ing redoubles the "life" it itself always simply is. With such identification, the displacements of diasporic suffering, and the dialectic of negativity it enforces, can melt into the undivided purity of an achieved revolutionary nation:

> John palpitating love notes
> in a lost-found Nation
> within a Nation . . .
> black people whose walls
> should be a hall
> A Black Hall of Fame
> so our children will know
> will know & be proud
> Proud to say I'm from Parker City, Coltrane City . . .

Thus, "How Long Has Trane Been Gone" arrives at its penultimate declaration, where the enclosed space of lineal self-presence is realized in a burst of memorial patronymics. The crisis of unheard sacral wisdom or undelineated communal meaning is dispelled by a circumscription of energy constituting a self-affirming circuit of cognition and re-cognition. In such a space, inscription is no longer fractured by the temporal disorder of deferral, but guarantees both the proximity of expression and meaning, and, through that transcendental identity, the connection of generation to generation. But the fragility of this ideality of Coltrane-as-Name, this conse-cration of the univocal nation through a reified sign, erupts in the poem's next, and concluding, stage, where the decision to forego a dialectical encounter with Coltrane's death in favor of a diacritical sublation of crisis into monumentalization pays its cost:

> How long will it take you to understand
> that Trane been gone
> riding in a portable radio
> next to your son lonely
> Who walks walks walks into nothing
> No City No State No Home No Nothing
> How long how long have black people been gone.

If – and here you should imagine the poem performed in Cortez's famously spellbinding manner[10] – the poet's bluesy out-chorus can be heard as a final sermonic exhortation upbraiding the inattentive congregants and encouraging them to responsible and rebellious praxis under the aegis of a Coltrane now himself "wrapped up" by the capricious boombox ("There was a time/when KGFL played all black music," begins the *ubi sunt* of an earlier strophe), in terms of poetic process these lines bring "How Long Has Trane Been Gone" to a starkly melancholic closure. Here the nega-tion mostly repressed in the earlier strophes' elevation of Coltrane as iconic realization discharges a surfeit of pain. Even, one feels, the dialectical potential of negativity has itself been expunged ("No Nothing") as the enriched stasis hitherto projected collapses into an abyss of shock, error, and loss.

A lesson of "How Long Has Trane Been Gone" might therefore be that the self-actualization and collective development seemingly modeled by Coltrane's music cannot be salvaged after his death if his 'truth' is treated as tautology, or, put in positive terms, unless his B-ing is imagined in continual movement rather than 'flattened' into uniform substance. In a sense, Cortez's poem exchanges the vulnerable complexity of Coltrane's materiality, his precarious habitation of a breathing body, for the certain-ties of apotheosis, only to find him walking beside the bodies left behind, like a spectral avatar of Whitmanian ruin. Declaring Coltrane the "true image of black masculinity," the poem seeks to fix meaning as an assured presence, claiming authority and power against "those dead white people" who African-Americans must efface in order to possess the City of Blackness. Such an image is not itself the site of racial struggle, but enables it from the outside as weapon and aim, succor and motivation ("John Coltrane/A name that should ring/words of comfort ... /words of welcome"). Nor is its "masculinity" particularly engendered, certainly not sexually mobilized or particularized; rather, it operates as a meta-physical instrument of natonalist instruction and construction. With no less fervor of collectivist racial identification, David Henderson's "Elvin Jones Gretsch Freak (*Coltrane at the Half-Note*)" sets forth in implicit contrast to Cortez's pithy memorialization precisely by foregrounding the 'jazzed' body as medium of restless expressivity.* In Henderson's poem, subjectivity emerges at the intersection of text and sex, of semantic and somatic outpourings linking Trane's explosive horn with Jones's pulsating tubs. Yet it is not the wholeness of physique or the certainty of phallic mastery that eroticizes jazz utterance, but its imbrication with the contradictions of African-American urban culture:

> The Half Note
> westside truck exhaust and spent breath
> of Holland Tunnel   exhaust   soot darkness jazz
> speeding cars   noisy/   noiseless
> speeding gretsch   tremulous gretsch ...
> four men love on a stage
> the loud orgy
> gretsch trembles and titters
>
> > > gretsch is love
> > > gretsch is love
> > > gretsch is love.
> > (David Henderson, "Elvin Jones Gretsch
> > Freak (*Coltrane at the Half-Note*"))[11]

Not unlike the opening segment of *for colored girls*, with its scattered "half-notes" evoking the terror of a violently repressed childhood, Henderson's poem opens a "tremulous" gap between chaos and purpose, abjection and affection, displacment and place. Thematically, imagistically, and visually, "Elvin Jones Gretsch Freak (*Coltrane at the Half-Note*)" announces itself as a work about breaking with and within contexts, about subversive transportation of meanings that can seem like antimeanings ("noisy/noiseless") to those outside its own terms of engagement, about a rhythm of inhalation and dissemination in which expenditure becomes indistinguishable from fulfillment (aptly enough, the poem was written in one breathless take, and remains, splendidly, unrevised).[12] Like Shange, Henderson begins

---

* See Appendix A (pp. 317–20) for full text.

in the realm of negation, but with greater inclination to embrace abjection as the means of creation and productive affiliation. For Henderson, the central ethos of Coltrane and Jones's orgiastic outburst is an uncompromising commitment to violent appropriation (which converts negation from mere form to defining force), to the very precondition of being as a ferociously accelerated metamorphic drive.

As the poem proceeds through an underground scene that smacks mimetically of waste, exploitation, and division ("clashing metal mad") but sings affectively of fecundity and guileful command ("tin frantic road of roaring/ gretsch/roar"), this translational dynamic stokes Henderson's version of the genre's "train" motif with mercantile, musical, and psychic significance, converting the "gretsch" trademark inscribed on Jones's drums into an instrument of economic rebellion, aesthetic insistence, and sexual assertion. The musicians' orgasmic effusions are so intense as to convert "la petite mort" of sexual "exhaust"ion into the *jouissance* of what Barthes calls "death liberated from dying."[13] The blinding speed of their expressive interaction blurs the boundaries separating pleasure and danger, convulsion and clarity, horn and drum, and even phallic authority and feminine receptivity, as we hear "Coltrane sane/cock" and "the feminine mystique/cymbals tinny clitoris resounding" each other in an ecastatic "chase" of cross-fertilization:

> lips snares flanked/   encircling
> thumping foot drum peter rabbit the fuck   take
> this   and take   that
> elvin behind the uterus of his sticks
> the mad embryo
> panting sweat-dripping embryo . . .

Here is no Oedipal economy in which patriarchal mastery is secured by yielding the self's most urgent impulses to the chaste(ning) law of symbolic exchange; nor is subjectivity founded in its transmutation of riotous energy to clarifying form. The incipient self is thrashed out to vigorous excess, refusing everything given, rending its way through every containment, founding itself in a self-confounding discharge of iconoclastic propulsions. Indeed, Trane's and Elvin's generative bodily surges revel in a kind of glorious ob-scenity, imposing themselves on the *mise-en-scène* of American urban oppression with an antithetical exuberance that flouts even its own formal achievements. Their anarchic spasms of self-assertion suggest that unanchored semiosis subsumes or overflows any structural value. So to understand what Jason Pikler aptly terms the "repercussive rhythm"[14] of the "gretsch love" arising from a highly-charged, libidinal exchange between "thumping" drummer and "screaming" hornman, the poet must, in the poem's incarnational logic, become en-"snared" in its "cymbalic" transformations, participating in the activity of its production rather than simply marking its observations at a distance:

Coltrane/Jones
Riffing   face to face
instrument charge
                stools to kneecap
many faceted rhythm structure   to   tomahawk
gretsch rocks n rolls   gretsch rattles
fuck gretsch/
                    we know so well strident drums
                    children singing death songs   /war . . .
                    sometimes late in silent din of night
                    I hear
                    bagpipes/   death march.

The duet's erotic fury screams not only the ecstasy of release but the outrage of history, where dark, elemental passion becomes an inhuman rather than liberating destruction. It becomes the poem's challenge, then, to work beyond this debilitating stridency to a dissonance that paradoxically redeems an unbridled negativity:

and the man elvin behind the baptismal tubs
that leap like cannons   to the slashing sound of knives
black elvin knows so well . . .
the kind of knives elvin talks about
downtown by the water
and uptown
near the park.

In closing thus, "Elvin Jones Gretsch Freak *(Coltrane at the Half-Note)*" seeks to retain its defining energy as a continual movement of repudiation, making its "truth" that of an antinomian extravagance that remains conscious, patent, and productive. The fall into metrical and stanzaic regularity, however, hints at a compromise formation that insinuates a subtle tension between "tremulous" and "slashing" intonations. The "loud orgy" has dwindled into "talk" about violent resistance; what Elvin *does* slides with an enervating precision into what he *knows*. Henderson's poem, rooting itself in a fecund negativity, has allowed Coltrane and Jones to rise again and again in sudden "leaps" of corporeal presence, establishing the ceaseless "deaths" of carnal expression as an effective basis of becoming. And yet, I would suggest, because this current of eruptive modality assumes always the fertility and exhilaration of negation, the poem cannot engage its substratum of death dialectically. Monumentalization has been duly shattered by the turbulence of uncompromised transgression, but the 'repercussive' savagery of history cannot, in turn, be effectively contested.

Sonia Sanchez's "a/coltrane/poem" converges on a similar crossroads of signifying energy and referential blockage through a radically different compositional strategy.* Rather than chasing the libidinal charge of Coltranesque performance to the impasse of historical resistance at the levels of anamnesis and exposition, Sanchez pursues a concept of form and meaning as indistinguishable activities of poetic articulation, championing the *reader's voice*, rather than the performing hero's body, as sensual medium of "Trane's" enduring implications. Indeed, the project of "a/coltrane/poem" is to unravel itself as textual structure, subsuming its representational tasks into continuously refashioned norms of invention and enunciation. At the poem's beginning, the speaker faintly hints at the process of 'writing aloud' by which the poem will soon "burst" forth from its inscriptive containment:

> my favorite things
>   is u/blowen
>   yo/favorite/things.
> stretchen the mind
>   till it bursts past the con/fines of
> solo/en melodies.
>   (Sonia Sanchez, "a/coltrane/poem")[15]

Though at first the speaker seems stationed in a merely receptive position, "My Favorite Things" is summoned not to repeat for its audience an accomplished revisionary performance (as we saw, for example, in Dancy's punning citation of Coltrane titles as instruments of preformed meaning) but to "blow" open a performative space for the reader to enter as jamming participant. By attending properly to Coltrane's "My Favorite Things," particularly its capacity to reshape inherited or heard melodies, the listener (like Trane's ensemble companions) is subtly enjoined to "stretch" her own consciousness as crucible of self-surpassing improvisation. But such an invitation can only be fully grasped once a more precise elegiac process is undertaken:

>   are u sleepen   (to be
>   are u sleepen   sung
>   brotha john   softly)
>   brotha john
>   where u have gone to.
>   no mornin bells
>   are ringin here. only the quiet
> aftermath of assassinations.

The inception of the performative activity through which Coltrane's loss is ultimately confronted (marked here by the gently falling stage direction,

* See Appendix A (pp. 321–23) for full text.

"to be sung softly") is accompanied thematically by a tension between sensations of expansion and dormancy, expectant release and the pathos of power cut short. The rising peal of *mornin* bells are replaced by the stunned uncertainty of a *mourning* that cannot yet complete itself in compensatory anger or action. "Frère Jacques" is, like Rodgers's showtune in Coltrane's rendition, appropriated for a vernacular exploration of graver matters, Sanchez's inflection of childish fare as lamentative carol for "brotha john" perhaps likewise recuperating a substratum of terror and resurgent potentiality buried beneath the popular ditty's sedimented sentimentality. But it does not readily attain this excavated vigorous immediacy, at first more declaring than enacting the incendiary rebellion by which elegiac quietude is to be transmuted to revolutionary passion:

> but i saw yo/murder/
> the massacre
> of all blk/musicians. planned
> in advance.
> yrs befo u blew away our passsst
> and showed us our futureeeeee
> screech   screech   screeeeech   screeech
> a/love/supreme, alovesupreme a lovesupreme.
> A LOVE SUPREME
> scrEEEccCHHHHH screeeeEEECHHHHHHHHH
> SCREEEEEEEECCCHHHHHHHHHHHHHHHHH
> a lovesupremelovesupremelovesupreme   for   our blk
> people.

Assuming like Dancy and Cortez the presence of a totalized, if incipiently betrayed, nation exalted in the martyred prophecy of black musical genius, "a/coltrane/poem" links thematic transgression with textual transformation, but as yet locates no agency for that conjunction's perpetuation outside the agile recollection of Coltrane's own performance. On the one hand, this enumeration of "murderous" scenarios that make of Coltrane the exemplar of seditious fury ("BRING IN THE WITE/MOTHA/ fuckas," the poem proceeds, "ALL THE . . . MAIN/LINE/ASS/RISTO-CRATS . . ./STOMPem. THEN/LIGHT A FIRE TO/THEY pilgrim asses . . ./till no mo . . ./raunchy sounds of MURDER . . ./come from they/throats") can be heard as a lapse into that instrumentalization of Coltrane's rebellious spirit that Henderson evaded only by pressing from such functionalist iconography an irreducible fluxional iconoclasm; on the other hand, we may be witnessing the (re)construction of Coltrane as the site of that conjunction of idea and passion necessary to the poem's own successful actualization as innovative *event*. That is, "a/coltrane/poem" evidently proceeds as if concerned that it not be a self-contained or self-fulfilled object, seeking instead to become a medium requiring acts of interpretive commitment – reading-as-nationalist-translation – that prepare for its consummation in acts of incarnational engagement – reading-as-revolutionary-transfiguration. Only after this transformation in the reading process takes place can the poem develop from transcription of Coltrane's energetic touchstones to appropriation of them in the speaker and reader's own situation. As the poem's collaborative shapers, speaker and reader now fill the musician's inherited vehicles with the energized meaning of the present, that space that Trane stretched out for us between the blown-away "passsst" and the momentarily glimpsed "futureeeeee." To enter this dilated space of possibility, we must move "in between the notes," as Sanchez has described the process by which she conceived the poem after witnessing a particularly moving performance of "My Favorite Things" by Alice and John Coltrane near the end of his life.[16] It is at this point that we can re-turn to the initiating trope of "my favorite things," a renewed activity of response to Coltrane's call that remains effectively hermeneutic, but in a pointedly performative manner:

```
(to be      rise up blk/people
sung                  de dum da da da da
slowly      move straight in yo/blackness
to tune               da dum da da da da
of my       step over the wite/ness
favorite    that is yessss terrrrrr day
things.)    weeeeeeee are tooooooooday.
(f          da dum
a           da da da (stomp, stomp) da da da
s           da dum
t           da da da (stomp, stomp) da da da
e           da dum
r)          da da da (stomp) da da da dum (stomp) . . .
```

As with Coltrane's improvisations, "a/coltrane/poem" accomplishes its shift of tenor by searching out an alliance of expression and structure that pressures the very medium of utterance into new configurations of ener-gized form. The invitation to metrical analysis borne by the mimesis of "My Favorite Things" must be set aside, for its methexis of essential Tranean practice overrides particular prosodic effects. One gets the sense here of poetic method being devised as perception affords and need demands, scatting beyond range of its enabling technology (here, the black-and-white fixtures of print) in cahoots with a specific – if elastic and iterable – instant of historical possibility. An authentic reading of the poem, then, can never be rehearsed (though my students have often wished they'd so prepared!), since the act of shaping sound *in and for the moment* is the funda-mental command of the poem, an imperative that is as much political ("move *straight* . . . weeeeeeee *are* . . .") as aesthetic. (Indeed, Sanchez has remarked that her first public reading of the poem, a famous impromptu presentation at Brown University in the Winter of 1971, was filled with surprise even for her, transforming her performance style beyond expectation, and forever.)[17] "Toooooooday" invades the textual border, shaping itself by the moving contours of each voice that riffs the poem's chart with its own inflections, 'stomping' not just the blues but the specific antagonist of a divided, overwhelmed "wite/ness." Each syllable signifies *as* enactment, the meaning of which inheres in the voice's 'movement to blackness.'

In effect, the poem has ceded elements of its narrative authority to readerly performance, maintaining ideological perspective while granting to another voice the responsibility and satisfaction of rhythmic embodiment. Sanchez has gradually destabilized poetic space in order to render it susceptible to pluralized redefinition, which opens the poem to the kind of temporalized risk that Dancy's and Cortez's works are hesitant to entertain. The pulse of modern black language, vernacular in tone and revolutionary in attitude, "rises" from within thematic presentation, becomes the poem *as utterance*. Discursive meaning and phonic density are, at least in a passage like that just quoted above, inextricable, as acoustic style becomes the very means of conceptual realization. In a subliminal way, then, point of view and cultural literacy become central concerns of the poem, since the agile, informed exchange of creative roles determines its progress. What the verse communicates to us is precisely itself as a shared medium of Coltrane's improvisational agency: in this sense, Sanchez has written, indeed, "a/ coltrane/poem." But once this turn to readerly engagement has been accomplished, the Manichaean content of nationalist uprising asserts itself with an anxiety that bestills the associated rhythms of interpretive inflection.

> yeh. john coltrane.
> my favorite things is u.
>   shown us life/
>   liven.
> a love supreme.
>   for each
>   other
>   if we just
> lisssssSSSTEN.

Explicitly recalling the opening lines' evocation of Trane as model, but substituting a proleptically expository "shown" for an imminently apocalyptic "blowen," the poem shifts gears in closing, its transgressive style unwinding into evenly paced, authorially directed stylization. Signifying, that boisterous activity of constantly reworked and musicalized idea, yields to significance, with its saliencies and directives. Narratorial surveillance overtakes the rumble of enunciation that had hitherto released and dispersed the quiescent potentiality of "brotha john." And most notably, the reader becomes again the consumer, not the producer, of "a/coltrane/poem," as the coda's echo of the opening's solicitous stillness calms the churning of syntax and sonority in the interests of a reclarified semantic order. Nevertheless, the poem's bold improvisational irruption has held out the promise of radical transvaluation, not only in the reader's habits of aesthetic response but in the sphere of social practice. As if in response to Sanchez's implicit invitation, still other Coltrane Poems seek to extend that promise, thus sustaining the revolutionary possibilities of Sanchez's vision.

In the concluding sections of this chapter, I will argue that A. B. Spellman's "Did John's Music Kill Him?" and Michael Harper's "Dear John, Dear Coltrane" best realize these prospects of challenge and change wrought by the experiments of Sanchez, Henderson, *et al.* But as a bridge to examination of those poems' achievements, I'd like briefly to glance at perhaps the most celebrated of Coltrane Poems, Haki Madhubuti's (Don L. Lee's) "Don't Cry, Scream," and especially to the reworking of one of its central motifs in its closural strophe.* Combining a Cortez-like exaltation of Coltrane as nation-building cipher with a performative (anti)textuality that rivals Sanchez for its ebullient translation of Coltrane's horn into (quasi)verbal effects, "Don't Cry, Scream" begins like Henderson's "Elvin Jones Gretsch Freak *(Coltrane at the Half-Note)*" in focusing Trane as a physical force of mobility, resistance, and rebirth:

> into the sixties
> a trane
> came . . .
> riding the rails
> of novation.
> > blowing
> > a-melodics
> > screeching,
> > screaming,
> > blasting –
> . . . music that ached,
> murdered our minds (we reborn)
> born into a neoteric aberration.
> & suddenly
> you envy the
> BLIND man –
> you know that he will
> hear what you'll never
> see.

> > > (Haki Madhubuti [Don Lee]
> > > "Don't Cry, Scream")[18]

* See Appendix A (pp. 324–27) for full text.

Above all, it seems, Trane incarnates a messianic potentiality, arriving upon the complacent scene of mid-century (Afro)America with a clarion call to modernity as refractory perception. In terms that reverberate with the portentous vehemence of archaic authority, his passion of unyielding innovation, suprahuman in its insistence, "blasts" the assumed wholeness of the speaker, who bears witness to Trane's razing onslaught. Thus assaulted and transfixed, we are told that one comes to "envy the/BLIND man": why? How does his "hear" transcend any possibilities of our "see"? And how does the Blind man's vantage affect the speaker's testamental project and his need for rebirth under the sway of Trane's "murderous" presence?

The poem doesn't seek answers to such questions by a systematic investigation of relations among musician, speaker, and Blind man; rather, it proceeds to chart "soultrane's trip" through a malignant white power structure and a snivelling black middle-class with vigorous, if programmatic, censure of all deemed inimical to an emergent blackness. Along the way, the blues, and its supposed tendency to "cry" piteously rather than "scream" rebelliously, are jettisoned ("we ain't blue, we are black./(all the blues did was/make me cry)"), and Coltrane is defended by the speaker against the uncomprehending black middle-class ("negro cow-sissies/who dig tchaikovsky &/the beatles . . ."). But in the poem's concluding lines, such tendentious binary formulations are set aside for a more challenging assessment of Coltrane's effect as scourging legislator of a "neoteric" dispensation. Most strikingly, the Blind man reappears and the speaker restages their encounter at the defining juncture of sight and sound:

> naw brother
> i didn't cry. . . .
> & that BLIND man
> i don't envy him anymore
> i can see his hear
> & hear his heard through my pores.
> I can see my me. it was truth you gave,
> like a daily shit
> it had to come.
>   can you scream – brother?   very
>   can you scream – brother?   soft
>
> i hear you.
> i hear you.
>
> and the Gods will too.

Though named only in the poem's frame, Madhubuti's Blind man suffuses the intervening passages as a figure for the surprising convergences of polemic and process in "Don't Cry, Scream": for its embrace of avant-gardist assertion over any particular espousal or position, and especially any memory or revery (the Blind man must commit himself to advancing without knowing with certainty where he is or looking back whence he came); for its guerilla movement toward discovery preceding actual perception (the Blind man must risk stepping awry in order to proceed); for its elevation of intuited authenticities over rational certainties (the Blind man must recognize feelingly before he can cognize rationally); for the necessity and covert superiority of processural vocalization, despite its repression by 'high culture' (to the Blind Man, the word is heard and understood in the aurality of time rather than through the inscriptions of space); and for its occult reclamation of Natural power by way of natural transgression (the Blind man, defined by sensorial deprivation, is traditionally vouschafed compensatory capacities that pose for us unsettling questions about the 'nature' of judgment, knowledge, and will). The Blind man hovers over the speaker's Trane-tracing journey through a landscape of craven betrayers of soul, huddled in their "split-level minds" like prisoners of Plato's cave, incapable of looking directly into the dazzling "truth" of Coltrane's blackness. As the speaker's initial envy retrospectively makes clear to us, the Blind man prefigures a need to reorient the will toward this radiant darkness, to free the voice from those visual enticements of racial self-hatred that make one forget the essence of being: "blonds had more fun –/with snagga-toothed niggers . . ./& the blond's dye came out . . ./anti-self in one lesson." Like Christ denouncing the scribes and the Pharisees ("Ye fools and blind . . . cleanse first that which is within the cup and platter, that the outside of them may be clean also" – Matthew 23:17, 26), the speaker angrily reproaches such seduction by external appearance in order to prepare for a moment of purgation and conversion that will restore the singular vocation of collective "selfhood." Only thus can the speaker join his audience in a resonant affirmation of "a people playing/the sound of me."

By virtue of his singular condition, the Blind man frames the poem as 'witness' to this sacrificial reformation, allowing the poem to become itself a testamental extension of the "soultrane"'s legacy of disruptive alteration. He makes accessible, in a paradoxically shrouded manner (that is, in a way at first invisible to the speaker), the connections among corporeal vulnerability, sensorial honesty, healing, and vision which the speaker ultimately can "hear through my pores." Introduced cheek by jowel alongside Trane "screeching/screaming/blasting," the Blind man stands as a figure of voluntary submission to mutation, even mutilation, in the interests of freedom and national mission (one is reminded here of Baraka's revery, in "Coltrane Live at Birdland," of a Samson-like Coltrane "destroying" the American urban "temple . . . with just a few notes from his horn," or of Jerry Ward's image, in his splendidly fierce poem "Jazz to Jackson to John," of "sheets of sound . . ./the aftermath of a fierce night . . ./something like a blind leviathan/squeezing through solid rock/marking chaos in the water"). In his mysterious resistance to the processes of desacrilization

and self-cancellation by which elements of black culture have lost themselves in contemporary American society, the Blind man bears within him
the apocalyptic potential of the tribe, its capacity to endure cataclysm
while remaining faithful to a "truth" that is always awaiting its unveiling,
needing only the readiness of the people to look upon themselves steadily
and unveiled. Mediated by the Blind man, or, more precisely, by the
speaker's gradual identification with the Blind man – a figurative *katabasis*
to the condition of a testamentary darkness, achieved by razing all false
idols of compromised blackness in America – "Don't Cry, Scream" turns
elegiac compensation to revolutionary commitment, naturalizing the
process through which the "shit" of everyday diasporic existence is turned
to a synesthetic capacity for radical perception (see–hear) and expression
(scream–soft). It is, finally, this mysterious but arduous process of election,
behind which can be felt the driving rhythms of "trane ... riding the
rails/of novation," that lifts the sometimes merely local aspersions of
Madhubuti's verse to the level of orphic transformation, as the poem
reaches a moment where its voice is not merely assumed but is re-generated.

The poem's *katabasis* is thus, too, an "Ascension" (as the speaker declares,
citing that 1965 Coltrane marvel of collective "neoteric aberration"), and in
this again we are reminded of Plato's prisoners' liberating ascent to blinding
intelligibility. But if, as Cornel West has reminded us, European culture has,
following Plato's foundational example, forged a semantic network bonding
the truth of *idea* to the authority of *sight*,[19] Madhubuti's insistence on blindness as site of enlightenment suggests a refusal of western mythos at the very
moment of its appropriative recollection. "Don't Cry, Scream" thus implies
a certain force or movement of black imagination that is not available to the
realm of what philosophy has termed the "visible" according to the light of
"Reason": the "truth" borne into the light of day. It is toward the night,
shadow, or darkness of another logic of experience and desire that the
Coltrane Poem turns in realizing the principles of election, discovery, and
transformation, principles that have been variously limned in the works we
have been tracing from Dancy to Madhubuti. The need to separate the self
from itself and to rejoin divided identities in renewed patterns of call-and-
response in the night of the Black Orphic ordeal – that is what motivates the
works by Spellman and Harper, to which we now turn. For they incorporate
at the very origins of their unfolding the principle to which we have now
arrived: that the "blindness" of Coltrane's suffering, fury, and insight is
already our "blindness" to "see" him, a blindness that can only be both
assuaged and, more deeply, realized in an act of methexic identification.

III

Listen ...
To his song
From the throat of future time,

Listen
To John.

Sharon Bourke, "Sopranosound,
Memory of John"[20]

Let us listen now to Spellman's "Did John's Music Kill Him?," which I
quote in full:

in the morning part
of evening he would stand
before his crowd. the voice
would call his name &
redlight fell around him.
jimmy'd bow a quarter hour
till Mccoy fed block chords
to his stroke. elvin's thunder
roll & eric's scream. then john.

then john. *little old lady*
had a nasty mouth. *summertime*
when the war is. *africa* ululating
a line bunched up like itself
into knots paints beauty black.

trane's horn had words in it
i know when i sleep sober & dream
those dreams i duck in the world
of sun & shadow. yet even in the day john
& a little grass put them on me clear
as tomorrow in a glass enclosure.

kill me john my life eats
life. the thing that beats out of
me happens in a vat enclosed
& fermenting & wanting to explode
like your song.

> so beat john's death words down
> on me in the darker part
> of evening. the black light issued
> from him in the pit he made
> around us. worms came clear
> to me where i thought i had been
> brilliant. o john death will
> not contain you death
> will not contain you
>
> (A. B. Spellman, "Did John's
> Music Kill Him?")[21]

From its title's opening question to its concluding prophecy of transcendence, "Did John's Music Kill Him?" displaces loss by a dialectic of death, a dialectic that transmutes the apparent finality of extinction into the creative deliverance of a perpetual dying. As in pastoral elegy, the lamenting poet so closely identifies with the dead musician that he becomes a reflection or "shadow" of the departed: "kill me john . . ." The poet and Coltrane are alike restricted; the musician's strife-tormented "ululation" is an image of the poet's own constrained expression, the poem itself. This complex identification with the dead, a fixation which becomes as problematic as it seems beneficial, will lead to the poet's own nocturnal descent and dismemberment ("so beat john's death words down/on me in the darker part/of evening"). But before the consequences of such doubled division are apparent, the opening of the poem attempts to envision a shared moment of fullness, imagining musician, ensemble, and community convened by the promise of Coltrane's "song," a ceremony of invocation now rendered conditional by the hero's imminent vanishing:

> in the morning part
> of evening he would stand
> before his crowd. . . .
> jimmy'd bow a quarter hour
> till Mccoy fed block chords
> to his stroke. elvin's thunder
> roll & eric's scream. then john.
>
> then john. . . .

The poem begins by returning to a time before Coltrane's disappearance, a time carefully imbued with historical particularity, assembled name by name, gesture by gesture, in the manner of the collective improvisation it evokes. And yet, as the many caesuras suggest, in building this precisely textured communal milieu the poem anticipates the hero's entrance with as much apprehension (perhaps, indeed, half-acknowledged foreknowledge) as attentive expectation. The off-stage figure becomes more distant, it seems, as the *déjà vu* of the setting becomes more populous, resonant, and precise. Within this scene-painting, the "calling" forth of Coltrane initiates the poem's pattern of beginning *again*, evoking as it does a kind of supplicatory restitution of the figure without whom performance is all mere prelude. But, despite these hesitations and a curious uncertainty of tense, the nourishment of the collective's call does at last appear to bring forth the longed-for being: "then john."

"then john": between the declaration concluding the first paragraph and the reiteration opening the second falls the shadow of the hero's absence. In that break between stanzas one and two, beginning has collapsed into silence, continuity has threatened to become closure: poet and reader alike face (through the tension of repetition and silence) what Leslie Brisman, in an illuminating reading of revisionism in Miltonic poetics, calls "the relationship of the poetic depiction of choice to the arrest of the present."[22] "Then," which seems at first to be affirmative annunciation signifying existence that we might have feared past (what Brisman terms a "temporal pointer"), now appears to be prelude to the catastrophic discontinuity of loss, and the gap between verse paragraphs places us on the threshold of a void: What happened to john? Can I locate and re-present his absent voice? Is his end an impediment to the progression of my own beginning?

The repetition of the phrase "then john" indicates the first, and indeed the defining, crisis of "Did John's Music Kill Him?" What value might we assign it? On the one hand, it may be a kind of stammer, a disembodiment of voice for both poet and musician expressing not merely the latter's extinction but the former's paralysis or ambivalence in the face of bereavement. As a reminder of the preceding silence, it confirms that rupture in the fabric of expectation and enactment, de-composing Coltrane and replacing him with a traumatic cut into the assumption of continuity and development that sustains our common view of "life." On the other hand, it might indicate the poet's capacity to begin once more despite the sudden shock of dislocation; the poet cauterizes the wound of john's denial by resituating the opening scene, moving it forward to the playing of familiarly funky sound. Thus, the stutter of repetition becomes instead the sly triumph of poetic grace; desolation is by revision made deferral. Such a positive reading of the repetition is encouraged by the music's own evolution, from the jocular and sassy "Little Old Lady" through the revisionary appropriations of "summertime" to the massive profundity of "Africa" which, in its self-interpreting essence, gathers around the reimaged performance a fully saturated blackness ("bunched up *like itself* . . . paints beauty black").

In a sense, then, the repetition of "then john" is what constructs the gap between strophes one and two (one can't, after all, know a pause to be other than permanent silence until it's over, cannot hear it as suspension until the abyss of its stillness has been crossed into the motion of resumed sound). This echoic structure thus constitutes the indeterminate space of john's absence in a peculiarly temporal way, articulating its historicity as a moment of sacrifice in which the double-edged uncertainty of exilic being resides. The silence of this space is a medium of desire, a call for responsive speech that marks simultaneously the concealment and revelation of presence after the yawning "middle passage" of tragic displacement. The reverberative summoning of "john," overtly made present *as* a temporal possibility ("then"), achieves appearance by rending the pure, blank space of nonpresence, thus articulating a *will-to-expressivity* that precedes articulation as such. Likewise, that space – a kind of visual wound in the poem's body that nevertheless makes evident that body's form – constitutes acknowledgement of john's representational status, his dependence on an Other who literally makes him possible by engaging him in the culturally sanctioned dialogue of listening and answering. But rather than suggesting Trane's entrapment in alien constructs or institutions, this enfolding of otherness and identity prepares for the musician's becoming a polyvalent, transdiscursive cultural agent, an expressive political force capable of changing those who enter with him into the crucible of self-challenging exchange.

This drama of hesitancy and echoic arrival establishes "john" as both performative consciousness and rhetorical effect. Indeed, the drama of transition enacted in the space of this stanzaic caesura suggests the need for speaker and reader now to probe the *relation* between consciousness and structure, identity and context, a connection that is itself played out in the speaker/reader's evolving relation to "john." For what we have witnessed is the production of "john" precisely as a *figure*, such that the projective impetus of his identity is bound to the reciprocal capacities of self and other to speak to and even for each other. In rhetorical terms, the poem composes "john" through an act of prosopopoeia, the ascription of voice to the absent or departed, but is also itself composed by *his* prosopopoeic gesture of return, without which "Did John's Music Kill Him?" quite literally cannot proceed and without which we (speaker/reader) cannot sustain our own proximity to his continuing productivity.

Spellman captures here (and soon puts to use in the poem's evolution) a cardinal philosophic dimension of Coltrane's improvisational method, which (as we discussed in the previous chapter) was itself striking for its strategic use of spacing within solo lines and, moreover, for what we might call the "then john" pattern of preparation and accession that often introduced those solos (e.g., in the weave between band and horn that opens "Africa," or, most dramatically, in the piercing moment of "Alabama" when Trane suddenly arrests the line, turns to direct a change of tempo in the band, then resumes the line in one of the most haunting, melancholic strains he was ever to pursue). After the reappearance of Trane in the repetition of "then john," his expression seems more powerfully immediate, more certainly a function of the exertions of his voice, than it might have been had Coltrane been simply conjured at the gitgo. In this respect, improvisation becomes a kind of inspiration, a sustained burst of breath that exceeds any determinate plan or expectation. That is, where john at first seems to be lagging, once present he seems to be ahead, guiding us toward the elusive absolute present by creating beyond the determinate moment. The manner of his emergence tells us that the instant of performance is a function of presence of mind, so that no external, atemporal concept of Coltrane's music can account for the fact of his playing within the poem. To perform is to take residence in a conditional state, where self and other, mind and experience, might yet be reconciled beyond the divided condition that hollows the present into an uncertain suspension, a silence ready to "explode" into song. It is within this acceptance of an irreducibly temporal existence that the utopic aspirations of an effulgent futurity ("as tomorrow in a glass enclosure") can ripen or "ferment." As a Scene of Instruction, the "then john" episode thus encodes the necessity of understanding as a temporal process, one that takes place not in the instant of pure perception (cf. Cortez's "whole of/life wrapped up in B flat") but through expectant awareness of what is lacking in the present: upon this *anticipatory* alertness are Trane's improvisatory power, and ultimately, the poem's revolutionary potentiality equally founded.

The second strophe thus asserts that what might have been a terminal rupture is but a stage of development, wresting through the acoustic power of echo the possibility that seeming loss can be transformed to unenvisioned gain. The shift in emphasis from visual to aural traces of the scene of performance is one dimension of this pursuit of a more authentic manifestation of Coltrane's essence. Another is the poet's acknowledged implication in the dynamics of immanence, a descent which, prefigured in the gap between the first two strophes, is accomplished through recognition of the hero's actual past-ness: "trane's horn had words in it/i know . . ." With this attachment to the fate and force of the hero's expression, the poem begins yet again, while the substitution of "trane's horn" for "john" begins the process of renewal by redefinition. Such displacement is only literally reductive, for the articulate horn is revealed as a kind of synecdoche of the musician's capacity for self-realization. Through its mechanism, the poet attains a freedom from the constraints of time and space which so bedeviled existence in the opening strophes. The resultant dream-vision, reversing classical elegy's priority of illumination to darkness (with a witty troping of nostalgic pastoralism by noctural reefer), answers the prior stanza's howl of discovered blackness with an easeful prospect of unoccluded futurity, the transparency of the "glass enclosure" suggesting an ultimate intelligibility of darkness which will later be named "black light."

At this point, the poem achieves a kind of stillness and composure. It seems itself to have become a crystalline sepulcher, a final form which sequesters an elusive, almost expended identity. But simile betrays the element of hypothesis ("*as* tomorrow . . ."), a post-lapsarian distance between desire and fulfillment. The poet has, in fact, struck a bargain with privation, dispossessing himself of Coltrane's transformative energy for the Clay-like "safety" of an unengaged seclusion. The dialectic of loss and recovery has been frozen by a gesture of self-consolation, and the poem's arrival at the period closure upon the thematic achievement of protective en-closure suggests a deadening monumentalizing of Coltrane which the poem's own attainment of "clear" structural containment presages. The poet and his subject, then, are equally constricted by the "knots" of completed identity. Physical demise has been redressed only by the tyranny of delimitation, while the sharpened sense of the moment conferred by the refulgence of Trane's synesthetic cry has threatened to be arrested by a false surmise of transcendence.

Thus, the poet tears himself free again, this time not merely miming but actually invoking the ruptures of discontinuity in the service of a paradoxically lethal continuity.

> kill me john my life eats
> life. the thing that beats out of
> me happens in a vat enclosed
> & fermenting & wanting to explode
> like your song . . .

The complacent assurances of delimited vision give way now to the harsher "clarity" of self-effacement: "Find the Self, then Kill it." Freeing himself from the impossible, if "beautiful," need to "paint" the hero's absent form, to reincarnate the literal body of his performance by the soporific lucidity of ekphrasis, the poet finds self-negation becomes a self-abnegation at once violent and fertile, self-consuming and self-engendering. The identification with musician is transformed to a liberatory, self-dispersing participation in music, just as the poem itself is about to dissolve structure into the "explosive" conversions of structuration.

Having entered at the ambiguous moment of past performance ("the morning part/of evening," recalling Sanchez's wry play on the "mourning" of incipient darkness) and having proceeded through a continuum of uncertain repetitions and reformulated certainties, the poet finally engages the spectral temporality of critical struggle ("the *darker* part/of evening"). The poet's consequent revision of being – for his subject, his people, and himself – requires experience, not just knowledge, of the self-endangering process of descent, fragmentation, and imagined release. For these dark voyagers (more wailers than whalers, undertaking ululating re-quests for meaningful presence) the 'self' remains occluded and unspirited until they have plunged into an ambiguously Ellisonian-Barakan underbelly of being. The poet, then, descends with Coltrane to the "pit" of deathly negation, seeking to deliver the classically oxymoronic "issue" of dark-light for both self and community:

> . . . black light issued
> from him in the pit he made
> around us. worms came clear
> to me where i thought i had been
> brilliant. . . .

The poet journeys through the underworld, submitting his own "brilliance" to the corrosive challenge of the worms, thereby restoring the brilliant image of john, no longer enclosed either by death or poetic artifice. The poet's speculative adventure leads toward a furious act of dynamic emancipation, yet one held in suspension by the ambiguous syntax of constrained desire and the submerged transumption of words by worms:

o john death will
not contain you death
will not contain you

Thus, the poem at once acknowledges the threat to sacramental liberation and attempts to marshall its energies to renew the opening stanza's
image of resourceful, improvisational vitality. On the one hand, death rises
up against will, taking position at the endline like an ever-swelling, impe-
rious blister upon the pleading tongue of the elegist. Seen thus, the poem
becomes the record of an iterative, increasingly compressed battle with an
antagonist whose presence is being denied (thematically, conceptually, and
psychologically) but who – in words worming into view with an insistence
that challenges the authority of any "you" – settles intractably into the
most prominent spaces of the putatively transcendental event.

On the other hand, the poem can be read as restablishing *life*, life as a
vigorous engagement and elimination of death (note the insistent enjambment and lack of closure in the last lines). *Life is the defiant, effervescent gesture
of death dying.* Concomitantly, "john" is not so much a musician as an
activity that quickens collective voice (despite the threat of discontinuous
silence), regenerative efflorescence (despite the eclipse of natural sustenance), and deliverance (despite the decomposing violence of an enclosure
suggestive of imprisonment and burial). Song – musical *or* poetic – must
be both discharge and product of this unconfining process; and the resumption of song in the repetitive conclusion is both formal and performative
evidence of catharsis. The ceremony it invokes, like that of the first strophe
which it echoes and fulfills, is a refinement of change, a revaluation of
deformation as the prelude to reformation. It thus creates, like the ceremonial *methexis* of modern black drama, a reflexively revisionary form, and,
like the spirit-dance of Shange's recomposed 'spook sonata,' it is efficacious
because it is an enriched *repetition* of the earlier truncated performance:
the "crowd" is reassembled with the 'named' hero; a given order of words,
expressions, and values is valid once again.

Coming after a radical reformulation of the import of self-annihilation,
this repetition does not convey the duplicitous stammering of the earlier
recitation of "then john." Incantational and intentional, it rather opens
the poem to unconditional stages of performance, the endlines providing
pointed visual reminder that "death" and not the poet is now enclosed by
the endless desires ("will") of a confidently apostrophized agency ("you").
Moreover, it facilitates the poet's surrendering of the desire to internalize
the musician's fate. Distance between self and other is abolished not by
the arresting seductions of literal identification, but by a purposive effacement of self in the clarification of "trane" as the very act of relinquishing
circumscribed identities – an effacement, we might add, that is (ironically)
mirrored by the conclusion's approach-avoidance of classical elegy's modes
of ordering, mediating, or otherwise mitigating the outrage of mortal

demise. On this view, we see that, for Spellman, passion and *poeisis* are woven into a single process, the displacements that transfigure Coltrane (from dead musician to music that kills) simultaneously turning the poet's tradition-shadowing plangency and self-regarding solace into phatic and subversive festivity.

The elegy therefore works through a series of subtle poetic modulations that together graph the relation between musician and poet. The poem is rife with temporal and visual (or spatial) oxymorons – the thematic center of which is the nocturnal radiance or revelatory/oracular "black light" – that suggest both the difficulty and potentiality of this relation. This linguistic tension is akin to the syncretism of words and song and to the release of silence into sound accomplished by the poet's submission to the essence of "trane's horn." But the momentary impression that Trane's word-song is past ("trane's horn *had* words in it") is, like the space before the repetition linking strophes one and two, an insinuated threat of expresssive discontinuity posed by the latent possibility of missing, or forgetting, the hero altogether. Thus, re-presentation of Coltrane might be viewed as recovery of an absent *name*. Or alternatively: as the disclosure of a *process* of naming which never finds absloute embodiment in a determinate shape.

We might think of these as, respectively, the Barakan and Ellisonian perspectives on performed blackness as developed in the dis/figurations of the Coltrane Poem. In the first reading, "john" becomes the Proper Name which, while authorizing the act of poetic recovery, stands beyond the strictly poetic domain; it is the singular and un-"contained" word assuring the musician (and the poet who mirrors him) a possible reappropriation of refocused being. Thus, too, Coltrane becomes the longed-for absent center, the recovered ground to collective history and revolutionary progress beyond the bounds of this realm's transactions. His death is thereby experienced as a kind of primordial violence, a splitting from original wholeness which the opening stanza images in its unfragmented state. The poem's task is therefore to be seen as a working through and against its own materiality in order to re-embody the salvific spiritual totality which obtained prior to the hero's particular performances and "words": here, we infer Clay's revolutionary aspiration.

The second reading would remind us that this desire for the unifying effect of a logos beyond temporal discourse is truly a *sign* of the will-to-expression, a necessary fiction of achieved sacralization which the paratactic repetitions of the poem's ending render indeterminate – propitiously so. The opening scene is thus the first in a series of reconstructions of Coltrane-as-performance; his being is seen from the beginning as nothing more nor less than the very possibility of performance, always inscribed into the cultural space which it itself also creates by playing "then," as "called" upon. This performance would be understood to have the power not only to refuse being characterized as belated but to "ferment" the nostalgia for a lost origin which such a characterization implies. On this view, Coltrane both engenders and then corrects the poet's desire to fix "him" as either a concrete body or ultimate ideal, suggesting that the dark vanishings of "trane" do not pre-exist the poem and its audience, but are, rather, the ongoing effects of such desire to wail: here, we verge on the Ellisonian critique and embrace of nonoriginary being.

It is perhaps the salient feature of "Did John's Music Kill Him?" that it enacts in this manner the tension, or, better, the dialogue of black modernism's double-voiced ideal. The uneasy movement from strophe to strophe in the poem represents the resultant torque of Barakan and Ellisonian visions, which might be further emblemized as a pursuit of vocal continuity in the face of ontological rupture seen from the alternative vantages of release from or recommitment to exilic struggle. And the salient unifying element throughout the poem's confrontation with these possibilities is nothing other than "john," the onomastic node of the hero's elusive, temporalized, and collectively improvised essence.

IV

> There is never any end. . . . There are always new sounds to imagine, new feelings to get at. And always, there is the need to keep purifying these feelings and sounds so that we can really see what we've discovered . . . So that we can see more clearly what we are. . . . But to do that at each stage, we have to keep on cleaning the mirror.
>
> John Coltrane[23]

Far from being either an unimpeded narration or a static imitative recitation of pastoral elegy's iconic lament, then, Spellman's Coltrane Poem must be read as a series of provisional or transitional hypotheses linking an actual to a virtual being. In some sense, each verse paragraph arises in response to premature closure which the poet either fears (as in the more awkward gaps, implied elisions, and caesuras) or miscasts (as in the projected plenitude of the second stanza). The poet's quest is thus a movement to catch a vanishing "Trane," an effort to (re)construct what was originally heard and felt by treating the scene of performance as a kind of communal palimpsest. Death proves not the 'end' of john as expressive medium but is instead a *turning* of voice, a deflection and recuperation of utterance centered in the apos-trophic vehemence of the concluding stanza. For if the suspension suffered between the doubled calls of "then john" suggests a turning away (either of Coltrane from communal summons or of Being itself – and the possibility of voice – from the musician), then the insistent entreaty and roar of "you" at the poem's close accomplishes the voice's ultimate recovery through relocation. By redirecting a possibly epitaphic account of john's disappearance toward this passionate avowal of his "beating" struggle for incessant emergence, the

closing exphonesis, or outcry to another, reveals the poem's inner motive
as that of dialogic resistance.

As we saw, the radical otherness of john initially overwhelms the poet,
hollowing him into silence. Yet as the poet recovers the capacity to grasp
that otherness not as a monumental fact to be known but as an occasion
for identification and the risk of intersubjective action, that silence becomes
retrospectively understood as the site of history and desire. Spellman's
Coltrane Poem is, we might say, pro-vocative, both thematically and ethi-
cally, founding as it does the empowering continuance of Coltrane, speaker,
and community equally on the *movements of voice* through which performance is carried over from an illustrative figure, place, and moment to
its successors. But whereas in "Did John's Music Kill Him?" it is only
in the final stanza's transition from third to second persons that this relation of rhetoric to form becomes fully apparent, from the instant of its
titular address, Michael Harper's "Dear John, Dear Coltrane" foregrounds
the activity of exchange between speaker and subject, thus entwining
speaking and subjectivity in the poem's pivotal explorations of loss,
meaning, kinship, and perpetuation (the work's key concerns, as we shall
soon see).* Beginning as a complex structure of address that evokes at
once private (or intimate) and public (or ceremonial) dimensions of the
hero's bearing (John/Coltrane), Harper's poem immediately posits the
dynamic of call-and-response as its thematic and procedural core. This
gesture of enunciation subtly posits the relation of two implicit subject
positions – the speakerly "I" and the receptive "you" so prominent in the
final stages of "Did John's Music Kill Him?" – as integral to the poem's
unfolding, intimating furthermore the possibility of reply from a figure
who, after all, is presumably now beyond reach of any direct discourse.

As Barbara Johnson has said, speaking generally of apostrophe, such an
implied ventriloquism, especially in an apparently "straightforwardly unfig-
urative" style of address, exposes "the desire for the other's voice."[24] The
opening invocation, at once gentle and formal, quietly establishes the poet
as someone fitted to issue an effective summons to the musician, someone
worthy of a *calling* whose very essence is articulate transaction – a calling
that, by inference, any capable listener must likewise share. Thus, Harper's
poem alerts us that its cause, like that of Spellman's Coltrane Poem, will
be that of a restoration against the diasporic distances and alienating
wounds imposed against the speaker and Coltrane, or, rather, that such
temporal and social revisionism is already intrinsic to the very initiation
of this present poetic project. The title's gesture of address, then, announces
what it exemplifies: the poem will operate as a desire for mutual recognition and continuity of expressive exchange.

But what does it mean to say that the dialogic assertion of apostrophe
is an enabling condition of expression whose very task is reparation of

---

* See Appendix A pp.329–30 for full text.

communication which has been mutilated (made "mute," as the poem says) by the harsh realities of black experience in America? How can we avoid taking the title's assumptions of poetic voice and responsive listening as anything other than the "embarrassment" that Jonathan Culler warns is the very hallmark of apostrophe, which seems "pretentious and mysti-ficatory" in its effort to make an optative plea appear to be a prophetic imperative?[25] This question bears upon two signal features of the poem's realization of "John Coltrane" as bearer of something precious, or "dear" (beloved, costly) – i.e., the spiritual and nurturing legacy of a "love supreme."

First, the embedded trope of address in "Dear John, Dear Coltrane" encodes precisely the *will* to reshape descriptive and naturalistic contin-gencies according to a larger design of collective vision. It purposefully foregrounds the status of exilic assertion as an urge to activate voice, rather than thoroughly binding it to a set of concrete desiderata. As the poem proceeds, Coltrane comes literally to embody a resolve that bends events to this overriding desire despite personal and communal ravages too terrible to be simply escaped or denied. In effect, Coltrane becomes the *genius loci*, or tutelary spirit, of an Afro-America capable of sustaining its orphic powers despite overwhelming appearances of dismemberment and dispersal.

Second, Harper constructs this will-to-voice under the aegis of an expressly *modal* interpretation of Coltrane, not only as musician but as exemplary life-force. In liner notes written for a compilation of Coltrane's first work as a bandleader, Harper says of modal perception that it "reveals its own truth on its own terms – one perceives it while integrated in the context of the mode."[26] The mode is an arrangement of claims, events, and insights, each of which possesses an idiosyncratic significance, but a significance which is fully intelligible only in *relation* to affiliated elements of a common structure of feeling and experience. As Paul Carter Harrison said of modal logic's function in his vision of modern black theater (aptly enough comparing dramatistic to musical forms), oppositions of "time/space, spirit/corpus, and social/moral [work] in a single force-field of reality, as if the event were located in a matrix of notes grafted on a B-flat scale."[27] The matrix, not the element alone, defines any given artic-ulation or episode enveloping a person or people.

Most crucially, temporality remains vital within modal understanding and invention, but not in the manner of narrative mimesis: referential temporality is displaced by an expressive discourse in which events circulate in consonance with hierarchies of meaning rather than according to strictly linear determinations. The sequential logic of empirical time is not thereby denied, but it can be cognitively overtaken by a discursive or figurative time governed by a play of presence and absence instead of by non-reversible succession. In short, modality is the methodology of (post)elegiac consciousness, in which history is defined not by death or its henchmen but by the refigurative energy of those who see and hear resonances of resistive will beyond the clamor of death's immediate sway.

Likewise, Harper remarked of his own work (referencing specifically the volume *Dear John, Dear Coltrane*),

> My poems are modal. By modality I mean the creation of an environment so intense by its life and force as to revivify and regenerate, spiritually, man and community. . . . The blues singer says 'I' but the audience assumes 'We'; out of such energy comes community and freedom. A Love Supreme!
>
> (Michael Harper)[28]

The self and its language attain their 'spiritualizing' vitality only when heard as elemental to dynamic social realization: it is at the junction of consciousness and culture that the singular voice of "creation" arises. "Coltrane," therefore, will stand for Harper as the name of this crossing of autonomous and collective experience, and his poem will take up from its titular hero the *respons*ibility of locating the modal link between the individual artist's tragic isolation and the community's "regenerative" perception. In this sense, the hero's voice will be heard as always potentially beyond any instance of its actual enunciations, inasmuch as it is always already spoken by accumulations of communal awareness (an awareness that might be lost to any given member of the group in the wake of particular bereavements and crises, but which is not, in the matrix of modal conception, thereby lost from the archive of cultural knowledge). Confined to the mimetically temporal, the axman's voice can say only so much, but immanent within its modal potentialities it reverberates with diachronic implications that we, his listeners, might ultimately sound within his music's continuing virtual present. Similarly, he and we exist, truly, only as potentialities requiring reciprocal appropriation in order to be effectively actualized and legitimated.

How does the poem choreograph this dialogue of self and culture in order to wrest, blues-like, modal affirmation from the surface evidence of grievous, if heroically confronted, privation? Our way into this question, in the manner of Harper's vision of modality as "creation of an environment" sufficient to such transformation, requires a corresponding contextualizing of the poem in a force-field of performances that suggests how Harper's work is itself crafted to be read as more than a solitary undertaking. Taking Harper's hint, we might note that the central node of the matrix within which "Dear John, Dear Coltrane" exfoliates is Trane's pivotal, epical composition, *A Love Supreme*, that quintessence of modal improvisation from which Harper draws the structurally framing chant, "*A love supreme, a love supreme / a love supreme, a love supreme,*" as only the most overt of many consequential inspirations. Perhaps the centerpiece of what Harper has called the "testamental" imperative of Coltrane's art,[29] *A Love*

Supreme (1964) served Coltrane as a touchstone of spiritual commitment through which he declared publicly the sacramental quest to which his art was thereafter openly dedicated. Designed as a synthetic – indeed, modally interdisciplinary – project comprising visual, narrative, poetic, vocal, as well as instrumental innovations orbiting the devotional themes of pilgrimage and regeneration, and fueled in part by the synthesis of confessional autobiography ("During the year 1957, I experienced, by the grace of God, a spiritual awakening," Coltrane writes in the opening of extensive remarks that accompany the original Impulse issue)[30] and elegiac passion (intimate associate Eric Dolphy had died less than half a year before the recording), *A Love Supreme* represents one of the most tightly integrated conceptions among all of Coltrane's late compositions. In effect, this complex work constitutes a kind of annunciation poem in which Coltrane made overt his belief that music is more a matter of spiritual than technical pursuit, and thus, by implication, that music is inextricably tied to the historical and moral continuum in which it takes shape. Music thus reflects the social and ethical contradictions of its compositional moment, tensions against which it might exert a (re)visionary pressure, properly conceived and performed. With *A Love Supreme*, the interior dynamic of search and renovation with which Coltrane's work had always been concerned becomes overt at every level of his art's presentation.

This increase in expressive candor, even abandon, gave rise necessarily to more complex formal design and conceptual arrangement. Structured as stations along a quest for enlightenment and purification, the suite's four sections unfold in a carefully organized dialectic, alternating movements of driving, incantational exploration (I: Acknowledgement/III: Pursuance) with segments of lyrical, searing meditation (II: Resolution/IV: Psalm). In themselves, but especially in their relation to one another, these pieces constitute one of Coltrane's most elaborate yet luminous investigations of melody as a function of temporal relations, as the work's dominant three-note cell,[31] doubled into a presiding scalar motif, is variously shifted, rotated, and spun through a variety of registers, runs, and riffs. Whether moving through the swing rhythms of "Resolution" or the jagged balladic tempo of "Psalm," for example, Coltrane fashions a continuously diverse yet cogent acoustic texture by troping the underlying motive in myriad formations. The result is a sense of collateral development and iterative revelation that affirms the voice in its simultaneous freedom and responsiveness to priority: the pilgrim of *A Love Supreme*, perpetually refigured in the primal three-note cell's transpositions from "home" to exilic resituation on a given scale or key, is, in short, a modal subject, bound to the often painful constraints of its historicity, but engaged continuously in transforming the negativity of this ordeal into the aching lyricism of an authentic askesis.

More than in any previous composition, Coltrane in *A Love Supreme* insinuates call-and-response as a thematic and structural principle, fashioning a plethora of conversations between vertical and harmonic patterns, while connecting the segments across their disparate coloristic values through many echoes of pitch and statement. Indeed, the suite concludes with one of the most technically subtle instances of internalized call-and-response in the Coltrane oeuvre, when a second saxophone enters at the end of "Psalm" to pronounce the final measures' dis/closure: this, it turns out, is Coltrane himself, overdubbed,[32] thus staging his departure as a reminder that the solo is always truly an ensemble achievement – when the axman says "I," his audience should hear "We." So, too, on a larger scale of modal construction, the album *A Love Supreme* works as an antiphonal play between musical and verbal assertion, a dialogic play internalized to the music itself with the eruption of the "love supreme" chant at the end of "Acknowledgement," appropriately intoned in double-voice style by Coltrane and bassist Jimmy Garrison. For Coltrane's liner notes – which are, like Harper's poem, framed as an epistolary appeal to a potentially responsive if literally distant audience ("DEAR LISTENER," they begin) – should be seen as an essential ingredient of the entire work. With their emphasis on narrative uncertainty ("As time and events moved on," Coltrane's confessional tale unfolds, "I entered into a phase which was contradictory . . .") resolved in the absolute present of God's enfolding Love ("HIS WAY IS THROUGH LOVE, IN WHICH WE ALL ARE"), these discursive and poetic inscriptions supplement the modal drama of temporal confusion and redemption marked by the music's fugal exposition.

Of especial interest is the long, sermonic poem that concludes these notes. Following the introductory epistle's dedicatory invocation of God as the emancipatory Love Supreme, these lines are themselves an intricate meditation on the relation of radical scepticism and resolute action, and, by way of that contingency, of solitude to interaction. Once recited by Coltrane in a church setting, after which reading he played the entire composition in an astounding long-breath enactment of the piece's call-and-response dynamic,[33] this meticulously designed versified prayer entangles theology with tropology and temporality in a manner wholly consistent with Harper's revolutionary-elegiac vision:

> It is most important that I know Thee.
> Words, sounds, speech, men, memory, thoughts, fears and emotions
> – time – all related . . . all made from one . . . all made in one.
> [. . .]
> Thought waves – heat waves – all vibrations – all paths lead to
> God. Thank you God.
> One thought can produce millions of vibrations and they all go
> back to God . . . everything does.
> Thank you God.

The "God" of Coltrane's chant-sermon is not a transcendental abstraction but the destination of a process enabling interrogation of the many in relation to the one, of inside to outside, of self to an Otherness that, possibly, is but clarified manifestation of self. The productive ambiguity here is whether God is celebrated for being beyond or within mundane experience. In either case, materiality and particularity are not dissolved but affirmed as the reverberative incarnation of that primal principle of modal relatedness: God, in effect, is the *rhythm of associations* through which meaning emerges. Thus, for Coltrane the fundamental principle of Being is activity, the endless becoming of all things in their infinite intermingling, the primal image of which is Love Supreme:

> God is.
> God loves. [. . .]
> I have seen God – I have seen ungodly [. . .]
> Thank you God.
> He will remake us . . . He always has and He
>   always will.

Love is the ceaseless transformative encounter of differences that shape the self, figuring God as the agency and supervening logic of perpetual transmutation. God is thus not a suprasensible master but a mode of self-completion without finality, not a referential order but a transferential transaction that defines but does not confine us by the boundaries of our (re)making. God is what situates our being as an ongoing performance, providing the manifold genres or milieux of our effort to locate ourselves in the right position. This divine manifestation thus provides a framework for the self's exertions of will, that quest for self-realization for which Love provides the motive energy and justification. God figures, in effect, the pilgrim's "way," which is the "path" from subjectification to subjectivity, from the "ungodly" to the "Elegance-Exaltation" of being on the road to "perfection" (LN/ALS).

In the totality of its modal improvisations, then, Coltrane's album articulates a principle of identity as incessantly repositioned performance for which *A Love Supreme* provides the ever-shifting but sustaining context. "God/a love supreme" names the modal configuration of being and temporality through which the episodic and contingent are "acknowledged" without loss of collective selfhood in the erosive linearity of irrevocable experience. In both its musical and verbal improvisations, Coltrane's composition seeks not to escape but to rethink the tragic contingencies of lived reality by displacing homogenous, punctiform duration with a felt sense of time as multidirectional *passage*. In both its music's approach to variation through repetition and its verse's insistence on possibility through recognition, *A Love Supreme* envisions self-expression as a quest liberated from time's diremptions by a willingness to undergo the exacting trials of self-revision. Appropriately, "Dear John, Dear Coltrane," unlike so many other Coltrane Poems, offers no determined representation of an already-centered subject, but rather, mimes performatively the ceaseless "cleaning of the mirror" through which the subject resolutely exerts its fealty to – indeed, its actualization as – *a love supreme*. Moreover, Harper follows Coltrane in imaging this process as one of endless purification wherein the abject residues of catastrophic violence are finally intelligible only within the presiding mode of their "exaltation."

A full rendering of the poem's modal landscape would include not only the many resonances with Coltrane's suite but a more extensive body of Harper's verse, including other elegies (especially those for artists and kin), other poems concerning jazz musicians (especially horn players, like Bird and Miles: "I was a horn man," he says of his earliest days listening to records copped from his parents' special record collection),[34] and other Harper Coltrane Poems (especially those in the volume *Dear John, Dear Coltrane* and its successor, *History is Your Own Heartbeat*). Read together, these works establish the deep relation in Harper's vision between the often painful exertions of craftsmanship and what Robert Stepto calls "kinship-in-process,"[35] the persistent tracing of familial continuity in the grace notes of cultural struggle. In "Here Where Coltrane Is," for example, Harper portrays Trane as an imaginative vector weaving bonds among personal and racial associations, linking the musician's elegiac response to the murder of children in Alabama with the poet's effort to discern possibilities of collective transmission in his son Roland's eyes:

> Soul and race
> are private dominions
> memories and modal
> songs, a tenor blossoming. . . .
> I play "Alabama"
> on a warped record player . . .
> For this reason Martin is dead;
> For this reason Malcolm is dead;
> For this reason Coltrane is dead;
> in the eyes of my first son are the browns
> of these men and their music.
>
> (Michael Harper,
"Here Where Coltrane Is")[36]

Musical and poetic anamneses combine, fusing Coltrane and Harper (" *I* play 'Alabama' . . .") into the warp-and-woof of a modality that allows Coltrane in effect to compose his own elegy as it radiates through the growing perception of Harper's bloodline. Of such interminglings is the matrix generating "Dear John, Dear Coltrane" fabricated, and while for our purposes a complete delineation of their many textures remains impractical, it is against the background of such an array of commitments that the following exploration of the poem should be best viewed.

In keeping with Coltrane's image of "God" as a constant revolving of will around regenerated possibilities of voice, Harper's poem works as an odic progression of turns and re-turns seeking to knit performative relations capable of surpassing an objectively irreversible narrative. Like *A Love Supreme*, it unfolds a pilgrimage that bespeaks a diasporic yearning for home's serenity alongside a courageous recognition that one life can seek no more than to sustain and pass on the journey's ardor. Thus, its structure is that of a quest-romance, but one that undergoes constant deconstruction in the crucible of testamental commitment – not because, as Paul Bové says of the anti-idealist demystifications of American modernists like Wallace Stevens, "the Romantic quest is self-deluding,"[37] but because the African-American passion for historical witness constantly disperses the mythos of origins and ends into the present's burden of articulate resistance. Accordingly, our voyage through the poem will both recapitulate the formal shape conferred by its motif of exploration and adventure – a formal design conveyed by strophes 1, 2 and 4 – and double back to a moment, strophe 3, that both ruptures and modally suffuses the encompassing sequential framework. From the vantage of that critical tension between quest and its dislocation by an event that both precedes and exceeds its telos – a tension that we might encapsulate as one between narrative and apostrophe – we will then be prepared to locate our own place within Harper's conception of *a love supreme*.

Like Spellman's "Did John's Music Kill Him?," "Dear John, Dear Coltrane" turns upon an effort to re-member the fragmented, departed Coltrane by an act of recreative signification. Again, the elegy begins with loss, but now imagined as the original, or defining nature of African-American life itself. The signal moment of that experience clearly revolves around the sparagmos, the literal dismemberment of self *and* community at the suggestively violent "marketplace":

> Sex fingers toes
> in the marketplace
> near your father's church
> in Hamlet, North Carolina –
> witness to this love
> in this calm fallow
> of these minds,
> there is no substitute for
> pain . . .

(Harper, "Dear John, Dear Coltrane")[38]

The hero's fragmentation is thus given elemental cultural prefiguration in a scene of racial horror and generative power. The breakup of community is traumatic yet incomplete; the auction block become church – linking slavery with Middle Passage, on one side of an historical continuum, and with the hero's spiritual and literal biography, on the other – is a site of contradictory, dangerous, and almost inexplicable potential. From the first, he faces the question, is division purely a catastrophe of estrangement or can it be the foundation of emergence – in other words, to what process of violent exchange, enervating or vitalizing, is he most "near"? Far from excluding the possibility of renewal, the violence threatening cultural and genealogical continuity (the latter established by the entanglement of sexual and familial imagery) is possibly enshrined as the enabling agent of an historically "witnessed" and specifically located 'Black Orphic' descent and return. Painfully challenged at the very extremities of mind and body – *sex, fingers, toes* – the hero will need to wrench metamorphic productivity from the terrors of social and somatic mutilation.

The dialectical reappropriation of productive "love," the "seeding" of his people's "fallow" consciousness, is the hero's task. Deprived and dispossessed, he too begins the journey for self-apprehension in crisis:

> genitals gone or going,
> seed burned out,
> you tuck the roots in the earth,
> turn back, and move
> by river through the swamps,
> singing: *a love supreme, a love supreme*;
> what does it all mean?

At once fugitive slave and riffing musician, Coltrane proceeds in the face of polarities expressing the need for creative destruction. The absent "seed" is countered by "roots" planted in previously uncultivated earth, and the very introduction of such heterogeneous elements by and into the questing body sets in motion a spiral of deformation and reformation that generates for the poem's environment a contradictory aura of abjection and rapture. Yet to the hero's less intrepid audience, as in the mourning processions of classical elegy, his absence seems final, his continued "singing" stilled in their ears by a failure to listen:

> what does it all mean?
> Loss, so great each black
> woman expects your failure
> in mute change, the seed gone.

The striving to achieve an undissolved totality of perception, an intuition of being, in the face of an unimaginable bereavement disintegrates expectation and dislocates accepted relations, semantic as well as epistemological. In performative terms, the communicative dynamic of address and answerability has been eclipsed by the shock of ruin and misrecognition. If, as Horkheimer and Adorno have asserted, "the history of [western] civilization

is the history of the introversion of the sacrifice,"[39] Harper prepares here
for a contrary motion, in which habits of private, domestic culture are
startled and stiffened, confronted by the victim's defilement, and forced
to reimagine and resituate what has evidently been wasted in its refusal
to accede to norms of quotidian survival. Imagistically, this signifies that
the unclean and transgressive must itself be sanctioned to achieve
that reversal of expectation that ensures the continuity of communal
consciousness and voice.

The question intervening between disappearance and lamentation –
"what does it all mean?" – blurs the poem's referential and reflexive
concerns, thereby energizing the poet's dialectic of "loss," transition
("change"), and recovery. The poet is thus allowed to image the hero's
mission as an anabasis, or 'ascension,' that transfigures threatened stillness
into the painful motion of time-changing song:

> You plod up into the electric city –
> your song now crystal and
> the blues.

The quest, then, contains the promise of renewal as the perpetuity of voice
not only despite but *through* negation. Thus, the perturbing "mute change"
issues redemptively in the 'ululating' (hence "blues"-inspired) clarity of song
– a song mystically "crystal" (cf. Spellman's "glass") yet funkily pastoral
("Dawn came and you cook" – the pun providing both musical and com-
mensal nourishment, dangerously spiced) and, because bending its notes
after the fashion of the blues, not solidified into a falsifying monumentality.

This musical incorporation of a surrounding stillness, a kind of self-over-
coming *poeisis*, is the key to the poem's effect of transcendence. Thus, the
originating crisis of the marketplace, and the fearful collapse into silence
that is redressed only by the "will" to *release* expression, are recapitulated
in the poem's climax in strophe 4. Coltrane approaches unavoidable death
as a return to the primal trope of affirmation, "*a love supreme*," that love
of self which endures in spite and because of all that has been taken, all
that has been given in suffering:

> So sick
> You couldn't play *Naima*,
> so flat we ached
> for song you'd concealed
> with your own blood,
> your diseased liver gave
> out its purity,
> the inflated heart
> pumps out, the tenor kiss,
> tenor love:

> *a love supreme, a love supreme —*
> *a love supreme, a love supreme —*

As in Spellman's work, liberation is figured as ritual catharsis, the repetition of "a love supreme" imitating the moment where loss and violation can be encountered without paralysis, and where "meaning" is grasped as an un-"concealment" that remains blessed — sacramentally wounded — in its very disjunction of "tenor" and vehicle. That vehicle here is, as the opening intimated, Coltrane's very body, which in the instant of its expiration has trans-muted into the expressive instrument of the horn's "kiss." The sense of openness, of bursting forward, is captured in the final strophe's expansion of the refrain heard at the end of each prior stanza (which, as with the closing chant of "Did John's Music Kill Him?," ends the poem *without* punctuated closure). Thus, the repetitive framing and stanzaic resolutions provided by the chant's lines are the poetic correlative of performance's spiritual purification of physical "disease." The impurity which infects Coltrane is only manifestation of the ambiguity and interstitial pain that threaten the hero's adherence to essence ("thick sin 'tween/impotence and death," as it is called in strophe 2). Conversely, the removal from experience of the accidental accretions and impositions of life in "the electric city" (a locus not of Whitmanian freedom but, rather, of Ellisonian disorder) is music's means of 'cleansing', of disseminating sacrificial energy through performative travail:

> the tenor sax cannibal
> heart, genitals and sweat
> that makes you clean —
> *a love supreme, a love supreme —*

So ends the second strophe, suggesting that, indeed, John's music *did* kill him, but only to give him birth through the labor of feral devotion to the instrument's call (note the implied paranomasia of *sex/sax*). Coltrane is diseased by that which roots his song; and yet, the site of devastation is the locus of genius: the tenor blows, we might say, as self-consuming event (not, indeed, as artifact). Thus, a principle of creative expenditure bursts upon the poem: the unclean founds, rather than confounds, comprehension, distributes, rather than disturbs definition; the impure enables, not just threatens, form. Implicitly seizing upon this uncanny and subversive insight, and thus inverting the basic formulations of the Symbolic in its effort to expel the abject, "Dear John, Dear Coltrane" gradually reveals the contradictory attainment of purity alongside the necessity of profanation, the loss and redefinition of the hero, and the poem's essential form (and, ultimately, as we shall soon, see, our role within that form) to be inextricable.

In this aesthetic-ethical complex, transgression and communality — the goals of black modernist rebellion and renovation — blend as voice signifies at one and the same time irreducible will and the residue of negation. Thus we come to the poem's key passage, the third strophe, where the call-and-response logic underlying that quest's purpose of shared self-production erupts into the text:

> *Why you so black?*
> *cause I am*
> *Why you so funky?*
> *cause I am*
> *Why you so black?*
> *cause I am*
> *Why you so sweet?*
> *cause I am*
> *Why you so black?*
> *cause I am*
> *a love supreme, a love supreme.*

Narratively, this stanza serves as a bridge between the opening sparagmos and the closing de/re-generation that together form the mobius strip of Coltrane's quest; performatively, these lines assert that the tersely eloquent self-under-siege permeates every instant of temporal succession. Harper locates Coltrane's being in a progressive series of hypostatized abstracts, wresting a *topos* of praise from the lexicons of racial abuse and identification. Orbiting that being is a cluster of propositions, which, in their association with specifically African-American language, establish the hero as the archetype or myth of African-American entelechy. Like "love," "Coltrane" is revealed as a nexus of differences, lucid in their individuality, but effective in their coming together through the agency of the hero's expressive insistence. It is his capacity to sustain this dialogic event – and, by way of that resolve, to discredit repressive oppositions of materiality and mentality, self and other – that, in fact, constitutes him as the poem's responsive addressee, guaranteeing his re-membrance despite evidence of interruptive molestation. As the synecdoche of process reaching toward a ritually purified black essence, this "I" bespeaking "We" imposes order or shape on the paradoxical chaos of African-American history: every specific sign of identity is subtended by the arch-signifier of motivated existence – "cause I am."

Coltrane's testamental "I am" thus enfolds the agonizing moment of speech – for which there is no "substitute," no symbolic evasion or monumentalizing alibi – with the historicity of collective experience. That history is for the New World quester inevitably a mongrelized, modalized palimpsest, layering (for example) biblical divinity ("I am that I am"), Coleridgean celebrations of primary Imagination (a human iteration of the "infinite I AM"), Bo Diddley's toast to insurgent manhood ("I'm a man, I'm a man, I'm a man . . ."), and the syncopated avowals of Harper's own initial Coltrane Poem, "Brother John" ("Trane, Coltrane; John Coltrane; . . ./it's black Trane; black;/I'm a black man; I'm black;/I am; I'm a black man – "). At the same time, the revolutionary immediacy of this thickly-textured assertion is the more powerful for its prosopopoeic disturbance of that mute-ation of speech which haunts Coltrane's unbridled affirmation: *I am dead*. Coltrane's exorbitant, if disciplined, reiteration of presence acts as an apotropaic defense against distortion, misnaming, depletion. It is thus that – to borrow a Coleridegean formulation under the aegis of the New Wave bluesman's improvisation of identity – somatic, semantic, and spiritual elements of being are "no longer absolutely heterogeneous but may . . . be supposed to be different modes . . . of a common substratum."[40] Achieved self-presence is itself the modal relation of desire and faith, the mutual troping of negativity and freedom. In this way, the (auto)biographical quest becomes both epitaphic and revolutionary, continuously preventing the erasure of consciousness by voicing the "cause" of voice from within that which would deny it.

Coltrane's exemplary activity of cathartic renewal – a displacement of inquisitional assault on identity by articulate self-identification – is the model for the poet's own creation. Harper's dialogic form, captured throughout the poem in the juxtaposition of discursive line and italicized refrain that extends the title's manner of dyadic address, "crystallizes" Coltrane. A kind of procession of African-American vocal convention, it is a provocative structure whose challenge is prepared by allowing the reader to look through the verse to the *process* that makes song of terror, mutilation, and silence. This coercion of private experience into objective order rescues the poem itself from the threat of malformation – and indicates why Coltrane is the signal mythic figure presiding over the contemporary thrust of African-American poetics. Coltrane's concluding performance, before which the poem widens to include reader and poet in an implicit communality of crisis ("*we* ached . . ."), is not a final but a continuing act. Past (loss) and present (life) are one ("liver *gave*/out . . . heart/*pumps* out"), the song enduring though the playing has ceased. The final chant is not unmistakably located "in" the mind or uttered by the voice of poet, hero, or reader/listener; the song does not fully complete itself in elegy, but the poem's elegiac intuition itself is precisely thereby completed: dismemberment and discontinuity are avoided by the poet-musician's capacity to move beyond the mute fixation of grief into new attachments with fresh energy.

Thus, as in the vernacular aesthetics to which Harper's form alludes (in terms that we will explore through our encounter with the chant-sermon in Chapter 7), dislocation of the center (here, the "marketplace" of literally human yet also eventually spiritual exchange) is ultimately seen exerting not a centrifugal but a centripetal force on the community (an implication adroitly served by Harper's metrical craft, with its trochees, spondees, and anapests registering elegiac grief but rocking us forward to the recuperated iambs of the chant). The consequence for both hero and poem is not disintegration but ceremonially sanctioned superintegration: in poetic terms, ceaseless formal experimentation bounded by a ritual manipulation of convention. Disruption, first suffered as assault, is grasped as a strategic necessity in a restructuring of experience: "there is no substitute for pain." It is in such a sense that "Dear John, Dear Coltrane," in the apostrophic ambiguity of its titular call – the prosopopoeia of its double address – functions as what Harper has called an "omen," the poem having actually been written as a premonitory oracle of Coltrane's death. The marketplace of Coltrane's performative death-birth is a place simultaneously of bereaving and conceiving. Reborn in creative grief, Coltrane's playing takes as its own condition the visionary conjunction of being and death, founding upon loss the cannibal heart's performative "cause I am." Likewise embracing an economy of death as the cost of its writing, Harper's poem becomes an omen of our own perpetual enactment of self-realization through a responsive rhythm of expressive identification and sacrificial effacement.

The abiding exemplum of "John Coltrane," then, as modal inflection of painful historical process and continued articulation, instructs us in the urge to create a new dispensation amid the fallowness of silence or the ferocity of discord. The hero's call and the poet's response, each provoked by loss, do not dissipate the vibrations of "a love supreme" but "pump" themselves back into the reader's world, where we now must take up the burden and opportunity, the pain and the passion, of founding collective identity in unyielding acts of transgressive affirmation. For, just as Coltrane's voice is joined by Jimmy Garrison's for the chant that concludes "Acknowledgement," and just as the rhythms and tonal variations of "Psalm" are (as Lewis Porter has demonstrated)[41] built upon the prosodic structures of Coltrane's liner-note verse, so "Dear John, Dear Coltrane"'s final refrain of *a love supreme* must surely no longer be Coltrane's, or Coltrane's alone, but now is ours, as we have been prepared to respond in kind to the poem's piercing call, "Why you . . .?" The final strophe's tense shift, in concert with the third strophe's exemplary performance by a departed but ever-immanent Trane, evacuates narrative commemoration into the performative present: the event-confirmed "I AM" must be the poem's own . . . and ours. In that collaborative present(ation), we participate not in a narrative mimesis of Coltrane's life but in the methexis of Trane's quest for "freedom and community." As Harper has written in a meditation on the "the humanization of an American audience": "The landscape of the poem is the contour of the face reading . . ."[42] If we accept that invitation to improvise expressive perception within the crafted environment of "Dear John, Dear Coltrane," this poem will have achieved that most revolutionary of transformations: the regeneration of life-force within the hitherto dormant voice of its listeners.

And, as it once was for other oracles of the voice and ax, even the "beasts" must pause and listen – and the gods will, too:

> *a love supreme, a love supreme –*
> *a love supreme, a love supreme –*

*

As they chase the Trane, modern black poets forge a poetics of redeemed abjection and excess in which extravagance of style, posture, statement, and action bespeak the double effort to "scream" the reality of historical pain and to invent alternative modes of expressive self-mastery. "Coltrane" thus emerges as a node of multiple, potentially conflicting, implications that, taken together, evoke black modernism's effort to reimagine relations of self and other, individual voice and communal performance. At the heart of these speculative poetic journeys is the relation of poet to subject, an unprescribed process of exchange that leads the writer to become, and not just measure, performative struggle. The next stage of our own journey requires us to follow exemplary patterns of this (r)evolutionary self-enactment, wherein the artist's own effort to speak reflexively stages the vagaries of ideological, narrative, and thematic concern. What better figure with which to begin than that most penetrating and restless of Coltrane's celebrants, Amiri Baraka?

Part III

Find the self, then kill it

Scripts and scores of self-enactment

> Trane was
> heavy   heavy
> because Trane did
> his thing
> Trane was in Tune
> with Trane
> and his God
> and his people
>
> Too many good poets
> are killing themselves
> trying to be
> like LeRoi
> Jones   Jones
> can take care of Jones
> Don Lee raps for Don Lee
> Larry Neal and Bill Russell
> create from Larry Neal and Bill Russell
>   (and we are all
>   blessed because
>   they do)
> Write *your* poem
> sing *your* song
> paint *your* picture
> Be your own Black self
> BE YOU
>
>   Norman Jordan, "Be You"

5 Sounding blackness

Vision and voice in the performative poetics of Amiri Baraka[1]

SOUND: A rant.
           A measure.
           A song.

                       Amiri Baraka, "Soundings"[2]

I Sounding niggas: signatures of voice

Our world is full of sound . . .
tho we suffer . . .
           We need magic
now we need the spells, to raise up
return, destroy, and create. What will be
the sacred words?

           Amiri Baraka, "Ka 'Ba'" – *SP*, p. 117

Nobody says *muthafucka* like Amiri Baraka. Whether excoriating spiritual enslavement to the "madness" of seeking exemption from history – *"preach!!/baldhead rip off/teach!!/chicken eatin metaphysical/loud talkin chained up mutherfuckas"* ("Reggae or Not!" – *TB*, p. 177) – or celebrating the anarchic energy of resistant black musicality – *"There was nothing left to do but/be where monk cd find him/that crazy/mother fucker/duh duh-duh duh-duh duh . . ."* ("Am/Trak" – *TB*, p. 191) – *muthafucka* rises and thumps, slithers and roils, slides and screams from Baraka's throat both as a vehicle of archaic power, evoking the irreducible violence of rupture, distance, loss, and restitutive transgression, and as a vessel of symbolic import, carrying the complex burden of ideological critique, reproachful admonition, and oracular fury. By turns witheringly ironic and brutally tender, scornfully embittered and slyly reverential, Baraka's *muthafucka* is a signature of a supple and sometimes self-divided voice that has for nearly four decades not so much graced America's imaginative ambitions as haunted its nightmare refusals, seductions, and betrayals, insistently ululating from the culture's subversive margins a long-breathed blues-tinged wail of prophetic outrage and utopic expectation, part Shine, part Br'er Rabbit:

The motherfuckin'
heart, of the
motherfuckin'
day, grows hot
as a bitch, on her
motherfuckin'
way, back home.

I want to go
back home.

I've got nothin'
against you. But I
got to get
back home.

("Lady Bug" – *SP*, p. 97)

America, likewise, is a signature of this rapping, cajoling, corrective Barakan
voice, one that rings throughout the poetry, prose, and drama in dialectical
relation with *muthafucka*, on the one side, *nigga* on the other. From his earliest
poetic efforts among the alienated modernists of the bohemian avant-garde
to his latest alarums as perdu of the Afro-socialist-anti-imperialist vanguard,
America has sounded in the Barakan lexicon as an intricate locus of limit and
transformation: now wistful and self-loathing ("You are/as any other sad
man here/american" – "Notes for a Speech" – *Preface*, p. 147), now
accusatory and dismissive ("All the pieces/drawn together/puzzle/nig-
ger/solved/by his self/A   merica/will break up/into a hundred
pieces/& Bloods will stand black whole bad swift cool fine" – "Whas Gon
Happen" – *SP*, p. 161), now exhortatory and almost secretly hopeful ("The
world can be changed . . . /America must change or be/destroyed" –
"Afrikan Revolution" – *SP*, p. 232), Baraka's *America* is spat toward his audience as a taunt and challenge, sick with the putrid legacy of slavery, yet
thickened with astonishing resources of survival and hope. *America*, uniquely,
is the landscape of the Barakan *nigga*, the "Afrikan" wrenched through
middle passage into the double consciousness of diasporic existence
("NewArk Afrikans (Niggers too)" – "Afrikan Revolution" – *SP*, p. 233),
redolent of ambivalent capitulation preparing collective renewal ("Unwilling
nigger actors/Heavy/Minstrels/this torture/Birth/of the/Black Nation" –
"Y's 18" – *TB*, p. 233), wildly alive with burgeoning consciousness of ancient
style and resurrected possibility ("The sanity of form is allness wholeness
rightness/Nigger form . . ./the pyramid speaks of niggers actually/the word
will be given to niggers . . ." – "Ask Me What I Am" – *SP*, p. 168). Echoing
and contesting one another in a polyrhythmic texture of overlapping accents,
rhymes, and shifting emphases, such hallmarks of the distinctive Barakan
intonation conjure a vision of African-American culture as a site of ceaseless
personal and social conflict. In their nexus Baraka envisions a dynamic meet-

ing ground of contrasting idioms and postures that vie for nothing less than the vital soulform of black historical consciousness while remaining subject to myriad contingencies of power, subjection, will, and desire. On this terrain, Baraka's expressive oeuvre orchestrates a multiplicity of distinct, sometimes antithetical, voices whose struggle is not simply economic and political – though the "actual" terms of sociality remain vitally, immediately central to Baraka's thematics – but always centrally an agon for utterance itself.

Surely, beyond the assonantal and conceptual constellation of *motherfucka, America, nigga* there are many other cardinal figures, critical touchstones, that signify the Barakan voice – or quest *for* voice – through its many turns of conceptual, aesthetic, and political perspective, chief among them: *revolution, change, real, why, crazy, we, sweet, scream, magic, filth, love, slavery, Africa, and, or.* Such locutions likewise evince the dialectical and self-contesting temper of Baraka's imaginative confrontations with history's perplexing emotional structure, his persistent effort to set history's cruel indifference to creative force in perpetual tension with revolutionary possibilities of collective avowal. Because Baraka's sensibility remains equally answerable to the apparently opposing imperatives of imagination and world, eschatology and history, reality and desire, voice in the province of Barakan vision seems to embody the very contradictions it would resolve. Even relatively brief and thematically univocal passages within long, intricate poems

> Renaissance
> Negritude
> Blackness
> Negrissimo
> Indigisme
>   sounding niggers
> swahili speaking niggers niggers in turbans
>   rna & app & aprp & cap black blacks
> & assembly line, turpentine, mighty fine female
>   blacks, and cooks, and coal miners
>   small farmers, iron steel and hospital workers
>   in the tradition of us
>   in the tradition of us
>   the reality not us the narrow fantasy
> in the tradition of african american black people/america
>
> nigger music's almost all
> you got, and you find it
> much too hot
>   ("In the Tradition" – *TB*, p. 208)

subtly intertwine cadences of seeming antithesis – polemical and parodic, lyrical and sceptical, epic and vernacular, constructive and apocalyptic –

shading their speaker in the multiple guises of dutiful griot, corrective demystifier, shamanistic mythmaker, rogueish liberator. What is striking, and directly challenging, about these braided inflections and prismatic self-images is their almost effortless simultaneity, or rather, their insistent focus upon the quicker-than-dialectical layering of heterogeneous perceptions and purposes. Whatever else Baraka's voice may be, it is *fast*, resolute in its very shifts and breaks, unwavering in its commitment to locate a precise pitch of new-old black expressivity, the elemental note of recoded blackness in the New World that would herald the supreme signature of revolutionary emancipation.

The counterpoint and tonal simultaneities of Barakan voice are not just stylistic, then, but figurative and theoretical. By spicing renovative proclamation with aggressively deconstructive sass, for example, Baraka establishes the necessary presence of realism to idealism, employing the grotesque as an instrument of the very subversive energies that would annul oppressive "ugliness" (see, e.g., "Heathens" or "A New Reality is Better Than a New Movie!"). Thus, Baraka's carnivalesque violation of aesthetic and social norms fractures assumptions about not only the progressive *récit* of ethnic progress in modern Euro-American culture but about the telos of revolutionary cultural performance as well. Refusing to fetishize even its own insights and assertions, Barakan voice establishes itself in the very space of its perpetual undoing, founding itself as a process of restless positing and interrogation. Syncretic, disruptive, and dis-located, this voice enfolds jocose impieties and incendiary affirmations as a manifesto of freedom not *for* transformation but *as* transformation:

> *African lullaby*
> Babenzele Pygmies
> S. Africa

Revolutionary War
gamed
   sold
      out . . .

English Departments
still
& the money & "culture"
in an "English"
accent . . . .

   Motion, the beat, tender mind
you humans even made music.
      But, our memory anywhere
as humans and beyond, parallel
to everything, is rise is new is
Changed, a glowing peaceful

Musical
World.

     What betrays revolution is the need
for revolution. It can not stop in life.
Whoever seeks to freeze the moment is

instantly, & for that instant, *mad!*
          ("'There Was Something I Wanted to Tell You.'
          (33) Why?" – *TB*, pp. 248, 250–1)

By distilling a thematic conjunction of music and memory, the desublimating demands of change – understood not as an indifferent or aimless drive but as a purposive historical vector – anchor Baraka's voice to its program of self-surpassing performance. For Baraka, "change" promises the often painful eradication of deceit or repression as the productive condition of a newly construed and constructed relation to the "actual." As we shall see, music – particularly the new wave music of bop and its inheritors – has always been for Baraka the advanced vehicle of this destructive alchemy,[3] the inner quest of which has been for a "moment," a radical present saturated with visionary potential, whose "instant" is not "frozen" but quickened by the bracing "terribleness" of vocal mastery. At the end of this preliminary exploration of Baraka's own soundings of such "nigga" musicality, I will hazard estimation of just how the musicality of Baraka's public performances, by blending the material, gestural, narrative, and theoretical qualities of Barakan "voice," establishes its own quicksilver and quickening adroitness in the realm of endless strife and change. But we must first acknowledge that the heteroglossia of Baraka's expressive stances bespeak, potentially, not just a complex insight into the contradictory temporality of revolutionary vision, but also, bearing their own equivocations, a continuous concern with whether poetic performance is itself an obstacle to the deliverance it foretells. To sound the depths of that which Baraka would profess as revolutionary aesthetician, we turn briefly to what I will term the "conversational matrix" of Barakan voice, where its programmatic allegiances and suspicions before the vaunted powers of imagination can best be "measured."

II   Sounding *Conversations*: aesthetic politics and the ideology of imagination

I am a meditative man. And when I say something it's all of me saying, and all the things that make me, have formed me, colored me this brilliant reddish night. I will say nothing that I feel is lie . . .

        today is the history we must learn to
desire.

                Amiri Baraka, "Numbers, Letters" – *SP*, p. 72

Whether as edgy (black) dadaist or Poppa-stoppa of the revolution, Baraka has always written within a sense of imminent crisis: his work derives much of its driving power from the assumption that apocalypse is always about to be, that its arrival requires nothing other than the conjunction of change's inevitable trajectories and his audience's decision finally to shed foolish delusions about the world and their own motivations. By the same token, as the necessary obverse of this poetics of prevision, Baraka has always understood his voice as arising within a network of cultural practices that as much constrains as enables its critical expression. To live in time, aligning oneself with what Baraka calls "the motion of history," means for him to serve a permanent apprenticeship in means for realizing socially viable forms of uncompromised desire. Pursuing a kind of metaphysics of the concrete, Baraka's art fuels the drive for collective liberation through a relentlessly unflinching observation and naming of fallen reality:

> Reality, is what it is. This suffering truth
> advertised in all men's loveliest histories. . . .
>
>   Bankrupt utopia sez tell me
> no utopias. I will not listen. (Except the raw wind
> makes the hero's eyes close, and the tears that come out
> are real.)
>
> ("History As Process" – *SP*, p. 68)

"Reality," mocking grand pretensions built of chimerical abstractions and overexalted self-expectation, brackets the predications and denials that would redefine or reposition it; at the same time, refusing the de-idealizing resignation of failed cultural systems, Baraka's work progresses as a search for transformative dialogue between the 'raw truth' of the real and aspirations for perfection. History and imagination are subjected to an intense mutual probe which sets perception against prescription, "wind" as pure intentionless force against the breezes of "in-spiriting" influence. Does the 'loveliness,' the self-promotional imagery, of "men's histories" simply belie actual experience? – or does its lyrical impulse exert some productive force against the "suffering" it helps chronicle, some possibility of reconfiguring the significance of events as more than stark data absolutely resistant to shaping imagination? Indeed, is "history" best understood as pure happening, which bestows meaning upon individuals from whom it moves apart, or as the mediation of occurrence, the narration of events through which culture is fabricated and power distributed?

Such questions converge equally on Baraka's aesthetic politics and philosophy of history by making central the problem, how is *meaning* identified in a continuum of change – by what means and agents, and at what cost, is meaning determined? Amidst his myriad mutations of artistic, spiritual, and polemical agenda, Baraka has maintained consistent focus on the essential conceptual tensions that emerge from this interrogation of meaning's conditions of possibility: ought we view art as a pretense or a paradigm of desire and truth, and, withal, are representation's mimetic and expressive impulses – the functions, respectively, of truth-recording eye and desire-asserting voice – contradictory or co-implicated elements of revolutionary praxis? In perhaps his most famous poetic manifesto, "Black Art," Baraka skips rope on this crux of aesthetic politics:

> Poems are bullshit unless they are
> teeth or trees or lemons piled
> on a step. . . . Fuck poems
> and they are useful, wd they shoot
> come at you, love what you are . . .
> > We want live
> words of the hip world live flesh &
> coursing blood. . . .
> > We want "poems that kill."
> Assassin poems. Poems that shoot
> guns. . . .
> Let there be no love poems written
> until love can exist freely and
> cleanly. Let Black People understand
> that they are the lovers and sons
> of lovers and warriors and sons
> of warriors Are poems & poets &
> all the loveliness here in the world
>
> We want a black poem. And a
> Black World.
> Let the world be a Black Poem . . .
> > ("Black Art" – *SP*, pp. 106–7)

Art as only a construction of misdirected will, an empty projection that affords no protection against the reality that its tepid abstractions cannot affect; art as the very medium of being, the very essence of the real, properly construed: thus arising as a double-edged and potentially self-cancelling poetics, "Black Art" enfolds rhetorics of negation and affirmation, wresting an incantational celebration of black will-as-representation from the initial curse against mediation's conventional fictionality. "Black Art" seems to valorize presence over representation, but by generating a rhythm of incandescent desire ("we want, we want, we want") capable of coalescing literal and figurative expression, the poem subtly declares its belief in a form of art that can attain full consciousness without succumbing to the intentional negativity of discourse. In progressing from corrosive theory to authorizing invocation, "Black Art" performs the meaning it seemingly prevents, enunciating in its own space the very fierce "love" that it earlier suspends, establishing itself through an insurrectionary defiance of its own negations. What begins as nihilistic invective modulates through serio-comic pragmatics into a kind of aesthetic theodicy. In effect, "Black Art," in its movement from deprecatory 'sounding' to millennial embrace of poetic practice, enacts a romance of black signification as transcendent potentiality. In this way, the poem fulfills its titular promise by making its scatological disillusionment the ground of "black art"'s eschatalogical immanence.

"Black Art" can be taken as exemplary of the contradictory yet productive aesthetic politics that permeate the poet's meditations on imagination and social change from LeRoi Jones to Amiri Baraka. Nowhere is this clearer than in the many interviews conducted with Jones/Baraka over the past 35 years or more, many of which happily have now been collected by Charlie Reilly under the title *Conversations with Amiri Baraka*.[4] Shrewdly selected and organized by Reilly to suggest a kind of autobiographical gyre described by the rotation of changing idioms and constant concerns, *Conversations* provides an indispensable sounding of Baraka's urge to find a language more materially effective than the very discourse within which he speaks in these interviews (a discourse strangely both public and parochial, both political and narrowly professional). What Baraka seems always to be seeking in these discussions is a language that is both "useful" and "lovely," and so throughout we hear Baraka speaking against his own voice . . . whatever *that* "is." In the early interviews, this inner dissension entangles assertions of absolute creative freedom with a nascent awareness that social contingency limits, if not fully delimits, voice:

> [A poem] can be made up out of any feeling. And if I tried to cut anything out of my life – if there was something in my life that I couldn't talk about . . . it seems monstrous that you can tell almost anything about your life except those things that are most intimate or mean the most to you. That seems a severe paradox. . . . I'm always aware, in anything I say, of the "sociological configuration" – what it *means* sociologically. But it doesn't have anything to do with what I'm writing at the time.
>
> (David Ossman/1960, Reilly, 5, 7)

We sense bubbling here subterranean recognitions that any representation claiming to be fully adequate to 'felt' experience can be self-deceiving, that poetic 'making' can be duplicitously artifactual ("made *up*"). But we hear, too, the habit of pressing bold assertion into its hidden "paradox," so that these conversations about the fate of "talking" constitute a dialogue between Baraka and his own conceptual assumptions. And so, in the next interview of Reilly's collection we hear Baraka seeking an idiom of subversive avowal that is not limited by the tone of "intimate," inward complaint that often characterized the writing of his "downtown" years:

The most valuable writing is by the outlaws like Ginsberg. The reason I always associate with the people thought of as 'beats' is that they are outside the mainstream of American vulgarity. . . . [O]ne of the great values of these writers is that they talk about the Americans who have a vested interests [sic] in maintaining some finally invalid image of what America really is.

(Judy Stone/1964, Reilly, 11)

As "talk" is directed outward from the self to the "sociological configuration" that would both sicken and void ("invalid") American imagination, Baraka's voice retains its hortatory and defensive tone, suggesting ambivalence about art's transformative power even as its moral import is being honed. As we move to conversations conducted after Baraka's 'conversion' to cultural nationalism, we find him seeking a 'spiritual' vernacular beyond tragic irony that remains responsive to the likelihood that any given expression remains to some degree framed by context, even trapped in illusion, as it strives toward a more effective synthesis of personal and collective consciousness:

The writing, from the earliest published work, is a concern with the identity of black – my identity of black and what is blackness and just the whole style of black people. You know, always. Any poetry – early poetry – I've ever written you will see that there. The focus is not always clear. Sometimes it's even self-deprecation, but it's always a deep concern there. It's a matter of developing, a matter of coming through . . . A striving to be what I am. . . . It's always been a struggle to determine what I am actually thinking and to discover how I can move on based on that.

(Theodore R. Hudson/1970, Reilly, 74–5)

Baraka's voice proceeds in these "Conversations," then, through a series of radically iconoclastic gestures whose vacillating emotional calculus derives from the ongoing interior dialogue between visionary purpose and demystifying critique. On the one hand, Baraka's voice is restless with ironic realism, scourging the culture's flaccid metaphysics, with their tendency to exalt abstraction; on the other hand, his iconoclasm does not simply turn against idealism in the name of materialism, for "the real" can quickly become another fetish. That is why Barakan idealism and Barakan irony are alike intermittent or, perhaps, simultaneous; always aware of the fictitiousness of his positions, yet equally committed to their fidelity to current perception, Baraka's talk about "talk" thematizes the effort to absorb doubt into belief, retaining a value for art that cannot always be justified in empirical or epistemological terms. Baraka cannot subscribe to the post-Kantian aesthetic ideology that prioritizes "thought" over life's brutalities; but neither can he see "thought" as anything less than an embodiment of the "identity of black"'s entelechy. Throughout *Conversations* he takes his stand on "developing" ground, and is therefore always susceptible to the charge of inconsistency (as his interlocutors endlessly remind him – e.g., C. W. E. Bigsby/1978, Reilly, 135; William J. Harris/1980, Reilly, 178; D. H. Melhem/1981, Reilly, 192–3). But the talk Baraka pursues – among audiences more varied than is implied by *Conversations'* retinue of 'expert' interviewers ("I stand on street corners and on platforms talking, that is as direct as I can get" – Bigsby/1978; Reilly, 136) – is committed to demolishing the idols of servitude enshrined in our "thinking" as much as the physical temples of oppression. Thus, *Conversations*, seen as a coherent project of "publicly redefining/each change in my soul, as if I had predicted/them" ("The Liar" – *TDL*, p. 79), is *at every moment* dialectical in form, graphing the growth of Barakan voice as a process of constant self-negation designed to generate a momentum toward superintegration.

Thus, notwithstanding the well-known changes in political affiliation and cultural influence that, one might note, are marked more obsessively by the category-obsessed interviewers (myself included: Kim Benston/1977, Reilly, 105–17) than by Baraka himself, one discerns from the earliest discussions a wariness of merely substituting one falsifying presupposition with another, an exacting scrutiny of hardwon positions that generates a self-critical tone sometimes bordering on the "self-deprecatory" but more often unruffled in accepting that "your perception of reality changes, just as reality changes" (Debra L. Edwards/1979, Reilly, 152). This revisionary questioning of imaginative claims services the progressive liberation, for conscious use by the poet, of areas of social and performative experience that had previously to be repressed or sublimated in accordance with a paradoxically more restrictive view of "pure" artistic production.

At the core of this evolutionary praxis is, conceptually, the confrontation of form and energy, structure and process. Considered as a reading of "sociological configuration," this opposition expresses itself as the call for violent "resistance" to oppressive "systems," while as aesthetic ideology it discloses itself in the strategy of briskly improvising rather than reifying those images that convey Baraka's current sense of imaginative necessity. The figures through which revolutionary purpose is enunciated, for example, are generally mimetic ("the artist represents the will of a particular idea" – Robert Allen/1967, Reilly, 22; "Any work that [whites] have – art, technical work – demonstrates who they are" – Marvin X and Faruk/1968, Reilly, 61; "the poet's function is as an interpreter of society and as a reflector of society" – Harris/1980, Reilly, 177), but the goal of aesthetic insight is always that of rectification, purification, and transformation. Baraka thereby explores the possibility of a functional rather than a transcendental agency for poetic language, defining his linguistic resources in terms of its activity, its capacity for "action, doing" rather than as a "passive kind of enterprise" (Harris/1980, Reilly, 168).

Accordingly, we never hear in *Conversations* the kind of extended expository or meditative voice that characterizes, by exemplary contrast, Ralph Ellison's interviews. For Baraka, such elaborated rumination would undercut the emphasis on self-discovery as a continuing act, a "violent" series of discoveries that can make few claims as finished products (Harris/1980, Reilly, 168). Rather, the interviews work as a kind of "talk poem" whose self-interruptive style varies tonal registers as a way of releasing the expressive energy latent in an ever-shifting poetics. The pages of *Conversations* are, to be sure, peppered with portentous announcements . . . but these come, for the most part, from the mouths of Baraka's interlocutors. One can often hear Baraka seeking his voice not in dialogue with his questioners but against the grain of their efforts – sometimes overt and captious (as with Stewart Smith and Peter Thorn/1966; Reilly, 12–19), sometimes subtly tendentious (as in Marvin X and Faruk/1968, Reilly, 51–61) – to turn him into a sounding-board for their own preformulated readings of Barakan purpose, fixing him to his own enunciations as absolute blunders or pieties. But this struggle between the interviews' pre-scriptions and Baraka's treatment of his work as pre-text for freshly vocalized interpretation is often valuable, yielding a clearer sense of Baraka's self-conception as evolving will.

At times, we find Baraka not so much exchanging "views" with his inquisitors as sounding their and his own presuppositions, working against the texture of a given query toward a differently-focused "question":

> *Smith/Thorn*: The question is, what happens to you as a creative person when you start to give yourself over entirely to protest activities, to the actual fighting for what you want? . . .
>
> *Jones*: . . . Building a new world is the creative work of our time – there is *nothing* more creative than that.
>
> *Smith/Thorn*: If you succeed in setting right these various social questions, are Negro Literature and Negro art and so on actually going to be submerged?
>
> *Jones*: No, no, no – it's not a question of that. You see, the white man tries to separate art from social protest simply because he has no real interest in hearing the protest. . . . Literature has to deal with men, with men's lives, with men's souls, with the way men live and are forced to live. These are crucial questions. . . . it's a question of who is doing the looking . . .
>
> (Smith and Thorn/1966, Reilly, 15–16)

Baraka's responses crackle with their nervous insistence on reformulating not just the import but the timbre and conditions of inquiry, driving toward an immediacy of purpose and perception denied by the interviewers' presumptive separation of "activity" from "art." One hears in them the urge to fuse political and aesthetic idea by making them audible within the instant's discourse, rendering them internal to the refashioned tonality of call-and-response by which Baraka seizes the stage from questioners whose own speech is redefined as a refusal to "hear." Baraka's sentences, by the same token, enact within themselves the inseparability of sound and sense, "protest" being indeed the very substance of his reformulated aesthetic ideology. Interrupting the thrust of antagonistic propositions with measured exclamations, contra-interrogations, and a forceful anaphoric syntax ("with men ... with men's lives/souls/live[s] ..."), his phrases establish for the conversation a counter-momentum that sweeps away the dismissive inquiries, built of unexamined but settled constructs, with which he is confronted.

Moments such as these pivot on Baraka's resolute occupation of positions of both questioner and interrogated, a dramatic 'turn' that transgresses generic decorum by exposing the interview format's unspoken structures of authority, hierarchy, and legitimation. Disrupting the interview mode's predilection for rehearsing the subject's preestablished shibboleths, Baraka parries the form's habitual complacency, ease, and empty repetitiousness, preferring tones bespeaking the verve and labor of a mind seeking precise, germane apprehension. Perhaps this is what lends *Conversations* its air of surprise and risk-taking, felt at once as moral obligation, performative strategy, and personal imperative. No less than in his poetry, drama, and prose, Baraka here forges a distinctive idiolect of imaginative worldliness that blends vocal with social freedom at the most particular level of utterance. Resisting any effort to arrest his expressive vision, to monumentalize his ever-changing commitment to emancipatory projects and articulations, Baraka appropriates the conversational medium for what we might call an antitextual manner of sounding.

III Sounding type: screaming beyond the text

LISTEN.
      SOUND.
The word *sound*-ed, in its quicker leap from the mind, as the cry or dancer, singer does, Making the voice leap past the machine. (Past the formality of "literature," which is a cracked white vahz ...)

                    Amiri Baraka, "Poetry and Karma"[5]

Art's epitome is thus consistently for Baraka temporal and oral, rather than visual and total, an act of *energeia* that inevitably undermines any of its specific forms. It is a continuous *movement* of what he often calls "actual speech," set against the very conventions which it erects only to alter, suspend, and transgress.

The page doesn't interest me that much – not as much as the actual spoken word. ... and I think that the whole wave of the future is

definitely not literary ... The question to me of a poet writing in
silence for people who will read in silence and put it in a library where
the whole thing is conceived in silence and lost forever in silence is
about over.

(Harris/1980, Reilly, 176–7)

Sounding the literary as the mausoleum of a fragmenting misrecognition of creative impulse, Baraka ironically reverses the customary account
of writing's institutional authority, casting it as the ephemeral counterpart
to a vibrant futurity of orality. For him, writing is always already agonal;
its disappearance is not just historical but congenital. Utterance, not just
as signified on the page but as embodied in performance, is by contrast
enlivening in its implicitly communal expenditure, its realization in and
for current circumstances, where it drives into time with a force that shatters the 'cracked white vahz' of Euro-American (post)Romanticism, that
Cold Pastoral Urn containing the unseen ashes of cultural waste. Only by
thus superseding its particular determinations can language escape its
hollowing into spurious permanence, becoming for Baraka instead a force,
activity, and spirit: thus established as a continuously refashioning process,
language-as-utterance aspires to its natural rather than conventional
'sound.' But this does not make Baraka an unreconstructed logocentrist,
for 'convention' here indicates the arid decorum of an alienating aesthetic
code, 'natural' the full range of resources forged in the African Diaspora.
Mimesis, then, does not thereby replace design; rather, Baraka seeks an
expressive realism in which language does not simply observe or confirm
experience but, instead, becomes a way of grasping and affecting the world.
Not a mediaton between self and world but an instrumental fusion of
power and perception, the Barakan word at its maximal pitch of lucid
(de)creation forges a nexus of intelligibility and desire, becoming the node
of an activated comprehension.

From the projectivist phase of Baraka's verse to the poetry's most recent
incarnation as a "transbluesnt" quest for "whys/wise" interrogations and
evocations, the movement of type along the pages of Baraka's writing
bespeaks this resistance of word to image, of voice to textual determination.
Even at the very level of materiality, then, Baraka's work seemingly moves
towards its own erasure. But this self-effacing vocality betokens no Euro-
modernist retreat from public display, no Mallarméan aphanisis in pursuit
of the perfectly-(de)composed Book. Indeed, it is the very commitment to
realize voice as a boisterous assertion of emotive, bodily, and expressive
presence that sparks Baraka's serio-comic clash with type's fixities:

A typewriter? – why shd it only make use of the tips of the fingers .
. . If I invented a word placing machine, an "expression-scriber," *if
you will*, then I would have a kind of instrument into which I could
step & sit or sprawl or hang & use not only my fingers to make words

express feelings but elbows, feet, head, behind, and all the sounds I wanted, screams, grunts, . . . I'd have magnetically recorded, at the same time, & translated into word – or perhaps even the final thought/feeling wd not be merely word or sheet, but *itself*, the xpression, three dimensional – able to be touched, or tasted or felt, or entered, or heard or carried like a speaking singing constantly communicating charm. *A typewriter is corny!!*

("Technology & Ethos",
Raise Race Rays Raze, 156)

A typewriter is corny – an unreformed apparatus of High Modernism (William Faulkner and Charles Olson, among others, gave telling testimony to the typewriter's central place in modernist visions of aesthetic labor), it offers merely a frustratingly inadequate medium of the stereo-typed and *hack*-neyed; as much barrier as broker between visceral and conceptual 'sense,' it provides only a provisional, creakily primitive mechanism of Baraka's raucous urge for unfettered expressivity. By re-"placing" the word-scriber such that it serves not as torpid hindrance but as quickening membrane for a mutually defining passage between sense and sensibility, Baraka would reverse the process, endlessly repeated in post-Renaissance metaphysics of the text, by which representational abstraction detaches itself from communicative purpose, by which consciousness stands beyond the substantial sphere that it purports to understand and ex-press. Such interwoven activity of sema and soma would allow Baraka to press together linguistic and corporeal impulses, to heal the breach between materiality and meaning that typically opens in western aesthetic theory (be it mimetic or expressive, classical or Romantic, modern or poststructuralist). In a kind of revolutionary catachresis of postmodernism's 'writing the body,' Baraka exuberantly flouts scriptorial decorum, making an unrestrained spectacle of his provocatively physicalized, nearly eroticized, fusion of linguistic and bodily registers. 'Communicating' itself as if propelled like a viral or sexual congress through a perpetually dancing organism, the poet's body signifies on the primordial *Ursprache*, with word and object, image and imago, interanimating each other in a vibratory performance of mutual transformation . . . just as the print itself skips across the page here in a breathless expansion of brash self-"inventions," text transformed to a "sheet" of "sound" (to appropriate Ira Gitler's famous description of John Coltrane's saxophonic *glissando)* in which paratactic proliferations of carnal activities ("step & sit or sprawl or hang & . . .") force a constant reframing of signifying conventions ("why shd . . . If . . . then . . . or perhaps . . .").

Baraka's reformed 'xpressive instrumentality' is deliberately, ex-statically outlandish: one feels in these twists of diction, syntax, and typographical convention the feral cunning of the poet claiming his elemental power as (re)maker (*poietes*), as he slams the typewriter toward becoming that which it nominally prohibits; or, perhaps, Baraka mimes his projected desire to merge form and intention by returning us to the root sense of 'type' as a *blow* or *impression* (*typos*), hammering his vision to a new 'beat' (*typtein*) that amplifies the machine as a more-than-metaphorical vehicle of voice.[6] Dashing among audacious propositions and poses, this a fugitive voice that crosses boundaries artificially delimiting interior and exterior, the felt and the said, to liberate the sounds muffled by their sedimentation in the textual environment itself. What is sought is not a mere stylistic modification but a redefinition of the spatio-temporal domain of expression *per se*: even the post-projectivist orthographic dislocations and contractions serve, paradoxically, to dislodge the page's visual logic (assumed and silenced in customary reading practice) and thereby assert a more inclusive, if disruptive, "recording" of animated inscription. In this way, poetic 'writing' no longer follows, or illustrates, thought and desire; it *is* the conjunction of conception and concretion, and as such deconstructs any priority of understanding to performance, making each modality or moment immanent to the other, each equally a means of achieving a renovative im-mediacy, a fully realized NOW where "xpression" and its 'translation' take place "at the same time."

The Barakan "text," so (re)conceived (and the passage's final image of a "carried" song – punning on the typewriter's one mobile element – subliminally suggests the body's impregnation with its own newly articulated bearing toward the incarnated word), is, then, both a strategic and illocutionary gesture. By eluding the dominant 'typographic' system's function as a regulative device structured to amputate or bind a full range of emotive utterance, this refashioned Barkan text operates as an instrument of productive iconoclasm, smashing through the restrictive economy of writing whereby repression and censorship occlude or postpone the arrival of meaning at the scene of immediate experience. In contrast to such a self-alienating system of deferral and conservation, the Barakan instrument enables a modal improvisation of self-authorizing power that transposes textuality from object to event, redefining performative legitimacy as a fearless capacity for continuous metamorphosis, an *attitude* of exorbitant self-expenditure. Transgressing its own "record" by subjecting it to myriad mutations, such legitimacy infuses the word with en-chanted possibilities only by desacralizing the word's relation to the truth it seeks, prodding it to speak always differently, always otherwise. A self-consuming artifact that none the less presses the cause of an empowered, if migratory, presence, the Barakan word affirms what it also contests, or rather, affirms itself as projected variation and transfiguration. The word thus doesn't mean in advance of its transient substantiation in performed gesture and sound; it means what it *says*.

But what are the implications of this performative confluence of craft ('techne') and character ('ethos') for a politics of self-reformation? When writing and identity meet in the newly configured terrain of tactile signification, the self verges upon a fully saturated, almost talismanic vocal determination. Yet the rewired typewriter charges toward this uninterrupted incantational performance of self *as song* (or "charm," *carmen*) through those punctuated evocations of metonymic embodiments and disembodiments that suggest a self-*shattering* repudiation of any given shape or moment within which an identity might establish itself. Likewise, Baraka's quest for a fully adequate, unchecked expressive form is fueled by an impatience with language as he finds it, a nervous dissatisfaction with the tendency of any name or posture to freeze into an illusory finality. Hence the conclusive and celebratory imagining of the "three dimensional" (post-paginal) self as a ceaselessly-enacted harmony of critique ("speaking") and idealization ("singing") is arrived at only by way of its radically negative semblable: the continuously scattered self conceived as a rupturing repudiation of all codes and abstractions – the self as *scream*.

Welling from within the icy-hot belly of the Euro-American beast, Baraka's scream rips through his oeuvre as a fundamental sounding of desire, pain, and insurgency, eventually evoking a whole historical and emotive range of black vocality, from the field holler and work call to the foulmouthed invective of streetcorner jive and resistant elegance of the homey's sass:

> Here at the bridge. 2
> bars, down the street, seeming
> to wrap themselves around my fingers, the day,
> screams in me;
>
> ("The Bridge" – *Preface*, p. 25)

> Grand
> dancers
> spray noise and disorder in these old tombs. . . .
> unfinished cathedrals tremble with our
> screams.
>
> ("Rhythm and Blues," – *TDL*, p. 46)

> Cold air blown through narrow blind eyes. Flesh,
> white hot metal. Glows as the day with its sun.
> It is a human love, I live inside. A bony skeleton
> you recognize as words or simple feeling. . . .
>
> It burns the thing
> inside it. And that thing
> screams.
>
> ("An Agony. As Now." – *TDL*, p. 16)

> . . . some possible image
> of what we shall call history. A jungle
> of feeling. . . .

And the windows of 5th street
scream.

("A Poem for Neutrals" – TDL, pp. 13, 14)

Begin on by Philly night club
or the basement of a cullut church
walk the bars my man for pay
honk the night lust of money
oh
blow –
scream history love

("Am/Trak" – TB, p. 189)

I still hear that
song,
that cry,
cries
screams
life exploded

our world exploding us
transformed to niggers . . .

("Wise 2"– TB, p. 221)

Echoing across the textures of Baraka's verse from *Preface* (1961) to *Wise, Why's, Y's* (1995),[7] the Barakan scream haunts the disparate spaces of black modernity, inhabiting alike tomb and womb, confounding alike the mercantile and the magical, transfusing alike the sacred and the secular. Interrupting the flow of symbolic commerce (often, in these poems, it is or 'has' the last word), the scream presses meaning back into the rhythmic, somatized arena of cultural conflict, simultaneously opening and 'bridging' gaps between music and language, love and history, "me" and "us." A paradoxically stylized disturbance of accepted ties between signs and things – disseminated through the text as both lexical and visceral cue, what *is* the scream, and how does it *sound?* – this intrusion into conventional textual space works both to diffuse and recenter possibilities of meaning for black vocality, repositioning significance (however now dispersed) in more proximate, more intimate relation to sound. By both signaling and substantiating a shift in discursive focus, intervening between Euro-American images of cultural power (cathedral . . . lust . . . money) and the possibility of alternative 'images' of historical value, such cries rudely reinflect political arrangements by mobilizing dormant emotive energies and erecting oppositional structures of "feeling."

Poised on the page between representation and performance, print and voice, the scream shortcircuits convention and mediation, disowns

institutionalized terms of social exchange, and sounds at the threshold of
an apocalypse that would "explode" blackness into a *nigga* "cry" of insur-
rection. Thus turning the West's mislocation of blackness as a "jungle"
into an anarchic zone for reclaimed cultural force, the scream makes sound
its own subject, its own aim; thus incarnating the demand for unfettered
self-determination via an irruptive 'blow' into the freezing "night" of diasporic experience, the scream sets in motion a subphonemic counterplay
to dominant culture's "lust" for "cold" semantic order, allowing signifyin'
to overflow signification, roughening the text's fabric as the voice asserts
the viscoelastic grain of its restive will.

As prelude to a recoded *nigga* presence, the scream springs from a longing
for expressive plenitude that reforms the medium of inscription into a pre-
text, a materium rather than a model for performance. Both thematically
and stylistically, it "calls" for a notion of text as ephemeral resource not
authorized source. This enlargement of tonal agency bypasses textual
semantics in pursuit of a more elemental language of history's "possible
image." As imprinted word, Baraka's "scream" is thus itself only a shadowy
re-presentation, a *type*, of a more fundamental expressive medium. In so
far as Baraka has championed African-American music as a vehicle of this
purifying blackness, the word becomes merely a fallen emblem, at best a
heuristic catalyst for a more essential, intrinsically seditious *song*. But such
a compartmentalizing reading of Baraka's aesthetic politics cannot account
for the persistence of his effort to dis-cover – often through the jagged
interruptions of the scream – a nexus of verbal and musical articulation
that resists reduction of ideal to discrete manifestation or, contrarily, prior-
itization of abstraction to actuality. The revelation of such a progressively,
enduringly revolutionary medium may depend precisely on changing the
nature of words not only on the page but in the "bars": on nothing less,
that is to say, than a murderously criminal rewriting of voice as it sounds
in music as well as in text. For finally, what is at stake is not the mode or
means of utterance *per se* but expression's meaning in time, its capacity to
strive against death (psychic, communal, spiritual) in the continuum of
historical change. Equally, liberated voice, Baraka insists, is the "scream
history love" of a praxis ready to die into the present of perpetual struggle.
Only thus can the metamorphosed and the re-membered self become one:
"New Black Music is this: Find the self, then kill it."[8]

IV   Sounding song: the sacrificial cadence of revolutionary voice

> The eye is useless. Sound, Sound,
> & what you smell
> or feel. . . .
>   Were you
> singing? What song
> was that? . . .

          What song
    is that The words
    are beautiful.

(Amiri Baraka, "The Clearing"
– *Preface*, pp. 29, 30, 31)

To thus shear textuality's authority with the clamoring materiality of the 'honking' voice situates the poet ambiguously as either exorcist or visionary, expending without reserve his breath in the present only as sacrifice toward a redeemed future. A vessel both of discontent and desire, the Barakan scream registers the entanglement of destruction and possibility in his vision of a revolutionary performative idiom. Can the scream portend a *language* of revolutionary blackness, or must it resist the structures of iteration and relation upon which rest the efficacy of shared idioms? Born of the withering belatedness that it would cure, Baraka's scream redoubles itself both as a violence of gesture that empties discourse and as a potential purity of speech stripped bare of even rebellious figurations. To hear it in its most pungent register, let's return to the site of Clay's repudiating howl:

> Bird would've played not a note of music if he just walked up to East Sixty-seventh Street and killed the first ten white people he saw. Not a note! Some kind of bastard literature . . . all it needs is a simple knife thrust. . . . If Bessie Smith had killed some white people she wouldn't have needed that music. She could have talked very straight and plain about the world. No metaphors. No grunts. No wiggles in the dark of her soul. Just two and two are four. Money. Power. Luxury. Like that. All of them. Crazy niggers turning their backs on sanity. . . . Would make us all sane.
>
> (Dutchman, 35)[9]

Clay, speaking himself from within the exilic veil of doomed self-division, images a mode of immediacy that renders even the richest vernacular breach of hegemonic decorum a symptom of continued enslavement, another condition of banishment from fully restored meaning. At the least, we feel in his anguished protest to Lula's misprized "belly rub" (34) an ambivalent view of black music as disclosure and as frustrated avoidance of revolution's *thing-in-itself*. Figuring a peculiar combination of sedition and evasion, idealism and nihilism, even the 'blackest' musical expression, according to Clay, sublimates what it reflects, erecting barriers to full psychic realization as it mediates insight and gesture. It fatally entwines the killing which ruins black culture with that which would cure it, obscuring the therapeutic pleasures of implacable upheaval with substitutive, if searing, compromise formations. Ultimately, Bird's bebop fury and Bessie's blues-people outcry refer not to the deprivations of experience, or to their ironic profanation, but to the very corrective violence from which the music itself is a detour.

Clay's African-American musical lexicon thus seemingly constitutes a simulacrum of the "I" who speaks through it, a site of self-distantiation more than self-display. The irony Clay insists upon – and which, not incidentally, will momentarily unravel his own voicing of black expressive power, when Lula's "knife thrust" cuts him off "like that," "his mouth working stupidly" as he slumps breathless toward oblivion (37) – is that the most forceful assertions of subaltern estrangement redouble rather than redress traumatic alterity, as much dis-integrating as furnishing forth ('performing') black identity. Hardening illusion into 'truth,' the very brilliance of music's metaphoricity becomes insidiously misleading, suggesting the necessity for re-creation of initial intentions by a renunciation of artistic forms. Housed in the fictions of "that music," Bird's and Bessie's identities are merely symbolic fragments of a primal agency that cannot itself be represented. Therefore, it will become the project of Baraka's musical aesthetics to reorient the search for this agency from contemplation of musical expression in its objective form to the *process* of playing, the askesis of imaginative desire carried along the movement from note to note, form to form.

This relatively early Barakan vision of black music in *Dutchman* suggests the potentially tragic limitation of black vocality as a fragile surface that nevertheless includes a resonant depth, an aesthetic foreground that conceals a background of anti-metaphorical desire for the directly liberatory act. Music remains a version, however elevated, of "bastard literature," since it functions as a restraint upon the absolute will-to-freedom that it expresses "in code" (36). It never arrives at the meaning to which it points – the decisive face-to-face encounter with spurious white power – but instead sees, or speaks, through a glass darkly, denying itself the raw satisfaction of apocalyptic aggression. Caught still in the metaphysics against which it speaks, black voice is ensnared in a potentially inalterable relation to death, arising from the negative foundations of replacement and exchange. Baraka's longstanding focus upon black musicality can be read, I suggest, as a continuously rethought effort to liberate the performance of voice from the metaphysics of death, substituting for the ordinary substitutive logic of language-as-'metaphor' another experience of voice, one where the displacements of expression no longer indicate the mere 'stupidities' of dislocation or decease, but instead attest to black consciousness's capacity to sustain an unlimited number of revisions, to undertake death as the possibility of the voice's freedom.[10]

Clay's speech itself, considered in dramatic context, is a fleeting intrusion of this revealed and unmasking voice-of-death, piercing as it does the demonic theatricality of Lula's minstrelsy. Hence the ambivalence of Baraka's attitude toward the tragic emplotment of Clay's argument is as important as the frustrated black aesthetics embedded in the argument itself. Unable (as yet?) to transcend indirect duplication of 'murderous sanity,' Clay's black music nevertheless images the presence within itself of a language more profound than its own discourse, a language capable of converting wiggling traceries of black desire into withering negations of all otherness ("No/no/no . . ."). A riddling double-helix of self-consuming defiance, it hints at Baraka's belief, here wistful or shrouded, in the necessity of an unequivocal affiliation of perception and performance. As structures of dissimulation, Bird's and Bessie's performances veil the'in-itself' or living insurgency behind the ameliorative fabrications that at once frighten and thrill "all the hip white boys" (35: one senses here in *Dutchman* a dig at Mailer's 'white Negro,' whose bebop minstrelsy Lula incarnates as a kind of mirror of this double-voiced black vernacular). The music is, as it were, an elaborate covering to an earlier mode of utterance, the residues of which disrupt the tone-deaf listener: "Before . . . anything you can explain, [Bessie's] saying, and very plainly, 'Kiss my black ass.' And if you don't know that, it's you that's doing the kissing" (35–6).

Clay's enigmatic exposure of the way cryptic resistance delays its own chiliastic investments can be seen as generated from the tension between two ontologies of black expressivity: one driven by the negativity attendant to the subversive masking of 'double consciousness'; the other consequent upon appropriation of this capacity for multivoiced insight, suggesting the value of black musicality for collective articulation, at once adversarial and renovative. And, when we examine Baraka's musical aesthetics as a *progressive* model of vocal determination, we find a rich development toward the latter position from the seeds of the former. Through the movement from an ironic-tragic to a performative-revolutionary vision, Baraka's musical aesthetic dialectically revises its assumptions by locating *in* avant-garde experimentation the very de/reconstructive energies that Clay's Pisgah account of Bird and Bessie can envision but not experience. What is sought is a sublime mode of performance that can blast the container of representation, freeing the community's sense of superiority to a hostile world. Musical transformation would thus be not tragically figurative but cathartic and prophetic; its disruption of received codes would be subsumed into a larger program of desublimation that restores the continuity of representation and truth. Black vocality would no longer be seen as a means of coping with existence, trapped in the repetitive cycles of illusion and disillusion, but instead would appear as a fusion of will and expression that sanctions violent demystification as a means of survival and renewal.

Baraka finds precisely this crossing of passion and purpose, intention and process, in the "New Black Music" of the Black Arts Movement era. Reshaping Clay's deceptive but despairing idealism, Baraka finds himself ready to privilege the sounds of such emergent innovators as Albert Ayler, Sonny Rollins, Sun Ra, and, especially, John Coltrane as a fresh mode of artistic endeavor, since its *raison d'être* is the negation of the very concept of 'art' that rests upon figural understanding. In Baraka's reading, the New Black Music promotes a style of imaginative exploration that perpetually breaks through its own limits and achieves something not habitually given

to 'art' within western aesthetic standards (indeed, the periodic deconstructive appropriation of popular musical 'standards' is a salutary element
of the new music's subversive ethos). Most striking for our purposes is
Baraka's insistence, especially in his detailed engagements with Coltrane's
"shattering" and reconstruction of popular balladic edifice, on the way the
novel manner of extended "free" improvisation achieved a new temporality for sound's intentional structure. By braiding the melodic and
harmonic statement, Baraka averred, Coltrane's "surging chordal line"
allows diachronic tonality to keep pace with the rhythm of linear narrative,
in effect liberating the subtextual disruptions buried beneath Clay's musical
masking ("A Jazz Great: John Coltrane").[11] Coltrane's uproarious yet
precise parsing of the never-yet-heard note buried within the tones of the
standard "bar" inaugurates a context for African-American performance
that inscribes the historical phenomenality of vernacular expression (Baraka
was the first critic to recognize the idiomatic roots of the freshly re-'bent'
chord) while suggesting the singularity of its own outrageous practice.

As the first principle of the New Music's inventive procedure, Baraka
cites "*Projection over sustained periods* (more time given, and time proposes a
history for expression, hence it becomes reflective projection" ("New Black
Music," 175), the unclosed parenthesis miming this intuition of temporal
suspension and openness to constant historical emendation. Positing within
Coltrane's infinitely particularized note the capacity to act as "bridge"
between exactly those discontinuous instants that so divide African-
American history from its eschatological destiny, Baraka finds *in* the New
Music the longed-for *revolutionary moment*:

> . . . after riding a subway through New York's bowels, . . . and then
> coming upstairs to the street and walking slowly, head down, through
> the traffic and failure that does shape this place, and then entering
> "The Jazz Corner Of The World," a temple erected in praise of what
> God (?), and then finally amidst that noise and glare to hear a man
> destroy all of it, completely, like Sodom, with just the first few notes
> from his horn . . . All the music on this album is *live*, whether it was
> recorded above the drunks and clowns at Birdland, or in the studio.
> ("Coltrane Live At Birdland," 64–5, 67)[12]

Trane's shimmering movements along the harmonic line re"shape" not
just the chordal network but the very space through which the poet moves,
redefining his own sense of direction and possibility. This awe-ful, resounding transfiguration of psychic and social being *charts* a remade relation
between past and present, echo and originality, transgression and spirituality that reconciles the wounds opened by Clay's disjunctive account of
musicality and the "plain talk" of rebellion. The reconceived moment of
performance is *live* because it cannot be reduced to any precise instant,
but articulates an assemblage of events that arise across spatial and modal

boundaries. It redeems the historicity of loss to which it gives witness by 'naturalizing' its protean habitations of 'convention': hence the second of Baraka's principles for understanding the New Music – "*Arbitrariness of form* (variety in nature)" ("New Black Music," 175).

The sheer *speed* of Trane's chordal *glissando* liberates his sound from strict bondage to preformulated meanings without yielding the instrument's powers of signification; establishing itself in the paradoxical tense of the future present, this rhythmic dissolution and reconstruction of the medium defines the music as a constant interfusion of transitive and material functions. No longer, as with Clay's account, are we turning our attention to the moment *before* sound, forcing song back upon itself to find an idiom that refuses translation into musical appearance. Instead, music becomes the argot of the *plenum* even as it wields itself as a 'destructively' emancipatory discourse threatening every manner of sense-making. The New Music orients us not to a veiled world of signs but to a revealed cosmos of effectual avowal, revealing in the moment of its own playing the unspoken value that the world's "noise" conceals beneath its cacophony of hardened 'truths.' Hence the third principle of Baraka's catechism: "*Intention of performance as a learning experience*" ("New Black Music," 175).

Implicitly, then, under the direction of the New Music's therapeutic restitution of engaged consciousness, performing becomes a mode of attention, listening an active enactment: "I got up and danced while writing these notes, screaming at Elvin to cool it" ("Coltrane Live At Birdland," 66). One can fairly feel Baraka rising to reform Clay's stance, suturing the rifts dividing the body's assertion from the voice's inscriptions, apocalyptic scream from communicative utterance. "Performance" now encompasses the physicality and communality of expressive production *and* the "intention" to signify: it becomes not just "notes" but the choreo/graphy of their taking (a) place ("I got up and danced *while* writing these notes").

Not that "these notes" – be they Baraka's or Trane's – can accomplish their millennial enterprise by themselves. Baraka's serio-comic evocation of call-and-response as he leaps from his desk to "wiggle" to Elvin's 3/4 scrambling of the conventional jazz beat's "straight two and two are four" betokens an urge to follow the music's inspiration as a reconception of authorship itself. The scene of performance extends itself improvisationally, rewriting the master text or score in a blurring of boundaries between maker and audience: neither player nor auditor remain a monolithic authority, but are instead mutually produced by the fluid dynamics of performance itself, each one 'arranging' the other through a continuously interwoven stream of "notes." The New Music materializes itself in Baraka's body, inspiriting it as a site of critical and creative activity, suggesting that the listener is not the limit but the beginning of the musician's generative heat ("cool it"!).

This insistence on collaborative invention resists the temptation to idolize or totalize Trane and the new musical vanguard, bursting the closure or expressive inhibition that reification of authorial mastery imposes on the rambunctious proliferation of unruly meanings. Refusing to occlude the rough-edged energies of cultural change behind a mask of aesthetic performance, Baraka grasps the New Music as a way for an emergent black consciousness to interpret itself to itself as an act of transgressive revision, spurring each communal member to tell another version of "these notes": ". . . almost anyone who's heard John and the others at a nightclub or some kind of live performance, has got stories of their own" ("Coltrane Live at Birdland," 65). "John and the others" in this sense designate not so much individual craftsmen (however much they are, indeed, "avant-guardians" of the ever-expanding black expressive lexicon) as an acoustic milieu for realization of boldly reimagined cultural identities. One feels here, in part, the recovery of a kind of innocence, the renewed capacity to believe in the self as pure potentiality. But, given the exacting crucible of stern discipline and interpretive confrontation in which are forged such reawakened possibilities, one senses the primacy in Baraka's responses to the New Music's call of the will-to-*choice*, the urge to create conditions for making the most momentous of personal and historical decisions. Above all, Baraka seizes upon the New Music not to idealize it in a style of counter-hegemonic ideological mystification but to intensify the present as the scene of revolutionary resolve. Through its apocalyptic innovations, Baraka's New Music leaves a trace of the future on the present, modeling in the music's radical reconceptualizations the appropriation of historical forces in an actual moment of performative experience. Redirecting Clay's portentous pessimism, these musical "poets of the Black Nation" ("New Black Music," 176) reinvigorate black expressive culture with a felt power of political efficacy and humane vision, interlacing realism (as attention to the endless demands of craft) and idealism (as breathless pursuit of the perfect "note") to display in their art the dialectical relation between historical circumstance and utopian aspiration:

> There is a daringly human quality to John Coltrane's music that makes itself felt, wherever he records. If you can hear, this music will make you think of a lot of weird and wonderful things. You might even become one of them.
>
> ("Coltrane Live At Birdland," 67)

V Baraka sounding: "thrash and moan" of the performing self

> I'm Everett LeRoi Jones . . .
> A black nigger in the universe. A longer breath singer,
> wouldbe dancer, strong from years of fantasy
> and study. All this time then, for what's happening
> now.
>
> Amiri Baraka, "Numbers, Letters" – *SP*, p. 72

At once destructive and creative agents of a new 'Afro-Blue' semiotic of feeling, the Black Arts musicians in Baraka's vivid portrayal play annihilating notes of a black Jeremiad in order to sing the creative sound of being – in this way, the "thrash and moan" of their furious pursuits do not oppose but resonate the "black rhythm energy blues feeling (sensibility)" of African-American culture *per se* ("New Black Music," 176; 175). The interfusion of dispersion and synthesis in their (de)compositional method makes possible for Baraka the reformulation of black expressivity as a simultaneously constructive and transitive adventure. Thus, Baraka has since reinflected his vision of Bird's and bebop's aesthetic negations in terms consistent with the New Music's capacity to revitalize, not just re-cover, a transformational relation to process and presence: with Bop, "another world had opened . . . [it] created a new speech, a new song . . . [in] black night laboratories of sound" ("Diz").[13] Linked by this impulse to animate the unheard of tradition, Bop and the New Music form in Baraka's aesthetic theory and history a single 'new wave' amplifying the ideal of immoderate vocal outpouring without loss of either expressive immediacy or cultural continuity.

For Baraka, then, the innovative jazz sound is the exteriorization of that moral energy that can quicken revolutionary insight, which might be further defined as an unbound consciousness assuming agency by subjecting imposed structures and interior norms to the dialectical play of critique and reparation. Like Trane, his poetry, in performance, tears through a variety of idioms in search of a nexus of praxis and being, (re)creating for its audience the experience of facing interpretive and moral options: recapturing the power of choice, a Baraka reading is designed to envision, if not achieve, nothing less than history's redemption. Even in the early stages of his career, when he was relatively bound to the text in hand, Baraka's verse registered a protest against 'literary' falsification of feeling and desire, declaring that the unfolding of alternatives, the ground of action as such, can only occur in the presentational moment. As they have evolved, Baraka's readings have sought to convey the feeling he recorded so strikingly in listening to Trane, *et al.* forge "the touchstone of the new world": that "something is really happening. Now" ("New Black Music," 175).

The ongoing history of Baraka's readings project over their span this ethos of progressive improvisation. Baraka's readings must therefore be approached as both structures and events, as utterances which possess their own principles of relation but whose intentional activity transpires, self-consciously, within a network of prior calls and imminent responses. They cannot be seen merely as rhetorical objects, but instead should be placed in numerous contexts of historically conditioned enactments, beginning with the still-evolving story of Baraka's performance stance itself. In tracing, for example, an arc of recitational style from the Living Theater reading of 1961 or Town Hall reading of 1964 to a recent gig in New

York (1995) or Philadelphia (1996), we find what a rendition of any given poem will display: *the poet's relationship to the work undergoing continual change in performance.*

Before undertaking a brief outline of this tracery, we must keep in mind our own entrapment, here, in the order of print. Especially as Baraka's texts increasingly provide more a catalytic than a scriptive function for his reading, my account will become a faint vestige of his voice's dramatic embodiments, becoming at best an allegory of their gestural vigor. What I need is an "expression-scriber, *if you will,*" but no, I haven't yet gotten up to dance while writing these notes – though my students have been jumping in the hallway to the mixed sounds of Baraka's taped voice and my own floating out the office door for the past few days! In reading what follows, then, it's best to think of his cited texts and my own responsive commentary as challenges to your inventive ingenuity and ethical bearing, treating them, too, not as static objects but as spectral scores for a fervid, if evanescent, production.

Something of this effort is mimetically apt, for we can see in Baraka's own performative development the emergence of a concern to locate and exploit the musical rather than semantic potential of his voice. Cognate with this augmented interest in the vocality of meaning is a shifting poetics of the self in – or *as* – performance. Both vectors of self-presentational revision involve, as we shall see, reorientation equally of his own rhythmic and tonal capacities and his audience's perceptual expectations. Let's begin with an exemplary poem from the 1961 Living Theater reading:

African blues
does not know me. . . .
        A country
in black & white, newspapers
blown down pavements
of the world. Does
not feel what I am. . . .
                Black
words throw up sand
to eyes, fingers of
their private dead. Whose
soul, eyes, in sand. My color
is not theirs. Lighter, white man
talk. They shy away. My own
dead souls, my, so called
people. Africa
is a foreign place. You are
as any other sad man here
american.

                        ("Notes For A Speech" – *Preface*, p. 47)

Sitting tightly wedged between chair and table, tautly-pressed, like Clay, into his careful dark suit (sharp, precise, 'tied down'), his eyes fixed keenly on the paper before him (see Plate 1 below), LeRoi Jones makes his appeal to the mostly white audience in an unwavering tone, the phrases pronounced with piercing exactness, uttered word-by-word, each syllable crackling with attention to the minutest demands of vocalic or consonantal inflection, each caesura carefully marked, each periodic closure given due emphasis – a very model of rhetorical and elocutionary control. Such eloquent rectitude and solicitous decorum befit all too well a poem depicting the alienation of the poet's "blues sensibility" into the dusty distances and ironic lassitude of writing, "African" immediacy having been dissipated into the middling passages of bleached-dry American "black & white." The poet's discourse manifests estrangement rather than communicative confidence, cramping him into the narrow privacy and even irrelevance of his self-display. Sharing with the landscape only an eviscerating colorlessness, the poet experiences himself as his own limit, the halting pace of the sentences indicating the failure of dialogue even within the self. One might ask of the poem's rhetorical and historical speakers both, whether they indeed fully occupy the present, whether their shared diasporic consciousness is not fragmented in the noncoincidence of "my" and "you," body and text, performer and audience. In some way,

Plate 1: LeRoi Jones reading at the Living Theater, 1961. Looking on are Allen Ginsberg, Joel Oppenheimer and Diane di Prima.

Photograph © Fred W. McDarrah

"Notes for a Speech," from its sardonically "shy" title through its dénouement of jaggedly insistent denial, is a poem that almost asks *not* to be read,
that requires a kind of suspension from the languid pulse of "white man's
talk" (oxymoron, that?) within which a living voice might arise.

Such, perhaps, is the unsaid of "LeRoi Jones"'s readings, their carefully
sculpted pauses – hollowed from lines delivered with such painful exacti-
tude – suggesting a space for a contra-dictory moment of inspiration, as
if *Baraka* were always about to irrupt from within "Jones" to read the
poem that would revivify "my own dead souls." Here, the privative laments
– "not know . . . not feel . . . not theirs" – can be heard as an effort to
stop the reading itself, to deaden the voice to the task of enacting its own
imprisonment in "foreign" space and language. Beneath the spare, self-
evacuating articulation, hovering between despondency and listlessness,
lurks a less ironically disposed figure. For the careful auditor might hear
a "note" of a different kind of "speech" in the seething undertow of the
recitation's measured insistence, the voice – almost impossibly young, it
seems now, when heard again on tape – wafting toward the audience in
the final lines with a slight upward, questioning intonation, as if registering
some subvocal, almost inaudible, plea, the body possibly not just impris-
oned by furniture and stage-isolation but rocking, almost imperceptibly,
with the nervous energy of a coiled rebel, his irony not a mark of fatigue
but a mask (*dissimulatio*) of violent desire: "And I sit here, in this buttoned-
up suit, to keep myself from cutting all your throats" (Clay; *Dutchman*, 34).

In content and style of declamation, such early poems as "Notes for a
Speech" are suffused with a wistful tone suggestive of the poet's equivocal
relation to his performative circumstances and his longing for a release
from postRomantic despair by the upsurge of rebellious disavowal. In such
works as "Green Lantern's Solo," "A Poem for Speculative Hipsters," "A
contract. (for the destruction and rebuilding of Paterson," and "A Poem
for Willie Best" (all *TDL*), this hesitant, garbled voice of repudiation is
given idiomatic inflection in sudden eruptions of vernacular exclamation
– "He said, I'm tired/of losing./'I *got* ta cut'cha" ("A Poem for Willie
Best," VII– *TDL*, p. 25) – and dada 'sounding' – "No, Nigger, no, blind
drunk in SantaSurreal's beard. Dead/hero/for our time . . ." ("Green
Lantern's Solo" – *TDL*, p. 68). In these lines, when read in Jones's even-
toned clarity and high-cultural diction, we feel the poet's ambivalent
aesthetic and political identifications as a conflict of idiomatic postures, an
emergent clash of linguistic sources and styles that is thematized with esca-
lating frequency in poems just preceding the move Uptown: like Willie
Best and the Green Lantern, Jones performs himself as a disguised but
potential 'hero,' increasingly compelled and willing to hazard the flourish
of subversive accents against the conspicuous petition for admission to the
modernist ranks of the certifiably 'poetic.'

This subliminal absorption of elegiac dejection into a dialectic of emancipatory exorcism becomes overt in both the subject-matter and changing

performance styles of the pivotal early poem, "BLACK DADA
NIHILISMUS." Appropriately, given the undertone of supplication
suffusing Jones's early recitational manner, the poem is cast as a kind of
hymn of the Black Arts, an invocation to a long-dormant Africanicity. As
with earlier poems like "Notes for a Speech," in "BLACK DADA
NIHILISMUS" voice and thought are intertwined, but here their ironic
contract is replaced by an incendiary covenant of "breath" and "purpose":

> .Against what light
>
> is false what breath
> sucked, for deadness.
> > Murder, the cleansed
>
> purpose, frail, against
> God, if they bring him
> > bleeding, I would not
>
> forgive, or even call him
> black dada nihilismus. . . .
>
> B. D. N., for the secret men, Hermes, the
>
> blacker art. . . .
> > Trismegistus, have
>
> them, in their transmutation, from stone
> to bleeding pearl, from lead to burning
> looting, dead Moctezuma, find the West
>
> a grey hideous space.
> > ("BLACK DADA NIHILISMUS,"
> > – *TDL*, pp. 61, 62)

Corresponding in all respects to the classical modes of hymnic evocation
– theurgic, celebratory, genealogical, mythic, and inventive – while playing
out what Paul Fry terms the "strange logic" of invocation and prolepsis,[14]
"BLACK DADA NIHILISMUS" cuts open a new space for Baraka's verse
at the threshold of "murder" and rebirth, banishment and empowerment.
Even so, "BLACK DADA NIHILISMUS" sustains its hymnic bearing
only so far, summoning its mythopoeic craft in order to provide a fresh
context for prophetic discourse within which the poet can recast his public
role (as Jonathan Culler reminds us, hymnal invocation is a figure for
vocation). Hence the poem's enthralled replacement of white mythology's
grey hideousness with a "blacker art" of incisive "transmutation" modulates the poem from divine summons to daemonaic origination, the
radically dissenting invocation of its second, concluding section – "Why
you stay, where they can/reach? Why you sit, or stand, or walk/in this

place . . ./Come up, black dada/nihilismus" – rising into proclamation of
the transgressive voice incarnate:

> Black scream
> and chant, scream,
> and dull, un
> earthly
> hollering. Dada, bilious
> what ugliness, learned
> in the dome, colored holy
> shit . . .
>
> ("BLACK DADA NIHILISMUS,"
> – *TDL*, pp. 63–4)

Touching the root violence of the 'sacred,' the sanguinary criminality of
the 'blessed,' the poem seeks to regenerate a sanctified collectivity from
conditions of defilement, to grow the seeds of deliverance from the
un/earthly ground of disgust. Its originating 'hermetic' discipline charges
the poet's priestly function with an increasingly ruthless task of purification that challenges the text's own deliberate techniques of enunciation.
By thus enlarging its vocative purpose from the valedictory aims of
hymnody to the full-throated "scream" of portentous divination, "BLACK
DADA NIHILISMUS" seeks to recover and embody the voice deferred
or submerged in the early works, to locate that cosmogonic "chant" of
blackness by becoming exactly what it announces. By proposing ever more
outrageous manifestations of this crossing of will and word – "Rape the
white girls. Rape/their fathers. Cut the mothers' throats" – the poem calls
into question the propriety of figuration itself (imaged most cunningly as
a shattering de-nigration of the Shelleyan–Yeatsian 'color-dome' of
Romantic vision), or perhaps allows for the use-value of representation's
negativity only in the ambiguously subjective-imperative mode of redemptive profanation:

> For tambo, willie best, dubois, patrice, mantan, the
> bronze buckaroos.
>
> > For Jack Johnson, asbestos, tonto, buckwheat,
> > billie holiday.
>
> > > For tom russ, l'overture, vesey, beau jack,
> > (may a lost god damballah, rest or save us
> > against the murders we intend
> > against his lost white children
> > black dada nihilismus
>
> ("BLACK DADA NIHILISMUS,"
> – *TDL*, p. 64)

Gathering momentum for release from the spectral, cynical, (mock)-meditative address of his 'bohemian' and even projective verse, Baraka floods the text with an alliteratively textured chronicle of 'proper' names drawn from a New World catalogue of black vernacular performance styles. Operating appropriately under the salvaged sign of "a lost god damballah" (the skin-shedding serpent deity of Creation and ancestral knowledge, the loa fed by sacrifice of white animals), this onomastic inventory reclaims a host of familial (tom russ), revolutionary (vesey), pan-African (patrice, l'overture), and even iniquitous (asbestos, buckwheat) entitlements from the indignity of oblivion and the minstrelsy of misdesignation. "BLACK DADA NIHILISMUS" thus offers itself as a kind of revolutionary semiosis whose capacity for 'long-breathed' invocation prolongs the aura of presence that putatively subtends the poem's fundamental project of reoriginating negation.

"Black dada nihilismus" is itself the name for the moment and instrument of transition, or the unnameable and uncanny rupture from one tradition that recalls another. It is a charm that signifies its own unmaking or overcoming, the riotous excess both internal (dada) and external (black) to the system in and "against" which it arises. Expunging the categories that it enumerates, "black dada nihilismus" names itself as an anomaly. As such, it can only be read in a double movement, as catachretic end and apocalyptic beginning, as though the poem were a *vévé* of the postmodern – or, as Baraka might later have put it, postwestern – damballah. And as a ritual for beginning *again* ("the *lost* god damballah"), "black dada nihilismus" occurs in the gap between cultural figurations, at the crossroads or agora where blackness redefines itself as a transvaluation of (de)creative energies.

One way of reading the play in "BLACK DADA NIHILISMUS" between the unnaming "call" that eradicates "bastard" authority ("i call them sinned/or lost/burned masters . . .") and the summons that restores communal aspiration ("we intend . . .") is to think of the speaker shaping the poem as a sufficiently dilatory space for him to eventually assume the lost god's power himself. What begins as an almost interrogative prayerful meditation designed to open some unstated closure (".Against what light . . .": note we begin here with a period, later 'ending' with no punctuation) extends toward an outpouring of shamanstic purgation ("against . . . against . . ."). The poem thereby aims to erase all traces of irony and pathos, becoming itself the spell that it would conjure.

If the poem exalts the energy to burst the word's boundaries as a circumscribed form, the poet would likewise exceed the enclosure of his own being. Reading the poem near the time of its composition at Town Hall in 1964, Jones displays in his voice commitment to a new emotive cadence, an intensified psychic discipline: setting aside the even stresses of his earliest diction, he gives special, delayed emphasis to such words as *light*, *sucked*, *God*, and *bleeding*; then, as the poem builds toward its climactic provocations, the voice becomes heavier and more bodily (the sibilants of *lips sucking splinters*, for example, tightening the ligature of tongue and agglutinating words), betraying a hint of pressured speech, the inclination to give end-lines a full, sober rest giving way to enjambment as the pace quickens slightly (slowed somewhat by the necessities of page-turning!) in anticipation of the final chanted spell. Though still well within parameters defined by conventional readings, the Town Hall rendition gives an indication of Baraka's desire to generate from within the poem a new disposition of voice adequate to thematic rearrangements of feeling, making the process of enactment the very 'meaning' of poetic production.

But we need only listen to the recording of "BLACK DADA NIHILIS-MUS" made late that year with the New York Art Quartet to the accompaniment of Roswell Rudd's composition "Sweet V" to see how much the Town Hall version remains enclosed in an alien, contradictory framework whose static presentational mechanisms remain essentially unresponsive to the poet's desire not merely to participate in reconceived voice but to *be* that voice.[15] At Town Hall, it is as though "black dada nihilismus" alludes to something which does not allow itself to be made fully present, in itself or in the poet's bearing. Style asserts itself at the level of theme, which resists assimilation to the norms and expectations governing Baraka's early verse: vision by dis-figuration, constitution by de-composition. "BLACK DADA NIHILISMUS" can complete or realize itself, then, as a breakthrough and not just a breach only when it has reoriented the materiality as well as the political epistemology of poetic practice. "BLACK DADA NIHILISMUS" becomes a fully original moment for Baraka when its ethos of collective resistance and engagement is given determinate form, bridging the distance it also marks between representation and action. With the New York Art Quartet performance of "BLACK DADA NIHILISMUS," Baraka's recitational style begins to assume this break with the textual ethos of its engenderment, as he undertakes active insertion of the poem into a new performative context (black audience) and modality (literal en-chant-ment in an environment of collective musical improvisation). Allowing accent and lineation to be defined by the percussional outline provided by Lewis Worrell's bass and Milford Graves's drums and cymbals, Baraka pushes the reading toward a rising emphasis that issues into the aching insistence of John Tchicai's alto and Rudd's trombone rumble. The poem's disruptive narrative, the unfolding of what Aldon Nielsen terms its "terrifying tensions,"[16] is thereby given new direction and sense, for all elements of exposition and rumination are *from the gitgo* subordinated to the *enactment* of rupture from received ideas of the 'proper' (propriety, property, propitiation – all no longer directed to an 'authoritative' white assembly,[17] but submitted for revaluation to a société of the poet-houngan's peers). With this performance, Baraka is, as it were, "given the asson," becoming in presentational manner a voice of revolutionary 'black magic.'

Such certainly is the Barakan posture of the Black Arts years, the years of classic performances like *Black and Beautiful . . . Soul and Madness* (1966) and *It's Nation Time* (1972), where the fragmentariness and heterogeneous irony of the early-middle readings give way to a pursuit of a hallowed blackness that effaces the poet's personality, making him a ritual per-sona of a common destiny. In these readings, Baraka begins to develop a kind of elocutionary athleticism, shaping his breath and body to the demands of extended litanies of envisioned power that hypertrophy the concluding appeal of "BLACK DADA NIHILISMUS":

> Time to get
> together
> time to be one strong fast black energy space
>   one pulsating positive magnetism, rising
> time to get up and
> be
> come
> be
> come, time to
>   be come ...
>   Boom
>   Booom
>   **BOOOM**
>   Boom
>   Dadadadadadadadadadad
>   Boom ...
>   Hey aheee (soft)
>   Hey aheee (loud) ...
>
> come out niggas come out
>   come out niggas come out
> It's nation time eye ime
>   It's nation ti eye ime
>   chant with bells and drum
>   it's nation time
>
> It's nation time, get up santa claus   (repeat)
>   get up roy wilkins
>   get up diana ross
>   get up dionne warwick ...
>   get up rastus for real to be rasta farari
>   ras jua
>   get up nigga come over here
>   take a bow brother
>
>   It's Nation
>   Time!
>   ("It's Nation Time")[18]

Accompanied – no, driven – by a cyclone of African and trap drummers, with Gary Bartz's alto sax lashing the upper registers in quick bursts of Trane-inspired runs, Baraka's voice attains here a strikingly fresh timbre and mobility. Moving with astonishing speed, his voice becomes another instrument within the ensemble, displaying polyrhythmic dexterity in negotiating rapid passage among shouts, call, wails, and declarations. Authorial mastery is decentralized or, better, distributed across the total fabric of collective improvisatory composition (as the call to the redefined niggah nation suffuses poet's voice and hornman's ax, one can't tell who's the straightman, who's the chaser), releasing an anarchizing vitality that "builds" collective purpose by razing the ossified rigidities of inherited terms and structures. Against the suffocating decorum of his earlier readings, Baraka refashions his voice as a ludic instrument of mimetic festivity, scatting the revolution as a resymbolized "dadadada" of aroused national consciousness, distending his enunciation of the temporal – tiiiiiiiiiiiii-eye-ime – with such vociferous abandon that it opens space for alternative vision (eye) and reasserted identity (ime). Moreover, by shifting the tonic accent, sliding and eliding certain syllables, and stretching himself through waves of percussive onomatopoeia, Baraka's voice 'bends' the diction so that there is no melodic contradiction between its spoken and sung resonances, just as Bartz and the drummers pattern their own riffs on the feints and darts of Baraka's ever-elastic poetic line. The performance proceeds to blur distinctions between instrumental and vocal articulation, the ax "speaking" as the voice "sounds." (One could almost transcribe Baraka's New *Nigga*, for example, on a stave, to wit:

Nig ga

. . . except that one would have to produce several such notations, making for a comically misplaced insight!) In this way, the poetry, as performed, becomes reflexive in its Africanicity, evoking the bond of speech and music that makes the slit-drum or *mvet*, for example, tunable to a linguistically comprehensible pitch understandable only in a community alive to its specific reference.

These kinds of works force a redefinition and retraining of 'reader' as well as audience, for the page is less a text anchoring meaning or an object to be dramatized than a chart initiating gestural and vocal inflection of unpredictable intensity, pace, and emphasis. Indeed, with Baraka's nationalist performances the poem is actually becoming the pre-text imagined in his critical reflections, both antecedent and occasion for exploring shared resources and perceptions. The text now inscribes itself in the body of the performer, who rewrites it in the dynamics of presentation. Look at the photo of Baraka reading with David Murray and Steve McCall at Soundscape (*New*

Plate 2: Baraka reading at Soundscape, 1981, with David Murray and Steve McCall.

Photograph © Bob Cummins

Music–New Poetry)[19]: the hints of nervous movement flickering in the sitting LeRoi Jones are now brought fully into view, the leg cocked forward in readiness for some movement aligned with the kinetic cadence of the "fast black energy space." Following this mutual generation of space (social and performative) and energy (political and expressive), syntax and signification emerge from rather than rule over sound. Vocality no longer either laments or stands beyond cultural milieu, but asserts its status *as* the histrionics of communal transformation: "take a bow brother/It's Nation Time!"

Criss-crossing the impulses to repudiate and renew, degrade and humanize, Baraka's nationalist performance ethos has remained the engine of his presentational practice through the succeeding stages of his political/ aesthetic journey. Retaining its utopic lyricality, that youthful sweetness of hope amidst degradation which surfaced in the edges of those carefully caressed vowels of the early years, Baraka's voice has only gained in texture and range, as was brilliantly evident in the Schomburg Retrospective (1995) and Philadelphia Clef Club (1996) readings. Now, in such works as "Reggae or Not!," "Am/Trak," "The Last Revolutionary (For Abbie Hoffman)," and the poems of *Wise, Why's, Y's*, Baraka operates within a complex matrix of communicative utterances and cultural idioms, adeptly sifting among formulae, quotations, inversions, and other shards of historically-charged diction as he spins polyphonic challenges to audiences sometimes all-too prepared to fix him (lovingly, to be sure) into some anticipated pose.

One of the most important elements of these performances, therefore, is the wry laughter and deceptively calibrated patter between pieces, which help sculpt the poem's own territory of reception. A piece of sermon here, a bit of stand-up there, some anecdotal spiel on the side, Baraka's chatter stretches context and modifies tone so that his audience is charged equally by critical and affective passion: directly after a stirring rendition of "So the King Sold the Farmer #39" in Philly, for example – in which, backed by Oliver Lake's screech-off-the-beat improvisations, Baraka intoned the climactic, choral dirge "We were slaves/slaves/slaves/slaves/..." with anguishing encyclopedic emotiveness – Baraka reminded us that federal welfare "reform" was putting more folks on the street for us to walk past on our way home ... only to strike up immediately (again with Oliver Lake in mad pursuit) an astonishingly nuanced version of "In the Tradition," which I cite once more at length to prepare an out-chorus for these notes on Barakan voice:

> Arthur Blythe
>   Says
>   it!
> *in the*
> *tradition*
>
> Tradition
> of Douglass
> of David Walker
> Garnett
> Turner
> Tubman
> of ragers yeh
>   ragers
>
>   (of Kings, & Counts, & Dukes
>   of Satchelmouths & SunRa's
>   of Bessies & Billies & Sassys
>   & Mas
> Musical screaming
> Niggers
> yeh ...
>
>   bee-doo dee doop bee-doo dee dooo doop ...
>
> ¼ notes
> eighth notes
> 16th notes
> 32nds, 64ths, 128ths ...

Yet in a casual gesture, if its talk you want, we can say
Cesaire, Damas, Depestre, Romain, Guillen ...
    What are you masochists ...
        I aint even mentioned
            Troussaint or Dessaline
                or Robeson or Ngugi

Hah, you bloody & dazed, screaming at me to stop yet,
NO, hah, you think its over, tradition . . .
               of those klanned & chained
     & lynched and shockleyed and naacped and ralph bunched

hah, you rise a little I mention we also the tradition of amos and andy
hypnotized selling us out vernons and hooks and other nigger
    crooks . . .
But just you rise up to gloat and I scream COLTRANE STEVIE
    WONDER!
            MALCOLM X!
            ALBERT AYLER!
            THE BLACK ARTS! . . .

               In the tradition of
all of us . . .
in motion forever . . .
don't tell me shit about a tradition of slavemasters
& henry james I know about it up to my asshole in it . . .
in the tradition, always clarifying, always new and centuries old
says
    Sing!
    Fight!

        Sing!
        Fight! &c. &c.
               Booshee dooooo doo doooo dee
                 dooo
               doooooooooo!
               DEATH T   O THE KLAN!
            ("In the Tradition" – *TB*, pp. 200–1,
               202, 203–4, 205, 206, 209–10)

In the tradition, indeed, of Barakan voice: old and new, singing and fighting, the "thrash and moan" of raucous, communitarian, demystifying, sacralizing, resisting, rejuvenating passion. But still we must speak not of Baraka's "voice" but rather of a layering of voices, as tone and attitude reply to and succeed one another with exceptional rapidity and precision. Performing "tradition" as a double-voiced continuity of betrayal and resistance, Baraka swoops through a heady succession of vocal effusions and signifyin' positions (all-the-while dipping into the Bird-to-Trane dialect of bop, cool, atonal, freeform – and R-and-B! – with cross-rhythmic agility), forcing us to experience the continuing opportunities of inherited expressivity at the intersection of the scatological and the honorific, the treacherous and the heroic, the ludicrous and the sublime. The litanies by which Baraka composes tradition as an aptitude for self-presencing "talk" in the face of crisis orchestrate a counterpoint of abuse and survival, subterfuge and assertion, as though "tradition" named a dialectical genius for abundant, unpredictable responses to oppression.

Such incongruities and sudden turns of perspective are not mere pyrotechnic display but render Baraka's voice the site of ideological contestation waged with irascible tenacity and hieratic stamina. For *being* "in the tradition" signals not arrival at some monumentalized truth but participation in an historically contingent project of revisionary transgression that cancels *all* delusions of permanent power. All the more remarkable, then, that Baraka's ability to sustain recitation of works like "In the Tradition" through unreserved profusions of "32nds, 64ths, 128ths" after all the years of battle, transit, and metamorphosis is not meant as sign of achieved meaning or mastery but as model for our own inspired active alliance with a tradition of progressive struggle. By pointing to his own pneumatic persistence in engaging this agonistic will-to-being – "Hah, you bloody & dazed, screaming at me to stop yet" – Baraka makes the audience experience the present-ness of tradition as a realization that one must always go forward; with a preacherly thump and gibe ("NO, hah, you think its over, tradition . . ."), he issues a call to shape time to desire in self-conscious recognition of what must be done *now*.

Today, when he steps up to exercise his chops, Baraka may sidle forward looking more like the old man of *The Slave* – nonchalantly scratching an old vest, porkpie cocked at cruisin angle – than the jittery *enfant terrible* or dashiki-clad, fierce-browed nationalist. Papers are shuffled alongside a low mumble, his first speech a little hoarse and sluggish; then the old sideways smile, sardonic and knowing, a quick gathering of the shoulders, a light-middleweight bounce to the feet, the voice suddenly strong again in its familiar demanding cadences . . . and off we go! More than ever, Baraka wields a style crafted to release the energies embedded in our conflicting idioms, intending to make language function as a medium of communal integrity that does not yet fully exist . . . even in the moment of the poem. From the beginning, his quest has been for that quintessence of sung-magic that would obviate all hesitancies, temptations, and duplicities that bind the tongue, preventing its message of freedom and love. Sounding this revolutionary utterance continues to be a work in progress: liberated from the most crippling chains of diasporic textuality, but never allowed simply to become its own object, Barakan voice remains at once adversarial – "DEATH TO THE KLAN!" – and attuned to the challenges of revitalizing our will to social transformation *in the present*, in the moment of our own *re*-sounding performances:

> . . . All the poems
> are full of it. Shit and hope, and history. . . .
> I'm here now, LeRoi, who tried to say something long for you.
>   Keep it.
> Forget me, or what I say, but not the tone . . .
>   ("Tone Poem" – *TB*, p. 131)

*

Oscillating between uniqueness and repetition, Baraka's vocalized present works toward a convergence of desire and meaning that would elide distinctions between stage and experience. Seeking that particular juncture of word, shout, and touch which would deliver African-American modernism from the limits of representation, his career of stirring performances nevertheless coheres as a sustained *rehearsal* of oracular conjuration. What happens when rehearsal, what Herbert Blau terms the "ghosting" of theatrical longing in its endless self-questioning, becomes the iterative mode of self-enactment?[20] Can the self emerge from the "play of appearances," perhaps wresting agency from the very spectral disturbances haunting black modernism's continuing improvisations? Such a question requires a shift of scene from the exuberant spectacles of Baraka's declamations to the subversive traceries of Adrienne Kennedy's self-stagings, where the dialectic between saying and being, and the shadow play between yearning and possession, shapes an equivocal but piquant mode of black modernist performance.

6 Rehearsing blackness

Spectre and spectacle in the
theatrical prefaces of Adrienne
Kennedy

Preface: I

> The rooms are my rooms; a
> Hapsburg chamber, a chamber in
> a Victorian castle, the hotel
> where I killed my father, the
> jungle. These are the places
> myselves exist in. I know no places.
>
> Sarah, *Funnyhouse of a Negro*[1]

Writing about Adrienne Kennedy is not unlike being written by her: one feels always already estranged from any clear point of departure, though a plethora of intellectual, psychic, and political themes suggest themselves as equally plausible centering concerns. Self-narration as crisis and quenchless need; the crossings of race and gender in the construction of identity; arresting but enigmatic juxtapositions of spectacle and verbal image, echoing ruptures between various historical and cultural formations – these are among the more encompassing issues which lend Kennedy's work its characteristic aura of irresolvable disturbance.[2] The ensuing temptation for the reader trapped in this funnyhouse of textual effects is to seize upon a specific representational category or structure in order the thematize Kennedy's project from some consistent conceptual position.

Nevertheless, the highly self-reflexive nature of Kennedy's writing forces any interpretive stance into immediate unease, opening questions about strategies of reading which are at once cognate with her characters' explorations and limitations upon whatever comprehensive account we might offer of them. The very conventions of narrative intelligibility and logical design by which we habitually organize critical response are often themselves the object of Kennedy's distorting critique. Nor, in yet another turn of the critical screw, is it quite sufficient to posit this polysemous elusivity as the very hallmark of Kennedy's confounding self-referentiality; her work's uncanny disturbance to our sense-making facility cannot be so easily deflected. It is not that we cannot produce a sufficient number of thematic, politicized, or contextualized readings to match the work's abundantly intricate figurations; rather, such a compendium of styles and effects can help only if we confront the way Kennedy's writing exceeds our formulations by putting the question of meaning itself into question.

When I first undertook to situate Kennedy's idiosyncratic mode of self-enactment alongside Baraka's within the stream of African-American modernism that she both enriches and radically challenges – thinking to work beyond the contribution she made to the dramatic movement traced in Chapter 2 – I sought to locate one instrumental norm of reading through some controlled understanding of Kennedy's "language." After suffering the topic's dispersal into a variety of substructures and classifications (language as image, as discourse, as narrative, as spectacle, etc.), attempting to organize my discussion around points of conflict between various discursive and symbolic expressions, I encountered the further bafflement of a discontinuity between assessment of a given work's 'linguistic' or paralinguistic means and the uncontainable effects and unaccountable intentions for which those means would conventionally serve as vehicle. Seeking to control this crisis of incommensurate interpretive tasks by establishing its limit through thematized configurations of specific conflictual linguistic performances – in particular, undertaking to establish the contrast in *Funnyhouse of a Negro* between the Jungle and the Room (emblems of reified stasis – statuary, walls, repetition – versus signs of wildness – hair, scream, movement) as synecdochic enactment of a larger defining tension between classicism (such as colonialism, the unified bourgeois subject, theater history) and its disruption or interruption by the Uncanny (such as revolutionary resistance, the subject-in-process, the Imaginary) – I experienced instead the frustration of any sure conceptual grasp as Kennedy's play continuously displaced my schema by its own ceaseless self-interrogations.

In further retreat, questing still for some authenticating source or design at the core of Kennedy's work by which to effect my own mimetic response, I began to pay closer attention to the author's own self-explanations, particularly those offered in the prefatorial statements appended in striking profusion to three texts that emerged in the aftermath of her stunning early drama: *People Who Led to My Plays*, *Adrienne Kennedy in One-Act*, and *Deadly Triplets*.[3] The present effort to define Kennedy's ongoing inflection of black modernist desire "takes place" at this juncture, taking as its subject Kennedy's "own" taking of herself as subject in writing which stands structurally before but logically outside of the main works they introduce. Not that any 'solution' to the critical dilemma here posed can be imagined in advance, for what the Prefaces offer, in themselves and taken together, is an interminable series of inscriptions upon the act of self-representation itself, a dazzling and dizzying layering of text upon text, such that any particular touchstone or origin of intention is unlikely to present itself. But as a meditation on the problems of repetition, quest, dissimulation, and self-origination which so haunt her plays' protagonists as exiles in quest *of* a position within the "room" of self-authorizing black expression, the Prefaces embody a striking record of the author's entanglement in her works' extravagant perplexity, and so warrant our best powers of engagement. In the process, we will experience a significant reorientation of perspective, a kind of echoic displacement, in our own quest for an expansive vision of African-American modernism.

People Who Led to My Plays: the self as supplement

> To know places is to
> know the emotion of
> hope is to know beauty.
>
> Sarah, *Funnyhouse of a Negro*

The "subject" of Adrienne Kennedy, in its many figurations and apparent embodiments, seems to us ever elusive, always beyond the traces imprinted before us. Often understood as an effect of her self-confessed penchant for 'non-linear,' discontinuous, and expressionistic form,[4] the uncertain notice cast by Kennedy's work might equally be felt as an obsessional evocation of the strangeness of writing itself, a disruptive preoccupation with consciousness conceived at once as uncanny and domesticated, mobile and paralyzed, lyrical and banal.

And yet there exists no lack of tracks and signs for the ardent pursuer of this evasive subject to follow, not least of which remain Kennedy's own recorded searches for self-origin. Autobiography, of the flesh and its inscriptions, is the very signature of Adrienne Kennedy's impossible though endless quest for a clarifying and stabilizing source. Much like her heroines, Kennedy's work seems driven by a search for an incandescent touchstone of self-reference, some primal image, story, or scene, which would heal the self's constitution as wound or lack, its entrapment in dramas scripted from elsewhere. And thus every Kennedy work appears as its own simulacrum or double, juxtaposing the fantasmatic with the empirical, setting fabulous interiorizations against the banalities of public display, casting an aura of compulsive self-exploration while leaving deepest concerns somehow excessive to representation, the subject neither quite present nor absent: familiar, veiled – spectral.

Among the most fascinating of these records of self-search, these charming spectacles of self-exposition, are the various "Prefaces" appended, like a delusory after-image, to several of the theatrical and fictional works. Their typical inaugurating gesture is the submission to a demand for self-explication, as exemplified by the opening paragraph of *People Who Led to My Plays* (the chronicle's *de facto* preface):

> More and more often as my plays are performed in colleges and taught in universities, people ask me why I write as I do, who influenced me.

... they continue to ask. Who influenced you to write in such a nonlinear way? Who are your favorite playwrights?

After I attempt to answer, naming this playwright or that one, as time progresses I realize I never go back far enough to the beginning. So I decided to.

(*People Who Led To My Plays*, 3)

As Stephen Greenblatt has remarked in his penetrating analysis of theatrical improvisation and discursive power in Shakespeare, the urge of self-narration is, paradoxically, the response to a call for public unfolding.[5] But if private rumination is potentially already social property, Kennedy implies a more complex dynamic by which the energy of persistent public inquiry may itself be turned to serve an inward quest for origins, the demand of self-performance yielding a 'decision' to interrogate the founding stages of that histrionic unveiling. The probing effort to define the author as an effect or echo is insistent, but no less so is the equivocating failure to name the self as the past's shadow and so tame the potential of self-origination.

That equivocation is perhaps the most compelling, if subtle, motivating impulse behind the subversively anti-narrative strategy of *People Who Led to My Plays*. In a sense, *People* is a collection of such introductory events, a chain of signifiers of the will-to-begin the process of self-location. Composed of lists of favored objects, compendia of memories both trivial and pivotal (the degree of importance must be inferred or imposed), visual fragments and labels (possibly parodic gestures to the school yearbook or celebrity scrapbook, with their cavalier commodification of the knowable subject), *People* makes the possibility of its meaning its most meaningful issue. So exhaustively banal are some of these catalogues, so paratactic are their juxtapositions, that we are left to wonder whether the life's meaning resides in some residue of silence, in what still remains to be said about and by an "I" which is consistent merely in its relentlessly prosaic quest for the source of careeristic renown.

Put differently, the autobiography's interest lies in what the narrative's dependence on discrete scenic representation cannot yield, and we must, if we desire it, supply some explanatory narrative perspective or significance, in short, a story. Because the life's data are given no hierarchical arrangement or relational balance (Jesus, Mrs. Miniver, Leslie Howard, *Little House on the Prairie*, favorite childhood belongings, childhood aversions, father, mother, Snow White, *et al.* compete for space in the text's and the author's imaginative order), the book frustrates the interrogative impulse of the opening query, refusing any clear reference to a conceptual design beyond the text's borders. Despite, if not because, of the persistence of the first-person pronoun in juxtaposition to these sketches and anecdotes, no comprehensive thematic structure coalesces around a perceptual center; no controlling consciousness focuses and justifies the details which would give it referential validity.

In this way, *People Who Led to My Plays* refuses the normative circular logic by which autobiographical enactment establishes an "I" through tautological pronouncement of that I's confirming incarnations. And yet *People* would be an entirely chaotic jumble of entries, equally devoid of and replete with significant events, were there not operating some principle of emphasis and subordination. And, in turn, any such hermeneutic principle implies behind it a phenomenological entity. But whether we find that centering notion in the unseemly thrust for fame, in the eventual material production of the plays which produce that fame, or in some more occult metaphoric apparatus,[6] the principle is never visible as part of the narrative's own appeal, remaining, like the central subject, like the I's perduring voice, suppressed or deflected. Rather, the subject of *People* is that voice's floating, fragmented inflections, which never cohere into the sort of continuity of belief or crisis or concern through which we normally infer a reflective subjectivity.[7] The very hermetic enclosure of each entry, the seeming finality of each catalogue, means that no overt thematizing of the entries can reduce them to the kind of consistent significance we associate with ontological wholeness. In short, what we're led to in these reflections is not a *person*, but only the author's own textual constitution as a locus of "people." Offering a theoretically infinite stock of self-revelations, Kennedy in effect tells no story of herself at all.

Even so, the reader, unguided by the spurious logic of narrative authority, becomes in some sense a version of the heroine, asking at every turn, "Where am I?", grasping at every moment for some preliminary outline or map. Its organizing voice perpetually decentering the very consciousness it claims to be re-presenting, *People* suggests how the subject responding to the opening injunction to tell is constantly reinvented. The obligation to self-representation hollows the identity it makes possible, nullifying any specific claim to a fullness of truth by the very proliferation of truthful data it engenders. The text is so relentless and nonsyntactically detailed that what might appear as total disclosure becomes instead a kind of occlusion: revealing subversively becomes re-veiling. By the same token, a narrative which seems wholly a collection of exterior manifestations (dates, objects, encounters, events) becomes the most unfathomable process of interiorization, as the project's subject becomes, as it were, secreted, placed outside the speculative invasion of the reader's eye.

Perhaps even this discourse of the seen and the hidden, with its structure of inside and outside, fails to clarify the way *People Who Led to My Plays* explores a new mode of self-representation by discrediting the available models for staging the marginalized self seeking position in public discourse. Just how tenacious is this demystification can be felt by setting the book's concluding entry against our memory of the prefatorial self-inauguration:

Myself:
We sailed back to New York on the *United States*. I had a completed play in my suitcase. How could I know it would establish me as a

playwright and change my life? After years of writing, I had finally written of myself and my family and it would be on a stage and in a book too, and I would be on the pages of *Vogue* and in Leonard Lyons' column.

And in a few months I would climb the steps to the Circle in the Square theater where I would see this play inside my suitcase performed, become a member of the Actors Studio (where Brando had been) and become a part of the Off-Broadway theater movement . . . a movement that in itself would come to occupy a powerful place in American theater history.

(People Who Led to My Plays, 125)

Is this a satire of the narrative implicit in the opening invitation for self-display, that reifying quest for value in the public exchange of recognizable personalities whose devastating costs of mutilated consciousness are explored so hauntingly in the very triumphant writings being brought 'home'? What effect does the echo of the slave narrative's topos of climactic self-realization in the acceptance of representativeness, marked by a merging of personal and public "places" on the historical scaffold, have upon such an evaluation?[8] Or ought we rather ask, might the implicit tension between the definitively subjective entry-title, *myself,* and the diffusion of that potent locus of well-catalogued desires, interests, possessions, wounds, expectations, etc. into the narrowed expression of public notice signal an unresolved conflict of self-representational decorum, a conflict which makes of the subject a peculiar rhetorical predicament? Form and consciousness, self and representation, structure and agency can be seen by the end of *People*, not as the unified, consumable entity complacently presumed by the opening query, but as mutually supplemental aspects of a mobile and transformative subject.

Adrienne Kennedy in One Act: performance in excess of itself

> I am a nigger of two generations. I am Patrice Lamumba. I am a nigger of two generations. I am the black shadow that haunted my mother's conception.
>
> MAN (Patrice Lamumba),
> *Funnyhouse of a Negro*

Already, we can say, autobiography is theatricalized, rendered as a play at the borders of revelation and concealment. The pronominal shifts and instability of tense evident in *People*'s framing passages alert us to the self's constitutive movement between the other's interrogating gaze, with its demand to render the self as a tellable entity – Who influenced you? Who are your favorite[s]? – and the ideal of subjectivity seeking an alternative space of enactment and, so, possibly, an alternative (kind of) story. Demanded disclosure threatens the closure of a misrecognition, but it is none the less the instigator of the quest for a less visible position of self-enunciation. The autobiographical project is inescapably, if indeterminately, dialogic, its scene a multivoiced nexus of subtle conflicts and purported confluences.

The Preface to the Minnesota edition of Kennedy's one-act plays (intriguingly entitled *Adrienne Kennedy in One Act*, in subtle affinity with the works' emphasis on the self's quest for an almost classically austere and definitive enclosure, a carefully furnished though generally distorted 'room of one's own') seems again a response to a query:

> More than anything I remember the days surrounding the writing of each of these plays . . . the places . . . Accra Ghana and Rome [. . .] the shuttered guest house surrounded by gardens [. . .] the sunny roof of the apartment on Via Reno . . . our wonderful brand new apartment in New York [. . .] and the enchanting Primrose Hill in London [. . .] Hadn't Sylvia Plath lived across the way in Chalcot Square? [. . .]
>
> Without exception the days when I am writing are days of images fiercely pounding in my head and days of walking . . . in Ghana [. . .] in Rome [. . .] in London, Primrose Hill (hadn't Karl Marx walked there?) . . . all of which seem to put me under a spell of sorts . . .
>
> (*Adrienne Kennedy in One Act*, Preface)

In languid, almost hypnotically recursive phrasing, Kennedy suggests how these plays are precipitates of a personal search for the continuity of self in time. Personality and history reflect one another as persistent, but self-interrupting, discourses (the ellipses are, quite frequently, Kennedy's own), a series of phenomena whose center lies in a recurrent questioning of their possible underlying necessity. Structured by a symmetry of personal re-locations and ghostly summonses, this Preface seems obsessed by evocations of an Other at once radically distant (as markers of specific, historicized, even monumentalized figures) and potentially self-mirroring (as anterior editions of the author's own perambulations and, covertly, ambitions). The unifying thread of these reflections is the juxtaposition of memory's pleasant resituation of activities *surrounding* writing's effects to what Lacan termed *aphanisis*, or the incipient panic of a fading from presence of those inspiriting authorities which legitimate one's enunciations. By evoking Plath (with her problematic identities as woman, writer, wife, American, modern) and Marx (an exiled revolutionary who died at his desk), Kennedy formulates the precariousness of the author's own writing subjectivity, which takes up uneasy (and temporary) residence along several locations of marginality. Seeing herself as if from the other's vantage, or as if recognized as an effect of another's incantation, Kennedy enmeshes the remembered writing subject in an irresolvable drama of identifications and distinctions. Catching glimpses of herself in the fading traces of such richly provocative spirits, she resists any precise self-location (spatial or temporal, psychic or political, formal or thematic), while teasing our own desire to resolve the quest in some specific ideological or biographical predetermination.

The implications of such insouciant exilic self-displacement are further "spelled"-out in the Preface's final lines:

> . . . I am at the typewriter almost every waking moment and suddenly there is a play. It would be impossible to say I wrote them. Somehow under this spell they become written.
>
> (*Adrienne Kennedy in One Act*, Preface)

Is the author, then, merely a *per-sona*, a mask through which language(s) (whose? from where?) speak(s)? And are we to understand such a spoken subject in a Plathian manner, as a willing if troubled participant in a pluri-voiced struggle for expression's grace, or in a Marxist sense, as a pure position within a system of utterances wherein subjectivity is only a fantasm of ideology? Thus fragmented into the writing itself, the spectacle outlined by the Preface's narrative of writing's genesis is emptied of its presumed intentionality. Or, rather, that intentionality is deconstructed, distantiated as the product of the very discourse it would claim to wield. Kennedy performs for us the structural dependence of the subject on some relation to an Other, its constitution as a locus of voices variously competing for presence and self-authorization . . . even from beyond the grave. Seen in this way, the subject is not an essence reporting on its self-discovery but a process of invention arising as a relation with itself that is mediated by time and circumstance. It is an infinitely open semiosis, a body and a ghost all at once, a maddening interchange of repetition and substitution. And, 'naturally,' it cannot help but be inadequate and excessive to its own scene or "home."

Deadly Triplets: the double scene

> He never tires of the journey,
> he who is the darkest one, the
> darkest one of them all.
>
> ALL, *Funnyhouse of a Negro*

This generative motif of narrative staged as endless self-supplementary quest is given sharper imagistic focus in the Preface to *Deadly Triplets*, a self-consciously disjointed fiction-cum-journal in which theatre, autobiography, meditation, and mystery mix into a generically fragmenting, thematically phantasmagoric enigma. Continuously rehearsing the book's own defining tensions between unity and dispersal, continuity and contingency, the

"Real" and the Imaginary, story and detail, gesture and body, script and event, this Preface finds compelling focus in moments of recollection, where memory and writing compete for the still-elusive center of the author's attention:

> This book contains two very different, though connected, writings that deal with my experience of London and the theatre. Although a theatre journal and a theatre mystery may seem an unlikely combination, they are united in the attempt to write about a time and set of experiences that for me continue to be significant. The real mystery is why London has occupied such an important place in my imagination and why it continues to haunt me. . . . Although I thought the sketches [vignettes of theatre personalities, echoing the style and format of *People Who Led to My Plays*, which comprise *Deadly Triplet*'s second section] I had written on London were complete, four years later when I reread them I decided the sketches only reminded me of the mystery I still felt existed around London and my three-year stay there in 1966–69. . . . I decided to try a short mystery novel. Perhaps fiction in this form would finally capture the complexity of my feelings toward London.
>
> (*Deadly Triplets*, viii)

The laconic style, which lends each compositional and even 'experiential' decision an air of casual improvisation, is belied by the 'haunting' sense of writing's endless struggle to contain the excessive imaginative dis-ease which is, ironically, writing's very spur. A pattern of desire and frustration inaugurates the book's effort to settle the self's accounts with time and place: desire for containment of experience's 'significance' in some formal mode, frustration at the inevitable rupture of narrative by those unnameable clusters of associational feelings whose appearance, in the fort/da rhythm of inscription and re-reading, in turn produce more narrative. And so the drive for, and of, narrative begins as the staged return to a doubled scene of writing:

> Writing short sketches on people had seemed natural to me so I had been surprised when a friend . . . asked me why I had written sketches rather than a long continuous piece. I think I had written sketches because the people I met in the theatre seemed to be dream interludes in my life. My real continuous story seemed to be that of my family. . . . The real me went out to Actor's Studio worrying about what to wear, running across the street to the cleaners, waiting for the babysitter, and met Geraldine Page, Rip Torn, Molly Kazan. These wonderful interludes of people excited me. But they were not quite real. Even with the passage of time most often the people I've met in the theatre seemed no more real to me than people I'd seen on stage at the old Palace Theatre in Cleveland when I was a kid.
>
> (*Deadly Triplets*, viii)

The putatively 'real,' anchored by the quotidian and the familial, becomes entangled, even syntactically, with the theatrical; repeated, doubled, the real and the 'seeming' mirror one another in an obfuscating iterative play, and distinctions of locale, time, and their memorializations (whether in dream or in the already quasi-hallucinatory or shadowy impressions of 'sketches') begin to be blurred – again (as in the opening to *People Who Led to My Plays*), under the slyly factitious pressure of arresting, if 'friendly,' inquiry. The theatre, a site of masks and illusions neither true nor false ("*not quite* real"), is itself characterized as an "interlude," an *entre act* interrupting and reflecting a presumably larger encompassing drama, that of the purportedly "real" life-story in which the act of doubling dramatic scenes by means of the quasi-performative mode of the "sketch" (the *splash* of pictorial representation) seems quite "natural." Impelled beyond the apparent security of domestic structure by some unspecified desire, the author experiences the intrusion into that realm's routinized histrionics (marked by the primoridal theatrical signifiers of dressing and waiting) of another order of personality and place, so that no absolute present or past is established. Rather, the present is suffused by the otherness of several alternative stages, and the self is, like its story, always incomplete, its 'significance' always an effect of narrative's partiality and excess.

Strangely compressed, specific yet ex-centric and mesmerizing in its repetitiousness, Kennedy's prose suggests here an almost therapeutic scene at which layers of past experience refuse repression by any systematic ordering of significance or any unbroken temporal schema. The author embarks on a hunt for encounters in the giddy world of theatrical "recognition" which would simultaneously derealize and establish her own identity as mother, wife, playwright, public figure.[9] But as the divisions or boundaries between private/public and real/hallucinatory dissolve into a montage of impression and recreation, we find ourselves everywhere in the domain of the Imaginary, where identity *is* structured as a fantasmatic scene which the subject immediately (though unsuccessfully) disavows. It is no wonder, then, that *Deadly Triplets*'s Preface proceeds to a series of doublings and reflections, replete with imagery of enclosure and alienation, which manage to complicate the very coordinates of identity they would firmly anchor:

> My plays were filled with the intricacies of race in my life. Why had I refused? [I.E., to write of race autobiographically when asked to do so] Was it because at that moment I had not wanted race to separate me from the Brontës, Wordsworth . . . Tintern Abbey? (I often felt deep down that I had once lived in Haworth.) . . . In Accra, Ghana, my husband and I had driven past the enclave of British homes surrounded by walls where British families had lived separate as they colonized the West African. Although in 1961, Nkrumah was Prime Minister, these enclaves still existed, and when we first arrived in Accra

we even lived briefly in a section of the city that had once been populated by Europeans, a district of large homes, walled in, gardens tended
by Ghanaians. I used this experience as the basis for plays and stories.

(*Deadly Triplets*, viii–ix)

But what, exactly, is "this experience"? On the one hand, it seems rea-
sonably clear that two disparate and antipathetic political and cultural
matrices compete for power and centrality in both landscapes. But, as with
Kennedy's own efforts to write of memory's continuity in the present's disjunctive moment (recorded in the Preface's opening ruminations on *Deadly
Triplets*'s form and origin), we discover a haunting continuity of effect despite
apparent revolutionary change. Not only do the architectural configurations
of colonial rule remain in place, their arrangements of labor and social hierarchy still effective; but, perhaps even more disconcertingly, the author's
own placement within that labyrinthine system of 'separations,' protections,
and containments stands in disturbing relation, first, to a lingering wish to
close the distance between herself and an imagined Anglocentric ancestry,
and then, to a structural re-placement of those European masters among
their African servants. "Race," a barrier to the black American woman's
'momentarily' idealized self-realization in the English domain, stands in
analogical relation to the Ghanaian walled garden, which, paradoxically,
enforces the suppression of the African by the European. And this remains
so even when the African has, presumably, undertaken a triumphant action
of reversal. But the irony of this oppositionality, too, is precisely to the point:
whoever stands within the enclave, under whatever empiric sign, the *structure*
of differences remains the same.

It is perhaps a strategic necessity that race remain inflected within a
structure of difference in such a way that, given a resistance to the logic
of reversibility, its value cannot be too easily calculated. Standing somewhere *between* African and European (in racial, historical, and physical
terms),[10] the author suggests that the work of self-realization arises along
an ever-shifting boundary 'separating' the vague evocations of a literary
tradition and the concrete (if still undecidable) data of political event. What
gives "unity" to such projections of contrast, repetition, and irony is the
structure of doubling itself, the compulsion to continuous transferences
and transformations which, though intoxicating in their proliferation, create
the illusion of balance, of a wholeness composed of fused oppositions – a
wholeness economically labeled "this experience." Once again, we might
think of this kind of seductively circumstantial exposition as a *staging* of
narrative self-exploration, a simulated inquiry into the definitive coordinates of the self understood as both consciousness and as social construction.
Once again, the "self" is above all a dramatic proposition, a derivative of
movement between positions, a series of displacements which adhere only
if seen simultaneously from differing perspectives of culture, temporality,
and place.[11]

It is also in this sense of writing-the-self as the scene of self-writing, as a restorative and effacing movement of an impossible self-scrutiny, that Kennedy's Preface becomes a confrontation with the historicality of self-construction. For race, like nationality, gender, and other categories of recognition and mis-construal, appears in these pages as an alternative mode at once of representing experience and of experiencing the self *as* a representation. "History," like its subjects, becomes then an irresolvable layering, or friction, or accretion among elements which might be at one moment felt as representation, at another termed experience. (It is for this reason that the Preface moves with obsessive nervousness from capturing experience in the discourse of writing – *sketches, rereading, writing* itself – and attempting to locate an exact experiential ground for the present's performative *activity* of writing.) The personal and the political become inextricably entangled, not because the self is either beyond or utterly produced by ideology and tradition, but indeed because it *is* the ongoing effort to locate itself between determinations, an effort which writing seeks ever to record and thereby materially enacts.

Thus problematizing the scene of its own enactment, Kennedy's "Preface" (dis)locates the self as something both within and beyond the discourse of self-representation, just as she was both in and absent to the legacy of Haworth, both within and foreign to the ambiguous walled gardens of post-colonial Ghana. The subject's formation is a conceptual dilemma of specific historical texture, since its failure to achieve satisfying harmony questions the violent closures of both traditional (imperial, Romantic) order and its transgression by revolutionary replacement. On the one hand, as Kennedy suggests in the conclusion of the "Preface," the old economy of colonial authority remains a fading but still enrapturing fantasm, a memory in dissolution, a literally in-spiriting landscape of the past's ghostly reinscription:

> . . . now I felt I did not know the English. I remembered all of this. I remembered . . . [and used as] the setting for my mystery novel: . . . squares shrouded in mist, fog rising over Primrose Hill, stories of dead writers, dead Kings and Queens, landscapes with names like Gloucester Gate . . . murders . . . betrayals . . . all of it still mesmerized me
>
> (*Deadly Triplets*, x–xi)

while on the other hand, still arrested by the spectacle of tradition's mutilations, secrets, and ravishments, the author suggests that contemporary subversions of this fading dream of feudal narrative figuring an exchange of power cannot yet offer any truly alternative "names" of self-empowerment. Stripped of any aura of natural cultivation either in the security of European lineage or the liberatory assertion of African sovereignty, the self, in its continued search for origination, becomes an unavoidably but undecidably political crux.

In this sense, too, Kennedy's 'experience' in Accra *is* paradigmatic: presenting a poignant juxtaposition of "home" and exile, this anecdotal hinting at a perpetual foreignness is everywhere duplicated in *Deadly Triplets*, especially in the Preface's own doublings in the opening paragraphs to each of the book's two main sections and in the framing epilogial entry. "Part One," the "mystery," is prefaced by the following account of an uncanny repetition, replete with the temporal confusions and spatial dislocations already familiar to us:

> Last night John Lennon was murdered at the Dakota apartment . . . four blocks from where I am now living. I find it a strange and terrible coincidence that several years ago I started writing a play based on Lennon's nonsense books . . . in a studio at the top of the Dakota apartments and that the writing of that play led to my being involved in a mysterious and brutal death. A murder most unexpected.
>
> My theatrical producers, who let me use the studio in the Dakota to write, put me in touch with Lennon's English publisher. The publisher liked the pages of the play I had written. This, and some reasons that I myself was not entirely aware of, reasons that dealt with the strange demise of my adopted mother years ago in England, convinced me that London was the place I wanted to go. I brushed aside the unfulfilled longing and curiosity that I had never satisfied about my adopted mother's illness and last days and accepted the more obvious reasons: I was recently divorced, in the throes of a new career . . . that was bringing me recognition . . . I was entangled in the deadly ambitions and desires of other people I was yet to meet . . .
>
> (*Deadly Triplets*, 5–6)

The clichéd outline of murder mystery's *mise-en-scène* notwithstanding (and that parody is itself characteristic of the book's constant evocation and displacement from its ostensibly enabling genres and voices), the passage again instances the "I"'s diffusion in a miasma of dislocations, refracted desires, dispersed projects, and incomplete perceptions. Typically, the subject introduced is occluded by the juxtapositions of portentous exposition and petty ambition, of self-assertion and self-deferral. Does the voice, or character, presented here consist merely in a range of impulses and movements, a process under constant erasure? Or is there a motivating center behind the "I"'s furtive gestures preserved apart from the continuing drama of separation and resituation? Though syntactically (even, on the page, visually) central, that *I* is perhaps superfluous or resistant to the symbolic order it variously invokes (as repository of careers, relationships, protections, judgements, recognitions, etc.), unable or unwilling to take up determinate position within it.

In the book's next prefatorial entry, the opening of the second section or "Theatre Journal," we see repeated the desire to repeat the self as the story of its telling:

In 1981 when I was teaching at Berkeley, I decided to write a piece entitled *People I've Met in the Theatre*. One evening [my writers' group] asked me about winning the Obie. . . . [O]ne of them said what a "glorious past" you've had. . . . So now sitting . . . in a lovely room facing a redwood tree and a creek, I started the first sketches about off-Broadway, choosing what I felt to be exciting moments of my life. . . . One of the reasons I chose sketches was a book I read when I was twenty-one, by Daniel Blum, called *Famous People in the American Theatre*. How I had loved the short, dense paragraphs about the actors and actresses accompanied by a black-and-white photo. How I had longed to be in that book.

(*Deadly Triplets*, 99–100)

The doubling of the prefatorial justification of *People Who Led to My Plays* is cannily further layered by the expressed desire to discover oneself in the enclave of another's account of oneself, to reside in the "book" of fame as character and commodity. In a sense, Kennedy here calls upon the conventional notion of identity as a reciprocal social construction, though here it is an exchange of representations that produces the thrill of identity. Or perhaps we should rather speak, with Elin Diamond, of Kennedy's desire for identification,[12] that mode of identity-as-reading in which the subject is both present and estranged, its presence an effect of that very otherness, of its (mis)recognition by the other-as-reader. Kennedy here further delineates her earlier expressed "entangle[ment] in the desires of other people" by suggesting how the self and its longings can reach fulfillment only by knowing itself in another place and by accepting the conflict between consciousness and its formal embodiment which lies at the core of mimetic desire. Where else can the author wish to be but "in" the book? But once in the book, however condensed and spatialized its form (the proclivity for the sketch and the photo expressing a resistance to invasion by narrative temporality), how can the authorial subject hope to escape the contingencies imposed by readers with their own inevitably transformative and unmastered desires?

Deadly Triplets concludes with a stunning answer to this perplexing contradiction of scriptive containment and transcendence; not surprising, it is in several senses a reflection and duplication of the strategies organizing the book's prior prefatorial performances, not so much an answer in fact as a response:

In one of my stories I gave myself an estranged twin sister, an actress whom I saw on stage (not realizing she was my sister because of her elaborate disguise). My children and I were also continual characters in my stories. . . . On some nights I wrote mystery stories . . . and made myself and the children characters. One included a description of our real house.

"Chalcot Crescent was beautiful: . . . It was furnished and belonged to an English family that was in Nigeria. The faded parlor faced a wild garden with a brick wall. . . . The children were thrilled because the television series 'The Avengers' was filmed on the Crescent.

Soon there would be rallies in Trafalgar Square against the war in Vietnam. More than once Vanessa Redgrave led them.

The crazed old woman living in the house on Rothwell Street screamed . . . "Go back to India where you belong." Despite the enchantment, there was a subplot to England that I couldn't perceive. And although I could never admit it, the hurt over the breakup of my marriage had never healed. I thought: Perhaps I should go home. And I did."

(*Deadly Triplets*, 121, 123–4)

Like the uncanny mists of the old English landscapes or the enclaves of colonial structure, *Deadly Triplets*'s own major thematic, imagistic, and narrative scenarios arise once again, enfolding one another in a dizzying play of the "real" and the represented so that writing becomes, as if for one 'last' performance, its own ghost, its own simulacrum, its own empty excess. Race, revolution, history; motherhood, marriage, authorship, career; nature, technology, commodification; discrete encounters, mass actions, uncertain relations – every category of self-constitution, every perceptual and representational strategy, and indeed every specific nexus of cultural and personal experience called upon heretofore to organize the book's rehearsal of a proper subject is once again summoned on-stage, "twinned" to a funnyhouse profusion of such evocations and projections. Kennedy stages a meta-narrative of multiplied depictions and receptions such that the referent of any given instant in this climactic self-explanation is both an 'experience' (meticulously dated and located) and a previous description of such 'experience' (available not only in *Deadly Triplets* itself but in other works bearing Kennedy's signature). Jostling for primacy are the effort to tame alterity's threatening potential by various tactics of containment and the concurrent urge to undo the strictures of such domestication by acknowledging a residue of uncertainty. The book ends in yet another reiteration of its inability to fully begin, for despite the marvelously productive intention to turn all desires and all strangeness into the tractable material of drama and story – to effectively confuse the boundaries of work and world and thereby formalize the characteriological quality of any identity – despite this imperialist annexation of experience by fabulation, the countervailing intuition of an otherness that remains unconditioned by the author's powers of appropriation saves the book from any complacent and deadly closure. Put differently, in more ideological terms, the self now emerges from the *failure* of the procedure of identification which gives rise to the "journal" of personal images, anecdotes, and other reflections, becoming instead a (re)commitment to its absence from any absolutely understood locale or relation. "Home" and the *unheimlich* become not so much fixed and mutually exclusive places of legible definitions and events as differential elements in a continuing entanglement of conflicting desires, plots, structures, affiliations. "Home" names the site of the next adventurous rearticulation of the subject in question; like "self," it names what is never there but always about to be.

Preface: II

> But he is dead
> And he keeps returning. Then he is not dead.
> Then he is not dead.
> Yet, he is dead, but dead he comes knocking at my door.
>
> (ALL, *Funnyhouse of a Negro*)

The "mystery" persistently presented in *Deadly Triplets* emerges as the desire for an authentic source of expression's own mimetic intention amidst the swirling welter of social, political, historical, psychic, familial, and cultural markers by which Kennedy seeks to "recognize" herself and gain recognition from others. Each scene of origination conjured as explanation of writing's responses to puzzlements of memory and desire can only repeat the subject's irresolution in a vertiginous play of inscriptions and mirroring revisions. In this sense *Deadly Triplets*, like *People Who Led to My Plays*, is composed of a *series* of mutually qualifying 'prefaces,' a succession of textual masks confusing the order of 'author' and 'character,' reified book and exorbitant world, spectral rehearsal and imagined performance.

Similarly, Kennedy's Prefaces, taken together, repeat the search for a subject that is somehow both reliably essential (repetition bespeaking the desire for the stability in time conferred by ontological continuity) and unpredictably inventive (the impossibility of fixing the self being the one reliably repeated topos). For her audience, such rigorously and openly contradictory "self"-exploration provides an instructive exemplum (this, too, a paradox, given the spectral quality of her own exemplars). We are enjoined to suffer the inadequacy of any narrative of the works' intentions, while standing warned that only silence, mutilation, or death can substitute for this disruptive process of hermeneutic displacement. More concretely, no discussion of Kennedy's work can fail to address her protagonists' arduous quests for anchoring signatures of time and place (be they sexual, familial, racial, or cultural); and no such discussion can fail to entertain risk of privileging a single order of significance in the desire to redress or cure or avenge those enduringly hopeful, if apparently unrealizable, explanatory journies. For the quest, the hope, and even perhaps the endurance is ours, as well. And so we, too, begin to preface the subject . . . again.

*

Perhaps nothing within the sphere of African-American cultural expression could seem further from Kennedy's elusive and defamiliarized landscape than the domain of vernacular utterance. Indeed, shards of vernacular imagery and idiom appear in Kennedy's work often in the shock of *mis*recognition, or as thwarted resources for a healing form of historical revisionism. But it is just this deeply rooted connection of fragmenting injury and agonistic consciousness that binds the elegant enigmas of Kennedy's rehearsals to vernacular culture's improvisational reparations of diasporic displacement. Moreover, if the question haunting Kennedy's self-inquisitions – *Who is speaking?* – highlights and troubles the specular positions of articulation and reception, vernacular enactments are equally concerned with the ethical and epistemological consequences of enunciative exchange. Therefore, though our final section returns in most overt fashion to the 'testifying' modality of modern black drama and the musical inspiration of contemporary African-American poetics, it is Kennedy's trope of 'funnyhouse negroism' that perhaps best prepares for the speculative praxis of vernacular performance, a blend of critical call and visionary response that is the quintessential mode of African-American modernism.

Part IV

I was myself within the circle

Vernacular and critical paradigms of expressive agency

> i go out to siren street
>> don't play no more
> me and willie beat a certain beat
>> aimin wood carvin shadows
>
> sometimes i knock on wood
>> with fist
> me and willie play *togetherin*
>> and we don't miss

Henry Dumas, "knock on wood"

7 Improvising blackness

Telling and testifying in the
modern chant-sermon

I

> There is no need to establish a "black aesthetic." Rather, it is important
> to understand that one already exists. The question is: where does it exist?
> And what do we do with it?
>
> Larry Neal[1]

On a crisp day in the early period of his New York exile, Ralph Ellison's
Invisible Man chanced upon the bluesman Peter Wheatstraw, that trickster-
rabbit pushing his cart valiantly through the "bear's den" of Harlem. The
following interchange between Ellison's narrator and Wheatstraw ensued:

> "What's all that you have there," I said, pointing to the rolls of blue
> paper stacked in the cart.
>
> "Blueprints, man. Here I got 'bout a hundred pounds of blueprints
> and I couldn't build nothing!" . . .
>
> "You have quite a lot," I said.
>
> "Yeah, this ain't all neither. I got a coupla loads. There's a day's work
> right here in this stuff. Folks is always making plans and changing 'em."
>
> "Yes, that's right," I said, thinking of my letters of introduction, "but
> that's a mistake. You have to stick to the plan."
>
> He looked at me, suddenly grave. "You kind young, daddy-o," he said.
>
> (Ralph Ellison, *Invisible Man*, 72)

Ellison's naive hero, a relatively young student of introductory "letters,"
might be forgiven his evident confusion. After all, practitioners and critics
alike of African-American culture have endeavored for generations to
expound a "blueprint for Negro literature." Indeed, the history of African-
American literary criticism, if not the story of black literature itself, could
be sketched in great measure as a succession of manifestos, paradigms,

and their various revisions. But the mere fact of the tradition's constitution as a dialectical sequence of such "new Negroisms" suggests how any blueprint, in the very act of its inscription, necessarily sets in motion the process of its own displacement. Each version of the envisioned ideal, precisely where it aspires to total coherence, seeds an unpredictable array of refinements and supplements. The blueprint, as a responsive inscription upon the template of African-American expressive desire, carries the imprint of revision as its guiding motive, thus bearing within its very assertion the trace of its own anticipated refiguration. As the projection of an historically marked struggle for effective meaning, the African-American blueprint cannot help but bear within itself the horizon of other, contestatory patterns: like Coltrane, it must be ever "cleaning the mirror" in a gesture of self-surpassing articulation.

Blueprint piled upon blueprint, the continuing history of contemporary African-American cultural theory will, according to the Peter Wheatstraw vignette, unfold as a series of partial visions, as every blueprint of the tradition can be at most a heuristic design of the tradition's unfolding history. As in the innovative improvisations of the New Wave musicians, every chart of meaning and its meaningful performance must turn about each other in a play of mutually transforming resignification. Any given blueprint is a preparation of an alternative scheme, an invitation to riff upon the chart; and any historical critique implicit in each remapping constitutes a nascent critique of its own historical position.[2]

Ellison's blueprint episode thus exerts a specifically performative and phenomenal pressure against conceptual and disembodied inscriptions. Thereby placing theory under the restraint of worldliness and practice, the parable likewise intimates the irreducibly political nature of performative designs upon ideal presence, implicating *all* modes of enactment in the enveloping *mise-en-scène* of social interests, needs, and histories. Understood as a stream of alternative perceptual instruments or images, Peter Wheatstraw's pile of blueprints deconstructs the delusions of classic representation into ever-growing fields of deferral and play, forging a parodic chronotope that distends the time–space constructions of normative power. But while the joke slips the yoke of classifying projects, it cannot elude the intricate bonds of remembrance and affiliation. In contrast to the absolute assault on representation animating (anti)paradigms of Euro-American experimental theater and avant-garde theory, Wheatstraw's seriocomic project interrogates the relation between structure and event, expectation and improvisation. His critique of scripted intentions displaces concern with text's 'essential' significance, calling attention instead to the process of meaning-*production*. Blueprint and experience, script and occasion, are equally subject to the ceaseless, unpredictable dialectic of intention and interpretation that dispels the lure of any self-enclosed textual metaphysic.

This complex interplay between mimetic aspiration and its continuous subversion, qualification, or transformation by performative 'rewriting' is, we have seen, characteristic of modern African-American theater, music, and poetry in their shared quest for a mode of self-realization that is both transgressive and integral, for a site of being that is both revolutionary and rudimentary. *Invisible Man* itself, in its persistent and ambivalent return to such performative modes as blues, jazz, and sermons for models of self-narration, participates in what has become the most consistent imprint of this modern African-American cultural blueprint: its aspiration to construction of a powerful cultural voice that receives its authority from creative imitation of vernacular exemplars. Like Peter Wheatstraw, Ellison inflects a vernacular-inspired suspicion of scriptorial paradigms as reified and falsified intentions while setting forth the possibility that such expressive irony might itself constitute a model of successful self-performance. Staking out a day's work among the crumbling fantasms of inherited texts, modern African-American expressive culture on this view confronts a challenge to theorize its alternative status from *within* the problematic of paradigm and performance sketched by Ellison in the encounter of hero and homeboy, the upright straightman and the uptight-but-allright bluesman.

My own design (!) in this final section is to explore the potential of vernacular theory and performance for effectively mobilizing, if not resolving, the tension endemic to modern black discourse between systematic and improvisatory expression, a tension this chapter will explore in the setting of the contemporary African-American church – specifically, in the genre of the chanted-sermon – and which I hope to show in the following chapter continues to spur the productive perplexities of today's critical daddy-os as they extend vernacular-inflected criticism into a fresh mode of modernist presentation. But at first hearing doesn't that phrase, *vernacular theory*, sound with an enigmatic, even oxymoronic, tone? Given, on the one hand, the habit displayed by a wide variety of post-Enlightenment cultural discourses (psychoanalysis; Idealist philosophy; and, as we shall further explore, ethnology, chief among them) of positioning nonwestern discourse as the "outside" to its various epistemological claims, and, on the other hand, the resistance of black studies to that cultural ideology's enabling role in the history of the subaltern's repression – given that radical mutual disregard we can hardly be surprised by the traditional tendency to view "theory" and "vernacular" as rival terms in an endless struggle to define expressive value. The continuing effort to articulate an African-American vernacular theory by such writers as Henry Louis Gates, Craig Werner, Karla Holloway, John Callahan, Hazel Carby, Houston Baker, and Gayle Jones,[3] then, constitutes a fundamental interrogation of those exclusionary and privileged terms by which competing cultural idioms have historically constituted themselves. While this call for a fresh model of black theoretical inquiry in part reproduces the antithetical rhetoric it would dismantle, it also can be seen as exemplifying the intricacy of negotiating between conceptual and expressive sources that, however apparently opposed, are often mutually implicated, even mutually constitutive. Crucial to this deployment of vernacular modalities as instruments of revisionary aesthetic and political visions is demystification of the binary divisions of "tradition" and "modernity," convention and innovation, for such figurations can neutralize the revolutionary potential of idiomatic resources, turning them into objects of merely commemorative or even nostalgic revery rather than releasing their transformative potential within the present. Just as Black Arts poets often chose between monumentalizing Trane as emblem of achieved nationalist patrimony and activating "Trane" as a somewhat unpredictable, ongoing process of refiguration, so black vernacular theorists have navigated between stabilized and processural images of their subject.

The central passage of Gates's manifesto for what he calls a "critical vernacular poetics" is exemplary, and worth dwelling over, with respect to this network of motives, choices, and effects:

> We must not succumb to the tragic lure of white power, the mistake of accepting the empowering language of white critical theory as 'universal' or as our own language, the mistake of confusing the enabling mask of theory with our own black faces. . . . Now, we must, at last, don the empowering mask of blackness and talk *that* talk, the language of black difference.
>
> (Henry Louis Gates, "Canon-formation and the Afro-American Tradition," 29)[4]

In form and content, Gates's assertion encapsulates the complexity, the doubleness and more than doubleness, of contemporary black criticism's call for vernacular paradigms. Generated from a continuous emphasis on the relation between language and power, the passage's structure of balance implies a poised, intelligible, calmly authoritative, and morally transluscent voice, one fully versed in the enabling verbal manners of a practice claiming "universal" status. On one level, that is to say, Gates makes it clear that he can frame his claim against "white theory" in tones normal to its "own" province. At the same time, the passage's penchant for antithetical formulations bespeaks an interest in oppositionality *per se*, in the eruptive "difference" that is in every sense the passage's end. Its diction and syntax, organized by a series of parallelisms and rhythmic repetitions, serve to highlight contrasts of resistance and ownership, complicitous loss and willed recovery, illusory enablement and authentic empowerment, "confusion" and deliverance. Underlying these tensions is the essentially reflexive contrast between theory and "talk" by which Gates subtly insinuates homology between the oppositions West/vernacular and writing/speech. But what complicates the nature of this oppositionality, the strategy by which the force of black cultural expression becomes the syntactical changeling of white power, are the slight variations amidst recurrent phrases – seen most emphatically in the contrast between the passive image of mistakenly accepting "white language" and the performative injunction to "talk *that* talk," and in the appearance of the crucial temporal sign, "Now, at last," that establishes the historicity of Gates's turn to the vernacular, announcing a liberating release from repetitive entrapment in the false harmonies of dominant critical discourse.

But perhaps the most suggestive locus of Gates's double-edged project is the figurative space traversed from "the enabling mask of theory" to "the empowering mask of blackness." In the first phrase – "we must not confuse the mask of theory with our own black faces" – we move from alien device to the proper being, the substitution of mask by face suggesting resolution to the "tragic" seductions of diasporic displacement. The differentiation of heuristic mask and authentic face, echoing Du Bois's notion of black double-consciousness formed within the Veil of African-American experience, displays, first, a knowledge that one begins in response to another representational system and, correspondingly, a desire to heal those imposed divisions by recuperating a lost center, plenitude, origin. Such a move from mask to face is generated by an essentially sacramental or epiphanic logic by which the vernacular is posited as a kind of Primal Scene or site of Originary and salvivic Truth. But the following phrase – "Now, we must, at last, don the empowering mask of blackness" – while making more overt the passage's eschatological undertone, initiates a new turn, suggesting how even the face may be another mask, a site of continued resistance, even of tricksterism, and not a revelation of final being after exile in the Egypt of white theory. By positing an authentic face beneath the various masks, white and black, while all the time speaking various languages – the idioms of *dis versus dat*, so to speak – Gates at once keeps race from being put utterly under erasure while reminding us that the vernacular, whatever its originary and material sources, operates for the African-American theorist as an enabling device, an ever shifting mechanism of critique and self-interpretation.

Gates's passage, ever turning upon its variously proposed and decomposed centers of attention, exemplifies how contemporary black criticism's interest in vernacular models marks a moment when African-American critical discourse confronts itself, opening a privileged though problematic space in which it can frame its own practice as performance while disturbing prevailing logics of cultural construction. The antithetical yet constructive torque of this project ought to be seen as extending the Black Arts Movement's speculative quest for a distinctively black modality of cultural assertion, notwithstanding salient gestures by many postBAM theorists (including Gates) to distinguish their efforts from the sometimes roughhewn parochialism of "black aesthetic" tracts. But in fairness equally to underappreciated connections between Black Arts and vernacular strategies of resistance and to later theorists' sophisticated extensions of those strategies through both intricate critiques of Euro-American modernism and self-scrutinizing engagements with the politics of positionality, we ought to enlarge the scope of our own inquiry into conceptual and historical parameters of the moment when vernacular theory becomes truly prominent among those many strands of performed blackness privileged earlier by Black Arts practitioners. In order to begin elaborating the conceptual and genealogical import of this moment – an elaboration that we will test in the forge of the preacher's sermon and then reinflect in the next chapter's return to the stage of critical performance – I'd like to label that double movement of disruption and self-predication "The Sandy Bottom Shuffle," as per the following vernacular anecdote, a parable made popular by Redd Foxx and most recently given pungent reinsertion into popular African-American culture by Richard Pryor:

Once a cop followed an unsuspecting black couple into lovers' lane. Having lost their trail at the opening of a thicket, he noticed a black man resting upon an adjacent perch. "Hey boy," called the cop. "Did you see a darky couple drive by here?"

He said, "Yes, I saw 'em drive by here."

"Well, what did they do?"

The man replied: "They went through the bushes and they did the Sandy Bottom Shuffle."

"Say What?!," the cop stammered. "You come to court and explain what you saw."

And the judge ordered the black witness, "Tell this court what you saw."

Said, "These folks went through the bushes and they did the *Sandy Bottom Shuffle!*"

The judge banged his gavel. "Say what?!" he boomed. And then, without waiting for reply, he announced, "We've got to make an affidavit in this case."

So the blood asked him, "Well, what is an 'affidavit of this case'?"

The judge answered, "That's a technicality in the law that you niggers don't know nothing about. You come back here again tomorrow. We're going to get beyond this impasse."

Next day the judge called him up: "Tell us what you saw!"

"I saw a couple go through the bushes and do the Sandy Bottom Shuffle."

So the Judge was *really* mad then. He stamped his foot: "Just WHAT do you mean by the Sandy Bottom Shuffle?!?"

Whereupon the brother shot back, "That's a technicality in screwin' that you white folks don't know nothing about."

Court was dismissed![5]

For Redd Foxx and Richard Pryor, this little tale at least partially expressed the paradoxical glee and vulnerability of the crossover black performer, moving gingerly along the frontier between disclosure and concealment in order to survive one sphere's judgmental gaze while announcing another's legitimacy. Following their lead, we can see how the parable offers a reminder that meaning, and the cultural authority it affirms, is never simply an object waiting to be recalled from its natural condition, but is rather a contingency of enunciative positions and the strategies they warrant. Notably, the tale makes this point by staging the confrontation of two modes of perception, understanding, and expressive control. I will suggest that these modes are themselves differential positions, susceptible to multiple recombinations and contradictory effects, but for the moment let us name them Writing and the Other, reading the tale as an allegory of western culture's ethnographic project of self-empowerment through the pursuit, collection, and containment of darker bodies and voices. Needing at once to establish and to capture difference, ethnography polices alternative cultural practices in order to regulate the defining terms of its own terrain's identity. In what James Clifford might call an "allegory of salvage,"[6] this narrative of retrieval and representation, the substitution of affidavits for occluded acts and impenetrable speech, founds the custodial and hermeneutic prestige of the tribunal space, while at the same time the object of interpretation is muted even as it gives compulsory witness to its world's activity.

Such a story of rupture between invisible or recalcitrant experience and its authentication by an alien refabrication enacts the rhetorical structure by which literary practice, in its canonical garb, has habitually asserted a fragile claim to cultural importance. Indeed, the aesthetic language of European identity has long grappled with the vernacular as an alternately debased and inspiriting, indecorous and refreshening, Other to its own projected image of authorative originality. In this regard, one can plot a line stretching from the Roman juridical designation of the vernacular as that which stands outside the domains of consumption and production, that is, outside the domains of desire and power, to postmodernism's location of the nonwestern Imaginary in an ironically privileged realm beyond the crisis-ridden Symbolic of European modernity: thus, in such formulations as Artaud's "dark prodigious reality," Sartre's "primordial simplicity" of Negritude, and Tyler's "breathing darkness of the antipodeal night," the European subject has projected an idea of vernacular alterity as part of a program of therapeutic self-narration.[7] Taking an alternative but complementary tack along the frontiers of an emergent vernacular literature *within* the domain of 'high' Euro-American culture – e.g., with the translational poetics of Dante, Chaucer, and Cervantes, and the improvisational lighting for fresh territory in Twain, Whitman, and Williams – we can see how the vernacular is called upon to inaugurate the challenge of modernism as a deliberate disturbance or expropriation of decorum, mastery, and received method. This fiction of a radical division between mainstream and vernacular expression is integral to the naturalization of canonicity itself, and forges a critical link between the ideologies of culture and colonialism, even where imperial power operates within local western spaces. Thus, for example, the emergence in the late eighteenth century of historicist and textual criticism, with the attendant focus upon categories of authorship, authenticity, and editorial accountability, was accompanied by the "invention" of what we still call folklore, the collection of putatively evanescent forms undertaken under the aegis of the written canon's contrasting stability. As the work of Susan Stewart and Roger Abrahams on the consolidation in early modernity of such genres as ballads and folktales suggests, the naturalization of literature's canonical authority as a substantial and permanent archive is achieved in great measure by construction of a contrasting "folk" realm as its undeveloped (often childlike) antithesis.[8] Properly collected and annotated, folklore helped anchor the project of canon, providing the literary a ready-made contrast with the supposed ephemerality and unmediated organicism of what we might call the "oral" class (the rural, the impoverished, the Welsh, etc.).

The early "writing of folklore" (*ethno-graphy*) thus emerges as a symptomatic anxiety of modernity itself, as an emblematic instance of that crisis of belatedness which we recognize more readily in the emergence of ethnology in the twentieth century. The rising prestige of ethnology among the "human sciences" accompanies a turn in European self-apprehension when the metropole is itself rattled in its perch atop a fantasized hierarchy of cultural value, shaken by worldwide war, economic uncertainty, and rumblings of third world resistance, and prodded by its own anthropological musings to rethink the relation between the "civilized" and "barbarian," the familiar and the foreign, the original and the servile. As Homi Bhabha has recently proposed in a critique of structuralist historicism, the so-called "science" of ethnology cannot be separated from attempts to secure European culture during the crisis of imperialism, itself the uneasy legacy of post-Enlightenment reason's effort to purify itself of other lesser or excessive impulses and desires.[9] Forced to summon the Other in order to establish its form of mastery, ethnology inevitably retells the contradictory fable of a cultural discourse split between its self-conception as primary and impervious to anxieties of influence, and its constant reinforcement by disastrous raids of distant cultures.

So the police get to the heart of the Jungle too late; failing to prevent the circulation of energy in an alien space, they seek to force description of the hidden event as a story of illicit desires that require textual discipline: Thou Shalt Not Shuffle . . . but none the less, tell us all about it! Yet, as our anecdote reminds us, this bringing of the transgressive into visibility is risky business, for the witness, in an act of parodic mimesis, reverses the very language by which he is compelled to speak. The ethnographic project meets a moment of embarrassing impasse: Court dismissed!

But if the anecdote seems to unwrite the ethnographic and revoice the vernacular in a distribution of agency that exceeds the judge's expectations, doesn't this reversal itself depend on just those oppositional strategies by which the vernacular is conscripted at the bidding of the literary? Generated by such structural antitheses as court versus nature, participatorial witness versus external Gaze, body versus language, desire versus law, speech versus text, doesn't the triumph of vernacular narrative depend here on the very notion of mutually exclusive mentalities and modalities upon which the judge's own presumption of mastery is founded? It is, I think, precisely the problem of conceptualizing difference without becoming trapped within the terms of a heritage one would redefine that has framed contemporary formulations of a "distinctively" African-American vernacular theory. For those who have worked toward such a revisionary stance have felt themselves to occupy variously the positions of participant, witness, *and* judge, which *together* figure the African-American modernist's peculiar relations to the very vernacular matrix being at once valorized and rearticulated. In this sense, the "Sandy Bottom Shuffle" can be said to designate the shifting site of a major topos of African-American modernist desire, a scene of vernacular textualization contesting ethnological "folk" genealogies of which I offer the following brief sketch.

In *Mules and Men*,[10] still one of the keenest contributions to African-American vernacular studies, Zora Neale Hurston crystallizes the positional drama of black vernacular theory. Practicing a form of what Alice Gambrell terms "ventriloquistic" self-critique,[11] Hurston stages her activity as emergent yet indiginous ethnographer in terms that prefigure the scenario of Ellison's blueprint parable:

> In a way [collecting "Negro folklore"] would not be a new experience for me [she writes in the Introduction]. From the earliest rocking of my cradle, I had known about the capers Brer Rabbit is apt to *cut*. But it was fitting me like a tight chemise. I couldn't see it for wearing it. It was only when I was off in college, away from my native surroundings that I could see myself like somebody else and stand off and look at my garment. Then I had to have the spy-glass of Anthropology to look through at that.
>
> (Zora Neale Hurston, *Mules and Men*, 1)

Though modelled from within the vernacular domain, Hurston's chemise, like Ellison's blueprint, becomes an enabling *and* constraining inheritance. Playing Brer Rabbit as college girl, she attempts to move beyond the cradle of the Imaginary to the "cut" of Symbolic meaning by surveying and not merely, as it were, assuming the vernacular garment – in particular, by seeing it from the place of the other, thus experiencing the epistemological split captured in the ambiguous grammar of the phrase "I could see myself like somebody else," an ambiguity subtly enforced by the chemise itself: is it a covering garb or an undergarment? is it a homespun smock or priestly cloak? (All these possibilities are latent in the term "chemise" – Like Brer Rabbit, Hurston uses shift-y terms!) But, she continues:

> Folklore is not as easy to collect as it sounds. The best source is where there are the least outside influences and these people, being usually under-privileged, are the shyest. They are most reluctant at times to reveal that which the soul lives by. And the Negro, in spite of his open-faced laughter, his seeming acquiescence, is particularly evasive. You see we are a polite people and we do not say to our questioner, "Get out of here!" We smile and tell him or her something that satisfies the white person because, knowing so little about us, he doesn't know what he is missing.
>
> (*Mules and Men*, 2)

Hurston stages the enthnographic encounter from a specific perspective, defining her terms from the implicated standpoint of identification rather than the invisible position of neutral 'objectivity.' The apparent anthropological gesture of peeling back the curtain on native folkways is in fact a covert reenactment of disguise, as the discussion of strategic masking re-inscribes the "seeming acquiescence" of the ethnographic subject in the writer's own deceptive tone of clarifying disclosure. Her "polite" gesture of explication is both affirmed and belied in the shift from disciplinary norms ("these people" as "source") to intimate association ("we" as those capable of transposing re-vealing into re-veiling), a move that allows her to become the vessel of repudiation ("Get out of here!") even as she smilingly erases this risky trespass against racially-charged rules of anthropological transaction. This defense against ethnological containment and mystification works also as a critique of cultural norms, as trickster deflection is defined as the defense of the civilized subject of home against the crude invasion by foreign interrogators. At the same time, the sly division between anthropology as textualization and as performance – "Folklore is not as easy to *collect* as it *sounds*" – with its subliminal contrast of transgressive dissent to custodial imperialism, deepens the subtle tension between Hurston and her own disciplinary authority. For in a fashion that Karla Holloway identifies as the knowing "dislocation" between standard and dialect idioms peculiar to black textuality,[12] this reverberating and unresolved play between potentially conflicting spheres' idiomatic registers cunningly signifies on the authenticating preface[13] of her mentor Franz Boas, which purports to celebrate the native researcher's unimpeded access to what he calls "the Negro's true inner life" (*Mules and Men*, xiii). Then, in a further destabilizing exchange of voices, Hurston proceeds to intensify her relation with that "inner life" by elaborating what she calls "the theory behind *our* tactics," illustrated immediately by a remark set in quotation marks but unascribed, as though her text has become a medium for shared self-disclosure:

> "The white man is always trying to know into somebody elses busi-
> ness. All right, I'll set something outside the door of my mind for him
> to play with and handle. He can read my writing but he sho' can't
> read my mind. I'll put this play toy in his hand, and he will seize it
> and go away. Then I'll say my say and sing my song."
>
> *(Mules and Men*, 3)

Employing what Barbara Johnson terms "featherbed resistance,"[14]
Hurston's collaborative voice reverses here the normative hierarchy of
knowing ethnographer and childlike native. The doorway defines the
liminal terrain on which such inversion takes place: on one side, the outsider
armed with knowledge (datum of the distant), on the other side, the homey
rich in understanding (substance of the situated). Writing is undone as
techne, becoming mere toy; its eminence is mocked in a parodic submission to its illusory certainty, while the "soundings" of self-representation
remain unheard by any but the attentive, even kindred, "mind." And
whatever that performance may present, it remains a reminder that there
can be no authentic practice "outside" the acknowledged actuality of its
discursive circumstance, the sphere of its agency.

Certainly, it is Hurston's project to participate in the agency her representation champions, yet that very dynamic of affiliation and mediation
suggests how her own authority remains suspended in the conflict between
she who sounds and she who collects. But it is not enough to say, with
many of Hurston's readers, that her life and work illustrate an illogical,
even tragic, commingling of so-called academic and popular perspectives.
Rather, as Gambrell notes in a compelling reading of Hurston's conjure
tales, the effort to reconcile the vaunted empirical objectivism of Boas with
alternative rhetorics of authenticity confounds such reductive antinomies
and compels transumption of ethnological writing, which emerges in *Mules
and Men* as an unsettling amalgam of fictional and scientistic narrative
procedures.[15] In this, again, she prefigures Ellison's strategy of juxtaposed
textualities through which *Invisible Man* 'dialectic-ally' (so to speak) ironizes
and historicizes reifying paradigms of African-American expressive culture.
Moreover, by foregrounding the interplay of performative and analytical
imperatives in the construction of her own authoritative yet contingent
voice, Hurston implies that the historical predicament of the African-
American theorist must be confronted and revised through its continuous
re-emplotment. In effect, mixing a kind of textual conjure from elements
of Boasian epistemology, New Orleans Hoodoo, and what Gates terms a
"speakerly" narrative stance,[16] Hurston affirms a paradoxically typical
subjectivity in the double gesture of the witness-participant rewriting
competing cultural narratives.

Mules and Men depicts its author operating across cultural, linguistic, and discursive boundaries in a manner that fuses critical praxis and nationalist consciousness. Perhaps Hurston "herself" has remained largely inscrutable because at every turn she destabilized norms of cultural legitimacy, undertaking the hazardous work of complicating, rather than validating, ideas of "culture" furnished by the disparate spheres of her continuing instruction. In her work, fueled as it is by Boasian restlessness with the cruder racisms of early modern ethnology[17] and by well-developed "capers" of deflection nurtured by her "rocking" origins, we see that the relation of inside and outside is not a prefatorial concern to be solved before the moment of ethnography, but the crux of ethnographic activity itself. If Boas and his followers were able to alter ethnographic practice by a liberal recognition of universal difference, the genuinely unassimilable difference of Hurston's presence among (and outside) them underscored the continuing implication of ethnology and modernism in the reduction of alterity to a structural principle of holistic, unvarying "tradition" (individual traditions might differ from one another, but each was finished and total in itself, as was, therefore, the very idea of tradition). Against the background of this schematization, *Mules and Men* accents the fabrication of culture as a series of decisions, selections, and negotiations, at times undertaken among a given group of participants, at times between figures with varying experiences inside and outside the sphere of defined cultural production. Beyond crossing boundaries, Hurston highlighted them, sketching their contours so as to magnify their status as constructed delineations while opening them to potentially liberating rewritings. Thus conceived, Hurston's image of vernacular culture anticipates the less guarded rebellion of Black Arts theorists who insisted on defining "culture" as a mobile and incessantly contested medium of ideologically charged (not organic or unchanging) values and "tactics." The vernacular emerges in her vision not as a realm of systematized or isolated 'authenticity,' but as an agile, collective medium of conflict, revision, and surprise, an improvisational artifice forged among institutional formations whose constraints can be guilefully transgressed to enable constructive movement and release fresh energies.

In the passages we've been examining, the motifs of collection versus critique, of sound versus script, of influence, generational encounter, schooled theorizing, and unlettered tricksterism all establish an affiliation between Hurston and Ellison – and indeed recall several instances of this speculative topos: one thinks, for example, of DuBois's movement from the isolating study's meditations to the Black Belt's songs at the end of *The Souls of Black Folk*, of this pattern's precise reversal by James Weldon Johnson's ex-colored man in the final chapters of *Autobiography of an Ex-Coloured Man*, and of the dialectical interplay of learned spectatorship and visionary performance in Toomer's "Kabnis."[18] But – as the very titles of Du Bois's, Johnson's, and Hurston's enthographic studies variously imply – all such vernacular theorists must be related to the slave narrative genre, which arises precisely to 'write the human' (ethnography) against the dehumanizations of servitude, but within which the conventional association of freedom and writing observed by many commentators is, as Vera Kutzinski observes, complicated by the desire to "maintain a dialogue with [vernacular] culture at the moment of writing."[19] Nowhere is the intricacy of the vernacular theorist's enablement by the expressive resources of slave society's "inner life" more evident than in the 1845 *Narrative*[20] of Frederick Douglass, where the political and affective resonance of literate power's dangerous dialogue with oral culture crackles on almost every page. One thinks most immediately of Douglass's explication of the slaves' songs, or "sorrows of the heart" as Douglass terms them (thus providing a pre-text, by way of Du Bois's "sorrow songs," of Hurston's vernacular expression as "that which the soul lives by"). Situating himself in a loosely delineated zone between the master's power and the sphere of slave expression, Douglass anticipates the stakes of vernacular theory's complex struggle within critical modernism:

> While on their way [to the Great House Farm], [the slaves] would make the dense old woods, for miles around, reverberate with their wild songs, revealing at once the highest joy and the deepest sadness. They would compose and sing as they went along, consulting neither time nor tune. The thought that came up, came out – if not in the word, in the sound; – and as frequently in one as in the other. They would sometimes sing the most pathetic sentiment in the most rapturous tone, and the most rapturous sentiment in the most pathetic tone. Into all of their songs they would manage to weave something of the Great House Farm. [. . .] This they would sing, as a chorus, to words which to many would seem unmeaning jargon, but which, nevertheless, were full of meaning to themselves. [. . .] I did not, when a slave, understand the deep meaning of those rude and apparently incoherent songs. I was myself within the circle; so that I neither saw nor heard as those without might see and hear. They told a tale of woe which was then altogether beyond my feeble comprehension; they were tones loud, long, and deep; they breathed the prayer and complaint of souls boiling over with the bitterest anguish. Every tone was a testimony against slavery, and a prayer to God for deliverance from chains. The hearing of those wild notes always depressed my spirit, and filled me with ineffable sadness. [. . .] The mere recurrence to those songs, even now, afflicts me . . .
>
> (Frederick Douglass, *Narrative*, 31–2)

Himself consulting both word and sound, Douglass measures the significance of the slaves' mobile and improvisatory composition as a fluid alternation among moods, postures, and idioms. At once inside and beyond the "circle" of slave performance, the ex-slave's own compositional dynamic echoes his people's in its simultaneous attention to mimetic and expressive impulses, 'weaving' awareness of contextual exigency and political impulse with appreciation of emotive resonance. In one sense, the entanglement of transcendent and implicated subject positions that characterizes this exegetical posture reflects the generic tension of seeking validation from an audience he must critique, that is, the white abolitionist consumers of testimonies stemming from, but written in a time and space beyond, the vernacular sphere of slavery. As Ronald Radano has pointed out, the slave narrator often "reinvented slave sounds" in the very moment of inscribing them in order to "fit the common sense of nineteenth-century Northern, literate culture" (which, to paraphrase Hurston, didn't know what it was missing).[21] The very "deliverance" desired by the songs themselves thereby threatens to dislodge the black freedman from the very source of his interpretive authority (where "source" loses its force of origination and becomes colored by the ethnographic idea of "informer"). In both the singing and its rehearsal through memory, legitimation and interpretation are mutually refractory concerns, and the pursuit of freedom is, correspondingly, a quest for meaning.

Douglass, of course, by deliberately entering an arena of impossible translation and then calling attention to significance that only he, "now," is capable of decoding is himself tuning an "apparently incoherent song," adopting what Marcellous Blount terms a "strategy of indirection"[22] in producing a multivalent response to the slave songs' play of determinate and indeterminate 'signifying.' The contradictions inherent in his present position lead along this double-voiced path of indirection to complexities in precisely determining the songs' "meaning" (or should we say, anticipating Hurston's crafty dis-location of anthropological expertise, *revealing* their "sentiments"?). "To many" the songs' "words ... would seem unmeaning jargon," Douglass writes, jabbing, no doubt, at much of his reading audience, which was susceptible to the Enlightenment view of *black culture* as an oxymoron, as a mute, non-historical body incapable of signifying itself.[23] But just what is this meaning? Is it subjective (it has meaning to *themselves*), or universal (*anyone* should understand its true import, he will conclude)? Is it beyond need of any interpretation at all (*full* of meaning) or a call for the rigorous intervention Douglass here supplies? Is it a property, a content to be expressed, or an act, something which can't be objectified outside what the song *does*? "The thought that came up, came out – if not in the word, in the sound," Douglass writes, pointing to the performative, rather than systematic, crossing of medium and meaning.

Douglass's rich instantiation of the African-American ethnographical topos suggests how crucial concerns of legitimacy, transmission, translation, and continuity of voice are conjured when vernacular theory is proposed from a self-consciously contemporary vantage upon collective struggle. And further, in its implication that vernacular performance and the consciousness it engages are likewise positional and plural rather than simply posited and polar, Douglass's seminal engagement with the slave songs offers us a possible route of return to the Sandy Bottom Shuffle as a parable of modernist critique and resistance, as well as to the Black Arts Movement as contemporary black theory's enabling "source." Having been tutored by Douglass in the self-transgressive energies of vernacular performance, and especially its insusceptibility to prefabricated 'understanding,' perhaps now we can hear the black witness's retort to the judge not simply as a parodic reversal but as a mimetic displacement of received strategies of vernacular reception and categorization. By *performing*, and not merely inverting, the judge's own reductive ridicule, he demonstrates just how local a dialect the language of power really is, as well as how theoretical an idiom vernacular expression can become. So conceived, the Sandy Bottom Shuffle figures "vernacular theory" not so much as a code of inversions but as a site where oppositional relations are interrogated, repositioned, or even decomposed into new forms of difference. It is this flexible insurgency that likewise makes the Sandy Bottom Shuffle a comrade of Black Arts' nationalist speculations orbiting diverse images of the blackness-of-blackness, for the presence of vernacular evocations in Neal, Baraka, Shange, *et al.* ought to be seen now more clearly as an index of motives more intricate than its surface Manichaeism allowed us to see at the time. Ethnography and its Other, the judging power and the participant-witness, the hierophant and homey, blackness as negation (aint) and as affirmation (is), can thus be seen as co-implicated if distinctively valued, rehearsing contestatory scenarios in a shifting dance which knows no bottom. It is to one such scene, as regulated now from *within* the circle, that I would like to turn in order to activate this reimagined vernacular 'paradigm' in the very midst of modernist African-American performance.

II

> When it comes to handling the Bible, I knocks down verbs, breaks up prepositions, and jumps over adjectives.
>
> Nineteenth-century vernacular preacher[24]

Vernacular performance, like the responsive subject who simultaneously recalls, reads, and becomes "afflicted" by it, vitalizes meaning as a production of a richly historicized present tense: to follow Douglass once again, "even now" can we perceive and experience the vibrant spatio-temporal reality, the dynamic chronotope, of vernacular tradition as it erupts into a living node of possibility. Refusing to become a fetishized object passed between competing judges and discourses, its meaning is not finally assignable to any single register, but situates black expressive intention in varied exchanges across diverse experiential, discursive, and symbolic economies. Vernacular performance, therefore, is as much a struggle *for* possibilities of meaning as 'about' any particular thematic ideographic content.

As we shall see, this chiasmal signifying on the meaning of performance as the performance of meaning energizes representative instances of the modern sermonic tradition, for the generative power of enactment is itself intrinsic to vernacular culture's own self-theorizing reflections. Take, for example, the old story about the good church-going sister who was asked by a friend who had been unable to attend the church services earlier that day, "Did Rev. Jones preach a good sermon this morning?" "Oh, yes," the sister answered. "Well, what was the sermon about?" her friend then asked; "I don't know what it was about," the sister shot back, "but it sure was a good sermon." Rippling with self-critical humor, the sermonic tradition incorporates such 'preacher tales' into the ongoing story of its own capacity to gain purchase on the attentive – if not, in this case, fully retentive – consciousness of its participants, foregrounding "The Message" as a means for realizing the call-and-response modality of communal authorship.

However, before beginning our exploration of the means and manner by which specific chant-sermons orchestrate such conjunctions of signifying and significance, it's worth pausing over the more corrosive element of the anecdote's wit, which tweaks the church's inattention to narrative clarity as a disregard and even incapacity for the kind of radical instructional program that a movement such as the Black Arts so vigorously propounded. If 'vernacular theory' seemed at first glance an odd coupling of idiomatic fluency and critical perspective, isn't it equally cause for pause to locate a fruitful exchange between African-American modernism's revolutionary vision and the unruly contingencies of vernacular enactment in the church, which to many commentators on the post-Civil Rights era remained wedded to anachronistic style and content in the face of fast-changing paradigms of black consciousness? W. Lawrence Hogue states succinctly the case against the church's relevance for an account of black modernism's emergent ethos of hard-edged social critique and radical action:

> The brand of Christianity that was fermented and preached under the slave conditions of the rural South, and that had lasted nearly a hundred years after Emancipation, simply could not have any real relevancy or meaning to the black youth growing up under the complex industrial systems of the urban centers. [. . .] [I]ts administration failed to keep up with the demands and realities of this new urban Afro-American social reality.
>
> (Lawrence Hogue, *Discourse and the Other*, 49)[25]

The shift from Martin Luther King to Malcolm X as charismatic center for insurgent discourses of black spiritual identity is likewise cited as emblematic of the waning of the church's influence within the new movement, while the Bible (*"what news from James' bastard Bible?"* – Henry Dumas, "harlem mosaic") and the Christian liturgy that promulgated its 'Word' ("I started talking/to the Bible/and it kept telling/me to Die" – Norman

Jordan, "Sinner") was often conflated with the lethal mendacity of white hegemony among younger artists and intellectuals of the time.[26]

No doubt the church became a visible site of communal self-criticism as arms of the black consciousness movement such as the Panthers and Black Arts Repertory/School sought their own institutional legitimacy and materialization. Indeed, as witnessed by the very tradition of preacher tales and other forms of anticlerical satire, the church, as privileged locus of black social and spiritual activity, has long been the sibling rival of more 'outlaw' kinds of personal and collective expression, not least that of self-consciously dissident modes of secular assertion. Nevertheless, the church ought not be so quickly hammered into an extraneous taxonomical niche carved out by Manichaean readings of African-American expressive culture that divide 'religious' from 'secular' inclinations, or institutional from 'street' imperatives. In The Life itself, such distinctions are more honored in the breach than in the conception: the 'crossovers' between musical styles, expressive mechanisms, performance atmospheres, and, more tellingly, belief systems and forms of critique are profound and persistent. With distance and documentation, historians have now described in textured detail the intricate crossfertilizations and mutual reinforcements among blues, spirituals, toasts, ballads, and other vernacular forms that practitioners and poets alike have exploited cannily and joyfully for generations.[27] Yet the period that continues to hover over the present moment is too often seen as one purified of such heteroglossic generic gumbos, a rather hasty assessment given the centrality of pulpit-oratory in the radical projects of King, Malcolm, and avatars such as Jesse Jackson and Louis Farrakhan, and in view of the functional evocation of 'preachment' in the Black Arts Movement's theatrical experiments that we observed in such practitioners as Kgositsile and Milner. And, indeed, one of the less-appreciated forms of such interfusion of modalities, separated from our view by too-quick historicist or ideological prescription but not by experiential complexity, is the chant-sermon's energetic participation in the performance of a reflexive black modernism every bit as politically charged and aesthetically resourceful as that envisaged by practioners of genres habitually associated with the Black Arts Movement.[28]

As the preachers would say, my texts for today are the sermons "The Eagle Stirs Her Nest," preached by Rev. C. L. Franklin, and "Build Your Own Fire," delivered by Rev. W. Leo Daniels,* each enacted in Northern urban centers (Detroit and Chicago, respectively) restless with rebellious energies of the post-Watts period. Already, of course, I've become enmeshed in the ethnographic thicket, preparing to speak of a performance by subjecting it to spatial, temporal, and formal displacement. The doubling of transcription and the audiotape from which it derives (redoubled in personal memory) just as much repeats as mitigates our distance

---

* See Appendix B (pp. 332–51) for transcriptions.

from the embodied realm of light, proximity, spectacle, temperature, locality, fortuitous sound, and innumerable other contextual features in which each sermon, as event, took place. How can we shuffle off such ideological coils? The question cannot be one of denying the institutionally framed authority and revisionary desire motivating my recollection of Rev. Franklin's and Rev. Daniels's sermons. However dialogic the following interplay of critical paradigm and vernacular performance might become, no conceptual advantage is to be gained by repressing the inescapable process of textualization upon which interpretation and performance alike are staked. Notably, no 'natural' resemblance can be inferred between sound or gesture and the transcriptions' notation: their relation is technically 'arbitrary,' though clearly 'motivated,' governed by an urge for interpretive inflection that makes the transcription a supplement not only of the performance to which it refers but of the readings which it here provokes. While I have made certain efforts to 'line out' the preachers' styles of utterance – to reframe that 'grain of the voice' through which they materialized a specific Message – the transcriptions necessarily retain their own symptoms of writerliness, and remain graphic signs of distance from those performative circumstances which they seek to retrace.

Still, we must be equally careful not to suppose that any contrast of 'original' event-utterance and 'secondary' citation will resolve the ambiguities of intention, code, and effect that lie at the core of these sermons: to borrow a metaphor crucial to Franklin's text, the preachers' performances "stir" rather than confirm assumptions about hierarchy, sequence, and priority, disrupting the logic of 'first-and-last' as they fashion a politics of spiritualized black consciousness. Too often, the opposition of vocalization and transcription has reinforced just these divisions between ontological and formal dimensions of language use, draining vernacular enactments of their capacity to script and analyze complex logics of signification and determination, while imagining writing as impervious to transitive effects embedded within its own grammatical organization.[29] To acknowledge, for example, that a Coltrane solo remains fundamentally untranscribable does not invalidate notation as a heuristic device of exploration and understanding, nor (to make a more important but more elusive point) ought it subtly deny that improvisation the possibilities of revision, the secondary operations of amendation and correction, covertly ceded to the pen in idealist accounts of orality's alienation from writing.

Clearly, then, doubts concerning transcription's propriety are not only, or even primarily, structural or epistemological; they are about power and legitimacy. As the often disgraceful history of ethnographic collection indicates – a history nowhere more charged by weighted economies of difference (governed by narrow canons of race, class, gender, and region) than in the vexed effort to translate African-American "dialect" into "literary" form[30] – it is ownership and manipulation of cultural utterance that is most at stake. But as participants in the African-American topos of vernacular reflection show, *not writing* is no less a contribution to enslaving institutions' sedimented mastery than is writing in the service of deleterious codes and decorums. Writing and utterance are equally efforts to question, reform, or extend the spheres from which they originate, and neither can be elevated over the other conceptually as preferable modes of sacrificial mimetism, that is, as distancing mechanisms by which representation substitutes for the very thing it seeks to make present. While it is true that the Other of ethnology has been not so much discovered as constructed by anthropological representation, it is just as much the case that the vernacular "self" is constructed through the conversational dynamic of imaginative transposition and recontextualization. What must be distinguished is not mediation and being, but rather representation as embalming theft seeking to reduce an active *now* into an encased *that was*, and representation as engaged praxis seeking to maintain the active *now* within the material reality of *then and there*. Thus, while we have passed the point in modernity when a naive defense of transcription as preservation can be mounted against a history of distortion and appropriation, so, too, have we moved beyond the compensatory naiveté that imagines one can protect a pristine vernacular sphere by first imagining it free of anxieties and strategies ascribed to writing and then leaving it untouched by supplementary inscription (especially when modern vernacular performances already understand their own hetereogenous composition as amalgams of 'voice' and 'text,' as we shall soon see with Franklin and Daniels). Thus, far from imagining either the adequacy *or* dispensability of transcription, it is precisely the possibility of the sermons' further carnivalizing my account of vernacular theory that gives their fragmented presence here a potentially productive urgency.

In fact, we owe a debt of insight to this crux of transcription since it alerts us to the *translational* drama that forms the sermons' nexus of thematic and performative concerns, concerns which focus upon the preacher's and congregation's shared capacity for transformative substitution, displacement, and re-vision. Indeed, "The Eagle Stirs Her Nest" and "Build Your Own Fire" are themselves meditations on these issues of representation and originality, especially as they map the juncture of communal performance and (re)appropriated authority. As deliberations on their own entanglements with prior, competing, and parallel discourses, Franklin's and Daniels's sermons together stage an inquiry into the very experiential and interpretive categories by which they proceed. Indeed, what emerges from the sermons as performances is a celebratory concern with their own constitution as mediated and effectual events, their own politics of form, their own empowerment and framing of agency.

Let us begin with C. L. Franklin's "The Eagle Stirs Her Nest," for it thematizes its very possibility as collective creation, blending design and composition in terms that progressively redefine the very meaning of sermonic performance. As recitation, the sermon can be quickly if

awkwardly summarized (indeed, so insouciant is it in its disregard of narrative development that "The Eagle Stirs Her Nest" could serve as illustration
of the style of preaching practiced by the good sister's Rev. Jones): riffing
on the passage from Deuteronomy proclaiming "the Lord's portion is his
people" – "As an eagle stirreth up her nest, fluttereth over her young,
spreadeth abroad her wings, taketh them, beareth them on her wings: So
the Lord alone did lead him [Jacob], and there was no strange god with
him . . ." (Deuteronomy 32:11–12) – Franklin enjoins his congregants to
enter the image's import as a vision of communal self-construction under
the stern nurturance of visionary guidance. Following venerable patterns
of African-American religious allegory, Franklin proceeds to sketch the
Jews' salvation in the time of the Babylonian Exile through formation of
a new 'synthesis' (72), an affirmation of 'wholeness' through 'reexamina-
tion of the Law' (68ff.) and re-collection of "their cultural background"
(196) that he will later explicate as the prototype for strategies of black
diasporic resistance and reconstruction. But this emblematic application
of Bible to lived reality does not unfold as a series of paradigmatic illus-
trations or narrative connections; rather, it is the process of making such
metaphors, the *symbolization* through which historical consciousness is itself
constructed, that Franklin makes both mechanism and matter of the
sermon. Thus, where in a more conventional Protestant service the text
would serve as a propaedeutic device, a fiction of convenience that would
then be carefully elaborated by exemplary reference to the Old Testament,
the Gospel, and the Epistles, leading to a recapitulatory proclamation of
a 'moral' carefully underscored throughout, "The Eagle Stirs Her Nest"
mimes its proof-passage in emphasizing the activity of its predication
over the prescription of its avowed subject, *stirring, fluttering, spreading, bearing,*
and *taking* its audience into a kairotic moment where medium and
Message are one.

In this sense, Franklin may be said to be activating rather than declaiming
the sermon, shaping a disposition toward preaching that clearly defines
the preacher's point of view as a social being. Every aspect of presentation – rhythm, gesture, bodily involvement, tone of voice (most notably
its *range* of inflection, from supplicatory to admonitory, from exhortatory
to celebratory) – signals his constitution as an active, aware, trenchant,
and emotively commited exemplar of communal consciousness, whose skill
is dedicated to quickening the congregation's own capacity for productive
engagement. At the heart of Franklin's vision, subtly embedded in the
eagle's prodding of her charges to autonomous flight, is the ideal of transformative exchange within the historically-charged space of the church-
become-diasporic forum. In beginning the sermon, therefore, the preacher
presents the "actual text" as a provocation to alternative readings, or
rather, to the boisterous *activity* of interpretation by which the community
comes to order as a collection of gently competing voices:

The eagle
Stirs
Her Nest.
A lot of people have come to me,
Uh, telling me, calling me about the subject
Some of them said, 'The eagle stirs his nest,'
One said 'The buzzard stirs his nest' (laughter)
Another one said 'You preacher the only chicken stirrin' his nest.'
  (laughter)
So I've heard all kinds of things
Concerning this subject but
According to the rendering
In the Bible it is the eagle stirs HER nest. (yes sir)

> (C. L. Franklin, "The Eagle
> Stirs Her Nest," 15–26)

Franklin's intimation of exgetical command as grounded in a material and prior – i.e., experientially historical – relation to the text before him situates that authority in a culture of robust response animated by a self-knowing capacity for critical humor. Franklin's guiding voice rises from a collective well of laughter that reaches its apex with the joke upon his own image as fallen emissary of divine inspiration (the eagle as chicken, replete with vernacular overtones of chicken-gorging preachers). Such mirth, upon which Franklin will frequently call as the sermon unfolds, often at strategic moments of assertion, possesses cognitive as well as performative value, projecting awareness of life in a world subject to surprise and reversal, as well as to continuous keen scrutiny. Such humor has its own kind of political and spiritual efficacy, demolishing fear and abject piety and thus clearing the ground for open-ended exploration of shared concerns. Raucous, discerning, and potentially subversive of the very primacy that it prepares for the reverend's preaching, the congregation's laughter sends a communitarian current through the church as it passes from individual to individual in a free and familiar atmosphere of collective contagion. At once critical and affirmative, this unabashed and knowing glee is early lit by Franklin so that it is throughout the sermon a mode of testing and extending the preacher's assertions, a choral instrument of nascent aesthetic and social judgment.

From the first, then, Franklin works to foreground the simultaneity of his own legitimacy as authorized deputy of the Word and his audience's capacity to sanction or repudiate his delivery of The Message. Ritual reproaches – "I don't believe you hear me tonight"; "You don't hear me"; "I don't believe you're going to pray with me tonight" (73, 123, 308) – self-interrupting shifts from biblical past to personal present – "It was then, that the priests and the Levis/Who found themselves in the throes of/A dilemma/In/A crisis/I see Mrs. Allibe Patterson over there, my daughter's

mother-in-law" (40–45) – and subtle entanglements of textual and performative temporalities – "*This* passage that I have read/In *your* hearing/
Comes from out of/*This* situation/*Now* I want . . ." (75–9; my emphases)
– combine to elevate the enactment of historical and communal *recognition*
over any received wisdom or liturgical script: indeed re-cognition, as the
convergence of remembered and lived experience in the present 'body' of
Franklin's congregation, is itself the 'reading' that his sermon produces.
Rather than illustrating the Deuteronomic text with corroborating scriptural passages or Gospel imagery, Franklin's discourse centers its interest
in its own relation to the passage's semiotic potential, generating preacherly
voice from presentational reflexivity rather than representational reflection: to borrow the language of our opening study of theater occuring at
the same moment of African-American cultural history, its mimetic aim
turns upon the quickening of methexis.

Most of "The Eagle Stirs Her Nest" therefore involves commenting on
the sermonic text's creation, rather than inhabiting it uncritically or merely
acting it out, exposing it as a story of meaning's creation, of the 'stirring'
of significance for and *by* an audience that becomes the very vehicle and
tenor of its 'World.' Franklin maintains a double-voiced dialogue with his
text and his audience as model of his congregation's ultimate tasks of
remembrance and engagement, foregrounding the dialectic of dispersion
and reunification by which an autonomous black consciousness can arise
"out of this situation/Now":

> You don't hear me, God is strong. (strong)
> Somebody said that this planet that we live on called earth
> There, we know by now that it's not built upon a platform
> It does not have anything to hold it up that's visible,
> But it is held in place by
> True countering forces
> Called trifugal and centrifugal forces. [. . .]
> You don't hear me.
> All they're talking about when they say that,
> They're just talking about how
> Strong God is [. . .]
> Well, in that way the eagle symbolizes God [. . .]
> You don't hear me.
>
> (148–54; 158–61; 180; 184)

At once eagle and fledgling, leader and aspirant, medium and expression,
Franklin joins his flock in submitting to a struggle for voice and meaning
among conflicting accounts of 'truth.' In response to the unstable terms
through which black culture comes into being as more than a disorderly
collection of inattentive nestlings, they must forge a polysemic idiom that
both acknowledges and exceeds the boundaries set by other discourses, an

expressive instrument capable of reopening established meaning without violating fundamental values of meaning-production:

> And what we need to do
> Is to reexamine the Law
> And the Prophets
> And reinterpret them
> And synthesize them into a whole
> Not only for ourselves, but for generations to come.
>
> (67–72)

Tradition becomes the ground of empowering self-expression in so far as it authorizes its own radical renovation through a vigorous, and decidedly temporalized, imaginary encounter. Notwithstanding the historical pressures toward fragmentation and occluded possibility, black consciousness remains sacred in its susceptibility to a forward-looking retrieval, especially in so far as it is itself grasped as a legacy of interpretive labor in alien and often hostile circumstances. A hidden implication of Franklin's glance against misplaced 'talk' about the centering force of this struggle for living 'truth' is that for the people's language to maintain what has been disclosed through the exegetics of call-and-response, it must itself be kept from solidifying into idle talk, or mere 'fabula.' That is, what Franklin seeks in the biblical passage to disclose and then appropriate is its interior demand for hermeneutical engagement, the encounter with conflicting meanings through which fledgling identity opens into unconstrained being. And in so far as tradition hardens into habit or inauthenticity, especially in the form of a complacent response to diasporic oppression, the preacher's "call" echoes the eagle's transitive intervention:

> . . . when
> Those eaglettes
> Have grown up and ought to be out
> Scuffling for themselves
> That parent eagle
> Push them out of the nest [. . .]
> It is said that she circles around
> Above them
> And watches them while they struggle [. . .]
> God does us like that sometimes
> I believe
> That
> Sometime we find ourselves
> In the comfortable nest [. . .]
> We don't bother to struggle . . .
>
> (250–5, 262–4, 275–9, 284)

Historical knowledge, scriptual allegory, and visionary semiosis converge in the preacher's summons to collective self-recognition as a community of revisionary resistance. Troping the eagle variously as embodiment of divine and human concern, and the eaglettes as progressively perceptive and independent disciples of an enabling instruction, Franklin proposes that revolutionary self-realization arises not beyond but within history. Represented world and contemporary experience find themselves in continual interaction as the necessity of interpretation, embraced as a complex balance of contending "forces," becomes the essence of the exilic condition. As the sermon moves towards its rousing conclusion, leaving behind the specific words and setting of the "actual text," the preacher enjoins the congregation to the challenge of change and risk which a fully temporal and hermeneutic encounter with black experience necessitates:

> The nest
> In history
> When, ah,
> We came as
> Slaves
> To this country, ah
> You don't hear me
> I know
> It was rough and, ah,
> I know it was hard, ah [. . .]
> That it was a LONG time, ah
> It WAS, according to OUR calender, ah
> But you see, ah
> GOD
> Doesn't work by our calendar, ah [. . .]
> Oh Lord
> For 400 years,
> That's a little while
> With God, ah . . .
>
> (338–47, 353–7, 360–3)

The compression of temporal perspectives afforded by Franklin's movement between God's and his people's measuring instruments doesn't obliterate his people's historical perception; quite the reverse – it legitimates that reading of black experience crucial to the Black Arts spirit which brings slavery into the present tense, opening the future from the reconsidered immediacy of a traumatic violence. History is thus not collapsed but reopened by the gesture of reclaiming for human possibility the energy of repudiation lost in evolutionary accounts of black accommodation and 'progress.' The eagle's stirring becomes a disclosure that refuses the conventional closures of official historiography, which cover up the constitutively embattled, hence intrinsically subversive, posture of black self-awareness. Fittingly, Franklin's own performative closure works toward a parallel self-disclosure as he insists upon the overlapping historicity of black experience and its interpreter:

> I don't believe you hear me
> What I'm, ah, 'bout to say that
> You know, preaching
> Means nothing
> Except, ah,
> Just reciting Bible stories
> Unless you can make it
> Ah
> Relevant
> To life TODAY. [. . .]
> My GREAT grandparents
> Were slaves, ah
> But look,
> Where her great grandson
> Stands tonight . . .
>
> (318–27, 370–4)

Neither tradition nor its heir is privileged unchanging center or reference point for the production of what is most vital, the continuity of black cultural consciousness in the living present tense; rather, each becomes audible through the agency of the other, such that black subjectivity arises as shared witnessing to an incomplete drama of "struggle." Recollecting the destiny of the past opens the possibility of transformation, just as freedom is imaged as a commitment to, not a release from, history as painful embodiment of communal value:

> For us to know ourselves
> Sometimes we have to suffer, ah [. . .]
> I see God
> Stirring the nest
> In labor . . .
>
> (387–8, 402–4)

No longer a mediator only but now also a participant in the divine travail of passionate negotiation with the traumatic lesions of historical violence, the preacher joins his responsive congregation, offering his own body to their self-engendering "labor," exchanging its authoritative distance ("but/ According to the rendering/In the Bible . . .") for a sacramental commingling. Privileged explication has been relinquished, exchanged for an interrogation into the possibility and condition of interpretation. In the process, African-American identity arises not simply within but *as* a framework of collective conceptualization of history, language, subjectivity, and experience. Not to be confused with postmodernism's embrace of an aimless 'indeterminacy,' such an identity *requires* identifications that are, in equal measure, ardent and heuristic: in effect, Franklin's sermon has served as blueprint for an interpretive experiment whose harmonious 'whole' is exactly the call-and-response of those contradictory forces, 'trifugal and centrifugal,' that comprise the ongoing history of black people in "the wasteland of America" (Malcolm X). Its 'meaning' arises in the quest for meaning among voices that both differ and cohere, as Franklin crafts a 'text' whose performance sounds the Other within a legacy of hermeneutic struggle. "The Eagle Stirs Her Nest," carefully situated within a specific social and historical condition defined as both dilemma and enablement, (re)generates that struggle, 'stirring' the encounter of blackness with its own potentiality for self-enactment.

III

> On the morning I stood up to speak I did not know what I was going to say, but when I started to talk my thoughts came faster than I could speak. I was filled up. The old meeting house caught on fire. The Spirit was there. . . . I used to wonder what made people shout, but now I don't. . . . It is fire in the bones. Any time that fire touches a man, he will jump.
>
> Ex-slave testimonial[31]

Crucial to the process by which "The Eagle Stirs Her Nest" becomes a dialogic meditation on freedom and power is a specific grammatical and narratological drama. As part of the instructional apparatus by which he establishes himself in the christological line of inspired teachers, Franklin offers the following lesson in narrative point-of-view:

> . . . when . . . any writing is in the third person
> It is written by somebody ABOUT somebody else.
> You see
> It is the FIRST person if I say 'I'm doing so.'
> That's the first person.
> If I say 'YOU are doing so and so,' that's the second person.
> [. . .] So this isn't Moses writing
> This is somebody writing about Moses
> This is somebody writing ABOUT Israel.
> You don't hear what I'm saying.
>
> (C. L. Franklin, "The Eagle
> Stirs Her Nest," 107–17)

Just as he will move beyond 'recitation of Bible stories' into the mode of authentically 'relevant,' that is avowedly performative, preaching, so

Franklin will *incarnate* the movement among narrative perspectives that he here outlines. The central problem of understanding the "actual text" becomes the task, first, of making, then of *being* the text of a revised personhood. If at first the preacher maintains a distance between himself and his material, foregrounding the text as a set of choices and stratagems, as the sermon proceeds he subtly metamorphoses perspectives, shifting from third to first person, and within first person from personal to plural pronouns. The early posture mimes the ethnographic tension between an autonomous, pure, knowing Gaze and the 'objects' of scrutiny, investigation, or knowledge. Such august narrative focalization works effectively by providing a sense of epistemological stability, the aura of a world not spinning into chaos but mastered by a panoptic authority. Such a world is, so to speak, already 'owned'; domination is both its conceptual foundation and political effect. By suspending and then dispersing the putative neutral 'truth' of this perspectival detachment, Franklin squanders the ethnographic privilege conferred by his role as divine emissary and pursues an epistemological politics that inscribes the necessity of participatory enunciation:

> *It is said* that [. . .]
> *I* believe
> That
> Sometime *we* find ourselves [. . .]
> For *us* to be ourselves [. . .]
> For *us* to know ourselves [. . .]
> *You* don't hear me tonight . . .
> (262, 271–2, 278, 379, 382, 401; my emphases)

This intertwining of *being* and *knowing* is cognate with the sermon's pronomial drama, which enacts the perception that individual consciousness can only emerge in conversation with the environment proper to it. No longer external and, as it were, invisible, the narrator moves from a realist perspective to an expressive involvement, reconstituting himself in dialogic interchange. As in those Coltrane poems that unravel collective enactment from apostrophic invocation, perhaps the crucial element of this refiguration of subjective voice, then, is the insistence upon the presence of the *second* personhood: summoned with a kind of rhythmic urgency, Franklin's omnipresent "you" emphasizes the impossibility of even conceiving identity independent from the engaged response of others. As both theme and enunciation, "The Eagle Stirs Her Nest" posits identity *as* the second person, for the subject appears in the care and recognition of historicized communality. In the call-and-response dynamism that defines both intention and agency for all performers in Detroit's New Bethel Baptist Church, self and other solicit one another until plural identity semantically (ful)fills the promise of Franklin's singular voice.

The ideological and creative import of Franklin's struggle with the very textuality needed to perform this revolutionary reversal of position is even more intricately developed in W. Leo Daniels's masterful chant-sermon "Build Your Own Fire," preached at Chicago's Shiloh Missionary Baptist Church after the fiery summer of 1968. If for Franklin narrative elaboration quickly yields to reflexive narrativity, for Daniels the development of an intricately conceived narrative identity is integral to its deconstruction into the ex-stasis of *communitas*. Again, in view of the chant-sermon's confusion of discursive and performative materials, we must start with a schematic overview of the sermon's multiform operations, concentrating on the narrative performance of the preacher's voice. Let us open to the first moment, a beginning which stages the problematic of beginning:

> God bless ya, God keep ya, living in a world of confusion
> A mixed up world in the midst of mixed emotion
> A sinful world
> A world where wars are going on in the ruins of wars
> I thought I would call your attention to the eighteenth chapter, the Book of St. John
> Let us notice the eighteenth verse, the eighteenth chapter, the Book of St. John
> (I see)
> "And the servants and officers stood there, who had made a fire of coals for it was cold; and they warmed themselves; and Peter stood with them, and warmed himself."
> (He did that)
> Our message today: build your own fire
> Build your own fire
> Why don't you say it after me: build
> (Build)
> Your own fire
> (Your own fire)
> God bless ya

> (W. Leo Daniels, "Build Your Own Fire," 1–16)

While "Build Your Own Fire" possesses no originating moment as such, the sermon arises from an elemental differentiation of World and Church, situating the congregation at their ever-blurring boundaries. However conventional, such a distinction must not go without saying, just as "living" is a sustained collective improvisation between ruinous "confusion" and blessed certainty. If this locates the sermon within the normative African-American mythos of diasporic fortitude and prophesied deliverance, it also serves to structure the sermon's setting as a Scene of Instruction, insinuating from within the prevailing religious language an inaugurating concern with political violence and the historical contingencies of the speaker's own enunciation. This dynamic of public and private voice is materially enacted through the citation of the biblical text, which enters the sermonic arena through the medium of the vernacular's mode of call-and-response. "I thought I would *call* your attention to the eighteenth chapter the book of St. John, *Let us notice* the eighteenth verse, the eighteenth chapter, the Book of St. John": foregrounding immediately the drama of personhood toward which Franklin's sermon gradually moves, Daniels prefigures the audience's response in his own pronomial movement from "I" to "us" (recall Hurston), in effect opening biblical text into communal performance. This inaugural gesture, solidified by the formal structure of a ring-composition, thereby suggests how any call is itself already a response to a prior expression, how entry into discourse is preconditioned by performative occasions which may themselves be recontextualized. Repetition becomes a means of appropriating and reopening scriptural authority, as Daniels effectively translates "the time of the text" (29) and the space of the present into each other. Call-and-response, a specific form of *cultural* "literacy," is thus immediately established as a mode of revision, both means and instance of the community's configuration as an exegetical and self-constituting power.

By thus declaring itself to be a transaction among inherited and personal visions, the sermon evokes and ratifies a structure of community in a single gesture, so that audience and preacher from the first share the task of confronting the Message as a test of legitimacy and voice. In effect, Daniels foregrounds the *construction* of himself as an authoritative mediator of this struggle, an exemplar empowered to interpret himself publicly. And by directing overt exchange between that voice and the congregation's, he underscores the intersubjective and vocative nature of its making.

The Bible thus serves not as an originary source of final meaning to which the congregation (re)turns for comfort *against* "the World." Any possible notion of such canonical purity is quickly ruptured by the critical absorption of the biblical passage into a freewheeling interplay of transmission and revision. (It is apposite to recall here Hurston's recollection that in the tales of her youth "even the Bible was made over to suit our vivid imagination" – *Mules and Men*, 3.) Privileged but not ultimate, the Bible enters the matrix of discourses and positions that together comprise "Build Your Own Fire"; as we shall see, it – though not it alone – is dramatically transfigured under the pressure of the service's exuberant activities of self-interrogation. The Message, Daniels repeatedly stresses, is "here," an immanent, not transcendent, challenge: thus, Peter's refusal to acknowledge Christ before the Pentecost, as well as his ultimate triumph as a *witness* of regenerative vocation, gain value not as a typological allegory of institutional intercession in the drama of wavering faith (as is common in the "mainstream" homiletic tradition extending from exegesis of the Gospels' eccelesiastical histories and, especially, of the Church's political and apostolic image in Pauline, Clementine, and Petrine epistles),[32] but as an initial episode of (auto)biographical narrative. Peter's story, and the divine presence it substantiates, figures and establishes the *historicity* of Daniels's instructional apparatus, its embeddedness in a narrative context which claims material pertinence to the congregation's own desire for self-realization. This deployment of the Message, in refusing to subordinate story to discourse, or invention to argument, releases Daniels from any obligation to scripture as prescriptive pattern, allowing his performance to proceed as an improvisational process, a process centered by the preacher's own evolving identity, or more exactly, by that identity's subtle collaboration with the congregation in its radical reformation. The sermon thereby unfolds as a series of autobiographical parables which, as an ensemble, illustrate, but also complicate, the Message of building one's own fire. By experiencing these tales as a carefully-patterend sequence, we can more precisely grasp the inner logic of Daniels's self-consuming narrativity. Here is the first story:

> And I'm not ashamed to (Come on) tell incidents that relates to me. I'd always been a lover of music and some of all kinds of music, and I was off in a meeting and the minister had placed me in a hotel there. They had one of these bands above the room where I was living; and each night I would try to sleep I just couldn' help but to hear the jazz music. (Come on; *laughter*) And every now and then they would start out on a song that I remembered when I was out in the world (*much laughter*) and the next night I said well I don't believe there's no harm if I was to go listen (*more laughter*) and instead of putting on my suit I had some sport clothes and put my (*more laughter*) my sport jacket on and I went on up and began enjoying the music. And the band-leader – you know you never know who knows you (*great laughter*) – I was sitting there sippin off my Coca Cola and the bandleader wanted the folk to get with him; said, I'd like for everybody to start crackin on this one like we used to do at church. And he said you know it just makes you feel good when you know the audience is with you. He said it does something to you and he hollered out, Idn't that right, Reverend Daniels. And everybody started looking around, looking for me, and I started looking like I was looking for Reverend Daniels (*Great laughter, clapping*) But soon's I got a chance I eased out the back door, put back on my suit, and I decided that it was best that I build my own fire.
> (Yeah, all right)

(73–8)

At both its diegetic and narrational levels, this story places Daniels on trial as a player and tester of social roles. Both the bandleader's surprise insinuation and Daniels's later narrative self-placement depend upon the space between what is known about a person and what they fail to perceive in themselves, a space that is bridged by each speaker's gleeful expansion of a controlled ritual of exposure. Through the split between Daniels-as-subject and Daniels-as-narrator of the story, the preacher constructs a paradoxical self-image as simultaneously divided and continuous . . . a paradox twice deepened, first within the story by the guilefully ironic image of a revealed Daniels looking for himself, and then in the story's telling by the preacher's implicit position of (re)conversion, which both widens and sutures the gap opened by humor between past and present, scepticism and affirmation. Beyond its ethical and social content, the tale links retro-spection with the possibility of prospective reformation, thereby making narrative shape a model for communal action. By thus forging a framing cultural critique from the details of individual history, Daniel's subtly inserts a covert instruction in the dynamics of remembrance and reconstruction, while fostering seemingly contradictory accounts of his own position that will be reconciled through collaborative energies such as those he left behind with the bandleader and *his* flock.

The next tale (106ff.) extends the anti-priestly humor, though now the object of deflation is not Daniels but an unnamed preacher who wants to get a drink (one can only wonder what concoction is winkingly euphemized by the "coca-cola" of the first story!). Thinking he can dash in to the bar for the booze before being seen by church members, he's greeted by the bartender with the line: "Reverend, what are you drinking today"! When we reach the next tale, beginning at line 145, Daniels's performance mode has changed from that of prose narrative to the chant form that he'll main-tain thereafter; with this formal shift comes a shift in the narrative's tone, as we're told of the preacher's visit to an old woman, trapped with seven kids in a freezing home (remember, the sermon is taking place in Chicago in the middle of December – and you don't have to have grown up on the South Side to know it gets damn cold in the middle of December in Chicago!). So the preacher gives her the money to get her heat cut back on, while noticing that, as he puts it, "her spiritual gas has been cut off also" (174), leading to his contrast between the undependable man from the power company and *The* Man, whose Divine Power is immanent – "I can see my Jesus," he intones at line 180, "conjuring" for his parishoners, as Theophus Smith might say, the "intersubjective" Africanicity of worship[33] – immanent and everlasting. Echoing the mixture of verisimilitude and won-der typical to biblical parable, Daniels's tale deftly unmasks the structure of spiritual longing within everyday experience, asking us not to dissolve the physical into the metaphysical but to see the familiar with an eye for multiple desires and possibilities. It is for this reason that Jesus can actively enter the narrative fabric at this moment, for Daniels will now more energetically pur-sue the performative implications of the divine messenger's allegorical strategies. For the tales have been almost imperceptibly edging toward the radical present tense of the Gospel's parabolic world, which presents to its listeners images of fellow pilgrims facing momentous choices. These are, characteristically, decisions of will and perception, so that the listener is made participant in the stories by virtue of a structural identification with figures facing the need to think and act in a new way by *reading* their lives in the light of life-determining transfiguration.

Daniels's final tale therefore presents for the first time the achievement of a new kind of existence, a new temporal bearing that forges a liberating prospect from the 'fire' of anamnesis. Linking itself to the prior tale while looking forward to the sermon's climax, it does so by elaborating the established contrast and intermingling of material and spiritual warmth:

> It's something about fiiii-re
> That'll make you move
> When you don't feel like movin'
> Yeaaaah!!
> (Yeaaah!!)
> Good God Almighty!!
> Share myself
> Oooooooooooh, yeah!!!
> It's just like fiiiiire
> Shut up in my bones
> Good God Almighty
> I'm closing here
> But let me tell you one thing
> It was said that there was a young man
> Who lived in a mountain country
> And, ahh, he was known to be a mountain climber
> And, ahh, one day
> He set out to climb the highest mountain
> In that land
> Ooooooh Lord!!
> (Yeah!!)
> (*Sung*) And he cliiiiimbed up that mountain
> Until he'd got so high
> He could not go any further, ah
> And he was just hanging there, ah
> Bout to fall to his death, ah
> Ooh Looooord!!
> And people gathered all round, ah
> (All right!!)
> And watching the young man there, ah
> Say he gonna fall to his death, ah
> And there was a old sheep keeper, ah
> Leading a flock of sheep, ah
> And he came round beneath that mountain, ah

Where the little boy was hanging, ah
And the little boy began falling, ah
He feeeell down, ah
And before he could hit the ground, ah
A sheep was up under him, ah
And he feeeeell down, ah
On that sheep, ah
It killed the sheep, ah
But the boy's life was spared
Yeaaaaaahhhh!!!
I remember in my life
When I was hangin' up high
(Yeah!!)
Good God Almighty!!
I was up above
My friend
I was way up
On my high horses
But Good God Almighty
(*Sung*) I remember
When I began to fall

(275–325)

Little dramas of identification and mis-recognition, Daniels's tales tell the story of identity denied, embraced, and finally recovered in being surrendered. Though perhaps implicit in each discrete narrative, it is a story conveyed by the preacher's changing role from parable to parable. In the first, we see the Reverend unmasked (all the while legitimating musical celebration in amiable rivalry with an alternative mode of vernacular performance);[34] in the second, he becomes a narrator whose neutrality is slyly complicated by the repetition of a debunking preacher tale; in the third, he becomes an engaged emissary of the Church, actively mediating the economies of World and Word; and in the last tale, he completes his transformation from Peter to Christ, from the insider who stayed on the outside to the scapegoat who fell into the Lord's joy. Charting a course from humorous self-negation to ex-static self-abnegation, the tales together enact a sacrificial yet redemptive process that ignites methexic consciousness from mimetic narration. In this way, they become a form of testamental modality, *à la* Harper's Coltrane, witnessing the construction and consumption of the preacher-as-voice. His "I," introduced as the instructional transcriber of biblical authority, becomes a series of versions and sub-versions, continuously dispersed into the voice of the other (the bandleader; the teller of preacher tales; the divine boy), finally undone and realized in the paradoxical gesture of a "self" (re)born in its "sharing."

In this ensemble unfolding, Daniels's tales can be read, too, as an appropriative critique of that method by which ethnography habitually produces its subject as Other. For the tales are at pains precisely to demonstrate that the link between representation and distance by which another is imaged bears ethical consequences for both speaker and character. By placing himself in *both* positions at once, and by generating a particular narrative of self-repudiation and self-recovery from those positions' changing relations, Daniels flaunts the autodestructive character of ethnographic figuration. Further, by establishing himself as a confident, but not masterful, traveler between realms (*à la* Douglass and Hurston), he underscores ethnology's generalized motive of converting experience into knowledge, but puts that insight at the service of communal self-fashioning. The plight of the ethnographic fieldworker is, as it were, remade into the *felix culpa* of learning to *go there to know there*, thereby effecting a critical reversal of ethnological practice that fuels the congregation's widened field of protocols and practices.

The opening Scene of Instruction is thus transformed into a site of multiple self-enactments and re-emplotments, as the sermon's exempla preach the cause of their own formal dissolution. The dramatic telos of this dispersion is, of course, the diffusion of the preacher's identity into those of the congregants, for they, too – especially in the story of the jazz audience that once got crackin' in Church and in the figure of the struggling woman visited by Reverend Daniels – have been offered opportunities for recognition which, together, suggest how negotiable and plural are their own subject positions. They are invited to stake their agency in the risk of dis-placement, whose climactic form is a dance at once spiritual and material. Having been summoned and reconceptualized by the preacher, they re-inflect and appropriate *his* place, enfolding witness and participant, and continuously regenerating the norms of legitimation put into play by the sermon's opening exchanges.

What, then, *is* "Build Your Own Fire"? *Where* does it exist? Who authors it, who speaks it, and who possesses (or is possessed by) it? Certainly it is not a "text" in the classic sense, assuming unity and referential ground; it is, rather, an arena or activity by which the referential as such is established and revised, while suspending any claim of autonomous production, whether bourgeois or priestly. More event than work, it coheres precisely by foregrounding the contingencies of its own integrity, founding itself in an act of *building* that is improvisational, but in no way unpremeditated or accidental. It is, if you will, the event of fire: that element which figures a multiplicity of enactments – the constant battle with poverty; an endless spiritual renewal; political upheavals of Chicago's hot summer of 1968 (the fire *this* time); the framed fluidity of a body that, as Ellison might put it, moves without movin' – without fixing its incendiary ferment to any singular mode of being. For as Shoshana Felman writes in a discussion of J. L. Austin's speech-act theory,[35] it is never ascertainable whether fire is thing or incident, contained as a spatial structure or unleashed as temporal occasion: whatever comes into contact with fire itself risks changing forever its 'original' contours. Extending the implications of Felman's insight, we might say that Daniels's fire reconciles the constative and performative valences of African-American experience, inflaming his congregation at the juncture of history and embodied consciousness. Put slightly differently, Daniels designates himself and his congregants, in their willingness to become the incarnate witness or "representative" of divine passion, as carriers of fire's contagion, the scandal of an agency that "civilization" (like the police at Sandy Bottom) thought to capture but which, set free, cannot be reabsorbed in its revolutionary ardor.

So any effort to locate or define the 'essential' "Build Your Own Fire" can't help but ensnare itself in the dilemmas of seeking an original and final vernacular being. In both Peter's thematic transgression and the preacher's enacted transfiguration, the sermon dramatizes a humbling of textual sovereignty and totality by exposing and then decentering the process of its own production as 'master narrative.' In this drama, no voice can be either neutral or final. Far from offering us a supreme discourse or vision, a primordial totality, such vernacular performance remains capable of self-difference which confutes whatever illusions of privation or plenitude might be spun in its name. Understanding itself as a provisional sounding on what was said or sung before, it calls, like the methexic modalities of modern black drama and the Coltrane Poem, for its own supplementation in our own partial responses. In this sense contemporary African-American expressive culture fashions the dilemma of positionality into an opportune feature of black modernism by theorizing *and* engaging the present, offering its participatory 'audience' the challenge of radically regenerating itself as a political society capable of confronting a world of confusion and struggle. Freed of any closure on its signifying productivity, but bound to its contestatory and dialogic project, such a society can enjoy no paradigmatic coherence in advance of its actuality as performance. For all of us, now, *court is in session.*

*

Through distinctively African-American strategies of self-difference and dialectical reversal, the modern chant-sermon as exemplified by "The Eagle Stirs Her Nest" and "Build Your Own Fire" absorbs the individual experience of trauma into collective historical meaning. Eschewing doctrines of apolitical transcendence for an exegetical idiom that both subverts (*stirs*) and constructs (*builds*) institutions and practices, Franklin and Daniels suggest how a resourceful blending of personal and communal autobiography can propel 'nationalist' agenda, opening new possibilities of desire, perception, and action. If, as we have seen in this chapter, vernacular performance thereby already conceptualizes a mode of positional identity envisaged by vernacular theory, something of the reverse has also emerged in recent annals of African-American cultural discourse: that is, we now see the performative project of African-American modernism extended into the very criticism that has sought to take its measure, replete with the pitfalls and possibilities innate to any movement perpetually submerged in the crossfires of historical engagement. As the quest for "black consciousness" carries forward into an era of "identity politics," the Black Arts Movement's performative ethos, especially in its effort to mesh revolutionary and vernacular rhetorics, surfaces most suggestively among its critical heirs, be they nationalist, humanist, poststructuralist, or feminist. It is toward that arena of critical self-enactment that we now turn in a gesture of provisional closure upon this study of black modernist performance.

8 Re-calling blackness
Recollection and response in contemporary black autocritography

I

> the tone of my life takes
> the future as a growl mingled
> with the groan of the past . . .
> the child of years from me
> the eyes of a grandfather days from me
> will know this strange word
> freedom ....
>
> Gaston Neal, "Today"[1]

There's an old army story – no doubt generic, but inflected in the Nipsey Russell version I'm about to tell by accents of power, voice, and self-enactment – regarding the black private who called the supply depot to complain about persistent lack of toiletries in the barracks: at first grimly polite, he quickly warmed to his anger, and before long let loose a stream of protesting profanity in mordant chords of vernacular vituperation. Finally, a voice growled back, "Do you know who this is?! This is Gen. Cornelius Egmont Filliport you're cussing at, boy!" A brief pause ensued, whereupon the private replied, "Well, do you know who *this* is . . . *sir?*" "No," the general shot back. A longer pause than the first followed. Finally, the brother said, "Good," and promptly hung up.

Let's imagine ourselves coming upon such a tale in, say, the mid-twenty-first century, practicing an advanced form of the now New and Improved Historicism (or Retro-Historicism as some will call it). Employing it as a spicy framing anecdote, what cultural narrative would it imply: The co-implication of power and parody in the phono-centrism of late capitalism? The echo-effect of subject and system in the dial-logics of early postmodernism? The constitutive "tragi-comic" inversions of communicative events in *really, really* late-capitalism, where speaking and listening refer not to essential differences but to the accidents of digitalized positions?

As Sterling Brown might have said, we'll know all answers, resolving all ambiguities and transcending all antinomies, when de saints go ma'ching home. But just now, trapped still in the *fin de siècle* regionalism of that vernacular known as American cultural theory, I'm more inclined to read the tale, following Nipsey Russell's coloration, as an exemplum of a particularly African-American response, at once critical and performative, to the conceptual logjams that clog the identity politics borne alongside the Black Arts era, logjams that I have tamely travestied in my para-prognostic speculation. As a kind of seriocomic transposition of black self-representation through call-and-response, Russell's tale refracts the crossing of critique and autobiography in contemporary African-American criticism that effects a revisionary engagement with the governing terms of identity politics advanced in the immediate wake of the Black Arts heyday. Often appearing within texts also devoted to interpretation of African-American literary and cultural performances, these autobiographical reflections – a mode we could call, after Nancy Miller and Aram Veeser, black autocritography[2] – themselves constitute a performative practice that dramatizes the roles of memory, reading, and translation in the construction of modern African-American subjectivity. Modal and improvisatory in temperament, this continuously emergent subjectivity, in the very interplay of critical and autobiographical voices, becomes reflexively dialogic, historical, and transformative, not only in relation to the contemporary scene of "postmodern" criticism but in collateral response to the abiding socio-aesthetic imperatives of the Black Arts Movement.

I'll go on to sketch in further the anecdote's pertinence to African-American critical modernism, but first a more equitable, if obviously reductive, account is in order of how identity politics arrived at its current impasse in the annals of Euro-American (post)modern critique, one that at least passingly acknowledges identity politics as itself a response to entanglements of irreconcilable elements in late twentieth-century theoretical discourse. After the displacement of humanism's Subject by the two-fisted engines of semiotics, and the ghastly disruption of that semiotic machine by post-structuralism's demystifications of *both* subject and language, identity politics arrived to declare the return of the repressed historical actor in quest of true value ... only to flounder between the Scylla of essentialism and the Charybdis of dissimulation. The persons recruited to fuel the politics have proven elusive or delusory, being either gasping, ill-disguised reanimations of humanism's bogey man, Mr. Ego, or such strategically (not to say opportunistically) essential stuff as to seem more the chorus line of a post-post-structuralist masquerade than the vanguard of efficacious public struggle. Against the portentous negative sublime of Foucauldian 'regimes of truth' and the chastening scopic mastery of the Lacanian Other we hear calls for an anti-aesthetic materialism so scorched of rhetorical agility and protean desire as to constitute a merely chiasmal reflection of power's totalizing discursive imperatives. Thus, founded as a reaction formation against hyperstructuralist denials of social agency, identity politics arises as a mode of opposition fated to mirror what it would displace, a countertheory of the subject committed to the logic of a negative dialectics generated from the syntax of repudiation: 'not this, but the other, not the represented, but the silenced, not the inside of authority but what remains outside of nominations and ideologies.' The subject of identity politics, no less than its 'hegemonic' opposition, must suppress or defer self-interrogation, excluding interior contradiction in order to assert and explain its function as a contra-dictory vector within the ruling order. Such a subject is thus constituted to ironize, challenge, and possibly even replace prevailing terms of the social 'real,' but it cannot fundamentally *transform* the conditions of its own articulation, making a difference rather than simply being different.[3]

Identity politics emerges, then, as an axis within that vein of Euro-American anti-Enlightenment that resists the tropological, translational, or performative possibilities of exchange. While interested, as a mode of ideological critique, in demystifying the transcendent claims of entrenched power, identity politics longs for the moment of absolute freedom, the irreducible act, that stands beyond semiotic indeterminacy or incompletion. Conforming structurally to what George Baker terms the "phenomenology of the modernist object,"[4] identity politics veers toward a kind of materialist metaphysics, locating the final 'cause' of social praxis in a stabilized, mimetic image of collectivity. As Baker notes (following Rosalind Krauss), this is the modernism of "indexicality," wherein meaning is determined by the physical bond of sign and referent. Indexes, Krauss writes, "are the marks [. . .] of a particular cause, and that cause is the thing to which they refer, the object they signify."[5] In the unbroken circle of identity politics' indexicality, then, the precoded signature of being – race, gender, ethnicity, *et al.* – is self-confirming ground of its own *raison d'être*, enfolding origin and end in a quest that has always already arrived at its destination.

Unsurprisingly, African-American cultural theorists, as frontline recruits in identity politics's foundering theoretical wars, have begun to plot alternative encounters of identity and modernity, forging a different disposition of critical consciousness to the drama of identity and difference. Mustering but also reinventing the oppositional postures of the Black Arts Movement, appropriating but also displacing the methodologies of modern and postmodern critical technologies, contemporary African-American critical voices have opened a space between structuralist and phenomenological visions of agency and praxis, a space where the specific impact of critical theory on defining norms of selfhood, kinship, and cultural value can be respecified. Such a space operates as a kind of bar or diacritical caesura between idiomatic registers – between the vernacular and the scholarly, the aesthetic and the ideological, the psychic and the historical, the subversive and the commemorative, the performative and the referential – and in that interstitial place and moment, in that revisionary pause, African-American critics have begun, as it were, to hang up on the general, or at least, to change the (perhaps over-general) terms of engagement.

In this final chapter I'd like to outline the argument that African-American criticism, cultivated in soil first claimed and enriched by Black Arts declarations, seeks to thus reconfigure its position in the terrain of identity politics – and, through that gesture, in the domain of modernity – by interweaving, or productively confusing, interpretive and autobiographical idioms. Practiced in diverse forms by writers such as Wahneema Lubiano, Hortense Spillers, Michael Awkward, bell hooks, Robert Stepto, Gayle Pemberton, Henry Louis Gates, Houston Baker, and Deborah McDowell (the last three of whom I shall discuss in more detail), this genre of black autocritography emerges, I suggest, as an effort to dislocate the structures of representation and agency that ground identity politics in the very oppositional syntheses that it would undo. We can better appreciate how and why this might be so by reconsidering the potential, if paradoxical, dynamism located in the very locution "identity politics." Juxtaposing as it does a term of achieved plenitude – *identity* – that figures continuity despite time's vicissitudes, and a sign of unruly desire – *politics* – that figures precisely a transformative and temporal commitment to reshape the given, "identity politics" is indeed an inscription always threatening to erase itself, bearing within itself the sign of its own undoing or overcoming. In that sense, "identity politics" figures well the moment of transition from which it arises and which perpetually threatens it, naming the excess and inadequacy that it combats, harboring the very contradictions that it is designed to resolve. In so far as it *is* critically productive, "identity politics" attains force through the torsion of this very duplicity, through its double claims to closure and development, its designation of its own will-toward-unity and commitment-to-struggle. Understood not merely as datum but as desire, as figure not just fact, its energy is not so much the assertion of a social logic but the restiveness of a visionary urge, the complex *need* for inviolable presence, the quest for a site of efficacious "authenticity." It can be effective, then, not as the name of an idea but as the evocation of a self-displacing style, not as a stabilized practicum but as a reflexive and self-subverting practice.

As a virtual site of insurgent speculation, where the hypothetical fusion of presence and action occurs as a provisional method of revision, "identity politics" doubles and displaces itself as an allegory of autobiography. For autobiography, too, confidence in authenticity and motivational integrity is at once founded and dispropriated through temporal acts of "self"-declaration. For autobiography, too, "identity" is a heuristic fiction that is both necessary and impossible, posited and deferred. What Sidonie Smith terms its "double scene,"[6] its event taking place in that ever-fluctuating gap between the present of writing and the inscribed past, renders autobiographical authenticity not a category of the transcendental subject but a mobile, ever-changing relationship of voice to signifying practices. And thus we return at last to Nipsey Russell and the unruly and self-effacing private, who blends identity and politics in a gesture of double-voiced ambivalence.

Assertive and evasive, confessional and concealed, Russell's nameless hero unnames the general authority of power only by performing his own absence to it, securing identity by first desginating and then performing the limits of recognition in a scene of asymmetrical antagonism. But this does-n't mean that his consciousness disappears into undifferentiated space, dis-located from meaning and mimesis. Rather, the possibility of determinate agency is defended by the private's abandoning the official scene of author-ity, leaving behind the empty echo of a semiotic cipher in favor of another performance, some other time, some other place.

Exile and the potential of self-realization thus converge, suggesting a discourse of political agency constituted in the twinned gestures of repu-diation and improvisational, if undetermined, revoicing. At the same time, the pauses in Russell's story remind us that such a reformulation of expres-sive resistance must, as Homi Bhabha has suggested, disrupt the enunciative 'present' through which aesthetic and imperial authority is established.[7] Those pauses, more than the private's invective, wiliness, or escape, are the signs of an oblique deflection of discursive closure, suggesting as they do another locus of passion or self-enactment. They figure the possibility of alternative alignments of time and place where negotiations of self and culture occur unlimited by strictly oppositional codes of difference. The private's pauses, marking the artifice of his own enunciation and the impos-ture of any closure, thus also figure a resistance within and against Euro-American modernism, a resistance to the latter's putative rupture with the historical that nevertheless still marks a gap in regulative conti-nuities. And it is to the imagined spaces and moments of those pauses that African-American criticism now journeys, seeking to transform the very conditions of speaking while continuing to interrogate and resist the framing discourses of cultural authority.

African-American critical autobiography thus recasts the ur-narrative of return as a means of reinventing the present, of reopening the discursive enclosures into which identity politics, as surely as any ethnographic or modernist aesthetic, has confined blackness in an inventory of otherness. The recast identity politics of African-American autocritography thereby poses Bhabha's question for subaltern self-figuration: To what in the present do I belong? In what time and place can I find resources for distinguishing my present from modernity's ideology of the new that is truly a return of the same, an ideology with which identity politics is complicit in its tendency to acknowledge differences only to repress their specificity in service of a generalized project? Nipsey Russell has a tale for that dilemma, too: A brother was leaving the South in the early days of the Civil Rights Movement because of all the unrest. As he sits in the bus station waiting to catch a bus going north to Chicago, he notices a scale that tells your fortune and weight on a little card that shoots out. He pops a quarter in the slot, and a card comes out that reads, "You weigh 150 lbs., you're a Negro, and you're on your way to Chicago." He's so surprised that he pops another quarter in, and the card again reads, "You weigh 150 lbs., you're a Negro, and you're on your way to Chicago." Shaken, he spies a Native American wrapped in a blanket; he quickly borrows the blanket, wraps it around himself and further disguises himself by sticking a feather in his hair. He slithers up to the scale again, pops in another coin, and another card shoots out, which reads: "You still weigh 150 lbs., you're still black, and by fucking around, you've missed your bus to Chicago"! Before Barbara Johnson, Nipsey Russell warned of too quickly blending "already-read" social identities by taking their specific textures as so many costumes to be easily shed or donned.[8] The performative body cannot be so quickly elided in favor of the theatrical character, whose representational logic, with its expectation of narrative and ontological coherence, denies that it appears in a cloak of temporalized signs: the subject-in-process, shivering its way to Chicago, can't route itself past reminder of its contextual and ever-signifying body. And yet Russell's gag, in the double-take of its irony, also hints that identification with blackness (which might equally necessitate missing that bus to Chicago) returns one not to blackness-as-purity but to an historically-charged site of struggle. Blackness may not be mere convention, but the consequences of self-presentation cannot be calculated in advance of its performance, and cannot be extricated from the play of signifying concealments and disclosures figured in the figure of blackness.

II

> Well, on my way to committing to memory the ABC reality
> I still couldn't forget all that motherly music,
> those unwatered songs of my babe-in-the-woods days
> until, committed to the power of the human voice,
> I turned to poetry & to singing by choice,
> reading everyone always & listening, listening for a silence deep
>   enough
> to make out the sound of my own background music.
>   Al Young, "A Little More
>   Traveling Music"[9]

Perhaps too easily, Russell's signifying on the irreducible materiality of black identity can be assimilated to the contemporary African-American critic's position within modern theoretical discourses and the institutions that house them, which likewise offer styles of self-displacement through which blackness can be differently presented. For the modern nonwestern intellectual, as Antonio Gramsci and Valentin Mudimbe have most trenchantly reminded us,[10] the snares set by western protocols of cognitive power, which conventionally locates conceptual mastery at a distance from its object of inquiry, are somewhat more costly than the two bits lost by

Russell's traveler: too often, the subaltern intellectual pays the price of communal alienation for the reward of institutional legitimation. Particularly in a moment less fired by passionate social upheaval than that in which Russell's restive brother finds himself, the black intellectual faces what we might view as the ethnographic paradox: who does one see when what Hurston termed the "spy-glass of Anthropology" works simultaneously to focus and estrange one's sight, returning the double-vision of a self-image that is at once perceptually present (the self looks like the Other *over there*) and ontologically absent (the self *looked* like the Other over [t]here)? Schooled in western epistemological assumptions and methodologies, the modern black intellectual focuses on patterns of collective self-invention and social praxis – which are themselves means of negotiating norms of authenticity – from a precarious, though potentially empowering, location, one fissured along temporal, economic, linguistic, and other defining borders. Whether the resources on either side of these liminal divides confront each other within black intellectual practice as a choice of both/and or either/or will do much to characterize that practice's rhetoric of knowledge, and its political ambitions.

Extending Black Arts Movement practitioners' concern to integrate liberation discourse with a "people's" revolution, African-American autocritography shapes this challenge as an encounter of "theory" and "experience" that tests the possibilities of their mutually qualifying, and reciprocally sanctioning, determinations. Indeed, the Black Arts' sensitivity to entanglements of expressive and institutional conditions in the development of a progressive communal agency prefigures and illuminates contemporary black criticism's effort to forge a mode of *materialist utterance* – that is, a conceptually daring instrument of cultural critique that is responsive, but not responsible, to prevailing idioms of Euro-American interpretive activity, while turned toward other audiences and purposes. The riddle posed by this effort is how to vitalize the nexus of personal and sociocultural meanings without eliding the ideological parameters in which the conjoined racial subject is then activated.

It is just at this juncture that vernacular genres offer most to black intellectual transformation: as we saw in the sermonic transactions of Franklin and Daniels, vernacular performance can exemplify a way of moving within and against modernity by making experience not just an epistemology (as it tends to become in Euro-American formulations of identity politics)[11] but a continuously scrutinized *method* of historical analysis and contemporary action. But as we observed with Douglass and Hurston, for the cultural theorist writing at a distance from the "indigenous" sphere itself this task is exacerbated by the fear of being excluded from the story told by their own discourse, internalizing the marginality so often turned to advantage by styles of vernacular irony and revision. For this reason, black autocritography, attuned to the liberating potential of vernacular sagacity, resounds a traumatic vibration, seeking as it does to excavate the *Nachträglichkeit*, or

290 "I was myself within the circle"

retroactive meaningfulness, that sutures natal past and urgent present into a narrative of realization. Specifically, this narrative is designed to convert the subaltern intellectual's experience of understanding as an oxymoronic enabling wound to an inspiriting provocation, fusing judgment and praxis. Its charge is therefore to bridge the gulf between culture and textuality, often figured as a gap between memory and mimesis, in order to render one's critical witness an effective political modality. Such narratives customarily orbit scenes of an original muteness that must be clarified as either incomprehension or embedded perception, and that must, in the manner of traumatic or sublime recognition, be animated later by moments of crisis and emergent insight – that is, by a moment properly termed "revolutionary." Remembrance in black autocritography is thus valued not for what it is but for what it permits: neither nostalgic reverie nor romantic evasion, it operates in these narratives as a means of revisiting and pressuring historical consciousness. Their concern with place must, then, be seen precisely as a way of rethinking (not sidestepping) the intersection of experience and ideology, infusing present intention with the temporalized nuance of shared perception nurtured in an alternative public sphere.

That said, as Hortense Spillers piquantly issues the challenge (following and amending the lead of Harold Cruse, whose momentous *The Crisis of the Negro Intellectual* served as historical conscience for Black Arts cultural theorists): "the black creative intellectual must get busy *where he/she is.*"[12] Possibly the most influential exemplar in contemporary African-American literary criticism of this locational necessity, and the positional drama it occasions, is Henry Louis Gates's path-breaking crossing of post-structural and vernacular linguistics, a theoretical gumbo elaborated around the figure of the Signifying Monkey. The annunciating manifesto of Gates's project, which receives its ultimate embellishment in *The Signifying Monkey*, is the much-anthologized essay "The Blackness of Blackness: A Critique of the Sign and the Signifying Monkey," where we find an instructive early instance of contemporary black autocritography.[13] Presenting what Gates calls a "tropological theory of formal revision," "The Blackness of Blackness," in its cunningly syncretic structuralism, seems at first glance an unlikely medium of autobiographical reflection, but in the essay's prefatorial gesture of historical exposition we find a subtle moment when the first-person peeks out from the text's guise of theoretical description: "Signification," Gates writes, "is a theory of reading that arises from Afro-American culture; learning how 'to signify' is often part of our adolescent education. I had to step outside my culture, had to defamiliarize the concept by translating it into a new mode of discourse, before I could see its potential in critical theory" ("The Blackness of Blackness," 286). Gates here constructs, and operates within, a double scene of expression and reconception, of in-struction and e-ducation, enacting a double movement of alienation and return. Western modes of discourse become here a belated but enlightening form of theorizing, while the vernacular Scene of

Instruction can be realized as productive process rather than inert "concept" only by being located "in" another cultural domain. Subtly, Gates implies a lag, a temporal gap that seems in fact a psychic and conceptual space, between that act of translational appropriation and the insight generated by braiding and mutually displacing cultural languages. Gates's own critical agency, his authority to move fluently between discursive realms, is lodged in that gap, in the passage between two sites of mediation and reception, between theory and translation, between culture as "African-American" and as 'mine,' between "had to" and "before," even between the collective knowledge of "our" and the individual vision of "I."

So who speaks here, and from where? Is the subject of enunciation a prediscursive self, ensconced within the amniotic enclosure of cultural origins, or a semiotic product of repeated and conflicting transformations, a figure born by being perpetually thrust from (e-ducere) the scene of its own beginning? These questions seem productively undecidable, suggesting at work a dialectical critique of both 'home' and the place from which it is freshly reimaged that forestalls reifying either founding cultural conceits or disengaged critical transposition. Vibrating between intimacy and disidentification, reading and translation, Gates's voice refuses to be bound to either place's demands, extending itself between competing terms of interpretation, social mediation, and authorial empowerment. Most importantly, as if himself signifying on the entangled routes and roots of the "verna-cular," Gates becomes not the 'slave born within the master's house' but the homeboy-scholar slyly choosing to inhabit the master's textual domain only to wield and improve upon its theoretical tools in a gesture that Gates terms "repetition and revision." Most intriguingly, Gates proceeds from this autobiographical reflection to offer his definitional matrix of African-American signifyin(g), emblemized by "that oxymoron, the Signifying Monkey [. . .] he who dwells at the margins of discourse . . . repeating and simultaneously reversing in one deft, discursive act" ("The Blackness of Blackness," 286). Gates's autocritographic performance thus reflexively doubles and masks itself, for who but the author himself dwells here at the margins of his own multiply textured discourse, "ever troping" himself as script and its enactment, voice and its interpretation, personal presence and its disappearance into a dazzling helix of explication and simulation.

Exile (and its implicit economy of loss) becomes, in Gates's 'deft act,' inextricable from discovery and restoration: diasporic consciousness enmeshes native knowledge, complicating the forms and origins of knowing *per se*. Even as he proceeds to enlist a Euro-American roster of theoretical masters of 'master tropology' to legitimate the privileging of signifyin(g) within a field of figural energies (no less venerable a genealogical procession than Vico, Nietzsche, Burke, Bloom, and de Man is called forth), he does so only for their linguistic systems (and, implicitly, the cultural capital those systems underwrite) to be subordinated to "the slave's trope," which "subsumes all other tropes." But more than a highstakes game of theoretical trope-a-dope is afoot; not surprisingly, the autobiographical passage that inaugurates this mercurial play of critical displacements must be heard as itself a double-voiced, or signifying, translation, one that recalls (this time covertly) an ambivalent Scene of Instruction already familiar within the terrain of African-American cultural theory. I refer, through the echo-chamber of Gates's own rhetoric and syntax, to Frederick Douglass's influential interpretation of slave songs from the *Narrative* of 1845, specifically to that passage which we earlier explored as a foundational site of vernacular speculation:

> The slaves selected to go to the Great House Farm, for the monthly allowance [. . .] [W]hile on their way would make the dense old woods [. . .] reverberate with their wild songs. [. . .] I did not, when a slave understand the deep meaning of those rude and apparently incoherent songs. I was myself within the circle; so that I neither saw nor heard as those without might see and hear. They told a tale of woe which was then altogether beyond my feeble comprehension. I have frequently found myself in tears while hearing them. The mere recurrence to those songs, even now, afflicts me; and while I am writing these lines, an expression of feeling has already found its way down my cheek.[14]

As we earlier saw, Douglass's description is only at first sight a straightforward defense of vernacular performance against alien appropriation or denial; the passage in fact dramatizes a complex movement of identifications and dislocations as the songs' "meaning" and the author's interpretive legitimacy reconfigure one another in a continuous process of renegotiation. His claim to legislative authority depends upon his simultaneous location beyond *and* within the scene he simultaneously recuperates and re-signs. The emergence of that authority from a confluence of critical and autobiographical voices is focused in the remarkable figure of the tear upon Douglass's cheek: here the disjunctive temporalities of the oral and the written seek mediation in a kind of body writing, the sentiment moving voluntarily through the writing subject as both a "feeling" and an "expression."

As in the moment from "The Blackness of Blackness" that responds to Douglass's passage, the multiple roles of boy, cultural traveler, and narrator, and the passage's oscillating tenses, suggest a constantly shifting authorial consciousness. Douglass's complex reflection on slave songs, like Gates's account of signifying, provides the insight that cultural performance, and not merely its textual interpretation, is always already a process of performative transaction and symbolic exchange. Participatory and continuously emergent, it can have neither predetermined form nor final significance. Correspondingly, Douglass's "I," like its later rearticulation in Gates's autocritographical passage, is not an absolved overseer of the cultural text,

an independent and steady node of awareness, but an engaged and implicated witness, occupying the place where the vicissitudes and jagged
continuities of African-American self-interrogation can be located in the
moment of expressive enactment ("while I am writing these lines . . .").
Site sanctions insight, as the modernist ideal of a singular perceiving being
discharges into the self's recognition of evolving identity in a re-cognition
of collectively enacted, plural, and contingent meanings. Such is what we
might term the mimetic residue of the "oxymoronic" vernacular method-
ologist operating in a 'defamiliarized' institutional arena. For what Gates's
citation of Douglass 'behind the veil' of New World academic discourse
posits is the vernacular scene's anticipatory marking within itself of the
absent presence of an interpretive beholder other than the Other, a
witnessing imagination that will come to know itself as having arisen from
within the veil of black expressive culture.

By thus founding an engaged criticism in such acts of cultural memory
and literacy, the black critic, occupying in the present a duplicitous and
unlocatable position, affiliates with a mode of political reading and self-
enactment resonant with genealogical particularity but irreducible to any
construct of foundation, code, or even determinate history or ideology.
For Gates, the gesture of affiliation is itself doubled, as recollection of
adolescent vernacular schooling also returns him to the slave narrator's
prefigurative translations of vernacular agency, resistance, authorial
control, and cultural deliverance. Citing Gates's procedural design for *The
Signifying Monkey* – "my movement [. . .] is from hermeneutics to rhetoric
and semantics, only to return to hermeneutics again" (44) – Sandra Adell
cannily asks, "how can one return to hermeneutics (the tradition) after
rhetoric?"[15] Gates's doubling of vernacular theory with autobiographical
performance, and both with a redoubled, historicized topos of modernist
and African-American critical self-revision (the latter rendered so as to be
audible only to one kind of audience), suggests a provisional answer to
Adell's question. By figuring the "return to hermeneutics" as the empowering recollection of vernacular soundings *and* their engagement by that
most theoretical of (ex)slave narrators, Douglass, Gates paradigmatically
crosses achieved meaning and linguistic performance, tradition and modernity, identity and difference. Hermeneutical and rhetorical processes
intersect in the realization that agency obliges the writer to take up residence both inside and outside competing frames of reference,
simultaneously occupying seemingly incongruous circles of understanding
according to their distinctive semantic and grammatical principles.
Vernacular and institutional scenes, like the past and the present, are alike
constituted by a performative dialectic of proximity and distance: to read
those scenes is to stand apart from them, just as (in the vernacular sense)
'to read' those scenes is to enter them. But the relation of these two scenes,
black and western, is asymmetrical: if the modernism of the latter variously exalts and shores the ruins of originary utterance, the former diffuses

the crisis of belatedness by remembering the disruptive questioning of propriety as its intrinsic endowment, its propers.

Gates's self-veiling self-revelation thereby pierces the notion of cultural authority as producing a closed and autonomous order, blurring instead the boundaries between mimesis and signifyin(g), thus situating black expressive praxis, and its revisionary notions of subject and context, at the thresholds of intention and iteration, text and intertext, call and response (notably, the very title of "The Blackness of Blackness" emblemizes this dialectic by signifying upon Ralph Ellison's prefatorial play of identity and difference, the underground sermon of "black is and black ain't" that, we recall, opens *Invisible Man*). The journey back thus discovers in "Afro-American culture" not the pristine ground of absolute value, but the uncanny home or "spirit house" of translation and transition, not an epiphanic origin beyond entanglements of power and desire, but an originary site of incalculable transformation. Such a journey suggests one means of moving us beyond the impasse of oppositional rhetoric out of which Gates's "chiasmal" tropology initially springs (*The Signifying Monkey*, 52; 63–4). Perhaps we can best follow, via the play of Gates's autocritographical allusion, *the slaves* along this route of return, as they compose their songs in an indeterminable space between home and the Great House Farm, a psychic and economic terrain marking the separation of desire and mastery, of freedom and servitude, even of life and death. A critical and contradictory arena, bounded by commerce but nurturing an economy of transgression, such a space destabilizes the unity of power without projecting some simple negating structure of counter-power. For the slaves, this site of "defamiliarization" is one simultaneously of subversive de-identification (their bar-barian or "wild notes" having in them always "something of the Great House Farm" while ever expressing "bitterest anguish" at their condition) and collective re-alignment ("they would sing, as a chorus, to words . . . full of meaning to themselves"). This is, Gates seems to suggest in his manner of summoning and resituating Douglass, the very locus of the vernacular *per se*, recalling again its root sense of an ambiguous, ambivalent relation to the house of mastery: a dual sign, it simultaneously inscribes itself in the discourse of judgment and sounds itself with the guile of resistance.

III

> We are always our best audience,
> resting on the breastbone
> of each performance.
>
> Michael Harper, "Sugarloaf"[16]

In citing a "journey back" to the "spirit house" of African-American refiguration, I mean not only to redirect Nipsey Russell's shaken traveler from the fortune-telling mechanisms of identity politics to an alternative scene of vernacular instruction, but to invoke the autocritographical language of Houston Baker, who, in *Afro-American Poetics*, has explicitly called for a practice of critical self-reflection that will "enable racial poetry to displace state philosophy."[17] Such a practice would be a specifically intoned mode of interpretation's constitutive circumstances, for, Baker avers, "critics eternally become and embody the generative myths of their culture by half-perceiving and half-inventing their culture, their myths, and themselves" (*Afro-American Poetics*, 8). Paralleling Gates's double-edged gesture of evoking Euro-American tradition while surreptitiously conjuring an African-American topos that prefigures his own critical enterprise, Baker fashions here a palimpsestic image of self-invention as call-and-response. Deploying Shakespearean and Wordsworthian formulations of imagination's relation to otherness, Baker reframes Ralph Ellison's troping of Stephen Dedalus's image of racial recreation as a process of forging "the uncreated features of one's face."[18] We shall return to the Ellisonian pretext of Baker's rumination, but for now it is important to note the complementary relation between self-invention and cultural origin proposed in Baker's apothegm, particularly in the charged connection between achieved embodiment and perceptual detachment: as a conceptual performative, the maxim's interchange of cultural references enacts the very creative fusion of homegrown and distantly forged mythographies that it describes.

Such layering of cross-cultural citations can become, as Baker admits, a mode of aestheticism, whose grand gestures of synthesis potentially neutralize the raucous energies released by displaced repetition. In his most recent autocritical performance, entitled "Everybody Knows the Real Thing, But Magic Brings us Home: Multicultural Notes," Baker addresses exactly this threat to the disruptive, hybrid possibilities of interpretive self-creation, a threat which he locates specifically in the more soothing discourse of multiculturalism, whose "implicit project [he defines as] a reconciliation of ever-proliferating American differences into a [spurious] harmony."[19] As his title suggests, Baker sees the present idealization of pluralistic identities as a form of realist ideology, which reiterates rather than reforms already-legible social narratives by minimizing the processural, historical, material, and figurative struggle for identity. Thus, conceiving the identity politics of multiculturalism as a covert form of "state" philosophy, Baker proceeds to seek its disruption and reconception via an autobiographical gesture of "racial poetry" (an African-Americanized *magical* realism) by staging a past scene of personal and cultural myth, memory, history, and self-creation. But the scene to which he travels through critical memory is not merely a repository for uplifting or oppositional images, but a locus of transformative mediation that functions in his essay as an expressive instrument for fathoming and reconfiguring the present. The narrative design of recollection and representation governing "Everybody Knows the Real Thing," a structure of 'half-perception and half-invention,' will suggest that a critically engaged blackness, because it is always actively amending prevailing social and signifying economies, can exert pressure against conditions of its performance and thereby alter its status as a mimetic practice. The journey back, in short, is designed as a movement forward, a means of reopening and reimagining the "real" at the moment of writing.

Splitting the difference between Nipsey Russell's traveler and the fortune-telling machine, Baker asserts that "'reality' manifests itself in the specificity of appearances," and so he frames his scene of autobiographical memory with readings of classical and contemporary contests to control the real in visual representation. Opening with Pliny's story, as mediated by Schiller, of Zeuxis' rivalry with Parrhasius for the prize of most realistic painter, and closing with a contrastive reading of John Singleton's sentimental, recuperative *Boyz N the Hood* and the Hughes brothers' self-reflexive and subversive *Menace II Society*, Baker weaves through his piece a flashback to his Louisville boyhood, when the great black diva, Carol Brice, came to town, "dazzling" the young Houston Baker with an extraordinary confluence of idiomatic narrative and classical song. Moving with consummate ease between the city's Memorial Auditorium, where she sang lieder with poise and pathos, and the Baker house of Louisville's Little Africa neighborhood, where she exchanged with Baker's kin "lies" that memorialized in living detail the daily drama of survival and celebration of mid-century black America (6f.), Ms. Brice becomes in Baker's reminiscence the quickening ancestor who, in Toni Morrison's formulation, "astonishes" with her "timeless" ability to dislodge the reifications of the present[20]:

> The scene of memory shifts from Little Africa to a street filled with lights, car horns honking, elegantly-dressed, surging crowds of dark people entering the glittering spaces of Louisville's Memorial Auditorium. [. . .] We wait like the rest of the audience for the appearance of [. . .] Carol Brice. She has studied at Juilliard, sung at the inauguration of Franklin D. Roosevelt in 1941, [. . .] debuted at Town Hall [. . .] One of Louisville's African-American sororities is her sponsor, performing fine community service by bringing the arts to us in a segregated city where, in 1947, the idea of a Negro as "Artist" was improbable as a white man who considered himself multicultural. [. . .] Yes, it was assuredly Carol Brice, whose folk wisdom and humor had been especially appreciated and seasoned for me [. . .] How could the magnificent contralto on stage be my Ms. Brice, or, indeed, *the real thing*?
>
> (Houston A. Baker, Jr., "Everybody Knows the Real Thing," 7, 9)

The great singer's visit not only provides a signal exhibition of African-American 'uplift,' whereby public performance emblemizes transcendence of social and statutory obstruction, but becomes the occasion for a complex, vibrant expression of collective imagination. The formal concert catalyzes a variety of acts, along a spectrum of economic enablement, organizational ingenuity, and aesthetic spiritedness, that evince a capacity for fraternal (and sororal!) self-display and self-affirmation (the 'show' clearly takes place before and outside, as well as within the concert hall). The worldly performer's sojourn enlarges the community's vision of *its own* status as "the real thing."

Reinfusing "her" lieder (Baker insists on characterizing the lieder as precisely "hers") with the passion of lived pain, and accenting her sassy tales of diasporic endurance with the elegance of her creative vocation, Carol Brice models for the young Houston Baker the translation of modern aesthetic idioms into an enabling performative montage. Migrating between concert hall and domicile of communal storytelling, Brice opens for Baker's consideration a multidimensional space that imbricates and redirects an assortment of dialects, postures, and images, demonstrating a strategy of appropriative quotation that serves not to recover some lost primal word but to release the potential for self-expressive authority. Performance becomes not enslavement to dominant scripts or to the involuntarism of their recitation, but a means of elaborating an anxious but shared story of initiation, deliberation, and recognition: the deathly servitude of repetition is thus transmuted into a collective journey of re-petition.

As with Gates's transformative journey from vernacular classroom to critical theory, the Scene of Instruction provided by Carol Brice's performance provides Baker passage to another way of seeing things, one which dislocates what he calls, in a catachresis of structural anthropology, his "preliterate" or aesthetic imagination (12). For when the boy, who (rather like a young Douglass entranced by a *white* donor of "instruction," Sophia Auld) first viewed on his doorstep the "robust [woman] with a shining face" and next heard her "rocking the house with songs and stories of lives that hadn't been no 'crystal stairs'" (6), again saw her in the auditorium, the scene was "so beautifully unexpected and strange that I was transported, carried away by vibrations of . . . voice" (8).[21] Learning from his mother that the ethereal singer of the auditorium and the soulful sister in the house were one and the same, Baker writes, "I was incredulous, undone, without words for the immensity of [the] revelation" (8). To transpose Cathy Caruth's insight regarding the necessity of traumatic forgetting for remembrance, it is almost as if young Baker experiences the voice's vibrations (recall, if you will, Coltrane's OM) exactly because of the momentary rupture between two disparate locales, with their distinctive stylistic and sociopolitical intonations.[22] His movement between contrasting orders of visual and oral presentation is both shock and illumination (one imagines that, in fact, a peculiar integration of ocular and aural experience marks each scene's singular resonance for the boy, and that it is the difference between these expressive conjunctions that erupts into his consciousness, making the moment a spot of time). Indeed, it is the interruption of "Ms. Brice" as a univocal referent, and the perplexity such referential suspension causes in the youth, that registers her presence as an *event*, disengaging her potential as a performative figure from any assumed pattern of meaning to which Baker had assimilated her.[23] Recalling a passage from *Invisible Man* in which Ellison's hero "sits with a lump in [his] throat" at the singing of a "thin brown girl" in his college choir (a passage that itself recalls Douglass's reading of slave songs, as invisible man is moved though he "could not understand the words" – *Invisible Man*, 114–15), this moment suspends the boy as well, setting him spinning in an equivocal state of fascination that the essay itself serves to constructively repeat and reread. As the Ellisonian context of enchantment haunted by incipient fetishization suggests, it will be the task of that rereading, that 'reinvention' of perception, to reimagine the Scene of Instruction not merely in order to decode the memory's enabling mythography, its cognitive stance, but also to claim for the present its persuasive efficacy, the subversive aberration of its performative force.

The vivid array of appearances that transmute the youngster's reality are contradictory not to her but to him, as he seems to have arrived on the scene as a kind of Aesthetic Child Prodigy, an infant Schiller all too ready to find a collapse of meaning into awe in this confusion of the everyday and the epochal, the vernacular and the classical. Truth to say, Baker's story teeters here at the edge of the very aesthetic modalities that he discerns in the eviscerating harmonies of multiculturalist ideology, as Brice is praised for the "plenitude" of her "beautiful" presence (9–10). But the potentially arresting lyricism of Baker's celebration serves to stage a more important narrative, the story of the boy's expanding consciousness – specifically, the instruction, by mother and artist, into the reciprocity and responsibility of cultural revision and transmission, undertaken at the crossroads of domestic and public spheres. Recasting Habermas's "life-world" as what Bhabha terms a *contra*-modern arena, Baker finally projects Carol Brice as tirelessly negotiating, not nullifying, differences, differences of perspective and intonation that arise not just between but within private and public domains. Her story becomes in his essay what her voice was in the Baker house and the Louisville auditorium: a provocative strand within the *mise-en-scène* of Baker's own temporally spaced experience of African-American expressive culture. That experience places him, too, in a double scene of figural and material enactment, a scene authorized by ritual and improvisational strategies of legitimation that persistently transgress the limits of the social "real."

Interweaving memory and cultural critique (Baker proceeds to situate Brice's expressive realism in genealogical continuum with the Hughes brothers' radical cinematography), "Everybody Knows the Real Thing" recalls and enacts the notion that the subject's beginning, as a beginning again, occurs in the space between idioms of identity, a place of crossing

– what Baker following Latino poetics terms the cultural "borderlands." Carol Brice is an heroic exemplar of unexpected movement across these borders, a culture worker who travels back and out not simply to import alien values into a new scene but to enact a transvaluation of the scene itself. As such, she functions for Baker not as a bearer of fixed cognitive or mythic value but as a model of the ceaseless will to self-performance grasped as a nexus of knowledges, and she models for him the distribution of that processual self-understanding to others in the spirit house of call-and-response. In doing so, she points his way toward a revaluation of the "public sphere" through which identity politics articulates its claims, for in the amalgam of presentations, displays, and expressions that render her a complex, mobile presence in and for the black community, Carol Brice demonstrates the mutual implication of body and voice, event and commentary, psychic and cultural process: the critic indeed comes to 'embody' the culture because the culture prefigures without predetermining that struggle as a ceaseless dialogue of perception and invention.

IV

> It's uh known fact, Phoeby, you got tuh *go* there tuh *know* there. Yo' papa and yo' mama and nobody else can't tell yuh and show yuh. Two things everybody's got tuh do fuh theyselves. They got tuh go tuh God, and they got tuh find out about livin' fuh theyselves.
>
> Janie in *Their Eyes Were Watching God*[24]

Implicitly, there can be no limit to the positions and voices adopted in this historically charged mode of critical performance. And so I'd like to bring our exploration of contemporary black autocritography to a conditional closure by briefly turning to a somewhat different instance of the genre, one that conscientiously turns the journey back into a more troubling source of reimagined and engaged identity, thus redirecting the topos's problematic of cultural authenticity and performative identity toward its congenital and generative uncanniness. In her meditative essay, "On 'Going Home'," Deborah McDowell also undertakes the journey back to the charmed circle of childhood instruction, only to find there the trauma of a stifling and declining community, rather than the invigoratingly disjunctive "shock" of ancestral wisdom.[25] If Gates and Baker, as genealogists of black criticism's primal scene of struggle and filiation, refigure institutional marginality as an empowering mode of cultural definition, McDowell renders the askesis of return a complication rather than cure of exilic critical consciousness. The perceptual gains of distance are measured anew in terms of loss as much as recovery. She finds therefore that the capacity to forge fresh visions of blackness as freedom and desire demands the potentially isolating discipline of perpetual movement, a mobility that threatens the shibboleths of memory and home with renewed awareness that such visions must be restlessly resistant to all constraining custom and expectation. Home, in short, may be not so much a place of bracing cultural transmission as another sphere of contested meaning and authority, the more startling for its pungent familiarity and ghostly lures.

The essay opens with McDowell driving her car to the airport for the flight down south. Another driver becomes obstructive and anger flares, but McDowell (in a moment that recalls Hurston accelerating "down the stretch into Eatonville" in her "little Chevrolet" at the end of the "Preface" to *Mules and Men*[26] – a germane allusion, as we'll shortly see) is soon speeding on: "I started laughing out loud – at myself, at her. What was the point of all that rage?" (351). That question haunts the visit home, where McDowell encounters the familiar assortment of elders, full of reminiscences of her unbecoming childhood postures, brusque questions about her unmarried and unchilded condition, and uncomprehending dismay at her insistence on working and living so far from them. With abundance of well-meaning emphasis but minimal delicacy, the homefolks craft an instructional scene that invites her to engage a ritual of filial repetition, wherein all modes of reproduction (spatial, professional, personal, biological) would establish identity as a return of the same. For McDowell, such a *nostos* insidiously challenges the commitment to ethical and intellectual decision, the discernment of differences by the agency of reflective and reflexive consciousness, through which her sense of value and voice have evolved. But the encounter between community and prodigy-turned-expatriate ("I might as well be in a foreign country, as far as [they're] concerned" – 352) cannot be reduced to this simple geometry of collective and individual. It is, rather, a drama of rival but consanguine voices, of the possibilities they proffer and the distinctions they etch, within the estranged homegirl herself. McDowell experiences the ancient spectacles, tastes, sounds, and moods of 'home' as both temptation and threat, perhaps even as a contest of idiomatic perspectives and authoritative registers. Intrigued at the prospect of resolving that interior drama by "fill[ing] the huge gaps in my memory" with narrative knowledge – memorial reconstructions that include insight into a slyly wicked paternal act of vernacular naming ("I was touched when Mrs. Emma Merriweather just volunteered a story about me [. . .] given my search, it was a precious tidbit. It gave me a clue as to why Papa called me Miss Priss" – 352) – McDowell confronts herself in the natal mirror with decidedly mixed motives and emotions: "I laugh and indulge them. [. . .] But even as I write this, I feel guilt and fear" (352).

Subtly informing and, perhaps, mitigating the sharpness of these confrontations is the essay's own subterranean encounter with its enabling African-American pretext, one which, like those of Gates's and Baker's reminiscences, situates the emergence of black critical consciousness in a scene of vernacular transaction. In chiasmal relation to scenes of instruction evoked by black male authors – who so often, from Douglass to Invisible

Man to Houston Baker, find themselves attending to the voice and visage of a displaced maternal figure[27] – the vernacular topos with which "On Going Home" is affiliated stages the crux of cultural authority and revisionary voice as a spry do-si-do between father and daughter, Papa and Miss Priss:

Robert Williams said:
Ah know another man wid a daughter.

> The man sent his daughter off to school for seben years, den she come home all finished up. So he said to her, "Daughter, git yo' things and write me a letter to my brother!" So she did.
> He says, "Head it up," and she done so.
> "Now tell 'im, 'Dear Brother, our chile is done come home from school and all finished up and we is very proud of her.'"
> Then he ast de girl "Is you got dat?"
> She tole 'im "yeah."
> "Now tell him some mo'. 'Our mule is dead but Ah got another mule and when Ah say (clucking sound of tongue and teeth) he moved from de word.'"
> "Is you got dat?" he ast de girl.
> "Naw suh," she tole 'im.
> He waited a while and he ast her again, "You got dat down yet?"
> "Naw suh, Ah ain't got it yet."
> "How come you ain't got it?"
> "Cause Ah can't spell (clucking sound)."
> "You mean to tell me you been off to school seben years and can't spell (clucking sound)? Why Ah could spell dat myself and Ah ain't been to school a day in mah life. Well jes' say (clucking sound) he'll know what yo' mean and go on wid de letter."
> (Zora Neale Hurston, *Mules and Men*, 40–1)

One of Zora Neale Hurston's more charged yet also playful anecdotes (re)collected in that masterwork of autocritographical ethnography *Mules and Men*, Robert Williams's story – and the story of Robert Williams's story – distills without reduction the politics of representation that flares in the gritty dialogue of habitus and homecoming, wherein the improvisational resources of tradition are put to school and are in turn tested by a new node of agency bearing an enigmatic techne. The father would remind his returning daughter of his encompassing, regulative command: having 'sent her off' presumably to acquire skill (and possibly stature) that would enhance his own social power (and possibly place), he cleverly puts her to the task of inscribing her own subjection to a paternal rule that always already circumscribes her worth and meaning. Or rather, by plotting the interruption of her newly-acquired capacity to inscribe, substituting the materiality of "tongue and teeth" for the alien technology of telling brought from outside the hereditary homeworld, the father compels his daughter to perform the gap between her "things" and their capacity to mark his experience. In directing her confession that she "ain't got it," he affirms his sphere's aptitude for strategic absorption and self-extension even when pressured by cultural diversification wrought by modernity and mobility. At first glance, it might seem ironic that he chooses the vehicle of writing, the letter, as the medium of (counter)educative assertion, but the mechanism is apt in that what most imperils cultural autonomy under such conditions of change is the introduction of heterodox articulations that menace traditional transmission of value and the mastery it ratifies. The father therefore crafts a jocoserious agon of *autho*rity, metonymically likening his amanuensis daughter to the mule made to 'move from de word' – the hybrid, and notably sterile, beast of burden (itself an often bleak metonym of the [ex]slave male laborer, suggesting the father's subtle displacement of stigmatization and socio-economic imprisonment to the feminine sphere)[28] is "another" taking the place of one now "dead," a figure of the father's ability to renew his mastery over lesser creatures through substitution and compulsory instruction.

Moreover, the mule, unlike the perhaps more stubborn daughter, "gets it": "When Ah say," he moves "from" the Word's mandate, confirming its speaker's causal and distancing sway. The father, we should note, opens the letter by defining his daughter as "all finished up," as though her exotic schooling has brought closure to the sense of potential and desire that likely quickened in her with the move beyond domestic surveillance. Defensively signifyin(g) on Miss Priss's presumed uppity bearing and the polish of her tutelage, the phrase, in its vernacular redundancy, renders completion as depletion, the daughter once again made a mere receptacle of paternal imperatives: a dead mule needing (re)transformation into an obedient one. Such a critique and recontainment of the daughter's wayward potentiality is conveyed not only by the dominance of the father's voice but by that voice's endorsement in the framing vehicle of Robert Williams's presentation, which provides and authenticates its diction (e.g. in the crucial phrase "come home . . . all finished up"), enforcing the impression insinuated by the letter's address to the father's brother that the daughter is constituted as an element of homosocial and intragenerational commerce.

But perhaps a certain wily obstruction inspirits the daughter's 'inability' to complete the translational task demanded of her. Perhaps she practices her own strategy of histrionic interruption, inserting her own breaks against the call for a certain 'saying' that would speak the conscription of her own expressive resources. It is she, after all, who halts the act of inscription, making it *in*complete by postponement of the father's intention: forcing him to "wait a while," she actually 'unsays' the smooth appropriation of writing, hollowing a space within his design that enigmatically re-calls him to the ethical immediacy of dialogue or marks a temporal distance that foregrounds his refusal of genuine exchange. By thus *diss*-'spelling' the father, the daughter sounds or specifies his signifying; her reiterated denials – "Naw suh . . . naw suh" – suggest recalcitrance as much as inability, a subversive resistance or scrupulous hesitation before the home regime's gibing, jiving interrogation. Against the letter's aim of circulating news of the daughter's reconfinement, her disarticulation of patrimonial determination enacts a guerrilla arrest of the word's movement and inserts an antiphonal alternative of uncertain notice.

Once we adopt the daughter's position, eschewing the identifications invited by the tale's privileged positions, the narrative opens to a reversal that draws suspicion of its evident emplotment of mastery and subjugation, pulling us into a more active, endangered relation to its play of prescriptions and (mis)recognitions. These concerns hint at yet another level of ambivalent identification, that between Hurston and both parties of her anecdote, most obviously the daughter (who may be adopting a stance rather like that of Hurston fending off expectations of her anthropological mentors), but also, subliminally, that of the father, who moves nimbly between realms of talk and text. Among its many resonances, Hurston's tale is a fable of ethnographic transcription,[29] one that reopens tensions within her own project and position as "native" anthropologist that are screened by the deft pronominal movements of the "Preface" discussed in the previous chapter. In this respect, we ought to be particularly attentive to inscriptions of her locational dilemma in the story's very textuality: reading the text aloud, how does one pronounce "(clucking sound of tongue and teeth)"?! Should one heed these marks as a kind of musical scoring or stage direction, *à la* Madhubuti's or Sanchez's directions for creating Coltrane-esque sounds in reading their Coltrane Poems? Or would that circumvention of the impasse of orality and writing precisely neutralize the dilemma that Hurston has carefully constructed for us? And ought we to adopt different strategies when such notation appears in the daughter's voice (she who claims inability to make the sound) and in the father's (he who likely makes an ostentatious display of his performative capacity by repeating the sound as often as possible, thus, as it were, flogging his 'mulish' daughter with his expertise)? The need to grasp and enact such decisions, maintaining their peculiar force without too quickly translating them into 'sense,' suggests how Hurston has crafted the anecdote to materialize the reader's cognitive dilemma as a performative crux, and, further, how that crux is shaped to foreground the drama of identification and distance that entangles vernacular culture and its traveling homegirls.

Taken in its complex and reverberative entirety, then, Hurston's fable of filial return to the defining crucible of cultural legitimation refuses closure on its dialectic of affiliation and alterity. Context becomes an ambiguous site of structuration and enablement, susceptible to multiple reframings that make it unclear whether imaginative acts must be reabsorbed by the traditional energies they engage. Most of all, the tale inflects the difficult necessity of clarifying the place from which one addresses relations of agency and system, experience and discursive understanding, embodied authenticity and performative semiosis. As the father and daughter enter a dance for position and authorial prestige, we are enjoined to see how emergent identities make choices within circumstances that are simultaneously concrete and overdetermined. Agency is inextricable from engagement with competing mediations, so that who one is or can become, what one says or imagines for utterance, depends upon the horizon of expressive possibilities confronted in the various scenes through which one moves.

This sense of tension between desire and scene, and specifically the pressure home exerts upon a critical consciousness formed equally by upbringing and migration, reconnects "On Going Home" to *Mules and Men*, though McDowell is if anything more emphatic about the need to refuse being "finished up" by the siren call of a place that hollows prospects for vitalizing speech. Everywhere in the town, there are signs of loss and lassitude – a church elder whose once-magnificent hair has declined into a "stingy row of stiff curls" (351); the stifling, formulaic church service conducted by "two old faithfuls" (351f.); her old elementary school dwindled to a single remaining room (353f.); the porches and living rooms no longer sites of ritual communal play and affirmation but sweltering and shuttered spots of isolation. These evocations of decay, emptiness, and, finally, of death, provoke no nostalgia, but rather a "fury" which quickly subsides into a sadness that poignantly contrasts with the rage-become-laughter of the opening highway episode. For the desiccated landscape and homefolks' narrow-eyed expectations suggest to McDowell little scope for spirituality or likelihood of repose in the house of origins. Instead, they tell a tale of disfiguration and effacement that threatens to swallow her own developing narrative as an intellectual traveler, and her potential for mobility and self-realization depends upon successful passage through the spectral milieu.

The essay's final scene, troping the initiating moment of speed and liberation, thus finds McDowell riding through the ramshackle streets of her once-sturdy neighborhood, "huddled in the back seat" of her aunt's ironically named Rambler, crying. In the last sentence, we read: "Children playing hopscotch step out of the road to let the car pass by, a passing car with unfamiliar faces which they watched until we were out of sight" (354). No more than she can abide the reassimilation of an altered self to the ghostly imprint of a surpassed childhood can she eliminate the distance between the moving vehicle and the transfixed children. The dislocation of voice and face, which in Nipsey Russell's army anecdote suggested the double-play of power and tricksterism, and in Houston Baker's essay catalyzed entry into a world of instructive transformation, is here for Deborah McDowell the chastening failure of autobiography to forge an idealist program of cultural renewal, the collapse of prosopopoeia into the crisis of identity as cultural mourning.

But that is really not the end of McDowell's autocritographical performance. I noted that the essay's beginning images her driving with energetic anticipation down the highway. In fact, that is only the story's first event; the story itself begins with these lines: "I am at home. I see the effects of the Alabama drought on Auntie's grass. It's brown, dry, patchy. . . . At least it's cool enough to sit here and take more notes for the essay on *Sula* that I have promised Nellie for her volume" (351). That essay, significantly entitled "The Self and the Other" – in which McDowell, to my mind, revolutionizes our ethical and conceptual view of black literary subjectivity by reading Morrison's heroine as an exemplar of uncompromising and liberating acts of self-displacement – that essay written in response to the call of her friend and colleague Nellie McKay, should be read, I think, as a transfiguring supplement of "On 'Going Home',," for it completes McDowell's mourning for communal loss, allowing her to move on productively with the narrative of a differently conceived, more mobile black communal identity that the old place couldn't fully digest or sustain.[30] Reading Sula as a heroine of exorbitant powers of liberatory assertion who converts exile from the familial household into a positive mission of self-fulfillment, McDowell brings her analysis of Morrison's novel to focus on Nel's return to the buried past of her and Sula's childhood friendship. In language that recalls Coltrane's evocation of "a love supreme" as the reverberative interchange of autonomy and connection, McDowell here returns implicitly to the incomplete project of traumatic recovery and collective regeneration forged in the revolutionary passion of the Black Arts Movement: "The 'circles and circles of sorrow' she cried at the narrative's end," writes McDowell of that final cemetery vignette, "prepare her for what Sula strained to experience throughout her life: the process of mourning and remembering that leads to intimacy with the self, which is all that makes intimacy with others possible" ("The Self and the Other," 85). If in "On 'Going Home'" the fiercely idiosyncratic, will-ful, self-inventing heroine sheds her own tears of elegiac apprehension, it is likewise the dialogic bond of that sorrow to a defining kinship with the absent-but-sustaining Nel(lie) that whets inspiriting critical performance.

Explicating the association of Sula with water, a fecund fluidity so unlike the parched Southern territory to which McDowell alludes in the opening of "On 'Going Home'," McDowell notes in particular the association of Morrison's hero with the tadpole, that figure of transition, of the in-between: "The image of the tadpole reinforces [the] notion of SELF as perpetually in process. Sula never achieves completeness of being. She dies in the fetal position welcoming this 'sleep of water,' in a passage that clearly suggests she is dying yet aborning" ("The Self and the Other," 81). Likewise embracing a posture of self-reflection through which the embryonic self is ambiguously lost and regained, McDowell locates the courage of Sula in herself by re-signing home while in the very clutches of a gripping re-memory. Grasped as an ever-emergent, mutable, and self-transgressive agency, such black expressive identity confutes the conventional oppositionality of identity politics by resituating vectors of resistance *within* subject ('self') and community ('other') that drive their mutual performative realization. In resolute dialogue with the layered contexts of familial history, cultural habitus, literary narrative, professional experience, fraternal communication, and autobiographical reflection, McDowell indicates how the quest for voice and place engages rupture and displacement in a ceaseless transformative dialectic. Her inability to reassimilate fully the still affecting terms of "home" squanders the illusion of restored coherence in an embrace of the scandal of history, which registers its drive to futurity precisely in its resistance to easy translation or transparency. In this, alongside Gates and Baker, McDowell offers for the contemporary politics and performance of African-American identity an alternative yet congruent model of renewal through interpretive struggle, working likewise in the pauses hollowed from modernity by the call-and-response of diasporic revision. . . .

"*Do you know who this is?*" each voice asks, from somewhere uncanny. And each answers itself, in admiring perplexity, "No." "Good!" comes the clincher, and the dialogue is momentarily complete, ready to begin again.

Epilogue
Re:presenting blackness

A theatre is transformed, fore and aft, into a slave ship, so that as soon as one enters the performance space one becomes enslaved to the dramaturgy of servitude. The drama itself moves inexorably not to an American historical domain but to a re-vision of neo-African liberation, accomplished by the whole audience collectively as it dismembers the play's one white character in an exorcistic festival called *boogalooyoruba*. The one white member of the audience is, in a necessary paradox, excluded from the festival; nevertheless, he survives it.

*

A (white) man facing a (black) comrade suffering public distress affects to console him with the following words:

> Good name in man and woman, dear my lord,
> Is the immediate jewel of their souls.
> Who steals my purse steals trash; 'tis something, nothing;
> 'Twas mine, 'tis his, and has been slave to thousands;
> But he that filches from me my good name
> Robs me of that which not enriches him
> And makes me poor indeed.

Two self-consciously histrionic scenes frame for us a final consideration of performance as cultural act, critical perspective, and political effect in African-American modernism's still-expanding panorama. The first, a 1971 production in West Detroit of Amiri Baraka's *Slave Ship* – likely the Black Arts Movement's fiercest vision of methexic realization – offers an apocalyptic spectacle that, in its very anti-narrative 'scripting' of a revolutionary ideal, inevitably acknowledges its status as mediating, temporal act: I could, after all, pocket my note-scribbled playbill and leave the play-decapitation behind me for the less predictable, if no less coded, streets. The second – Senator Alan Simpson's lofty reminder to Judge Clarence Thomas of Iago's speech on reputation (misattributed by Simpson to Iago's victim, Othello)

during the 1991 ("high-tech lynching") Supreme Court nomination hearings – displays a deliberate, if inadvertently ironic, conjunction of "citation"
and "confirmation," offering an Imaginary blend of narrative coherence
and authority, character and history. Here, the script is appropriated to
recover, not dissolve, narrative authority, but fulfills its intended mission
as ambiguously as does Baraka's play.

   Slave Ship and the Thomas hearings bracket two consequential decades
of tumultuous encounters between blackness and spectacle, thereby
suggesting the contradictory pathways confronting African-American
cultural experiment at the threshold of a millenial turn. With *Slave Ship*
we experience that nationalist and visionary assault on representation in
which "performance" connotes a revolutionary liberation from all prior
codes. Rejecting distance as the medium of knowledge, this transformational theater abolishes traditional connections, from relations among
script, playbook, and choreography to the very perspectival sightlines
assuring traditional audience perception. On one hand, it collapses all
manner of position, material, and concept into the *mise-en-scène* itself: expression *is* interpretation, event *is* meaning. On the other hand, it mistrusts
its very processes of enactment, coherence, and closure. The scene is staged
only to be disavowed as mere gesture; refusing contextualization in any
temporal continuum, it is ultimately ob-scene.

   By thus fetishizing the denial of any sublimated performative significance, *Slave Ship* emblemizes a range of modernist black practices from
agitprop actions (with their conflation of power and critique) and the
abstractive soundings of The Last Poets (with their dissolution of semantic
into 'natural' expression), to mixed-media, vernacular-inspired hiphop
improvisations (with their anamorphism of perception and production) and
choreographic extravaganzas of vogueing (with their merger of intention
and materiality in the performer's body). At the heart of these experiments
with a nonlogocentric relation of audience and play is the negation or
expropriation of 'legitimate' epistemology, often explicitly expressed by the
practitioners as a refutation of textuality. As first the writer, then performer
and ensemble, seek to enlist the spectator in subverting institutional claims
of authority over manifold spheres of enactment, the conventional script
is variously metaphorized and metamorphosed – as palimpsest (Kennedy),
as score (Madhubuti), as motif awaiting elaboration (Neal), as improvisational cue (Harper), as blocking agent (Stewart); the text evaporates as
anything more than a spectral design for enactment conceived along the
axis of Baraka's envisioned "postwestern form." Evacuated of its material
and motive authority, writing is superseded by an ideal of *mise-en-scène* as
intrinsic value unfettered by any regulative mechanism from afar, any
command to repeat itself as alibi, any dictation from another scene.

   As the canniest practitioners understand, however, this radical emphasis
on immediacy, be it enunciated as a spooky or rainbow-colored occupation
of the theatrical domain, cannot seek merely to invert the order that it

opposes. For the suspension of literal script cannot annul the immanence of textuality as such. The substitution of will for idea, with its attendant acknowledgement of perception as arbitrary rather than logically positional, is itself a phenomenon susceptible to critique. In fact, these experiments clearly seek no immunity from reframing commentary. Comprising a network of interpretations, conventions, and sayings, the de-institutionalized scene of African-American modernist assertion supplements, as well as transgresses, received narratives of collective understanding.

Slave Ship, in fact, distinguishes itself from its pale specular twins in the "living theatre" of Euro-American avant-garde performance by its relative thematization of historically determined relations of power, a concern that provides a tenuous generic link between its Black Arts insurgency and the mediatized funnyhouse of the Thomas hearings. But the Thomas hearings, which began as a placid staging of a well-plotted ceremony, ultimately unfolded as a power struggle that privileged no narrative or perceptual position as does *Slave Ship*'s climactic improvisation. With the appearance of Anita Hill and her "obscene" depictions of lurid misconduct, the hearings were suddenly appraised in bursts of performance metaphor: "political melodrama," "media circus," "morality play," "theater of the absurd," "soap opera," "poisonous spectacle," and other evocative, if contradictory, images of high and popular theatricalism. These terms captured the American public's sudden consciousness of being spectators to an agon, arbiters of legitimacy. Yet what Anita Hill's testimony sparked was clearly not the transformation of a "real" event into a performative one but, more precisely, a shift from one mode of performance to another. Perceived *character* assassinations thrust upon participants and audience alike the awareness that they had been always 'in performance' – performance that, as Senator Simpson adventitiously noted, had everything to do with "reputation."

To live by reputation is to impersonate a "good name" that can be (as Iago understands to vicious advantage) "but sign." The self of reputation commodifies identity, readying it for exchange in the public commerce of social power. But it is successfully launched into circulation only when etherialized as the "something" of a non-reciprocal, private self-"enrichment." To be effective, then, the well-reputed public persona must present itself as the product of "natural law," appealing to a belief in the availability of non-mediated origins, purposes, and meanings. Thomas's autobiography, a collage of bourgeois tales of self-origination, was a calculated 'misrecognition' of his position as a conflictual product of the very social struggles his presence in the Senate supposedly belied. Having risen "up from" childhood deprivation at the hands of systematic racism, he now endorsed that very system "in spite of its contradictions" (*NY Times*, 9/11/91, A22). Notwithstanding the potential ironies of his "deep gratitude" for John Danforth and others' patronage (let alone the actual mechanisms of his advancement through the ivy halls of academic certification and ivory corridors of public policy), Thomas's self-portrayal as an authentic presence transcending the messy indeterminacies of historical violence embraces the aestheticized politics of the idealized *High* Modernist (Kantian) spectator free of active implication in the scene from which he himself has arisen ("I watched as my grandfather was called 'boy.' I watched as my grandmother suffered the indignity of being denied the use of a bathroom").

Anita Hill's arrival swept Clarence Thomas into the scene, antagonizing his story with less dismissable "contradictions" – and, for our purposes, turning the hearings into a model of black performance less 'purely' collective than that exemplified by *Slave Ship*. It is precisely not pertinent that the "truth" be "known" in calculating the impact of this performative sparring, but rather that the participants, clashing over a scene easily visualized but never visible, necessarily remain suspended within a tangle of narratives that cannot be neutrally adjudicated. It is entirely appropriate, moreover, that Anita Hill's story is redolent of its own array of narrative formulae, echoing a patchwork of American parables of seduction, violation, and betrayal, from *Incidents in the Life of a Slave Girl* to *The Exorcist* to a case of sexual harassment heard before the Tenth Circuit Court of Appeals in Sedgewick County, Kansas.

It is no wonder that Clarence Thomas felt himself trapped in a "Kafkaesque" labyrinth of ungovernable "fictions," nor that his rebuttal sought to restore the "real Clarence Thomas" by dramatic means (*NY Times*, 10/12/91, A10). First he absented himself from the arena of accusation, thereby evading not only the role of spectator in picturing an alleged scene, but also his own witnessed role as the accused. Then, seizing the stage to reassemble the fragments of his inaugural narrative, he repositioned himself from heroically transcendent judge to "lynched" victim under the white glare of the dominant "technological" gaze (thus seeking to substitute one vivid spectacle of violent American repression with another). Like *Slave Ship*'s violation of ethnological topography, Anita Hill's supplementary challenge punctured the state tribunal's metadramatic posture. But unlike *Slave Ship*, this dispropriation did not reconstitute legitimacy in another guise, restoring a hierarchy of primordial meanings. Having unmasked the serene neutrality of the proceedings, Anita Hill's dismantling of Thomas's "reputation" rendered impossible any 'repackaging' of the referential chaos.

So conceived as an interminable series of displacements offering no final resolution of identity and difference, the Thomas hearings exemplify a notion of the "performative" that frustrates the representational theology that helped spur the experimental fury of the Black Arts Movement. Such performance is no longer either a slavish extension of an immanent cause (text) nor the denial of external influence through a reduction-expansion of presence (*mise-en-scène*), but acts instead as a subversive intercalation of these opposing functions. If traditional performance can be termed a 'theater of identity,' returning all meaning to an "original" source registered under the trademark of occidental interests; and the performance of black modernist revolt (as exemplified by *Slave Ship*) a 'theater of difference,' exalting antinomian postures in the interests of another ideal of redeemed subjectivity; then the disruptive performance of post-Black Arts resistance (as witnessed in Anita Hill's appearance) might be termed, to borrow Lyotard's language, a 'theatre of differends':[1] a theater of dispute from irreconcilable positions that ruptures yet provokes representation.

Thus, the terms of engagement binding Baraka's Clay and Ellison's preacher in their fraternal struggle over the logic and telos of performed blackness remain pertinent as the twenty-first century opens, but the terrain on which they do respectful battle has become increasingly mottled by the mutual access of African-American actors (social as well as artistic) and complex mechanisms of image-production. More than ever, performance erupts within frames of perception that are both quickly disseminated and paradocially overlooked: because one is almost always *watching* (like young Clarence Thomas) new images of blackness in the public sphere, responsive acts of *witnessing* become more difficult to share and sustain over a technologically shrinking but psychically fragmenting national landscape. Correspondingly, just as identity politics might now best rearrange itself as what Peggy Phelan calls "visibility politics" to resuscitate its progressive ambitions,[2] so are the lengthening shadows of the Black Arts performance agenda extending themselves with impressive reach into the province of the image, variously conceived. This development takes residence in numerous forms, from the videographic tractates of Adrian Piper to the text-paintings of Greg Ligon, from the photomontages of Lyle Ashton-Harris to the docu-masquerades of Anna Deavere Smith. But in every instance, these dilations of the Black Arts Movement's crossing of critique and praxis are in edgy dialogue with quite different, and differently authored, images of 'performed blackness': Willie Horton; Rodney King; Michael Jackson; O. J. Simpson.

"Performance criticism" that addresses itself to the continued evolution of black modernist strategies in an era of magnified technological, discursive, and narrative intricacy – an era in which we experience increasingly complex entanglements of commodification and spectacle, race and other markers of emergent identity like gender and class – must therefore be all the more aware of the inevitable imbrication of textuality with revolutionary desire, while following the lead of black autocritographers in sharpening sensitivity to its own inception at the juncture of signifying practices. In an era of crossover rappers, guerrilla sampling and commercial reappropriation, and pan-American Africanicity, "performance" – and the idealized, if stratified, *blackness* that has recently underwritten it – can no longer be so quickly assumed to operate as part of a "revolutionary" critical structure, but must be employed ever more keenly as a discriminating measure of proliferating conflictual codes. More than ever, we must frame our own performance as an implicated practice within a boisterous welter of fast-changing idioms and postures. Thus proceeding with vigilance and humility, ever constant must remain our struggle for *a love supreme, a love supreme.*

Appendix A
Coltrane Poems

Jayne Cortez

*How Long Has Trane Been Gone**

        Tell me about the good things
you clappin & laughin

Will you remember
or will you forget

Forget about the good things
like Blues & Jazz being black
Yeah Black Music
all about you

And the musicians that
write & play about you
a black brother groanin
a black sister moanin
& beautiful black children
ragged . . . underfed laughin
not knowin

Will you remember their names
or do they have no names
no lives – only products
to be used when you wanna
dance fuck & cry

You takin – they givin
You livin – they
creating starving dying
trying to make a better tomorrow
Giving you & your children a history
But what do you care about
history – Black History
and John Coltrane
No

All you wanna do
is pat your foot
sip a drink & pretend
with your head bobbin up & down
What do you care about acoustics
bad microphones or out-of-tune pianos
& noise

You the club owners & disc jockeys
made a deal didn't you
a deal about Black Music
& you really don't give
a shit long as you take

   There was a time
when KCFJ played all black music
from Bird to Johnny Ace
on show after show
but what happened
I'll tell you what happened
they divided black music
doubled the money
& left us split again
is what happened

John Coltrane's dead & some
of you
have yet to hear him play
How long how long has that Trane been gone

and how many more Tranes will go
before you understand your life
John Coltrane who had the whole of
life wrapped up in B flat
John Coltrane like Malcolm
True image of Black Masculinity

Now tell me about the good things
I'm telling you about
John Coltrane

A name that should ring
throughout the projects mothers
Mothers with sons
who need John Coltrane
Need the warm arm of his music
like words from a Father
words of Comfort
words of Africa
words of Welcome
How long how long has that Trane been gone

John palpatating love notes
in a lost-found nation
within a nation
His music resounding discovery

signed Always
John Coltrane

Rip those dead white people off
your walls Black People
black people whose walls
should be a hall
A Black Hall Of Fame
so our children will know
will know & be proud
Proud to say I'm from Parker City – Coltrane City – Ornette City
Pharoah City living on Holiday street next to
James Brown park in the State of Malcolm

How Long
how long
will it take for you to understand
that Tranes been gone
riding in a portable radio
next to your son whose lonely
Who walks walks walks into nothing
no city no state no home no Nothing
how long
How long
Have black people been gone

David Henderson

Elvin Jones Gretsch Freak (Coltrane at the Half-Note)*

To Elvin Jones/tub man of
the John Coltrane Quartet.
GRETSCH is outstanding on
his bass drum that faces the
audience at the Half-Note,
Spring Street, New York City.

gretsch love
gretsch hate
gretsch mother   father fuck
fuck gretsch

The Halfnote should be
a basement cafe like the "A" train
Jazz/drums of gretsch
on the fastest and least stopping
transportation scene in NYC
subways are for gretsch
"A" train long as a long city block
the tenements of the underground rails
west 4th
34th   42nd   125th
   farther down in the reverse
                        local at west 4th
   waterfront   warehouse   truck/produce   vacant
   the halfnote
                        our city fathers keep us on the right track
zones/   ozone
                        fumes of tracks   /smokestacks
The Halfnote
westside truck exhaust and spent breath
of Holland Tunnel   exhaust   soot darkness jazz
speeding cars   noisy/   noiseless
speeding gretsch   tremulous gretsch
Elvin Jones the man behind the pussy
four men love on a stage
the loud orgy
gretsch trembles and titters
                  gretsch is love

gretsch is love
gretsch is love

Elvin's drum ensemble the aggressive cunt
the feminine mystique
cymbals tinny clitorous   resounding
lips snares flanked/   encircling
thumping foot drum peter rabbit the fuck   take
this   and take   that
elvin behind the uterus of his sticks
the mad embryo
panting sweat-dripping embryo
misshapen/   hunched
Coltrane sane/   cock   the forceps
the fox and the hare
the chase
screaming and thumping
traffic of music on Spring Street
'Trane says to young apprentice Ron Ferral "Fill in the
solids, get it while it's hot and comely; Elvin fucks almost
as good as his Mama."

The Halfnote is as packed as   rush hour on 42nd & 8th
 "A" train territory
coltrane is off with a hoot
directed supine
nowhere in generalness
into the din and the death
between   bar and tables   reds silver glass molten mass shout
tobacco fumes across the boardwalk
                    (coney island is the "D" train change
                    at west 4th if you want it)
Coltrane steps the catwalk
                    elvin jones drums gretsch
                    gretsch shimmy and shout
elvin drums a 1939 ford
99 pushing miles per hour/   shoving barefoot driver
                    in the heats
Coltrane/   Jones
riffing   face to face
instrument charge
      stools to kneecap
many faceted rhythm structure   to   tomahawk
gretsch rocks 'n rolls   gretsch rattles
fuck gretsch/
                    we know so well strident drums

children singing death songs   /war
tenor and soprano   high
tenor soar/   flux of drums   chasing
      keen inviolate   blue
the model "T" ford & air hammer
                  Holland tunnel
                  "Avenue of the Americas"
                  cobbled stones/   din   of rubber
                  of tin
to the truck graveyard
line-up of Boston Blackie nights/   deserted
right here model "T" & tomahawk
                  sometimes late in silent din of night
                  I hear
                  bagpipes/   death march
                     music of ago/   kennedy

gretsch   gretsch tune optical color-jumping gretsch
   Elvin's F-86 Sabre jet/ remember Korea/ Horace Silver
   the fine smooth jackets the colored boys brought back
            blazing the back   – a forgotten flame
   from the far east with 'U.S. Air Force' a map of Japan
            blazing the back   – a forgotten flame
Elvin tom-tomming
bassing the chest   "E/ gretsch   "J"/ gretsch
                  clashing metal mad
                  tin frantic road of roaring/   gretsch
                  roar
peck morrison
the *bass* player
told me once about a drum set
with a central anchor/   every drum connected
      unable to jump or sway
      drums like the cockpit of a TXF spy plane
      ejaculator seat and all
                           (call up brubecks joe dodge,
                                 al hirt
                  Lester Lanin et al)

pilot conflict
and the man elvin behind the baptismal tubs
that leap like cannons to the slashing sound of knives
black elvin knows so well
the knives the Daily News displays along with the photo
of a grinning award-winning cop
the kind of knives elvin talks about

downtown by the water
and uptown
near the park.

Sonia Sanchez

*a/coltrane/poem**

my favorite things
                    is u/blowen
                                        yo/favorite/things.
stretchen the mind
                        till it bursts past the con/fines of
solo/en melodies.
                        to the many solos
of the
        mind/spirit.
                        are u sleepen   (to be
                        are u sleepen   sung
                        brotha john   softly)
                        brotha john
                                        where u have gone to.
                        no mornin bells
                        are ringen here. only the quiet
aftermath of assassinations.
                                        but i saw yo/murder/
the massacre
                of all blk/musicians. planned
in advance.
                    yrs befo u blew away our passsst
        and showed us our futureeeeee
screech   screeech   screeeeech   screeech
a/love/supreme. alovesupreme a lovesupreme.
            A LOVE SUPREME
scrEEEccCHHHHH screeeeEEECHHHHHHH
        sCReeeEEECHHHHHH SCREEEEECCCCHHHH
        SCREEEEEEEEECCCHHHHHHHHHHHH
a lovesupremealovesupremealovesupreme for our blk
people.
                BRING IN THE WITE/MOTHA/fuckas
                ALL THE MILLIONAIRES/BANKERS/ol
MAIN/LINE/ASS/RISTOCRATS (ALL
THEM SO-CALLED BEAUTIFUL
PEOPLE)
            WHO HAVE KILLED
WILL CONTINUE TO
                    KILL US WITH
THEY CAPITALISM/18% OWNERSHIP

OF THE WORLD.
                    YEH. U RIGHT
THERE. U ROCKEFELLERS. MELLONS
VANDERBILTS
                    FORDS.
                              yeh.
GITem.
          PUSHem/PUNCHem/STOMPem. THEN
LIGHT A FIRE TO
                    THEY pilgrim asses.
TEAROUT THEY eyes.
                    STRETCH they necks
till no mo
          raunchy sounds of MURDER/
POVERTY/STARVATION
                         come from they
throats.
screeeeeeeeeeeeeeeeeCHHHHHHHHHHH
SCREEEEEEEEEEEEEECHHHHHHHHHH
screeEEEEEEEEEEEEEEEEEEEEEEEE
EECCCCHHHHHHH
SCREEEEEEEEEEEEEEEEEEEEEEEEEEEEEE
          EEEEECHHHHHHHHHH
BRING IN THE WITE/LIBERALS ON THE SOLO
SOUND OF YO/FIGHT IS MY FIGHT
                    SAXOPHONE.
                         TORTURE
THEM FIRST AS THEY HAVE
                    TORTURED US WITH
PROMISES/
          PROMISES. IN WITE/AMURICA. WHEN
ALL THEY WUZ DOEN
                    WAS HAVEN FUN WITH THEY
ORGIASTIC DREAMS OF BLKNESS.
                    (JUST SOME MO
CRACKERS FUCKEN OVER OUR MINDS.)
                    MAKE THEM
SCREEEEEEAM
          FORGIVE ME. IN SWAHILI.
DON'T ACCEPT NO MEA CULPAS.
                    DON'T WANT TO
                    HEAR
BOUT NO EUROPEAN FOR/GIVE/NESS.
DEADDYINDEADDYINDEADDYINWITEWESTERN
          SHITTTTTT

(softly da-dum-da da da da da da da da da/da-dum-da
till it   da da da da da da da da da
builds   da-dum- da da da
up)   da-dum. da. da. da. this is a part of my
           favorite things.
           da dum da da da da da da
           da da da da
           da dum da da da da da da
           da da da da
                da dum da da da da
                da dum da da da da – – – – –
(to be   rise up blk/people
sung   de dum da da da da
slowly move straight in yo/blkness
to tune   da dum da da da da
of my   step over the wite/ness
favorite that is yesssss terrrrrr day
things.) weeeeeeee are tooooooooday.
(f   da dum
a   da da da (stomp, stomp) da da da
s   da dum
t   da da da (stomp, stomp) da da da
e   da dum
r)   da da da (stomp) da da da dum (stomp)
           weeeeeeeee (stomp)
                     areeeeeeeee (stomp)
                               areeeeeeeee (stomp, stomp)
           toooooooday   (stomp.
                  day   stomp.
                  day   stomp.
                  day   stomp.
                  day   stomp!)
(soft   rise up blk/people. rise up blk/people
chant) RISE. & BE. what u can.
           MUST BE.BE.BE.BE.BE.BE.BE-E-E-E-
                     BE-E-E-E-E-
                     yeh. john coltrane.
my favorite things is u.
                     showen us life/
                               liven.
a love supreme.
                for each
           other
           if we just
lisssssssSSSTEN.

Haki Madhubuti

Don't Cry, Scream*

>   (for John Coltrane/from a black poet/
>   in a basement apt. crying dry tears
>   of "you ain't gone.")

into the sixties
a trane
came/out of the
fifties with a
golden boxcar
riding the rails
of novation.

>   blowing
>   a-melodics
>   screeching,
>   screaming,
>   blasting –

>   driving some away,
>   (those paper readers who thought
>   manhood was something innate)

>   bring others in,
>   (the few who didn't believe that the
>   world existed around established whi
>   teness & leonard bernstein)

music that ached.
murdered our minds (we reborn)
born into a neoteric aberration.
& suddenly
you envy the
BLIND man –
you know that he will
hear what you'll never
see.

>   your music is like
>   my head – nappy black/
>   a good nasty feel with
>   tangled songs of:

we-eeeeeeeeeee   sing
WE-EEEeeeeeeeeee   loud &
WE-EEEEEEE EEEEEEEEEE high
                             with
                             feeling

a people playing
the sound of me when
i combed it. combed at
it.

i cried for billie holiday.
the blues. we ain't blue
the blues exhibited illusions of manhood.
destroyed by you. Ascension into:

scream-eeeeeeeeeeeeeee-ing   sing
SCREAM-EEEeeeeeeeeeeee-ing   loud &
SCREAM-EEEEEEEEEEEEEE-ing   long with
                                 feeling

we ain't blue, we are black.
we ain't blue, we are black.
                (all the blues did was
                 make me cry)
soultrane gone on a trip
he left man images
he was a life-style of
man-makers & annihilator
of attache case carriers.

Trane done went.
(got his hat & left me one)

naw brother,
i didn't cry,
i just –
            Scream-eeeeeeeeeeeeee e-ed   sing loud
            SCREAM-EEEEEEEEEEEEEEEEEE-ED   & high with
            we-eeeeeeeeeeeeeeeeeeeeeee   feeling
            WE-E-EEEEEeeeeeeeee EEEEEEEE   letting
            WE-EEEEEEEEEEEEEEEEEEEEEEEE   yr/voice
            WHERE YOU DONE GONE, BROTHER? break

it hurts, brown babies
dying. born. done caught me
a trane. steel wheels broken
by popsicle sticks. i went out
& tried to buy a nickel bag

with my standard oil card.

blonds had more fun –
with snagga-tooth niggers
who saved pennies & pop bottles for week-ends
to play negro & other filthy inventions.
be-bop-en to james brown's
cold sweat – these niggers didn't sweat,
they perspired. & the blond's dye came out,
i ran. she did too, with his pennies, pop bottles
& his mind. tune in next week same time same station
for anti-self in one lesson.

to the negro cow-sissies
who did tchaikovsky &
the beatles & live in
split-level homes & had
split-level minds & babies.
who committed the act of
love with their clothes on.
> (who hid in the bathroom to read
> jet mag., who didn't read the chicago
> defender because of the misspelled
> words & had shelves of books by
> europeans on display. untouched. who
> hid their little richard & lightnin'
> slim records & asked: "John who?"

> instant hate.)

they didn't know any better,
brother, they were too busy getting
into debt, expressing humanity &
taking off color.

> SCREAMMMM/we-eeeee/screech/teee   improvise
> aheeeeeeeee/screeeeeee/theeee/ee   with
> ahHHHHHHHHH/WEEEEEEEE/scrEEE   feeling
>   EEEE
> we-eeeeeeWE-EEEEEEEEWE-EE-EEEEE

the ofays heard you &
were wiped out. spaced.
one clown asked me during
my favorite things if
you were practicing.
i fired on the muthafucka & said,
"i'm practicing."

naw brother,
i didn't cry.
i got high off my thoughts –
they kept coming back,
back to destroy me.

& that BLIND man
i don't envy him anymore
i can see his hear
& hear his heard through my pores.
i can see my me. it was truth you gave,
like a daily shit
it had to come.

> can you scream – brother? very
> can you scream – brother? soft

i hear you.
i hear you.

and the Gods will too.

A. B. Spellman

Did John's Music Kill Him?*

in the morning part
of evening he would stand
before his crowd. the voice
would call his name &
redlight fell around him.
jimmy'd bow a quarter hour
till Mccoy fed block chords
to his stroke. elvin's thunder
roll & eric's scream. then john.

then john. *little old lady*
had a nasty mouth. *summertime*
when the war is. *africa* ululating
a line bunched up like itself
into knots paints beauty black.

trane's horn had words in it
i know when i sleep sober & dream
those dreams i duck in the world
of sun & shadow. yet even in the day john
& a little grass put them on me clear
as tomorrow in a glass enclosure.

kill me john my life eats
life. the thing that beats out of
me happens in a vat enclosed
& fermenting & wanting to explode
like your song.

> so beat john's death words down
> on me in the darker part
> of evening. the black light issued
> from him in the pit he made
> around us. worms came clear
> to me where i thought i had been
> brilliant. o john death will
> not contain you death
> will not contain you

Michael S. Harper

*Dear John, Dear Coltrane**

> *a love supreme, a love supreme*
> *a love supreme, a love supreme*

Sex fingers toes
in the marketplace
near your father's church
in Hamlet, North Carolina –
witness to this love
in this calm fallow
of these minds,
there is no substitute for pain:
genitals gone or going,
seed burned out,
you tuck the roots in the earth,
turn back, and move
by river through the swamps,
singing: *a love supreme, a love supreme;*
what does it all mean?
Loss, so great each black
woman expects your failure
in mute change, the seed gone.
You plod up into the electric city –
your song now crystal and
the blues. You pick up the horn
with some will and blow
into the freezing night:
a love supreme, a love supreme –

Dawn comes and you cook
up the thick sin 'tween
impotence and death, fuel
the tenor sax cannibal
heart, genitals and sweat
that makes you clean –
a love supreme, a love supreme –

Why you so black?
cause I am
why you so funky?
cause I am
why you so black?

*Copyright 1970, 1985 by Michael S. Harper. Reprinted by permission of the author.

cause I am
why you so sweet?
cause I am
why you so black?
cause I am
a love supreme, a love supreme:

So sick
you couldn't play *Naima,*
so flat we ached
for song you'd concealed
with your own blood,
your diseased liver gave
out its purity,
the inflated heart
pumps out, the tenor kiss,
tenor love:
a love supreme, a love supreme –
a love supreme, a love supreme –

Appendix B
Sermon transcripts

"The Eagle Stirs Her Nest"

C. L. Franklin
Recorded August 23, 1973
New Bethel Baptist Church
Detroit, Michigan

The line divisions of Reverend Franklin's oral presentation are determined both by his pauses and the congregation's input. Usually, there is a little doubt to these divisions as the congregation and the preacher play off one another to form the text; when there were short pauses which were not interpreted by the congregation as metrical divisions, three periods (. . .) are used to indicate the pause. Please note the following typographical usages: "( )" = the congregation's response; italicized words in parentheses indicate qualities of action, much like stage directions in a play text: e.g., "(*sung*)." As these responses were persistent throughout most moments in the sermon, they are recorded here in a schematic, representative way. Punctuation was added only when obvious. Spelling is occasionally 'bent,' like a blues note, to provide a better description of Franklin's pronunciation.

> (*Song*: "Ever My Heart in Care")
> I had to sing that for ME tonight
> That's what I been doing all these years
> I want to read to you
> Um
> 5 From the
> 32nd chapter
> From the book of Deuteronomy
> Deuteronomy, the 32nd chapter,
> The 11th and 12th verses.
> 10 Uh, you are familiar by this time with the . . . subject that I want
>   to . . . just read . . . for you the . . . actual text.
> "As an eagle stirreth up her nest, fluttereth over her young, spreadeth
>   abroad her wings, taketh them, beareth them on her wings, so
>   the Lord along did lead him, and there was no strange god with
>   him" (my Lord, my Lord)
> 15 The eagle
> Stirs
> Her nest
> A lot of people have come to me,
> Uh, telling me, calling me about the subject
> 20 Some of them said "The eagle stirs his nest,"
> One said "The buzzard stirs his nest." (laughter)
> Another one said "You preacher the only chicken stirrin' his nest."
>   (laughter)

So I've heard all kinds of things
Concerning this subject but
25 According to the rendering
In the Bible it is the eagle stirs HER nest. (yes sir)
Ya see
Now, may I just by introduction say . . . that this particular passage
that I have chosen . . . comes out of the Bible which we call the
Pentitude. (yes sir)
30 Or more commonly called "The Books of the Lord" (yes sir, yes sir,
my Lord)
Uh This part of the bible according to . . . lay people,
uh, Was written as events took place (uh huh)
But it wasn't written like that. (no, no, not at all)
It was written
35 uh, Time after time and track after track (yes)
And some of it was preserved and some of it was lost (yes sir)
And it did not come into a whole
Or a syn-the-sis
Until the Babylonian exile (yes sir)
40 It was then, that . . . the priests . . . and the Levis
Who found themselves in the throes of
A dilemma (yes sir)
In
A crisis (yea)
45 I see Mrs. Allibe Patterson over there, my daughter's mother-in-law.
They found themselves in trouble, and it's a funny thing that most
People don't think too much about God (no)
Or themselves or their destiny (no sir)
Until they get in trouble.
50 So
When they were carried off (yes sir)
To Babylon by the Conquest (yes sir)
And enslaved,
They did a very unique thing (yes sir, uh huh)
55 They . . . did not do what most . . . of the people in this part of the
world did (no)
Usually, people in that part of the world (yes sir)
In the Euphrades Valley or in the Mediterranean area, (yes sir, yea)
When their gods fell (uh huh)
Or when they were conquered by other people (yea)
60 They FORSOOK their gods because they considered their gods had
fallen.
The Jews or the Hebrews did a very unique thing
When THEIR nation fell (yes)
They said "we are responsible for

Our sins
65 That have brought this calamity
Upon us."
And what we need to do
Is to re-examine the Law
And the Prophets
70 And reinterpret them
And synthesize them into a whole
Not only for ourselves, but for generations to come.
I don't believe you're goin' to pray with me tonight.
So that, uh
75 This passage that I have read
In your hearing
Comes from out of
This situation
Now I want . . . you to understand that the writer here
80 Is personifying
The nation
And he's using
Great symbolism
Now
85 Jacob, who is called here,
Is a personification of Israel
The eagle
Is a personification
Of God
90 The nest
That the eagle was stirring
Is a personification of history
He is saying, "Just as the eagle stirs her nest,
Fluttereth over her young,
95 Spread abroad her wings and protected THEM
He has done that over history for Israel." (laughter)
That's what he's sayin', uh
'Bout personification you say, sometimes you say, "well the negro
does this" – you're not talking about one person (right)
100 You talkin' about the whole ethnic group.
And this is what
Is going on here, uh
Moses did not write this
Well you see, as I referred to our teachers who teach us English, uh
105 Will agree with me when I say this is
In the third person
And, when . . . any writing is in the third person,
It is written by somebody ABOUT somebody else.

You see
110 It is the FIRST person if I say "I'm doing so."
That's the first person.
If I say "YOU are doing so and so," that's the second person.
But if I said "such and such thing," that's the third person.
So this isn't Moses writing
115 This is somebody writing about Moses
This somebody writing ABOUT Israel
You don't hear what I'm saying. (preach it, preach Reverend, preach)
Now,
He talks about
120 The protection . . . of the eagle
And . . . symbolizing . . . the eagle with God, uh
The eagle is . . . a regal bird.
You don't hear me.
The eagle is a regal bird
125 And by "regal," I mean kingly, royal
Royal. (royal)
And, why in this way the eagle symbolizes God because God is not
    just a king,
He is THE king.
And I'm glad it's that way because kings and rulers got to, uh, have
    somebody over them;
130 They've got to be accountable to somebody . . .
So in this way . . . the eagle symbolizes God
In his regal nest
And then in the next place, the eagle is strong
Is strong
135 It is said that
The eagle can fly long
Look down
And see a young lamb
Or a young animal grazing in a meadow . . . by a mountain side
140 And swoop down upon that unsuspecting lamb or animal
And grab him in the strength
Of his paws of feet
And fly away to yonder cliff,
And devour it, hummmch.
145 He's . . . just . . . that . . .
Strong
God is strong,
You don't hear me, God is strong. (strong)
Somebody said that this planet that we live on called earth
150 There, we know by now that it's not built upon a platform,
It does not have anything holding it up that's visible,

But it is held in place by
True countering forces
Called trifugal and centrifugal forces
155 And they,
They
They balance each other.
You don't hear me.
All they're talking about when they say that,
160 They're just talking about how
Strong God is
So strong that somebody called him a "leaning post"
That MILLIONS could lean on
And he, uh, substantiated, an' he secured, ah
165 Somebody called him a city of REFUGE
An' then they called him a fortress
An' you know that's talkin' 'bout strong
Well, in that way the eagle symbolizes God
Then,
170 You see the eagle is swift
Swift
It is said that the eagle can fly
With such swiftness
That his wings can be heard rowin'
175 In the air
And at the approach of a storm
He can
Zoom up above the storm
Get out of the fury of the storm
180 Well, in that way the eagle symbolizes God
For God,
You see,
Is swift
You don't hear me (swift)
185 He's swift
Well I could tell you many many instances of his swiftness,
but I'll just tell ya' about one.
One day down in Babylon
Three Hebrew boys got in trouble
190 They got in trouble with the king,
Because they would not recognize and respect
The ceremony
Dedicating a new god.
Somewhere
195 In their history,
In their cultural backround,

They had something that said,
"Thou shalt have no other gods
Before me."
200 And they wouldn't bow.
By that time they
Had made it clear that they wouldn't bow
And were sentenced
To a fiery furnace.
205 God was so swift (so swift)
He was there before they could get them
From court
To the furnace,
And was walkin' around in the furnace
210 Air-conditioning
The fiery furnace
So that it didn't singe a hair
On their head.
For He's swift
215 uh-huh
He swift.
Sometime He will
Hear ya and answer ya before you get through answering
Before you get through asking him
220 The answer is already there.
Peter had that experience (uh huh)
Along with the Christians
One time when he was in jail
He swift! (swift)
225 And I'll tell ya
Another thing
About the eagle
Uh-huh!
The eagle, it is said
230 Builds, ah
Her nest
In a peculiar way.
It is said that the eagle builds her nest, ah
In a kind of a huge fashion, ah
235 To fit
Her own anatomy and that of her young
But basically, the nest
Is rather crude
And rough
240 But then as that nest
Graduates towards a finish

It is said that
The material becomes finer
And finer and finally
245   Soft and balmy
Like cotton
So that the little eaglettes
Can be com-fort-able
In the nest
250   But when
Those eaglettes
Have grown up and ought to be out
Scuffling for themselves
That parent eagle
255   Push them out of the nest
Take them upon her back
Fly out into the blue yonder
And when they are unsuspecting
She DIVES from beneath them
260   And leaves them flapping their little wings,
Trying to stay aloft.
It is said that she circles around
Above them
And watches them while they struggle
265   And she knows when
They have become exhausted
She knows when they can't stay aloft
Anymore.
And when they are
270   About to go down
She dives beneath them
And catch them on
Her back
I think God does us like that
275   God does us like that sometimes
I believe
That
Sometime we find ourselves
In the comfortable nest
280   Of circumstances
Luxury or security or both
And we get
So comfortable
We don't bother to struggle
285   We're satisfied
Right where we are

Then God
Take us out
Allow some circumstances
290 To develop to push us out of our nest of security
And then when we find ourselves
We on our own
Wings.
Well have you felt like that sometime?
295 (*singing, here until end*) Sometime in prayer
You reach out and it doesn't seem that He is there
Like Job you go out
Ahead
And you turn to the right and left
300 You go back over your past
And it doesn't seem that He is there
Or
He's there, alright,
As He's everywhere
He's above us
305 He's lookin' down on us
But He's allowing us
To try our own wings
I don't believe you hear me tonight
And, ah
310 Before weeeeeeeeeee are
Ready
To fall
Why, ah
He
315 Will come in
And catch us when we are
Descending
I don't believe you hear me
What I'm, ah, 'bout to say that
320 You know, preaching
Means nothing
Except, ah,
Just reciting Bible stories
Unless you can make it
325 Ah
Relevant
To life TODAY
Now, the question is
Is God
330 Still

Stirring the nest?
That's what I want to ask you.
YES!
He's still
335   Stirring the nest
ummmmmmmnn
He stir the nest
The nest
In history
340   When, ah,
We came as
Slaves
To this country, ah
You don't hear me
345   I know
It was rough and, ah
I know it was hard, ah
And I know that we had
A hard time
350   Oh, Lord,
And, ah,
We feel
That it was a LONG time, ah
It WAS, according to OUR calendar, ah
355   But you see, ah
GOD
Doesn't work by our calendar, ah
He works by Eternity, ummmm
Oh Lord
360   For 400 years,
That's a little while
With God, ah
You don't hear me tonight,
Looking back, ah
365   It look like the night was too long, ummmm
But God
It was just a minute
In eternity, ummmm
Annnnnnd,
370   My GREAT grandparents
Were slaves, ah
But look,
Where her great grandson
Stands tonight

³⁷⁵ Oh Lord
While
God
Has been stirring the nest
Oh Lord,
³⁸⁰ In suffering
There is redemption, ah
Oh Lord
Unfortunately,
For us to be ourselves
³⁸⁵ We have to suffer, ah
Unfortunately,
For us to know ourselves
Sometimes we have to suffer, ah
Oh Lord
³⁹⁰ And
My great grandparents, ah
And their parents
Suffered vicariously
For me, ummmm
³⁹⁵ And for you, ummmmm
You don't hear me tonight
I see God
Stirring the nest
In labor
⁴⁰⁰ God
Stirred the nest
You don't hear me
I said in labor. . . .
(*leaves pulpit to preach from side of stage, then joins the congregation; all continue in vociferous collective elaboration of the sermon*)

"Build Your Own Fire"

W. Leo Daniels
Recorded December 13, 1968
Shiloh Missionary Baptist Church
Chicago, Illinois

This transcription again risks the gap of text and event, perhaps even more ostentatiously than did that of "The Eagle Stirs Her Nest," attempting to capture the flavor of live performance by: (a) breaking the lines according to Rev. Daniels's own rhythm, rather than according to "meaning"; (b) including the congregation's response in parentheses with special attention to the development of their involvement in the sermon; (c) spelling the more expressive, accented exclamations with vowel elongation (e.g., "I feeel"). Please note again the following typographical usages: "( )" = the congregation's response or activity; italicized words in parentheses indicate qualities of action, much like stage directions in a play text: e.g., "(*sung*)."

1   God bless ya, God keep ya, living in a world of confusion
    A mixed up world in the midst of mixed emotion
    A sinful world
    A world where wars are going on in the ruins of wars
5   I thought I would call your attention to the eighteenth chapter,
      the Book of St. John
    Let us notice the eighteenth verse, the eighteenth chapter, the
      Book of St. John
    (I see)
    "And the servants and officers stood there, who had made a fire of
      coals for it was cold; and they warmed themselves; and Peter stood
      with them, and warmed himself."
    (He did that)
10   Our message today: build your own fire
    Build your own fire
    Why don't you say it after me: build
    (Build)
    Your own fire
15   (Your own fire)
    God bless ya
    Our Lord Jesus Christ here during the time of our text had already
      been convicted and arrested
    (Uh-huh)
    He was taken before Pilate
20   To be judged
    His disciples went along with him

To the judgment hall
John, one of his very close friends, followed Jesus all the way on the
    inside
But Peter stopped on the outside near the door where some of the
    officers of the enemy had built a fire and were warming themselves
25 John said it was very cold
You see there are two types of coldness
A physical coldness and you have to look at the spiritual coldness
Evidently here Peter was cold both ways
We know that in and around Jerusalem during the time of the text
30 The temperature around Jerusalem had fallen below zero
Both inside and outside
If a person had gotten cold there was not but one way to get warm
He had to build his own fire or warm by somebody else's fire
(Yes sir, yes sir)
35 The enemies of Jesus here we noticed had their own fire
And we notice here when Jesus passed by they were standing there
Warming by the fire
John went in with Jesus but Peter was so cold he couldn't wait
Therefore he stopped outside and began
40 Warming by the wrong fire
He warmed by the wrong fire at the wrong time
    and with the wrong people
(Yeah, preach it – *laughter*)
We find here today that (preach it Reverend) we can get a great
    lesson out of this message
For, ahh, don't you see if a child of God gets cold
45 He should build his own fire
For it's not necessary to get embarrassed by standing around warming
    by the enemy's fire
One of the biggest mistake which most church folk makes
We warm by the devil's fire
Instead of building our own fire
50 (Yes sir)
Idn't that right
(Uh-huh)
And sometimes we afraid to identify ourselves
We notice here in the Message
55 Peter will ask a question
And sometimes when you in the wrong place
Doing the wrong thing at the wrong time
It puts you on the spot
Idn't that right
60 (Yeah)
They, they wanted to know if he was one of the society of Jesus

And you know the Message, he said I'm not
Immediately he realized that he was warming by the wrong fire
Being there and being with Jesus they could not understand why he
    was standing around there warming by their fire while his Savior
    was on the inside being tried
65 (Yeah)
Idn't that right
(Yeah)
Sometimes we all come to the point that we
You might experience this
70 That we try to sometimes be what we're not
(Yes sir)
I recall being off
And I'm not ashamed to (Come on) tell incidents that relates to me.
I'd always been a lover of music and some of all kinds of music, and
    I was off in a meeting and the minister had placed me in a hotel
    there. They had one of these bands above the room where I was
    living; and each night I would try to sleep I just couldn' help but
    to hear the jazz music.
75 (Come on; *laughter*)
And every now and then they would start out on a song that I
    remembered when I was out in the world (*much laughter*) and the
    next night I said well I don't believe there's no harm if I was to
    go listen (*more laughter*) and instead of putting on my suit I had
    some sport clothes and put my (*more laughter*) my sport jacket on
    and I went on up and began enjoying the music. And the band-
    leader – you know you never know who knows you (*great laughter*)
    – I was sitting there sippin off my Coca Cola and the band-leader
    wanted the folk to get with him; said, I'd like for everybody to
    start crackin on this one like we used to do at church. And he
    said you know it just makes you feel good when you know the
    audience is with you. He said it does something to you and he
    hollered out, Idn't that right, Reverend Daniels. And everybody
    started looking around, looking for me, and I started looking like
    I was looking for Reverend Daniels.
(*Great laughter, clapping*)
But soon's I got a chance I eased out the back door, put back on
    my suit, and I decided that it was best that I build my own fire
(Yeah, all right)
If a Christian gets cold he should build his own fire
80 Because we notice here in the text
They asked Peter art thou one of this man's society and Peter said
    I'm not
You see he placed himself in a position where he had to deny his
    identity

(Yes sir)
You see the enemy could tell that Peter was in the wrong place
He just didn't look right
85 And when you in the wrong place people can tell it
Idn't that right
(Yes, uh-huh)
You see the Lord wants us to act like a Christian
Wherever we are
90 The Lord sees everything we do
And he hears everything we say
Idn't that right
(Yes sir)
Peter here just hated admitting
95 Warming by the wrong fire
(That's right)
And he could not understand why the people pointed him out
He was warming by the wrong fire
While his Savior was on the inside
100 Being tried
And all up and down the devil's highway
And up and down life's highway
The devil has fires built
And he's waiting for someone to get cold and warm by the wrong fire
105 (Yes sir)
It was once said that there was preaching a deacon and they wanted to get together and have a little social activity. And they discovered that they needed a little drink to go along with this little get together, and they were going to try to figure out how to get it (I see). And they didn't have but one liquor store in that small town and the deacon suggested to the preacher, said, I'm going to drive up to the store, now you got to go in quick because church members are all around. (*Laughter*) And he drove up and the preacher looked all around and ran right quick and ran up to the bar and the man stood there and he said, Reverend what are you drinking today?
(*Long, loud laughter*)
Did you not know, if we are Christian
(Ah-hah)
We might as well be a Christian twenty-four hours a day
110 Idn't that right
(Yes sir, yes sir)
Because don't you see the world is standing watching
(Yeah, yes sir)
And you can't fool folks anymore

115   Because people know who you are
      (Uh-huh)
      Idn't that right
      (Yes sir)
      It's not wrong to go anywhere
      (*Here begins Rev. Daniel's musical cadence*)
      Because the Bible say go ye into *all* the world
      But it's one thing about it
      You must represent Christ
      (Yes sir!)
125   Idn't that right
      (That's right!)
      And I believe here if a child of God would make up his mind that
          he really had been born again
      And not be ashamed to own it
      We'd of had a better world to live in
130   (Yes Reverend!)
      Idn't that right
      (Yes sir!)
      Peter here was all mixed up
      Because he decided to warm by the enemy's fire
      And most dances and most worldly affairs that we have
135   If you don't mind
      They're supported mostly by church folks
      (Yes sir! What you say!)
      Y'all excuse me for saying that
      But I believe that we ought to build our own fire
140   (Yes sir!)
      And did you not know if a fire's not built to the Holy Ghost
      It might go out on us
      Is that right
      (Yes sir!)
145   Everyone says that an old lady
      And I recall in our church once
      That I was sent
      (Yes sir!)
      To look after an old lady whose gas had been cut
150   (Yeah)
      Her gas had been cut off
      And they sent me down there to look after her
      And when I got there she had seven children in the house
      And she said, Reverend I'm glad to see you come
155   Because they come and cut the gas off
      And the children were sitting round there shaking because it had
          gotten very cold

(Yes sir!)

And I ran my hand in my pocket and began to count out a few
    dollars

I said the church sent it to ya

160 And she said well now I can go and cut it back on

But I found out after she had gotten her gas cut back on

She still had another problem

(Uh-huh)

She did not know what He says

165 (Whoo-yeah!)

And therefore she was still cold

I asked her

I said have you ever thought about uniting with the church

(Preach it!)

170 I said I would like to recommend Jesus to ya

And I said not only does your, ahh, physical body need warmth

But your spiritual soul need warmth also

And I told her I said

Your spiritual gasoline has been cut off also

175 (*Sung*) But the man I'm talking about

You don't have to worry

About the gas man coming

Cuttin it off if you ever turn it on

(*Back to chant*) Because you see over nineteen hundred years ago

180 I can see my Jesus

Going up to Calvary Hill

Wearing a Cross on his shoulder

(Yeah!!)

People only wait to

185 Cut on the everlasting gas, y'all

(Uh-huh!!)

Idn't that right

(Uh-huh!!)

And I told her I said

190 If you'll accept Christ today

You don't have to worry 'bout your gas bill

Because it's already been paid

All you need to do is give your life to Jesus

Is that right

195 (Oh yeah!)

It might be somebody here

You might be cold also

Because don't you see we're living in a cold world

And everybody's so hard hearted

200   (Yeah!!)

And so cold
But I've stopped by to say
That I know a man
Called Jesus
205 If you will only trust him
I'm a living witness
That he will make you warm today
(Oh yeah!!)
Is that right
210 (Yesss!)
Some people are so cold
Until they're too mean to say
Thank you Jesus
They're too mean to say
215 I speak to ya
Is that right
(Yeah!!)
I would like to tell ya
That Jesus is on the main line
220 (Yess, yess!!)
Is that right
(Yess!!)
And there are some folks
Worshipping in the same church
225 And can not get along
Is that right
(Yeah!!)
But did you know
(Come on then)
230 That Jesus has done so much for us
Is that right
(Yeah!!)
And, ahh, I don't know about you
But I decided one day
235 To build my own fire
(Ooooooh yes!!)
And you know when I was a boy
We used to have to carry wood
To build a fire in the house
240 And I remember
My brother and I used to have to saw wood
And, ahh, there was a little splinter
That we called kindlin'
Aaaand, a good way to start a fire
245 Is to use that kindlin'

And every now and then I spray a little coal oil
On the wood
Well I'd like to tell ya
That Jeesus has a good method
250 Of building a fire in the church
Is that right
(Yeah!!)
Ooooh Loooord!
Jesus himself
255 Is the kindlin'
Oh isn't that right
(Yeah, yeah, all right!!)
And the Holy Spirit
Is the coal oil, Yeaah!
260 And Go-oood! Is where we have to leave 'em
(*Shouting, clapping, movement all throughout the congregation*)
Yeeah!!
I'm glad today
That I wanted to build my fire
Yes I am
265 Jeeesus fixed me
Where I can catch on fire
All by myself
It's something wrong
With a child of God
270 Who can sit up under the Gospel
And hear God's word preached
And then never catch on fire
It's something about fiiire
That'll make you get happy some time
275 It's something about fiiii-re
That'll make you move
When you don't feel like movin'
Yeaaaah!!
(Yeaaah!!)
280 Good God Almighty!!
Share myself
Oooooooooooh, yeah!!!
It's just like fiiiiire
Shut up in my bones
285 Good God Almighty
I'm closing here
But let me tell you one thing
It was said that there was a young man
Who lived in a mountain country

290   And, ahh, he was known to be a mountain climber
And, ahh, one day
He set out to climb the highest mountain
In that land
Oooooh Lord!!
295   (Yeah!!)
(*Sung*) And he cliiiiimbed up that mountain
Until he'd got so high
He could not go any further, ah
And he was just hanging there, ah
300   'Bout to fall to his death, ah
Ooh Looooord!!
And people gathered all round, ah
(All right!!)
305   And watching the young man there, ah
Say he gonna fall to his death, ah
And there was a old sheep keeper, ah
Leading a flock of sheep, ah
And he came round beneath that mountain, ah
310   Where the little boy was hanging, ah
And the little boy began falling, ah
He feeeell down, ah
And before he could hit the ground, ah
A sheep was up under him, ah
315   And he feeeeell down, ah
On that sheep, ah
It killed the sheep, ah
But the boy's life was spared
Yeaaaaaahhhh!!!
320   I remember in my life
When I was hangin' up high
(Yeah!!)
Good God Almighty!!
I was up above
325   My friend
I was way up
On my high horses
But Good God Almighty
(*Sung*) I remember
330   When I began to fall
I feeeell down
To wonders and prayers
I feeeell down
To happiness
335   I feeeeell down

To joy
I fell down
To love
Whoaaaaa-ooohhh Lord
340 I'm so glad
I'm so glad
That God so loves the world
Ooooooowwwwww!!!!!
(Oooooowwwwww!!!!!)
345 He gave
The Word that God is Love
Jeeesus diiiiiied
That I may live
Jeeesus diiiiiied
350 To get me down
Jeeesus diiiiiied
That (*high falsetto scream*) Oooooooooooooooooooooooo!! Oooooooo!!
I know he did
(Yeaaaaaahhh!!!! Oooooooooooooooooo!!!!!)
(*Everyone and everything here dissolves into an ecstasy of scream, shout, dance, movement as Rev. Daniels and his congregation move 'possessed'.*)
355 Ever since that day
I've had my own fire built
(*Shouts continue*)
Let me tell you what it'll do
It'll pick you up
It'll chuuuuuuuurrrnn
It'll chuuuuuuuurrrnnn
(*Long "falsetto" howl*) Yeeeaaahhhooooooowwwww!!!!!!
Turn you all around
Praaaaaaise Lord!!!!!!!!
(*Rev. Daniels, after he and his congregation have "come down" from the height of ecstatic "happiness," sings "Someone to Care".*)

Notes

Prologue: performing blackness

1 Ralph Ellison, *Invisible Man* (New York: Random House, 1952), p. 22.
2 Amiri Baraka [LeRoi Jones], *Dutchman and The Slave: Two Plays* (New York: William Morrow, 1964), p. 44.
3 Haki R. Madhubuti [Don L. Lee], *Dynamite Voices* (Detroit: Broadside Press, 1971), p. 38.
4 Baraka, *The Slave*, p. 66.
5 Peter Labrie, "The New Breed," in *Black Fire*, eds. LeRoi Jones and Larry Neal (New York: William Morrow, 1968), pp. 64–77.
6 Larry Neal, "And Shine Swam On," in *Black Fire*, p. 655.
7 James T. Stewart, "The Development of the Black Revolutionary Artist," in *Black Fire*, pp. 4–5.
8 Marvin X, "Don L. Lee Is a Poem," cited in *The Black Aesthetic*, ed. Addison Gayle, Jr. (New York: Doubleday, 1972), p. 196.
9 Trey Ellis, "The New Black Artist," in *Callaloo* 12, no. 1 (Winter, 1989), 33–42.
10 See Eric Lott, "Double V, Double Time: Bebop's Politics of Style," *Callaloo* 11, no. 3 (Summer, 1988), 597–605.
11 See Houston A. Baker, Jr., *Modernism and the Harlem Renaissance* (Chicago: University of Chicago Press, 1987).
12 Blyden Jackson, "From One 'New Negro' to Another, 1923–1972," in Blyden Jackson and Louis D. Rubin, *Black Poetry in American* (Baton Rouge: Louisiana State University Press, 1974), p. 93.
13 David Smith's nearly decades-old lament in an important essay that "there is a paucity of literature" on the Black Arts Movement remains essentially as true today as it was then (see David Smith, "The Black Arts Movement and its Critics," *American Literary History* 3, no. 1 (Spring, 1991), 93–110). Kalamu ya Salaam's (forthcoming) *The Magic of Juju: An Appreciation of the Black Arts Movement* (Third World Press) promises an important response to Smith's call for a comprehensive account of the diverse strands of the Movement's activities, including a fresh appreciation of its national (beyond New York) parameters and a careful historical rendering of its ill-appreciated regional foundations. See also Reginald Martin's *Ishmael Reed and the New Black Aesthetic Critics* (New York: St. Martin's Press, 1988) and Phillip Brian Harper's "Nationalism and Social Division in Black Arts Poetry of the 1960s," *Critical Inquiry* 19, no. 2 (Winter, 1993), 234–55, both important contributions to any assessment of the period.
14 Michael Harper, "Apollo Vision: The Nature of the Grid," in Harper, *History is Your Own Heartbeat* (Urbana: University of Illinois Press, 1971), p. 91.
15 Herman Melville, *Moby Dick*, ed. Harrison Hayford and Hershel Parker (New York: W. W. Norton, 1967) pp. 17–18.

16 Mari Evans, "*Vive Noir!*" in *Understanding the New Black Poetry*, ed. Stephen Henderson (New York: William Morris, 1973) p. 248.

17 Henderson, ed., *Understanding the New Black Poetry*, pp. 3–69.

18 Houston A. Baker, Jr., *Blues, Ideology, and Afro-American Literature* (Chicago: University of Chicago Press, 1984), pp. 74–88.

19 Sun Ra, "To the Peoples of the Earth," in *Black Fire*, p. 217.

20 By way of contrast with the present study, see Craig Werner's *Playing the Changes: From Afro-Modernism to the Jazz Impulse* (Urbana and Chicago: University of Illinois Press, 1994), which offers an insightful account of twentieth-century African-American aesthetic development in "polyrhythmic" relation to Euro-American postmodernism. In Werner's suggestive reading, "the jazz impulse" functions as a vector of cultural subversion that cuts across racial barriers in (post)modernist literary production, shaping a "genealogy" that comprises often 'invisible' nodes of cross-fertilization – for example, Barthes and Morrison, Derrida, and Chesnutt.

21 Throughout this discussion I assume the following distinction between the terms "modernity" and "modernism": where "modernity" refers to the conceptualization of the subject in the Cartesian and Enlightenment revolutions of epistemology – and to the juridical, liberal, and imperialist discourses by which that notion of the subject becomes enfranchised in the aftermath of Enlightenment – "modernism" refers to cultural practices produced self-consciously in struggle against modernity's conceptual regime and its continuation in post-Romantic cultural history. As we shall see at various points in this study, African-American modernism both echoes these modernist practices insofar as they are conceived as revolts against modernity's sway, and departs from them insofar as they are themselves perceived to be evasions of a liberation praxis responsive to perceived conditions of "blackness." Though, as noted above, my reference to "African-American modernism" throughout this study is meant to conjure the period known as the Black Arts Movement (including the frame of its immediate prelude and continuing aftermath), I believe this general distinction between African-American expressive culture and Euro-American modernism applies to earlier periods, as well, such as those explored by Lott, Baker, and Werner, among others. See also Aldon Lynn Nielsen's *Black Chant: Languages of African-American Postmodernism* (Cambridge: Cambridge University Press, 1997), which echoes Werner's work in offering an innovative and penetrating approach to the imbrication of black and western (post)modernist poetics in the period following World War II.

22 See, respectively, Jonas Barish, *The Anti-theatrical Prejudice* (Berkeley: University of California Press, 1981) and David Marshall, *The Figure of Theater: Shaftesbury, Defoe, Adam Smith, and George Eliot* (New York: Columbia University Press, 1986).

1 Sighting blackness: mimesis and methexis in Black Arts theatrical theory

1 Amiri Baraka, "The Revolutionary Theatre" in Baraka, *Home: Social Essays* (New York, 1966), pp. 210–15. "The Revolutionary Theatre," commissioned by *The New York Times* at the end of 1964, was refused publication by the *Times*, and subsequently published in *Black Dialogue* and *Liberator*.

2 In *The Magic of Juju* (Chicago: Third World Press, forthcoming), Kalamu ya Salaam makes the historically apt observation that the movement's roots can be traced to the Free Southern Theatre's early projects, which began in the Mississippi Delta during the freedom drives of 1963. Cf. *The Free Southern Theater: A Documentary of the South's Radical Black Theater*, ed. Thomas C. Dent, Gilbert Moses, and Richard Schechner (Indianapolis: Bobbs-Merrill, 1969).

My heuristic is not meant to contest Kalamu's insight, but rather to situate a certain conceptual focus of the movement's activities.

3 Robert Stepto, "Teaching Afro-American Literature: Survey or Tradition," in *Afro-American Literature: The Reconstruction of Instruction*, eds. Dexter Fisher and Robert B. Stepto (New York, 1978) pp. 8–24.

4 Lucius Outlaw, *On Race and Philosophy* (New York: Routledge, 1996); see especially chapter 2, "Philosophy, African-Americans, and the Unfinished American Revolution."

5 See, for example, Lance Jeffers, "Bullins, Baraka, and Elder: The Dawn of Grandeur in Black Drama," *CLA Journal* 16 (September, 1972), 32–48; Lloyd W. Brown, "The Cultural Revolution in Black Theatre," *Negro American Literature Forum* 8 (Spring, 1974), 159–64; and Robert J. Willis, "Anger and Contemporary Black Theatre," *Negro American Literature Forum* 8 (Summer, 1974), 213–15.

6 See, for example, Louis Phillips, "LeRoi Jones and Contemporary Black Drama," in *The Black American Writer, Vol. II*, ed. C. W. E. Bigsby (Baltimore, 1969), pp. 203–17; Toni Cade, "Black Theater," in *Black Expression*, ed. Addison Gayle, Jr. (New York, 1969), pp. 134–43; Shelby Steele, "Notes on Ritual in the New Black Theatre," *Black World* 22 (June, 1973), 78–84; and Darwin T. Turner, "Visions of Love and Manliness in the Blackening World: Dramas of Black Life from 1953–1970," *The Iowa Review* 6 (Spring, 1975), 82–99. For an excellent effort to evaluate contemporary black theater along both didactic and thematic lines see Geneviève Fabre's *Drumbeats, Masks, and Metaphor: Contemporary Afro-American Theatre*, trans. Melvin Dixon (Cambridge, Mass.: Harvard University Press, 1983).

7 Among the most vigorous and pungent of these critiques is that of Harold Cruse in *The Crisis of the Negro Intellectual* (New York: William Morrow, 1967) – see especially chapter 3, "Mass Media and Cultural Democracy."

8 Though thematic in emphasis, several studies of contemporary black drama offer excellent analyses that bear on my project here, including C. W. E. Bigsby's *The Second Black Renaissance: Essays in Black Literature* (Westport, Ct.: Greenwood Press, 1980), chapter 8; Helene Keyssar's *The Curtain and the Veil: Strategies in Black Drama* (New York: Burt Franklin & Co., 1981), chapters 6–8; Fabre's *Drumbeats, Masks, and Metaphor*; Mance Williams's *Black Theatre in the 1960s and 1970s: A Historical-Critical Analysis of the Movement* (Westport, Ct.: Greenwood Press, 1985); Leslie Catherine Sanders's *The Development of Black Theater in America* (Baton Rouge: Louisiana State University Press, 1988), chapters 3 and 4; Samuel A. Hay's *African American Theatre: An Historical and Critical Analysis* (New York: Cambridge University Press, 1994); Tejumola Olaniyan's *Scars of Conquest/Masks of Resistance* (New York: Oxford University Press, 1995); and most recently Nilgun Anadolu-Okur's *Contemporary African American Theater* (New York: Garland, 1997).

9 Sparks from such occasions, generating both light and heat, were captured in such timely venues as the journal *Black Theatre*, founded in 1968 under the auspices of the New Lafayette Theatre and edited by prominent playwright Ed Bullins. I discuss one of the journal's most lively debates, the controversial forum on Bullins's "We Righteous Bombers," in chapter 2.

10 Abiodun Jeyifous, "Black Critics on Black Theatre in America," *TDR* 18 (September, 1974), 34–45. While Jeyifous surveys the writings of black critics from the Harlem Renaissance to the present, he is centrally concerned with the earlier criticism, particularly that of Alain Locke. For a complementary survey-analysis of the same period and its preludial relation to the Black Arts Movement see Errol Hill's "The Revolutionary Tradition in Black Drama," *Theatre Journal* 38, no. 4 (December, 1986), 408–26.

11 Jacques Derrida, "Plato's Pharmacy," in *Disseminations*, trans. Barbara Johnson (London: Athlone Press, 1981), pp. 61–171.

12 Elin Diamond, *Unmaking Mimesis: Essays on Feminism and Theater* (London: Routledge, 1997).

13 See Peter Bürger, *Theory of the Avant-garde*, trans. Michael Shaw (Minneapolis: University of Minnesota Press, 1984) and Andrea Huyssen, "The Hidden Dialectic: Avantgarde-Technology-Mass Culture," in *After the Great Divide: Modernism, Mass Culture, Postmodernism* (Bloomington: Indiana University Press, 1986), pp. 3–15.

14 Zora Neale Hurston, "Characteristics of Negro Expression," in *Negro: An Anthology (1931–33)*, ed. Nancy Cunard (New York: Negro Universities Press, 1969 [1934]), p. 39.

15 See Farbre, *Drumbeats, Masks, and Metaphor*, chapter 3.

16 I borrow the term from Robert Brustein's study of the classic modern stage, *The Theatre of Revolt* (Boston, 1962), which applies well to the black theater typically bypassed by such scholarship.

17 Michael Harper, *Images of Kin: New and Selected Poems* (Urbana, Ill.: University of Illinois Press, 1977), p. 200.

18 Antonin Artaud, "The Theatre and Culture," in *The Theater and Its Double*, trans. Mary Caroline Richards (New York: Grove Press, 1958), p. 13.

19 See, e.g., "No More Masterpieces," in Artaud, *The Theater and Its Double*. Sanders (pp. 126–31) conducts a general comparsion of Artaudian dramatic theory and Baraka's aesthetic theory, with especial emphasis on the relation of "No More Masterpieces" to Baraka's essay "Hunting Is Not Those Heads on the Wall" (*Home*, pp. 173–8).

20 Amiri Baraka [LeRoi Jones], *Dutchman and The Slave: Two Plays* (New York: William Morrow, 1964), *The Baptism and the Toilet* (New York: Grove Press, 1967).

21 Ed Bullins, "The So-called Western Avant-garde Drama," in *Black Expression*, ed. Addison Gayle, Jr. (New York, 1969) pp. 143–6 (written in 1967).

22 K. William Kgositsile, "Towards Our Theater: A Definitive Act," in *Black Expression*, ed. Gayle, pp. 146–8 (written in 1967).

23 See, for example, the plays collected in the anthology *New Plays from the Black Theatre*, ed. Ed Bullins (New York: Bantom, 1969).

24 Ron Milner, "Black Theater – Go Home!," in *The Black Aesthetic*, ed. Addison Gayle, Jr. (New York, 1972 [1968]), pp. 288–94; p. 291 quoted.

25 See Erving Goffman, *The Presentation of Self in Everyday Life* (Garden City, NY: Doubleday, 1959); Victor Turner, *The Anthropology of Performance* (New York: PAJ, 1980).

26 Larry Neal, "Cultural Nationalism and Black Theatre," *Black Theatre* 1 (1968), 8–10; "Toward a Relevant Black Theatre," *Black Theatre* 4 (1970), 14–15; "New Space," in *The Black Seventies*, ed. Floud Barbour (Boston: Porter Sargent Press, 1970), pp. 9–31; "The Black Arts Movement," *TDR* 12 (Summer, 1968), 29–39. The entire Summer, 1968 issue of *TDR* was devoted to plays, essays, and documents related to black theatre and became, as Jeyifous points out, a kind of "collective manifesto" of the movement.

27 See, e.g., Amiri Baraka, "Myth of a 'Negro Literature'," in *Home*, pp. 105–15.

28 In addition to "The Black Arts Movement" see especially Neal's "Some Reflections on the Black Aesthetic," in *The Black Aesthetic*, ed. Gayle, pp. 12–15.

29 Such insistence on retrieving and revaluing vernacular forms of what Milner calls "fruitful memories" lies at the heart of Neal's furious dispute on the blues with such austere nationalist theorists as Mualana Karenga. Writing in response to Karenga's assertion in "Black Cultural Nationalism" that the blues "are invalid" as a living mode of cultural struggle (see *The Black Aesthetic*, p. 36, and

passim), Neal asserted "[the blues] do *not* . . . *collectively* 'teach resignation.' . . . The blues are basically defiant" ("The Ethos of the Blues," in *Visions of a Liberated Future: Black Arts Movement Writings* [New York: Thuder's Mouth Press, 1989], p. 108; written in 1971). If, for Karenga, the bluesman represented a fossilized icon of tragic submission and capitulation, valuable only as an historical warning against "acceptance of reality," for Neal, as Anadolo-Okur has suggested, the bluesman was the very archetype of improvisational agency (see *Contemporary African American Theater*, pp. 51–2). Cf. Houston A. Baker, "Critical Change and Blues Continuity: An Essay on the Criticism of Larry Neal." *Callaloo* 23, no. 1 (1985), 70–87.

30 I extrapolate the term "surrogation" to designate the process of vernacular enactment – neither purely imitative nor ahistorically 'original' – from Joseph Roach's splendid study of "circum-atlantic performance" in *Cities of the Dead* (Columbia University Press: New York, 1996).

31 Clayton Riley, "On Black Theater," in *The Black Aesthetic*, ed. Gayle, p. 309.

32 Amiri Baraka, "What the Arts Need Now," in *Raise Race Rays Raze: Essays Since 1965* (New York, 1971), p. 33.

33 Geneva Smitherman, "We are the Music: Ron Milner, People's Playwright," *Black World* 25 (April, 1976), pp. 4–19; p. 4 quoted.

34 See Marvin Carlson, "Theatrical Performance: Illustration, Translation, Fulfillment, or Supplement?" *Theatre Journal* 37, no. 1 (March, 1985), 5–11.

35 Larry Neal, "Cultural Nationalism and Black Theatre," p. 10.

36 Ibid.

37 Ishmael Reed, "19 Necromancers from Now: Introduction," in *New Black Voices*, ed. Abraham Chapman (New York: New American Library, 1972), p. 518.

38 I employ here Gregory Ulmer's coinage designating "the needs of multi-channeled performance" in a postmimetic program, the aim of which is to "decenter disciplinary identities" by "scripting" a pedagogy outside the borders of "the book" of western philosophy. See Gregory Ulmer, *Applied Grammatology: Post(e)-Pedagogy from Jacques Derrida to Joseph Beuys* (Johns Hopkins University Press: Baltimore, 1985).

39 This is Neal's term for the black Christian philosophy that stresses assimilation. Three plays which Neal singles out as particularly critical of the "Old Spirituality" are Milner's *Who's Got His Own* (in *Black Drama Anthology*, eds. Woodie King, Jr., and Ron Milner (New York: New American Library, 1971), pp. 89–145), Jimmy Garret's *We Own the Night* (*TDR* 12, no. 40 (Summer, 1968), 61–9), and Ben Caldwell's *The Militant Preacher* (Newark, N. J.: Jihad, 1967).

40 See Carlton Mollette II, "Afro-American Ritual Drama," *Black World* 22 (April, 1973), 4–12.

41 I refer here to a tendency to commingle fashioning of vernacular-inspired literary theory with denigration of the Black Arts Movement for its purported conceptual rigidities and radical elevation of a newly-declared "racial purity" over "ancestral" inspiration. Houston Baker, tracing the blues impulse of the black aesthetic, provides the corrective recognition that "the Afro-American masses became, in the late sixties and early seventies, both subject and audience for the utterances of black political spokesmen moved by a new ideology" (*Blues, Ideology, and Afro-American Literature* [Chicago: University of Chicago Press, 1984], p. 72). We will further explore inflections of vernacular expression by African-American literary and cultural criticism in Part IV (Chapters 7 and 8).

42 Paul Carter Harrison, *The Drama of Nommo* (New York: Grove Press, 1972), p. 203. Quotations of Harrison are from this text unless otherwise noted.

43 See Janheinz Jahn, *Munto*, trans. Marjorie Grene (New York: Grove Press, 1961).

44 Harrison has collected a number of plays under this title (*Kuntu Drama* [New York: Grove Press, 1974]), which he feels are representative of the new aesthetic of ritual. His own play, *The Great MacDaddy* (pp. 257–352), is probably the most precise of this aesthetic included in the anthology.
45 Paul Carter Harrison, "Who Knows Beauty Rests in the Souls of Men? The *Shadow* Do!," in *Black Review No. 2*, ed. Mel Watkins (New York, 1982), p. 147.
46 Paul Carter Harrison, *Kuntu Drama*, pp. 7, 8.
47 Ed Bullins, "Introduction," *The New Lafayette Theatre Presents*, ed. Ed Bullins (New York: Doubleday, 1974), p. 4.
48 Sonia Sanchez, "A Conversation with Sonia Sanchez," in *The New Lafayette Theatre Presents*, p. 163.

2 Site-ing blackness: abjection and affirmation in modern black drama

1 Larry Neal, "Into Nationalism, Out of Parochialism," *Performance* 1, no. 2 (April, 1972), 40.
2 Amiri Baraka [LeRoi Jones] *Dutchman and The Slave: Two Plays* (New York: William Morrow, 1964), p. 61.
3 Ed Bullins, "Theatre of Reality," *Negro Digest* 15 (April, 1966), 60–6.
4 All quotations from *Clara's Ole Man* are from *The Drama Review* 12 (Summer, 1968), 160–71. The play was first performed in August, 1965.
5 Lance Jeffers, "Bullins, Baraka, and Elder: The Dawn of Grandeur in Black Drama," *CLA* Journal 16 (September, 1972), 32–48; p. 35 quoted.
6 James Baldwin, *The Amen Corner* (New York: Dial, 1967); Amiri Baraka, *The Toilet* in *The Baptism and The Toilet* (New York: Grove Press, 1967).
7 Big Girl (cf. Big-ger?) also suggests the association of her entrapment in oppressed, ghetto life with hell: "Christians . . . HAAA . . . always preachin' 'bout some heaven over yonder and building a bigger hell here den any devil have imagination for." (163)
8 Defining features and the prevailing ethos of the carnivalesque are explored in a number of Bakhtin's works, most densely in *Rabelais and His World*, trans. Helene Iswolsky (Cambridge, Mass.: MIT Press, 1968 [1940]). For an elaboration of the translation of medieval, peasant misrule into an urban carnivalesque see Peter Stallybrass and Allon White, *The Politics and Poetics of Transgression* (Ithaca, NY.: Cornell University Press, 1986).
9 Cf. Sanders's discussion of Big Girl's "nurturing power," which analyzes the play's refiguration of the black matriarch (Leslie Catherine Sanders, *The Development of Black Theater in America*, Baton Rouge: Louisiana State University Press, pp. 208–9). Cf. Geneviève Fabre, *Drumbeats, Masks, and Metaphor: Contemporary Afro-American Theatre*, trans. Melvin Dixon (Cambridge, Mass.: Harvard University Press, 1983), p. 173.
10 See René Girard, *Violence and the Sacred*, trans. Patrick Gregory (Baltimore: Johns Hopkins University Press, 1978).
11 Craig Werner, *Playing the Changes: From Afro-Modernism to the Jazz Impulse* (Urbana and Chicago: University of Illinois Press, 1994), pp. 117–23.
12 Audre Lorde, "Coal," in *Understanding the New Black Poetry*, ed. Stephen Henderson (New York: William Morrow, 1973), p. 284.
13 Ed Bullins, *We Righteous Bombers* in *New Plays from the Black Theatre*, ed. Ed Bullins (Bantam: New York, 1969), pp. 21–96.
14 Neal, "Toward a Relevant Black Theater," p. 15. The New Lafayette symposium's transcript follows under the title, "Reaction to *We Righteous Bombers*," *Black Theatre* 4 (1970), 16–25. For Neal's remarks about the play as a "confusion

of form," see "Reaction to *We Righteous Bombers*," 19, 25, and "Toward a Relevant Black Theater," 14–15.

15 Neal, "Toward a Relevant Black Theatre," 14.

16 For a suggestive, sensitively argued alternative reading of black women's *unassimilated* relation to the Black Arts agenda, especially in the realm of poetry and fiction, see Madhu Dubey's *Black Women Novelists and the Nationalist Aesthetic* (Bloomington: Indiana University Press, 1994), especially (in context of the present discussion) chapter 1.

17 See Elin Diamond, *Unmaking Mimesis*, chapter 5 and "Mimesis, Mimicry, and the 'True Real'," *Modern Drama* 32 (1989), 58–72.

18 Leo Bersani, *Balzac to Beckett: Center and Circumference in French Fiction* (New York: Oxford University Press, 1970), p. 38.

19 Peter Brooks, *The Melodramatic Imagination: Balzac, Henry James, Melodrama and the Mode of Excess* (New Haven: Yale University Press, 1976).

20 Amiri Baraka, *Experimental Death Unith #1* in Baraka [LeRoi Jones] *Four Black Revolutionary Plays* (New York: Bobbs-Merrill, 1969), pp. 1–15; Salimu, *Growin' Into Blackness* in *New Plays from the Black Theatre*, ed. Bullins, pp. 195–200.

21 Adrienne Kennedy, *Funnyhouse of a Negro* [1964] in *Adrienne Kennedy in One Act* (Minneapolis: University Press of Minnesota, 1988), pp. 1–23; Kennedy, *A Movie Star Has to Star in Black and White* [1976] in *Adrienne Kennedy in One Act*, pp. 79–103.

22 Paul Carter Harrison, ed., *Kuntu Drama* (New York: Grove Press, 1974), pp. 23–4.

23 All quotations from *The Owl Answers* (1965) are from *Kuntu Drama*, ed. Harrison, pp. 169–90.

24 I allude here, with some modification, to a distinction elaborated by Bonnie Marranca in her discussions of Foreman, Breuer, and Wilson in *The Theater of Images* (New York: Drama Book Specialists, 1977).

25 In this concern with the poisonous inheritances possible within a given familial structure *The Owl Answers* resembles such plays as Milner's *Who's Got His Own*, Elder's *Ceremonies in Dark Old Men* (Lonne Elder III, *Ceremonies in Dark Old Men*, (New York: Farrar, Straus, and Giroux, 1969)), William Wellington Mackey's *Family Meeting* (in *New Black Playwrights*, ed. William Couch, Jr. (Baton Rouge: Louisiana University Press, 1968), pp. 217–55), Baraka's *Great Goodness of Life* (in *Four Black Revolutionary Plays*, pp. 41–63), and, most intriguingly, the somewhat earlier *The Owl Killer* (in *Black Drama Anthology*, eds. King and Milner, pp. 301–24) by Philip Hayes Dean. Almost certainly Kennedy's play is intentionally troping Dean's, which shares with *The Owl Answers* an interest in a confluence of naturalistic and surrealist modes designed to suggest nightmarish repressions pulsating beneath the stifling surfaces of the black bourgois family. But whereas Dean's play – which depicts the vengeful demise of the father under the mysterious aegis of the exiled son – focuses social critique through a standard oedipal conflict, Kennedy's implicates the narrative and ideological assumptions of oedipalized resistance in an encompassing scrutiny of black subject formation. As I hope to show, the relatively expansive parameters of Kennedy's exploration delineate significant consequences for the formal as well as ideological development of modern African-American drama.

26 'Haint' is an African-American term for a ghostly trace, an apparition, or haunting figure.

27 See, e.g., Paul Carter Harrison, *The Drama of Nommo* (New York: Grove Press, 1972), 216.

28 The term is developed by Herbert Blau to describe experiments in the enactment of *Hamlet* by his Kracken Theatre Company. See Herbert Blau, *Take Up the Bodies: Theater at the Vanishing Point* (Urbana: University of Illinois Press, 1982).

29 See Frantz Fanon, *Black Skin, White Masks,* trans. Charles Lam Markmann (New York: Grove Press, 1967 [1952]).

30 Nathaniel Mackey, "Song of the Andoumboulou: 12," in *School of Udhra* (San Francisco: City Lights Books, 1993), pp. 9–10.

31 Jacques Derrida, "The Theater of Cruelty and the Closure of Representation," in *Writing and Difference,* trans. Alan Bass (Chicago: University of Chicago Press, 1978), pp. 232–50.

32 Ntozake Shange, *for colored girls who have considered suicide/when the rainbow is enuf* (New York: Macmillan, 1977). The play's period of gestation, leading from the first poems' writing and partial performances to the famous New York production, stretches from 1974 to 1976. Shange's 'biography' of this process in the play's preface is discussed below.

33 Adolphe Appia, *Music and the Art of the Theatre,* trans. Robert W. Corrigan and Mary D. Dirks (Coral Gables, Fla.: University of Miami Press, 1962), p. 66.

34 Iris Young, "The Scaling of Bodies and the Politics of Identity," in *Justice and the Politics of Difference* (Princeton: Princeton University Press, 1990), pp. 122–55. Cf. Julia Kristeva, *Powers of Horror: An Essay on Abjection,* trans. Leon S. Roudiez (New York: Columbia University Press, 1982).

35 Pierre Nora, *Realms of Memory: Rethinking the French Past,* trans. Arthur Goldhammer (New York: Columbia University Press, 1996), pp. 1–19. Cf. Roach's discussion of dance in New Orleans's Congo Square in Joseph Roach, *Cities of the Dead* (Columbia University Press: New York, 1996), pp. 63–8.

36 A. M. Opoku, "Thoughts From the School of Music and Drama," *Okyeame* 2, no. 1 (1964), 51.

37 See Susan Foster, *Reading Dancing* (Berkeley: University of California Press, 1986), esp. pp. 167–85.

38 On the relation of gender to modern dance's formal imperatives see Mark Franko, *Dancing Modernism/Performing Politics* (Bloomington: Indiana University Press, 1995).

39 Here I borrow from Kenyan novelist Ngugi wa Thiong'o's analysis of oral expressivity operating within a matrix of "literate" forms. See his "Okot p'Bitek and writing in East Africa," in *Homecoming: Essays on African and Caribbean Literature, Culture, and Politics* (New York: Lawrence Hill and Co., 1972), pp. 67–77, where Ngugi develops the discourse on "orature" introduced by Ugandan linguist Pio Zirimu.

40 Ntozake Shange, "unrecovered losses," in *Three Pieces: spell #7: geechee jibara quik magic trance manual for technologically stressed third world people; a photograph: lovers in motion; boogie woogie landscapes* (New York: St. Martin's Press, 1981), p. xi.

41 For a judicious review of conflicting receptions of the play, especially after its early New York productions, see Neal A. Lester, *Ntozake Shange: A Critical Study of the Plays* (New York: Garland, 1995), chapter 2.

42 Tejumola Olaniyan, *Scars of Conquest/Masks of Resistance* (New York: Oxford University Press, 1995), p. 120. Cf. Claudia Tate's interview with Shange in *Black Women Writers at Work,* ed. Tate (New York: Continuum, 1983), pp. 151–3.

43 See Jonas Barish, *The Antitheatrical Prejudice* (Berkeley: University of California Press, 1961) and Jean-Christophe Agnew, *Worlds Apart: The Market and the Theater in Anglo-American Thought, 1550–1750* (New York: Cambridge University Press, 1986).

44 Tate, "Interview," 163. See Olaniyan's nuanced commentary on Shange's resistance to "standard" punctuation, lineation, spelling, and other linguistic conventions in *Scars of Conquest/Masks of Resistance,* pp. 126–8, and Houston Baker's discussion of what Olaniyan calls her "ubiquitous, eccentric, exasperating virgules" as a "riff" on the closures of standard grammar (*Workings of the*

Spirit: The Poetics of Afro-American Women's Writing [Chicago: University of Chicago Press, 1991], p. 171).

45 Laura Mulvey, "Visual Pleasure and Narrative Cinema," *Screen* 16, no. 3 (Spring, 1980), 6–18.

46 See Homi K. Bhabha, "Of Mimicry and Man: The Ambivalence of Colonial Discourse," *October* 28 (Spring, 1984), 125–33. For a suggestive critique of Bhabha's formulations, which subjects their Fanonian inspiration to a feminist inflection of the "politics of mimesis," see Diana Fuss, "Interior Colonies: Frantz Fanon and the Politics of Identification," *Diacritics* 24, nos. 2–3 (Summer–Fall, 1984), 20–42. See also Diamond's analysis of Irigarayan *"mimétisme"* in *Unmasking Mimesis*, pp. 172–4.

47 Eleanor W. Traylor, "Two African-American Contributions to Dramatic Form." In *The Theater of Black Americans, Vol. 1*, ed. Errol Hill (Englewood Cliffs, N. J.: Prentice-Hall, 1980), p. 51. Cf. Eric Lott, *Love and Theft: Blackface Minstrelsy and the American Working Class* (New York: Oxford University Press, 1993). For an insightful exploration of Shange's overt use of minstrelsy in another play, *spell #7*, see Karen Cronacher's "Unmasking the Minstrel Mask's Black Magic in Ntozake Shange's *spell #7*," *Theatre Journal* 44 (1992), 177–93. At a more general level of application, an intriguing deployment of vernacular norms of reception in a reading of twentieth-century African-American drama is provided by Sandra L. Richards's essay "Writing the Absent Potential: Drama, Performance, and the Canon of African-American Literature," in *Performativity and Performance*, eds. Andrew Parker and Eve Kosofsky Sedgewick (New York: Routledge, 1995), pp. 64–88.

48 For a balanced summary of opinion surrounding this depiction of gender relations within a continuum of social forces see Lester, *Ntozake Shange: A Critical Study of the Plays*, pp. 61–4.

49 Kate Malin, "On Playing Crystal," private communication with the author.

50 The segment's susceptibility to parody, exposed with keen particularity by George Wolfe in "The Last Mama on the Couch" segment of *The Colored Museum*, only underscores the ideological charge of the fine line separating "hysteria" from trauma as Shange traverses it throughout *for colored girls*. The confusion between mournful ekstasis and lurid histrionics, intrinsic to the very structure of impersonation upon which tragic drama has long depended, is itself thematized by Shange as early as the "distraught laughter" of "dark phrases": from that moment, the audience is alerted to its implication in any decision by which the colored girls' laments are thought to be "funny . . . hysterical" (3) or otherwise construed. For a precise analysis of the relation between Wolfe's play and its predecessors in and before the Black Arts Movement, see Harry J. Elam, Jr., "Signifyin(g) On African-American Theatre: *The Colored Museum* by George Wolfe," *Theatre Journal* 44, no. 3 (October, 1992), 291–303.

51 This was most vibrantly the case at the conclusion of the work's early performances in bars and small theatres, and has been particularly the case in its later presentations on community-based stages in such locales as Newark, New Haven, and Philadelphia. In the large production on the Broadway stage – a setting that Shange both authorized and disclaimed – such participatory energies were less often in evidence.

3 Innovating blackness: praxis and passion in (late) Coltrane

1 David Henderson, "Elvin Jones Gretsch Freak (Coltrane at the Half-Note)," in *Understanding the New Black Poetry*, ed. Henderson (New York: William Morris, 1973), p. 265.

2 Haki Madhubuti, "Don't Cry, Scream," in Madhubuti, *Groundwork: New and Selected Poems from 1966–1996* (Chicago: Third World Press, 1996), p. 41.

3 Addison Gayle, Jr., ed., *The Black Aesthetic* (New York: Doubleday, 1972).

4 Amiri Baraka [LeRoi Jones] and Larry Neal, eds., *Black Fire* (New York: William Morrow, 1968).

5 James T. Stewart, "The Development of the Black Revolutionary Artist," in *Black Fire*, 7.

6 Amiri Baraka [LeRoi Jones], *Blues People* (New York: William Morrow, 1963).

7 Quoted by Bill Coss in his liner notes to *My Favorite Things* (Atlantic 1361–2).

8 See, respectively, Robert Farris Thompson's *Flash of the Spirit* (New York: Random House, 1983), and John Hollander's *The Untuning of the Sky* (Princeton: Princeton University Press, 1961).

9 "takin a solo/a poetic possibility/a poetic imperative," in Ntozake Shange, *Nappy Edges* (New York: St. Martin's Press, 1978), p. 12.

10 Michael Harper, "Dear John, Dear Coltrane," in *Dear John, Dear Coltrane* (Pittsburg: University of Pittsburg Press, 1970), pp. 74–5.

11 Amiri Baraka, "A Poem for Willie Best," in Baraka, *The Dead Lecturer* (New York: Grove Press, 1964), p. 26.

12 Frederick J. Bryant, Jr., "Black Orpheus," in *Black Fire*, eds. LeRoi Jones and Larry Neal (New York: William Morrow, 1968), p. 397.

13 Cited by Paul F. Berliner in *Thinking in Jazz* (Chicago: University of Chicago Press, 1994), p. 157 (my emphasis).

14 Quoted by Nat Hentoff in his liner notes to "Om" (Impulse-9140).

15 A phrase popularized by John Tynan and Leonard Feather in a series of articles in various jazz publications; see, e.g., Tynan's "Take 5," *Down Beat*, November 23, 1961, p. 40 and Feather's "Jazz: Going Nowhere ('anti-jazz')," *Show*, January 1967, pp. 12–14. Tynan's remarks, which include an infamous characterization of Coltrane's new mode of articulation as "gobbledegook," are particularly illuminating of the pervading aura of iconoclasm, not to say extravagance and even irrationality, surrounding these early compositions and performance dates: Coltrane's performance, he wrote, had "overtones of neurotic compulsion and contempt for an audience," and seemed "bent on an anarchistic course" with the "intent on deliberately destroying" the foundations of swing upon which "jazz" *per se* purportedly rests.

16 Amiri Baraka, "A Jazz Great: John Coltrane," in Baraka, *Black Music* (New York: William Morrow, 1967), p. 59.

17 For a representative range of such critical views – alongside many of the most brilliant appreciations in the ongoing tradition of Coltrane criticism – see *The John Coltrane Companion*, ed. Carl Woideck (New York: Schirmer Books, 1998).

18 Frank Kermode, "Secrets and Narrative Sequence," in *The Art of Telling: Essays on Fiction* (Cambridge, Mass.: Harvard University Press, 1983), pp. 133–53.

19 Quoted by Joe Goldberg in "John Coltrane," in *Jazz Masters of the Fifties* (New York: Macmillan, 1980), p. 211.

20 Cited by J. C. Thomas in *Chasin' the Trane: The Music and Mystique of John Coltrane* (New York: Da Capo, 1975), p. 207.

21 Quoted by Nat Hentoff in "John Coltrane," *Jazz Is* (New York: Random House, 1976), p. 210.

22 Ibid.

23 Zita Carno, "The Style of John Coltrane," *Jazz Review*, October, 1959, 17–21; November, 1959, 13–17.

24 For a counterview, see Frank Kofsky, *Black Nationalism and the Revolution in Music* (New York: Pathfinder Press, 1970), chapter 7.

25 Quoted by Nat Hentoff in his liner notes to *Giant Steps* (Atlantic SD 1311).

26 Cited by Bill Cole in *John Coltrane* (New York: Schirmer Books, 1976), p. 95.

27 The album, and its liner notes by Orrin Keepnews citing Rollins's political intentions, were considered too incendiary for the producers of Riverside records, who recalled the first pressing and reissued it under the title *Shadow Waltz* with a diluted version of Keepnews's commentary; see Kofsky's scathing account of this scandal, which provides an enticing hint of the felt connections between what Baraka called the New Black Music and the unfolding drama of Black revolutionary culture, in *Black Nationalism and the Revolution in Music*, pp. 50–1.

28 Cited by Goldberg in *Jazz Masters of the Fifties*, p. 239.

29 Valerie Wilmer, "Conversation with Coltrane," *Jazz Journal*, January, 1962, 2.

30 See Ira Gitler, "Trane on Track," *Down Beat*, October 16, 1958, 16–17.

31 George Russell, *The Lydian Chromatic Concept of Tonal Organization for Improvisation* (New York: Concept Publishing, 1959). Note, too, Russell's remarks on Coltrane's innovations as cited by Goldberg, *Jazz Masters of the Fifties*, p. 204.

32 Quoted by Dom Cerulli in his liner notes to *Africa/Bass* (Impulse A-6).

33 Critics such as the acutely perceptive, but sceptical, Martin Williams (see, e.g., *Jazz Changes* [New York: Oxford University Press, 1992] and *The Jazz Tradition* [New York: Oxford, 1993]), fall prey to that Kingfish of Black Culture syndrome which, as Sterling Brown long ago observed, one sees so often in American politics and sports. Rooted in the plantation spectacle of enforced boxing matches between slaves, the staging of such an opposition as that between Coleman and Coltrane (who were, in fact, close friends and mutual admirers) serves primarily to situate the (usually white) critic as master and guardian of the genre's essence, a stance nowhere more embarrassingly evident than in the atmosphere of shrill advocacy and strident censure that permeated jazz criticism in the early 1960s.

34 For insightful musicological versions of these positions, see, respectively, Ingrid Monson, "'Doubleness' and Jazz Improvisation: Irony, Parody and Ethnomusicology," *Critical Inquiry* 20, no. 2 (Winter, 1994), 283–313, and Lewis Porter, *John Coltrane: His Life and Music* (Ann Arbor: University of Michigan Press, 1998), pp. 181–4.

35 Don DeMicheal, "Coltrane on Coltrane," *Down Beat*, September 29, 1960, 27.

36 See "Milton and His Precursors," in *A Map of Misreading* (New York: Oxford University Press, 1975), pp. 125–43.

37 Cecil Taylor, "John Coltrane," *Jazz Review* January, 1959, 34.

38 For equally rich but contrasting approaches to the methodology of such 'conversational' improvisation see Berliner's, *Thinking in Jazz*, and Ingrid Monson's *Saying Something: Jazz Improvisation and Interaction* (Chicago: University of Chicago Press, 1996).

39 Elvin Jones, remarks recorded in the film *The Coltrane Legacy*, directed by Burrill Crohn (Jazz Images, 1985).

40 Don DeMicheal, "John Coltrane and Eric Dolphy Answer the Jazz Critics," *Down Beat*, April 12, 1962, 22. Cf. his remarks in the first DeMicheal interview: "I've got to keep experimenting. I feel that I'm just beginning. I have part of what I'm looking for in my grasp but not all." "Coltrane on Coltrane," 27.

41 Cole, *John Coltrane*, p. 117.

42 Quoted by Nat Hentoff in his liner notes to *Coltrane – "Live" at the Village Vanguard Again* (Impulse-9124).

43 Porter, *John Coltrane: His Life and Music*, p. 277.

44 For an excellent discussion of the place of the drum in African and neo-African societies, see Jon M. Spencer's *Protest and Praise: Sacred Music of Black Religion* (Minneapolis: Fortress Press, 1990).

45 I borrow the term "deep memory" from Lawrence L. Langer's reading of Charlotte Delbo's holocaust memoir, *La mémoire les jours*. Developing Delbo's terminology, Langer distinguishes the "layered" and inexpungeable grain of metaphorical memory from the narrative, metonymical chronicle of "common memory." See Langer's *Holocaust Testimonies: The Ruins of Memory* (New Haven: Yale University Press, 1991), pp. 1–38.

46 John Cage, *Silence: Lectures and Writings* (Middletown, Ct.: Wesleyan University Press, 1961), p. 10.

47 Ihab Hassan, *The Literature of Silence: Henry Miller and Samuel Beckett* (New York: Knopf, 1968), p. 173.

48 Kofsky, *Black Nationalism and the Revolution in Music*; see esp. chapter 4.

49 "John Coltrane: An Interview," in *Black Nationalism and the Revolution in Music*, p. 233.

50 Cited by Nat Hentoff in *Jazz Is*, p. 214.

51 Cole is especially sensitive to these strategies in his analysis of "Giant Steps"; see *John Coltrane*, p. 107.

52 See Fela Sowande, *The Role of Music in African Society* (Washington, D.C.: Howard University Press, 1969).

53 Kenneth Burke, *A Grammar of Motives* (Berkeley, 1945), p. 228.

54 "John Coltrane: An Interview," p. 242.

55 Cage, *Silence*, p. 109.

56 Amiri Baraka, "New Black Music: A Concert in Benefit of The Black Arts Repertory Theatre/School Live," in *Black Music*, p. 176.

57 "Coltrane on Coltrane," 26.

58 "John Coltrane: An Interview," p. 235.

59 Quoted by Nat Hentoff in his liner notes to *New Thing at Newport* (Impulse-94).

60 See Cole, *John Coltrane*, pp. 94, 139, 171, passim.

61 "John Coltrane: An Interview," p. 226.

4   Renovating blackness: remembrance and revolution in the Coltrane Poem

1 I cite the text from *The Norton Anthology of African American Literature*, eds. Henry Louis Gates, Jr., and Nellie Y. McKay (New York: W. W. Norton, 1997), pp. 1957–9. The poem was written in 1968 and first appeared in *Pisstained Stairs and the Monkey Man Wares* (New York: Phrase Text, 1969).

2 See Walter A. Strauss, *Descent and Return: The Orphic Theme in Modern Literature* (Cambridge, Mass.: Harvard University Press, 1971), esp. chapter 1.

3 *De Arte Poetica*, 75ff. in *Satire, Epistles, and Ars Poetica of Horace*, ed. and trans. H. Rushton Fairclough (Cambridge, Mass.: Harvard University Press, 1978 [1926]) pp. 456–8.

4 Helen Vendler, *The Odes of John Keats* (Cambridge, Mass.: Harvard University Press, 1983), p. 78.

5 Amiri Baraka, *The Autobiography of LeRoi Jones/Amiri Baraka* (New York: Freundlich Books, 1974), p. 176.

6 Giorgio Agamben, *Language and Death*, trans. Karen E. Pinkus, with Michael Hardt (Minneapolis: University of Minnesota Press, 1991).

7 Quoted by Natt Hentoff in his liner notes to *Coltrane – "Live" at the Village Vanguard Again* (Impulse-9124).

8 I cite the text from *We Speak as Liberators*, ed. Orde Coombs (New York: Dodd, Mead, 1970), pp. 31–2.

9 On the origins of elegy see C. M. Bowra's *Early Greek Elegists* (Cambridge, Mass.: Harvard University Press, 1938) and Georg Luck's *The Latin Love Elegy* (Methuen: London, 1959).

10 Cortez recorded the poem on a 1974 album entitled *Celebrations and Solitudes*, with bassist Richard Davis (Strata-East, SES-7421). See Aldon Lynn Nielsen, *Black Chant: Languages of African-American Postmodernism* (Cambridge: Cambridge University Press, 1997), pp. 220–32, for a fine account of Cortez's recorded readings, one of the most compelling archives of jazz performance poetry produced over the past quarter century.

11 I cite the text from Henderson, *Understanding the New Black Poetry* (New York: William Morris, 1973), pp. 264–67. The poem originally appeared in David Henderson's *De Mayor of Harlem* (New York: Dutton, 1970).

12 Conversation with David Henderson, 7/3/99.

13 Roland Barthes, *A Lover's Discourse: Fragments*, trans. Richard Howard (New York: Hill & Wang, 1977), p. 12.

14 Jason Pikler, "The Repercussion of Rhythm in the Poetics of David Henderson," Haverford, PA, 1992. Unpublished ms.

15 I cite the text from Henderson, *Understanding the New Black Poetry*, pp. 274–8. The poem originally appeared in Sonia Sanchez's *We a BaddDD People* (Detroit: Broadside Press, 1970).

16 Conversation with Sonia Sanchez, 8/10/99.

17 Conversation with Sonia Sanchez, 8/10/99.

18 I cite the text from Madhubuti, *Groundwork: New and Selected Poems from 1966–1996* (Chicago: Third World Press, 1996), pp. 41–4. The poem first appeared in Haki Madhubuti's (Don Lee) *Don't Cry, Scream* (Detroit: Broadside Press, 1969).

19 See Cornel West, *Prophesy Deliverance! An Afro-American Revolutionary Christianity* (Philadelphia: The Westminister Press, 1982), esp. chapter 2.

20 Sharon Bourke, "Sopranosound, Memory of John," in *Understanding the New Black Poetry*, p. 376.

21 I cite the text from Henderson, *Understanding the New Black Poetry*, pp. 228–9. The poem is also grouped with others discussed here in Appendix A.

22 Leslie Brisman, *Milton's Poetry of Choice and Its Romantic Heirs* (Ithaca, 1973), p. 67.

23 Quoted by Nat Hentoff in his liner notes to *Meditations* (Impulse – 9110).

24 Barbara Johnson, *A World of Difference* (Baltimore: The Johns Hopkins University Press, 1987), p. 185.

25 Jonathan Culler, "Apostrophe," in *The Pursuit of Signs* (Ithaca, NY: Cornell University Press, 1981), pp. 135–54.

26 Liner notes to *John Coltrane* (Prestige 24003).

27 Paul Carter Harrison, *Kuntu Drama* (New York: Grove Press, 1974), p. 10.

28 Michael Harper in *Natural Process: An Anthology of New Black Poetry*, eds. Tom Weatherly and Ted Wilentz (New York: Hill & Wang, 1970), p. 43.

29 Liner notes to *John Coltrane*. Cf. Harper's statement that "All great art is finally testamental, and its technical brilliance never shadows the content of the song," which emblemizes for his own craft Coltrane's capacity to render his artistry a witness to the lived details of collective experience. See "My Poetic Technique and the Humanization of the American Audience," in *Black American Literature and Humanism*, ed. R. Baxter Miller (Lexington, Ky: University of Kentucky Press, 1981), p. 31.

30 Liner notes to *A Love Supreme* (Impulse S-77). Cited hereafter as LN/ALS.

31 I borrow the term from Lewis Porter. See his intriguing and impressively detailed musicological analysis of *A Love Supreme* in *John Coltrane: His Life and Music* (Ann Arbor: University of Michigan Press, 1998), pp. 232–49.

32 See David Wild, "John Coltrane: The Impulse Years," in Carl Wiodeck, ed., *The John Coltrane Companion* (New York: Schirmer Books, 1998), p. 199.

33 See J. C. Thomas, *Chasin' the Trane: The Music and Mystique of John Coltrane* (New York: Da Capo, 1975), p. 194. Curiously enough, the poem also became the car-

dinal document in the liturgy of San Francisco's St. John [i.e. Coltrane!] African Orthodox Church. See Porter, *John Coltrane: His Life and Music*, pp. 296–7.

34 See Harper "My Poetic Technique and the Humanization of the American Audience," p. 28.

35 Robert B. Stepto, "Michael S. Harper, Poet as Kinsman: The Family Sequences," *Massachusetts Review* 17, no. 3 (Fall, 1976), 478.

36 Michael Harper, "Here Where Coltrane Is" in Harper, *History is Your Own Heartbeat* (Urbana, Ill.: University of Illinois Press, 1971), pp. 32–3.

37 See Paul Bové, *Destructive Poetics* (New York: Columbia University Press, 1980), esp. chapter 5.

38 I cite the text from *Dear John, Dear Coltrane* (Pittsburg: University of Pittsburg Press, 1970), pp. 74–5.

39 Max Horkheimer and Theodore W. Adorno, *Dialectic of Enlightenment*, trans. J. Cumming (New York: Seabury Press, 1972 [1944]), p. 55.

40 Samuel Coleridge, *Biographia Literaria, Vol 1*, ed. John T. Shawcross (Oxford: Oxford University Press, 1907), p. 91.

41 See Porter, *John Coltrane: His Life and Music*, pp. 246–9.

42 Harper, "My Poetic Technique and the Humanization of the American Audience," p. 31.

5 Sounding blackness: vision and voice in the performative poetics of Amiri Baraka

1 Unless otherwise noted, citations to Baraka's poetry in this chapter will be from the following volumes, with specific citations noted as pertinent: *Preface to a Twenty Volume Suicide Note . . . (Preface)* (New York: Totem Press, 1961); *The Dead Lecturer (TDL)* (New York: Grove Press, 1964); *It's Nation Time (INT)* (Chicago: Third World Press, 1970); *Hard Facts (HF)* (Amiri Baraka, 3rd Printing, 1973–5); *Selected Poetry (SP)* (New York: William Morrow, 1979); *Transbluesency: Selected Poems 1961–1995 (TB)* (New York: Marsilio, 1995). The abbreviations that follow each title will be used to indicate sources for individual poems quoted in this chapter.

2 Cited from performed version, August 31, 1996, The Clef Club, Philadelphia, Pa. Cf. text in Amiri Baraka, *Funk Lore: New Poems (1984–1995)* (Los Angeles: Littoral Books, 1996), pp. 15–19.

3 My remarks below on Baraka's vision of jazz performance (section IV) should be read in a continuum of excellent commentary regarding the function of music in his construction of a "black aesthetic" program, including Nate Mackey, "The Changing Same: Black Music in the Poetry of Amiri Baraka," In *Amiri Baraka (LeRoi Jones): A Collection of Critical Essays*, ed. Kimberly W. Benston (Englewood Cliffs, N. J.: Prentice-Hall, 1978), pp. 119–34; and Werner Sollors, *Amiri Baraka/LeRoi Jones: The Quest for a "Populist "Modernism"* (New York: Columbia University Press, 1978), passim; Lloyd Brown, *Amiri Baraka* (Boston: Twayne,1980), pp. 51–5; William J. Harris, *The Poetry and Poetics of Amiri Baraka* (Columbia, Mo.: University of Missouri Press, 1985), especially chapter 1.

4 Charlie Reilly, ed., *Conversations with Amiri Baraka* (Jackson: University Press of Mississippi, 1994).

5 Amiri Baraka, *Raise Race Rays Raze* (New York: Vintage, 1971), p. 26.

6 A pertinent, but not necessarily ironic, fact of the moment is that the typewriter remains for Baraka, as Kalamu ya Salaam puts it, "the instrument of choice." Kalamu reports having tried to attune Baraka to the corrective wonders of the laptop PC, only to witness a comic misadventure leading, ultimately, to the "misplacement" of the computer at an undiscovered location.

One imagines that Baraka remains wedded to the typewriter as at least a relatively tactile vehicle of expressive immediacy . . . old dog/old tricks!

7 Amiri Baraka, *Wise, Why's, Y's* (Chicago: Third World Press, 1995).
8 Amiri Baraka, "New Black Music" in Baraka, *Black Music* (New York: William Morrow, 1967), p. 176.
9 Amiri Baraka [LeRoi Jones], *Dutchman*, in *Dutchman and The Slave: Two Plays* (New York: William Morrow, 1964).
10 This provides one way of re-reading the quasi-Hegelian dynamic of Baraka's early (and still classic) study of African-American music, *Blues People* (New York: William Morrow, 1963), allowing us to see the dialectic charted there between 'authentic' ("blues"-cast) blackness and its sublation into "mainstream" cooptations as a struggle between voice and its textualization, a struggle that requires the 'death' of one mode of blackness as prelude to its resurfacing in a 'higher' form of expressive force. *Blues People* thus mirrors, or inverts, Clay's catastrophic ratio of elegy and prophecy.
11 Amiri Baraka, "A Jazz Great: John Coltrane," in *Black Music*, p. 61.
12 Amiri Baraka, "Coltrane Live at Birdland," in *Black Music*, pp. 64–8.
13 Amiri Baraka, "Diz," *African American Review*, 29, no. 2 (Summer, 1995), 249–52.
14 Paul Fry, *A Defense of Poetry* (Stanford: Stanford University Press, 1995), p. 12.
15 New York Art Quartet (Base-ESP, 1004, 1965).
16 Aldon Lynn Nielsen, *Black Chant: Languages of African-American Postmodernism* (Cambridge: Cambridge University Press, 1997), p. 191. Cf. Nielsen's account of this recording, which elegantly contests Barry Wallenstein's reading of the poem as a "rant" (Aldon Neilsen, "Poetry and Jazz: A Twentieth Century Wedding," *Black American Literature Forum* 25, no. 3 [1991], 612).
17 The Town Hall reading, for example, is followed by a question period presided over by Kenneth Rexroth, during which Baraka is subjected to analyses emitted by members of the American professoriate as though in the poet's absence and questions of the 'How did you come to be so angry' variety. Looking as if he was late catching an uptown train, Baraka tersely responded by characterizing the pundits as exercising "a kind of parasitical function that certain, let's say, almost-poets can perform for school children."
18 Performed version from *It's Nation Time* (Motown-B457, 1972).
19 *New Music–New Poetry* (Indianavigation-1048, 1981).
20 See Herbert Blau, *Blooded Thought: Occasions of Theatre* (New York: Performing Arts Journal Publications, 1982), and *Take Up the Bodies: Theater at the Vanishing Point* (Urbana: University of Illinois Press, 1982).

6 Rehearsing blackness: spectre and spectacle in the theatrical prefaces of Adrienne Kennedy

1 Adrienne Kennedy, *Funnyhouse of a Negro* [1964] in *Adrienne Kennedy in One Act* (Minneapolis: University Press of Minnesota, 1988), p. 7.
2 Among the more insightful and stimulating thematically-oriented studies of Kennedy's work are the following: Paul Carter Harrison's effort to locate an Africanist modality throughout Kennedy's drama in *The Drama of Nommo*, pp. 216–20; Robert L. Tener's discussion of various mythic topoi in Kennedy's work, in "Theatre of Identity: Adrienne Kennedy's Portrait of the Black Woman," *Studies in Black Literature* 6 (1975), 1–5; Geneviève Fabre's examination of racial ambivalence and Kennedy's "hallucinatory" dramatic imagery, in *Drumbeats, Masks, and Metaphors*, pp. 119–22; Herbert Blau's reading of Kennedy's "politics of the unconscious," in "The American Dream in American Gothic: The Plays of Sam Shepard and Adrienne Kennedy," *Modern Drama* 27 (1984), 520–39; Timothy Murray's analysis of the mediation of the

"historical," in "Screening the Camera's Eye: Black and White Confrontations of Technological Representation," *Modern Drama* 28 (1985), 110–24; Rosemary K. Curb's interpretation of Kennedy's exploration of the temporality of identity, in "Re/cognition, Re/presentation, Re/creation in Woman-Conscious Drama: The Seer, the Seen, the Obscene," *Theatre Journal* 37 (1985), 302–16; Margaret B. Wilkerson's comparison of interiority in Hansberry and Kennedy, in "Diverse Angles of Vision: Two Black Women Playwrights," *Theatre Annual* 40 (1985), 91–114; Elin Diamond's situating of Kennedy's dramas of identity with respect to a feminist critique of mimesis, in "Mimesis, Mimicry, and the 'True Real'," *Modern Drama* 32 (1989), 58–72; Jeanie Forte's related study of subversive desire in Kennedy's plays, in "Realism, Narrative, and the Feminine Playwright – A Problem of Reception," *Modern Drama* 32 (1989), 115–27; and Diamond's re-reading of Kennedy in terms of "history" and "hysteria," in "Rethinking Identification: Kennedy, Freud, Brecht," *Kenyon Review* 15, no. 2 (Spring, 1993), 86–99.

3   Adrienne Kennedy, *People Who Led to My Plays* (New York: Knopf, 1987); *Deadly Triplets* (Minneapolis: University of Minnesota Press, 1990).

4   See Kennedy's "A Growth of Images," *The Drama Review* T76 (1977); Elin Diamond, "An Interview with Adrienne Kennedy," *Studies in American Drama* 4 (1989), 143–57; and scattered remarks on compositional method in *People Who Led to My Plays* and *Deadly Triplets*.

5   See Stephen Greenblatt, *Renaissance Self-Fashioning* (Chicago: University of Chicago Press, 1980), especially chapter 6.

6   Lesley Wheeler, in an unpublished paper on *People*, has, for example, suggested a synecdochic relation between the opening's striking image of a shuffling of Old Maids cards and the autobiography's persistent thematic tension between control and disruption.

7   Cf. Leo Bersani's discussion of realist ideology of character in *Baudelaire and Freud* (Berkeley: University of California Press, 1977).

8   The classic theatricalized instance of this topos is to be seen at the conclusion of Frederick Douglass's *Narrative of the Life of Frederick Douglas* [1845] (New York: Signet, 1968), but it is present as well in such narratives as those of Harriet Jacobs, William Wells Brown, and Samuel Ringgold Ward.

9   Here, a confession: the most difficult interpretive dilemma faced in reading both *People* and *Deadly Triplets*, I have found, is evaluation of authorial *tone* in the heroine's gushing recollections of awards garnered, compliments gleaned (no matter how trivial or ambiguous), encounters with renowned figures, and other detritus from the journey through the Anglo-American culture of celebrated achievement. Indeed, penetrating reflections on matters of race and politics are often interrupted, even disrupted, by a return to enumeration of the author's adventures in an almost comically Baudrillardian carnival of specularized, fetishized, commodified realm of "fame" and "success" (e.g., a discussion of the trial of Michael X is framed by comments on, first, what Bianca Jagger wore to the opening of *Hair* and, then, the domestic charms of the John Arden household – *Deadly Triplets*, p. 120). The inference that irony is in the air is an effect entirely of narrative juxtaposition and readerly desire rather than any rhetorical performance – an effect which makes the reader uneasy, perhaps even exposed, in her effort to stabilize the text's ethos through assertion of that inference.

10 Near the end of the "Preface" Kennedy records the following scene (a scene echoed in the book's final paragraph [p. 124]):

> During my time [in England] no one except a very old crazy woman in Rothwell Street had spoken to me negatively about race. And she in her half-consciousness had referred to me as Indian. Yet race was present in our

> consciousness. We talked about . . . Malcolm X, Martin Luther King . . . went to the Ambiance and saw plays by Ed Bullins, discussed Michael X. At the same time I was treated grandly as a Guggenheim Fellow. (*DT*, p. x)

Here, again, we are in a liminal and contestatory arena where "*half* consciousness" marks an otherness that invades and even seeks to define one's own "consciousness," where authority remains ambiguously distributed across many voices, and where the author's own "race" is pointedly, if comically, located along a boundary between absolute terms ("Indian" suggesting a figural, if non-logical, mediation of black and white). The alternation between political concern and personal aggrandizement and comfort (discussed in the previous note) only heightens the rhetorical aura of indeterminacy.

11   The possibilities of feminist appropriation of such displaced self-stagings are provocatively explored by Barbara Freedman in "Frame-Up: Feminism, Psychoanalysis, Theatre," *Theatre Journal* 40 (1988), 375–97.

12   Diamond, "Rethinking Identification." Diamond's argument derives from a subtle effort to expose Brechtian theories of distantiated performance and Freudian notions of self-transformation to the pressure of mutual critique, resulting in the startling formula of an "hystericized/historicized" spectator. In the terms we have been exploiting above, we might say that Diamond posits a disruption of the classic subject-stage opposition which has structured Marxist and psychoanalytic accounts of reception alike, if from diametrically opposed perspectives.

7   Improvising blackness: telling and testifying in the modern chant-sermon

1   Cited in Hoyt W. Fuller, "A Survey: Black Writers' Views on Literary Lions and Values," *Negro Digest* (January, 1968), 35.

2   Cf. William Ray, *Literary Meaning* (Oxford: Basil Blackwell, 1984), chs. 1 and 11.

3   See, e.g., Houston A. Baker, Jr., *Blues, Ideology, and Afro-American Literature: A Vernacular Theory* (Chicago: University of Chicago Press, 1984); Henry Louis Gates, Jr., *The Signifying Monkey: A Theory of Afro-American Literary Criticism* (New York: Oxford University Press, 1988); Hazel Carby, "It Jus Be's Dat Way Sometime: The Sexual Politics of Women's Blues," *Radical America* 20, no. 4 (1986), 9–21 and "The Politics of Fiction, Anthropology, and the Folk: Zora Neale Hurston," in *New Essays on Their Eyes Were Watching God*, ed. Michael Awkward (New York: Cambridge University Press), pp. 71–93; John F. Callahan, *In the African-American Grain: Call-and-Response in Twentieth-Century Black Fiction* (Middletown, Ct.: Wesleyan University Press, 1990); Gayle Jones, *Liberating Voices: Oral Tradition in African American Literature* (Cambridge, Mass.: Harvard University Press, 1991); Karla F. C. Holloway, *Moorings and Metaphors* (New Brunswick: Rutgers University Press, 1992); Craig Werner, *Playing the Changes: From Afro-Modernism to the Jazz Impulse* (Urbana and Chicago: University of Illinois Press, 1994). See, also, Bernard W. Bell, *The Folk Roots of Contemporary Afro-American Poetry* (Detroit: Broadside, 1974) and Keith Byerman, *Fingering the Jagged Grain: Tradition and Form in Recent Black Fiction* (Athens, Ga: University of Georgia Press, 1985).

4   Henry Louis Gates, Jr., "Canon-formation and the Afro-American Tradition," in *Afro-American Literary Study in the 1990s*, eds. Houston A. Baker, Jr. and Patricia Redmond (Chicago: University of Chicago Press, 1989), p. 29.

5   Cf. the version collected by Daryl Cumber Dance in *Shuckin' and Jivin': Folklore from Contemporary Black Americans* (Bloomington: Indiana University Press, 1978), p.207.

6 See James Clifford, *The Predicament of Culture: Twentieth-Century Ethnography, Literature, and Art* (Cambridge, Mass.: Harvard University Press, 1988).

7 See, respectively, Antonin Artaud, *The Theater and Its Double*, trans. Mary Caroline Richards (New York: Grove Press, 1958); Jean-Paul Sartre, "Orphée Noit," in *Anthologie de la nouvelle poésie nègre et malgache de langue française* (Paris: Presses Universitaires de France, 1948); and Stephen A. Tyler, *The Unspeakable* (Madison: The University of Wisconsin Press, 1987). On the 'vernacular' in Roman law, see Ivan Illich, *Gender* (New York: Pantheon Books, 1982), chapter 3.

8 See Susan Stewart, *Crimes of Writing: Problems in the Containment of Representation* (New York: Oxford University Press, 1991) and Roger D. Abrahams, *Singing the Master: The Emergence of African American Culture in the Plantation South* (New York: Pantheon Books, 1992). For some interesting suggestions about how African-American 'folklore' might itself already encode a response to this process of containment see John Roberts, *From Trickster to Badman: The Black Folk Hero in Slavery and Freedom* (Philadelphia: University of Pennsylvania Press, 1989).

9 Homi K. Bhabha, *The Location of Culture* (New York: Routledge, 1994).

10 Zora Neale Hurston, *Mules and Men* (New York: Negro Universities Press, 1969 [1935]).

11 Alice Gambrell, *Women Intellectuals, Modernism, and Difference: Transatlantic Culture, 1919–1945* (Cambridge: Cambridge University Press, 1997), p. 104.

12 Holloway, *Moorings and Metaphors*, pp. 78–9.

13 Cf. Robert B. Stepto's study of framing texts in the slave narrative in *From Behind the Veil: A Study of Afro-American Narrative* (Urbana, Ill.: University of Illinois Press, 1979), chapter 1.

14 Barbara Johnson, *A World of Difference* (Baltimore: Johns Hopkins University Press, 1987), p. 180.

15 See Gambrell, *Women Intellectuals, Modernism, and Difference*, pp. 116–24.

16 Gates, *The Signifying Monkey*, chapter 7.

17 A topic best expounded in a series of works on Boas and related anthropologists by George W. Stocking, Jr. See Stocking's *Race, Culture, and Evolution: Essays in the History of Anthroplogy* (New York: Free Press, 1968), *Volkgeist as Method and Ethic: Essays on Boasian Ethnography and the German Anthropological Tradition*, ed. Stocking (Madison, Wis.: University of Wisconsin Press, 1996), and Stocking's compilation of Boas's work, *The Shaping of American Anthropology, 1883–1911: A Franz Boas Reader* (New York: Basic Books, 1974); cf. Gambrell, *Women Intellectuals, Modernism, and Difference*, pp. 101–4.

18 W. E. B. Du Bois, *The Souls of Black Folk* (New York: New American Library, 1969 [1903]); James Weldon Johnson, *The Autobiography of an Ex-Coloured Man* (New York: Hill & Wang, 1960 [1912]); Jean Toomer, "Kabnis," in Toomer, *Cane* (New York: Harper & Row, 1969 [1923]).

19 Vera M. Kutzinski, *Against the American Grain: Myth and History in William Carlos Williams, Jay Wright, and Nicolás Guillén* (Baltimore: The Johns Hopkins University Press, 1987), p. 53.

20 Frederick Douglass, *Narrative of the Life of Frederick Douglass* [1845] (New York: Signet, 1968).

21 See Ronald Radano, "Denoting Difference: The Writing of the Slave Spirituals," *Critical Inquiry* 22 (Spring, 1996), 507–8, passim.

22 Marcellous Blount, "The Preacherly Text: African-American Poetry and Vernacular Performance," in *PMLA* 107, no. 3 (1992), 588, passim.

23 See *Race and the Enlightenment: A Reader*, ed. Emmanuel Chukwudi Eze (Cambridge, Mass.: Blackwell, 1997) and Paul Gilroy, *The Black Atlantic: Modernity and Double Consciousness* (Cambridge, Mass.: Harvard University Press, 1993).

24 Cited in Blount, "The Preacherly Text," 582.

25 W. Lawrence Hogue, *Discourse and the Other* (Durham: Duke University Press, 1986).

26 See Mercer Cook and Stephen E. Henderson, *The Militant Black Writer in Africa and the United States* (Madison: University of Wisconsin Press, 1969).

27 See, e.g., Lawrence W. Levine, *Black Culture and Black Consciousness: Afro-American Folk Thought from Slavery to Freedom* (New York: Oxford University Press, 1977) and Berndt Ostendorf, *Black Literature in White America* (Brighton, Sussex: Harvester, 1982).

28 The African-American sermon has, *per se* (i.e., in its historical development and technical procedures), received interesting treatment in several works, chief among them Bruce A. Rosenberg's *The Art of the American Folk Preacher* (New York: Oxford University Press, 1970); Henry H. Mitchell's *Black Preaching* (Philadelphia: Lippincott, 1970); Charles T. Davis, "The Heavenly Voice of the Black American," in *Anagogic Qualities of Literature*, ed. Joseph Strelka (University Park, Pa.: Penn State University Press, 1971), pp. 107–19; Gerald L. Davis's *I Got the Word in Me and I Can Sing It, You Know: A Study of the Performed African-American Sermon* (Philadelphia: University of Pennsylvania Press, 1985); Jon Michael Spencer's *Sacred Symphony: The Chanted Sermon of the Black Preacher* (Westport, Ct.: Greenwood Press, 1988); Dolan Hubbard's *The Sermon and the African American Literary Imagination* (Columbia, Mo.: University of Missouri Press, 1994); and Albert J. Raboteau's *A Fire in the Bones: Reflections on African-American Religious History* (Boston: Beacon Press, 1995), chapter 7.

29 See, e.g., Walter Ong, *The Presence of the Word* (New Haven: Yale University Press, 1967) and, for a more challenging version of such views, Roland Barthes's *The Grain of the Voice*, trans. Linda Coverdale (New York: Farrar, Straus, and Giroux, 1985).

30 Among the most important engagements with this history are James Weldon Johnson's Preface to *The Book of American Negro Poetry* (New York: Harcourt, Brace and Company, 1922), pp. vii–xlviii; Sterling Brown's *The Negro in American Fiction* (Washington, D.C.: Associates in Negro Folk Education, 1938); Zora Neale Hurston's "Characteristics of Negro Expression," in *Negro: An Anthology (1931–33)*, ed. Nancy Cunard (New York: Negro Universities Press, 1969 [1934]), pp. 39–46; and, in a more contemporary context, Henry Louis Gates, Jr., "Dis and Dat: Dialect and the Descent," in *Figures in Black* (New York: Oxford University Press, 1987), pp. 167–95; Eric Lott's *Love and Theft: Blackface Minstrelsy and the American Working Class* (New York: Oxford University Press, 1993), and Michael North's *The Dialect of Modernism* (New York: Oxford University Press, 1994).

31 Clifton H. Johnson, ed. *God Struck Me Dead: Religious Conversion Experiences and Autobiographies of Ex-Slaves* (Philadelphia: Pilgrim, 1969), p. 74; cited by Raboteau, *A Fire in the Bones*, p. 183.

32 See Oscar Cullmann, *Peter: Disciple, Apostle, Martyr: A Historical and Theological Study*, trans. Floyd V. Filson (Philadelphia: Westminster Press, 1953) and *Peter in the New Testament: A Collaborative Assessment by Protestant and Roman Catholic Scholars*, eds. Raymond C. Brown, Karl P. Donfried, and John Reumann (New York: Paulist Press, 1973). I am grateful to Laurel Bollinger for pointing me to this material.

33 See Theophus H. Smith, *Conjuring Culture: Biblical Formations of Black America* (New York: Oxford University Press, 1994), p. 122, passim.

34 Note, too, that this first tale's motif of costume change signals to the listener an overarching interest in re*fashioning* identity. See Alan Dundes's "Defining Identity Through Folkore," in *Folklore Matters* (Knoxville: The University of Tennessee Press, 1989), pp. 20–33.

35 Shoshana Felman, *The Literary Speech-Act: Don Juan with Austin, or Seduction in Two Languages*, trans. Catherine Porter (Ithaca: Cornell University Press, 1983), pp. 150–1.

8 Re-calling blackness: recollection and response in contemporary black autocritography

1 Gaston Neal, "Today," in *Black Fire*, eds. LeRoi Jones and Larry Neal (New York: William Morrow, 1968) p. 413.
2 See Nancy K. Miller, *Getting Personal: Feminist Occasions and Other Autobiographical Acts* (New York: Routledge, 1991); Aram H. Veeser, "Introduction: A Case for Confessional Criticism," in *Confessions of the Critics* (New York: Routledge, 1996), pp. ix–xxvi.
3 For exemplary struggles to establish a viable identity politics amidst the conflicting imperatives of structural critique and productive agency see Paul Smith, *Discerning the Subject* (Minneapolis: University of Minnesota Press, 1988); Mark Poster, *The Mode of Information: Post Structuralism and Social Contexts* (Chicago: University of Chicago Press, 1990); *Cultural Studies*, eds. Lawrence Grossberg, Cary Nelson, and Paula Treichler (New York: Routledge, 1992); Diana Fuss, *Essentially Speaking: Feminism, Nature, and Difference* (New York: Routledge, 1989); and bell hooks's review of Fuss, "Essentialism and Experience," *American Literary History* 3 (1991), 172–83.
4 George Baker, "Decoration and Detection," *Performing Arts Journal* 57 (1997), 53.
5 Rosalind Krauss, *The Originality of the Avant-garde and Other Modernist Myths* (Cambridge, Mass.: MIT Press, 1985), p. 198.
6 Sidonie Smith, *A Poetics of Women's Autobiography: Marginality and the Fictions of Self-Representation* (Bloomington: Indiana University Press), chapter 1.
7 Homi Bhabha, *The Location of Culture* (New York and London: Routledge, 1993).
8 See Barbara Johnson, *A World of Difference* (Baltimore: Johns Hopkins University Press, 1987), esp. part 4: "Other Inflections of Difference."
9 Al Young, "A Little More Traveling Music," in *New Black Voices*, ed. Abraham Chapman (New York: New American Library, 1972), p. 366.
10 See respectively Gramsci's essay "The Intellectuals," in *Selections from the Prison Notebooks of Antonio Gramsci*, ed. and trans. Quintin Hoare and Geoffrey Nowell-Smith (New York: International Publishers, 1971), pp. 3–13; and V. Y. Mudimbe's *The Invention of Africa: Gnosis, Philosophy, and the Order of Knowledge* (Bloomington: Indiana University Press, 1988).
11 See Elizabeth J. Bellamy and Artemis Leontis, "A Genealogy of Experience: From Epistemology to Politics," *The Yale Journal of Criticism* 6, no. 1 (1993), 163–84.
12 Hortense Spillers, "*The Crisis of the Negro Intellectual*: A Post-Date," *boundary 2* 21, no. 3 (Fall, 1994), 92 (and cf. passim, 65–116). Cf. Harold Cruse, *The Crisis of the Negro Intellectual* (New York: William Morrow, 1967).
13 Henry Louis Gates, Jr., "The Blackness of Blackness: A Critique of the Sign and the Signifying Monkey," in *Black Literature and Literary Theory*, ed. Henry Louis Gates, Jr., (New York and London: Methuen, 1984), pp. 285–321; *The Signifying Monkey* (New York: Oxford University Press, 1988).
14 Frederick Douglass, *Narrative of the Life of Frederick Douglass*, pp. 31–2. In the "Introduction" to his first collection of essays, *Figures in Black* (New York: Oxford University Press, 1987), Gates makes overt the connection between his effort to retheorize black culture through strategies of "defamiliarization" and this passage from Douglass's *Narrative*: "As Frederick Douglass figured the matter, I wanted to step outside the circle so I could trace [the black text's]

contours" (p. xxiv). I am grateful to Marcellous Blount for a conversation that
helped clarify for me intricacies of this intertextual dialogue.
15 Sandra Adell, *Double-Consciousness/Double Bind* (Urbana and Chicago: University
of Illinois Press, 1994), p. 135.
16 Michael Harper, "Sugarloaf," *Healing Song for the Inner Ear* (Urbana, Ill.:
University of Illinois Press, 1985), p. 75.
17 Houston A. Baker, Jr., *Afro-American Poetics: Revisions of Harlem and the Black
Aesthetic* (Madison: University of Wisconsin Press, 1988), pp. 3–9 and 169–78.
18 Ralph Ellison, *Invisible Man* (New York: Random House, 1952), p. 347. The
lurking Shakespearean text is *A Midsummer Night's Dream* V.1.12–17 (and cf.
211–12), Theseus' commentary on the imagination's capacity to "body forth"
and "amend" "the form of things unknown"; the more overt Wordsworthian
echo can be traced to "Tintern Abbey," 102–6: "Therefore am I still/A lover
of [. . .] all the mighty world/Of eye, and ear, – both what they half create,/
And what perceive."
19 Houston A. Baker, Jr., "Everybody Knows the Real Thing, But Magic Brings
us Home: Multicultural Notes," Ms., 3.
20 See Nellie McKay, "An Interview with Toni Morrison," *Contemporary Literature*
24, no. 4 (1983), 413–29; cf. Bessie W. Jones, "An Interview with Toni
Morrison," in *The World of Toni Morrison*, ed. Bessie W. Jones and Audrey L.
Vinson (Dubuque, Iowa: Kenall/Hunt, 1985), pp. 127–51.
21 The relevant passages of Douglass's *Narrative* are from the end of chapter 5
and beginning of chapter 6, when Douglass is transferred by "the interposi-
tion of divine Providence" to the Aulds of Baltimore:

> Here I saw what I had never seen before; it was a white face beaming
> [. . .] the face of my new mistress, Sophia Auld. I wish I could describe the
> rapture that flashed through my soul as I beheld it. [. . .] Her face was made
> of heavenly smiles, and her voice of tranquil music. (46, 47, 48)

22 Cf. Caruth: "The historical power of trauma is not just that the experience
is repeated after its forgetting, but that it is only in and through its inherent
forgetting that it is first experienced at all." Cathy Caruth, *Unclaimed Experience:
Trauma, Narrative, and History* (Baltimore: Johns Hopkins University Press, 1996),
p. 17.
23 Cf. Paul de Man, "The Purloined Ribbon," *Glyph* 1 (1977), 28–49, and Walter
Benn Michaels's reading of de Man in "'You Who Never Was There': Slavery
and the New Historicism, Deconstruction and the Holocaust," *Narrative* 4, no.
1 (January, 1966), 1–16.
24 Zora Neale Hurston, *Their Eyes Were Watching God* (Urbana: University of
Illinois Press, 1979 [1937]), p. 285.
25 Deborah E. McDowell, "On 'Going Home'," in *Life Notes: Personal Writings by
Contemporary Black Women*, ed. Patricia Bell-Scott (New York and London: W.
W. Norton, 1994), pp. 350–4. The circumstances, landscapes, and textures of
"On 'Going Home'" have since been expansively elaborated in McDowell's
lush and moving memoir, *Leaving Pipe Shop* (New York: Scribner, 1996).
26 Zora Neale Hurston, *Mules and Men* (New York: Negro Universities Press, 1969
[1935]), p. 4.
27 Cf. Michael Awkward's incisive proposition of a "black male feminist" critical practice, in which, following suggestions made by Hortense Spillers in her
pathbreaking essay, "Mama's Baby, Papa's Maybe: An American Grammar
Book" (*Diacritics* 17 (Summer, 1987), 65–81), he suggests viewing the "female"
not as "other for the Afro-American male . . . [but as] an important aspect
of the repressed in the black male self." In a searing and illuminating enact-

ment of black autocritography leading to this formulation, Awkward draws the principles motivating his own critical agenda from the wellspring of his own mother's "horrific stories" that spurred him to "understand who my mother was, perhaps also who my father was, what 'maleness' was and what extra-biological relationship I could hope to have to it." See "A Black Man's Place in Black Feminist Criticism," in *Negotiating Difference* (Chicago: University of Chicago Press, 1995), pp. 43–57.

28 Cf. Hurston's *Their Eyes Were Watching God*, where the heroine, Janie, receives the following lecture from her ex-slave grandmother, Nanny:

> [D]e white man throw down de load and tell de nigger man tuh pick it up. He pick it up because he have to, but he don't tote it. He hand it to his womenfolks. De nigger woman is de mule uh de world so fur as Ah can see. (29)

Hurston here signifies on texts such as James Weldon Johnson's *The Autobiography of an Ex-Coloured Man* (1912), in which the phlegmatic hero confronts an image of his own predicament when watching four men desperately trying to save a mule from a morass of mud – texts which in turn signify upon the post-Reconstruction betrayal of the promise to freedmen of "forty acres and a mule."

29 Cf. Johnson, *A World of Difference*, pp. 181–2.
30 Deborah E. McDowell, "'The Self and the Other': Reading Toni Morrison's *Sula* and the Black Female Text," in *Critical Essays on Toni Morrison*, ed. Nellie Y. McKay (Boston: G. K. Hall, 1988), pp. 77–90.

Epilogue: re-presenting blackness

1 Jean-François Lyotard, *The Differend: Phases in Dispute*, trans. G. Van den Abbeele (Minneapolis: University of Minnesota Press, 1983).
2 See Peggy Phelan, *Unmarked: The Politics of Performance* (London/New York: Routledge, 1993), esp. chapter 1.

Index